Religion and Democratizations

This book examines key debates on religion and democratization from three main perspectives:

- Religious traditions have core elements which are more or less conducive to democratization and democracy;
- Religious traditions may be multi-vocal – but at any moment there may be dominant voices more or less receptive to and encouraging of democratization;
- Religious actors rarely if ever determine democratization outcomes. However, they may in various ways and with a range of outcomes be of significance for democratization.

The contributions are divided into two sections: (1) religion, democratization and democracy, and (2) secularization, democratization and democracy. Overall, they examine the three assertions in the bullet points above. The book's starting point is that in general around the world, religions have left their assigned place in the private sphere. This means they have in many cases become recognisably politically active in various ways and with assorted outcomes. This re-emergence from political marginality dates back until at least the 1980s. At that time, the US sociologist, Jose Casanova noted that 'what was new and became "news" … was the widespread and simultaneous refusal of religions to be restricted to the private sphere'. This involved a remodelling and re-assumption of public roles by religion, which theories of secularization had long condemned to social and political marginalization.

This book was published as a special issue of *Democratizations*.

Jeffrey Haynes is Associate Head of Department with responsibility for Research and Postgraduate Studies, Department of Law, Governance and International Relations, London Metropolitan University.

Religion and Democratizations

Edited by Jeffrey Haynes

Routledge
Taylor & Francis Group
LONDON AND NEW YORK

First published 2011 by Routledge
2 Park Square, Milton Park, Abingdon, Oxon, OX14 4RN

Simultaneously published in the USA and Canada
by Routledge
711 Third Avenue, New York, NY 10017

Routledge is an imprint of the Taylor & Francis Group, an informa business

First issued in paperback 2013

© 2011 Taylor & Francis

This book is a reproduction of *Democratizations*, vol. 16, issue 6. The Publisher requests to those authors who may be citing this book to state, also, the bibliographical details of the special issue on which the book was based.

Typeset in Times New Roman by Value Chain, India

All rights reserved. No part of this book may be reprinted or reproduced or utilised in any form or by any electronic, mechanical, or other means, now known or hereafter invented, including photocopying and recording, or in any information storage or retrieval system, without permission in writing from the publishers.

British Library Cataloguing in Publication Data
A catalogue record for this book is available from the British Library

ISBN13: 978-0-415-58694-8 (hbk)
ISBN13: 978-0-415-85030-8 (pbk)

CONTENTS

Notes on contributors   vii

Abstracts   xi

1. Religion and democratizations: an introduction   1
   Jeffrey Haynes

   Section 1: Religion, democratization and democracy
2. The multi-faceted role of religious actors in democratization processes: empirical evidence from five young democracies   18
   Mirjam Künkler and Julia Leininger

3. 'Catholic waves' of democratization? Roman Catholicism and its potential for democratization   53
   Jodok Troy

4. Democratization in Israel, politicized religion and the failure of the Oslo peace process   75
   Claudia Baumgart-Ochse

5. Democratizing state–religion relations: a comparative study of Turkey, Egypt and Israel   103
   Amal Jamal

6. Spiritual capital and democratization in Zimbabwe: a case study of a progressive charismatic congregation   132
   Gladys Ganiel

   Section 2: Secularization, democratization and democracy
7. Islam and democratization in Turkey: secularism and trust in a divided society   154
   Ioannis N. Grigoriadis

8. The Fethullah Gülen movement and politics in Turkey: a chance for democratization or a Trojan horse? 174
   İştar B. Gözaydın

9. A rights-based discourse to contest the boundaries of state secularism? The case of the headscarf bans in France and Turkey 197
   Amélie Barras

10. The problematic nature of religious autonomy to minorities in democracies – the case of India's Muslims 221
    Ayelet Harel-Shalev

11. Conclusion: religion, democratization and secularization 242
    Jeffrey Haynes

    Index 253

Notes on contributors

Amélie Barras is currently finishing her PhD thesis at the London School of Economics in the Department of Government. She specializes in comparative politics, with a focus on secularism, Islam and human rights.

Claudia Baumgart-Ochse is a Research Fellow at the Peace Institute Frankfurt (PRIF), Germany. Her research interests include religion and politics in the Israeli-Palestinian conflict, the Democratic Peace, and transnational religious activism in global governance. She holds a PhD from Goethe-University Frankfurt and was a visiting research fellow at the Kroc Institute for International Peace Studies, Notre Dame University, in spring 2010. She is the author of *Democracy and Violence in the Holy Land: Politicized Religion and the Failure of the Oslo Peace Process* (Campus 2008, in German).

Gladys Ganiel lectures in conflict resolution and reconciliation studies at the Irish School of Ecumenics, Trinity College Dublin at Belfast. Her research interests include Pentecostal/charismatic Christianity, evangelicalism, religion and politics in southern Africa, and the Northern Ireland conflict. She is the author of *Evangelicalism and Conflict in Northern Ireland* (Palgrave 2008), co-author with Claire Mitchell of *Meet the Evangelicals: Journeys in a Northern Irish Religious Subculture* (UCD Press, forthcoming) and numerous articles about religion and politics in Northern Ireland, South Africa and Zimbabwe.

İştar Gözaydın is Professor of Law and Politics in the Department of Humanities and Social Sciences at Istanbul Technical University, Turkey. She is also the head of the Political Studies programme affiliated with the Department of Humanities and Social Sciences at Istanbul Technical University. She has studied at Georgetown University International Law Institute, and holds a MCJ degree from New York University School of Law and a LLD degree from Istanbul University. Her book titled *Regulating Religion in Turkey* will be published by University of Utah Press in 2011. She is also She is the author of numerous articles about religion, gender and politics in Turkey.

Ioannis N. Grigoriadis is Assistant Professor at the Department of Political Science, Bilkent University. He completed his undergraduate studies at the University of Athens, where he studied Law. In 2002 he obtained a Master of International Affairs (MIA) and a Certificate of Middle Eastern Studies from the School of International & Public Affairs (SIPA), Columbia University. In 2005, he earned a PhD in Politics at the School of Oriental and African Studies (SOAS), University of London. Between 2004 and 2007 he taught as Instructor at the Faculty of Arts and Social Sciences, Sabanci University and as Assistant Professor at the Department of International Relations, Isik University in Istanbul. Between 2007 and 2009 he was Lecturer at the Department of Turkish and Modern Asian Studies, University of Athens. His research interests include European, Middle Eastern and energy politics, nationalism and democratization.

Ayelet Harel-Shalev is a Post-Doctoral Fellow in the Politics and Government Department, Ben-Gurion University. Her forthcoming book is titled The Challenge of Sustaining Democracy in Deeply Divided Societies: Citizenship, Rights, and Ethnic Conflicts in India and Israel (Rowman & Littlefield 2010). It is based partly on her PhD dissertation, which won the Israeli Political Science Association (ISPSA) prize for outstanding doctoral dissertation, 2006. She is specializing in comparative political studies; Indian politics and society; ethnic conflicts; and Israeli politics and society.

Jeffrey Haynes is Associate Head of Department with responsibility for Research and Postgraduate Studies, Department of Law, Governance and International Relations, London Metropolitan University.

Amal Jamal is a senior lecturer at the Political Science Department at Tel Aviv University and chair of The Walter Lebach Center for Arab–Jewish Coexistence. His research fields include political theory and communication, nationalism and democracy, civil society and social movements, indigenous minority politics and civic equality. He has published extensively on Palestinian and Israeli politics and society. Three of his recent books are: *Arab Politic Sphere in Israel* (Indiana University Press); *The Palestinian National Movement: Politics of Contention, 1967–2005* (Indiana University Press); and *Media Politics and Democracy in Palestine* (Sussex Academic Press).

Mirjam Künkler is Assistant Professor in Near Eastern Studies at Princeton University. She obtained her Ph.D. in political science from Columbia University in New York, with a dissertation on Islamic political thought and social movements in Iran and Indonesia. Apart from contributions to political science journals, the *Encyclopedia of Islamic Thought* and edited volumes, Künkler's work appears in the recent book publications of Mirjam Künkler and Julia Leininger (eds.), *Zur Rolle von Religion in Demokratisierungsprozessen [On the Role of Religious Actors in Democratization Processes]*, VS-Verlag für Sozialwissenschaften

(2010), and Mirjam Künkler and Alfred Stepan (eds.), *Indonesia, Islam and Democratic Consolidation* (Working title), forthcoming 2010.

Julia Leininger is a Senior Researcher at the German Development Institute/ Deutsches Institut für Entwicklungspolitik (DIE). Her research focuses on governance, politics and conflict resolution in Sub-Sahara Africa and on religion and politics in the developing world.

Jodok Troy is a Researcher and Lecturer at the Department of Political Science at the University of Innsbruck/Austria and Affiliated Scholar at the Swedish National Defence College, Stockholm.

Abstracts

The multi-faceted role of religious actors in democratization processes: empirical evidence from five young democracies
Mirjam Künkler and Julia Leininger

The article comparatively investigates the role of religious actors in the democratization processes of five 'young' democracies from the Catholic, Protestant, Christian-Orthodox and Muslim world: West Germany after World War II (1945–1969), Georgia and Ukraine post-1987/9, Mali (post-1987), and Indonesia from 1998. The analysis provides an overview of the roles religious actors played in the erosion of authoritarian rule, the transition to democracy and subsequent democratic consolidation processes, as well as de-democratization processes. Our three paired comparisons, including one in-country comparison, show that the condition which most affected the role of religious actors in all three phases of democratic transitions was the de facto autonomy they enjoyed vis-à-vis the political regime as well as the organizational form these actors took. Their aims, means, and the political significance of their theology were highly dependent on the extent to which they benefitted from de facto autonomy within the state.

'Catholic waves' of democratization? Roman Catholicism and its potential for democratization
Jodok Troy

The aim and scope of the article is to examine if Catholicism is or can be a major force in democratization. And if so, what are its core values and motivations? To examine this issue, it is also necessary to evaluate democratization outcomes where the church was not involved. We shall see that it is unavoidable to take into account fundamental Christian and thus also Catholic values and doctrines which are – despite all 'earthly' constraints – in favour of both liberal and democratic values. In the case of the Catholic Church this is primarily because it perceives the social message of the gospels not merely as theory but also as a call to action, followed by many of its adherents. The article argues that the main reason for this was the result of the church's changing political theology, following the Second Vatican Council (1962–1965), which enabled the church's adoption of a pronounced focus on: human rights, religious freedom, democracy, and economic development.

Democratization in Israel, politicized religion and the failure of the Oslo peace process
Claudia Baumgart-Ochse

While the positive relationship between democracies and peace is by now a commonplace of international relations (IR) literature, the possible dangers of democratization processes for international peace and security have only recently become a focus of IR research. This article argues that some of the mechanisms prevalent in democratizing states' ambivalent conflict behaviour help to explain why the state of Israel initially entered into the peace process with the Palestinians, but soon reverted to former hostile policies. In the initial stages of the peace process in the early 1990s, the Labour-led government based its efforts towards peace on the typical norms of democratic peace and thus explicitly stated the need to improve Israel's defective democratic regime. This involved amending the electoral system by ending the de facto control of the Palestinians in the territories, who did not participate in Israeli democratic politics. However, the prospect of 'land for peace' threatened the politicized religious Jewish settler-elite in the territories who feared not only the destruction of the basic tenets of their religious identity, but also the loss of both power and resources in Israeli politics. As a consequence, this threatened elite engaged in fierce religious-nationalist mobilization in order to derail the peace negotiations and at the same time subvert the process of improving Israel's democratic regime.

Democratizing state–religion relations: a comparative study of Turkey, Egypt and Israel
Amal Jamal

This article examines the complex relationship between state, religion and democratization in Turkey, Egypt and Israel. It demonstrates that binary and static models of separation and integration between state and religion are not sufficient to understanding the complex relationship between them and chances of democratization. Based on examining the democratization processes in the three Middle Eastern countries, the article argues that separation or integration between state and religion, although different, does not precondition democratic transformation and democratization. It is the form, the measure and the direction of separation or integration that makes the difference. The article demonstrates that democratization is not a one dimensional linear model, but rather can take two opposing directions when it comes to religion and state relations. Whereas in some cases the public return of religion and the subsequent representation of religious groups reflect democratization, in other cases, where state and religion are tightly integrated, democratization means the decoupling of state and religion and the downgrading of religious control of public institutions and individual personal status. Moreover, the examination of the three Middle Eastern countries demonstrates that democratization could involve the return of religion to the public sphere, as part of the basic democratic right of social groups to be represented and their right to participate in determining their cultural and ideological environment.

It could also involve the deinstitutionalization of religion as exclusive authority and identity in the public sphere and in the private life of individuals. Based on such understanding the article claims that dynamic models of state–religion relations are necessary in order to anticipate the chances of democratization and consolidation.

Spiritual capital and democratization in Zimbabwe: a case study of a progressive charismatic congregation
Gladys Ganiel

Throughout Africa, charismatic Christianity has been caricatured as an inhibitor of democratization. Its adherents are said either to withdraw from the rough and tumble of politics ('pietism') or to preach a prosperity gospel that encourages believers to pour their resources into their churches in the hope that God will 'bless' them. Both courses of action are said to encourage such people to be politically quietist, with no interest in democratization or other forms of political activity. This is said to thwart democratization. This article utilizes an ethnographic case study of a 'progressive' charismatic congregation in Harare, Zimbabwe, in 2007, to provide evidence that 'pietism' and 'prosperity' are not the only options for charismatic Christianity. Drawing on the concept of 'spiritual capital', it argues that some varieties of charismatic Christianity have the resources to contribute to democratization. For example, this congregation's self-styled 'de-institutionalization' process is opening up new avenues for people to learn democratic skills and develop a worldview that is relationship-centred, participatory, and anti-authoritarian. The article concludes that spiritual capital can be a useful tool for analysing the role of religions in democratizations. It notes, however, that analysts should take care to identify and understand what variety of spiritual capital is generated in particular situations, focusing on the worldviews it produces and the consequences of those worldviews for democratization.

Islam and democratization in Turkey: secularism and trust in a divided society
Ioannis N. Grigoriadis

The history of Turkish modernization has been inextricably linked with the question of secularism. From the advent of the Turkish Republic in 1923, Islam was held responsible for the underdevelopment and eventual demise of the Ottoman Empire. Based on the laïcité of the Second French Republic, the secularization programme of modern Turkey's founder, Kemal Atatürk, entailed the full subjugation of Islam to the State, its eradication from the public sphere and its limitation into a very narrowly defined private sphere.

The transition of Turkey to multiparty politics in 1946 was linked with a rising role of Islam in the public sphere. Islam became a crucial element in the political vocabulary of peripheral political forces which challenged the supremacy of the secularist, Kemalist bureaucratic elite. While a number of military coups aimed – among other things – to control religion, Turkish political Islam showed remarkable resilience and adaptability.

Most recently, the transformation of the Justice and Development Party (Adalet ve Kalkınma Partisi – AKP) into the strongest proponent of Turkey's European Union (EU) integration brought Turkey closer than ever to EU membership, challenged the monopoly which the Kemalist elite enjoyed as the representative of Western political values and suggested a novel liberal version of secularism. Yet Turkey has been embroiled since 2007 in successive political crises which had secularism as their focal point. This article argues that the transformation of Turkish political Islam has produced an alternative, liberal version of secularism; yet, it has not resolved deep social divisions. Building a liberal consensus between religious conservatives and secularists is imperative for the resolution of deep social divisions in Turkey. The European Union as a guarantor and initiator of reform could play a major role in building trust between the secularist and the religious conservative segments of society.

The Fethullah Gülen movement and politics in Turkey: a chance for democratization or a Trojan horse?
İştar B. Gözaydın
Since 1923 the official ideology of republican Turkey has been strictly secular. However religious networking has always been a very important component of the socio-structural system in the country. Over time, the republican regime sought to stifle development of such networking, while at the same time also promoting changes in this regard. For 50 years – between 1930 and 1980 – Islamic networks in Turkey developed market relations that promoted strategies to improve the economic position of their members. In this context, several 'new' religious groups emerged, including the Fethullah Gülen movement. This article is concerned with the democratic involvement of the Fethullah Gülen movement in recent democratization in Turkey.

A rights-based discourse to contest the boundaries of state secularism? The case of the headscarf bans in France and Turkey
Amélie Barras
For the last two decades the human rights discourse has been increasingly used across the world – one could argue that there has even been a globalization of human rights. This discourse has also been intrinsically linked to positivism, enlightenment and secularism. It is with this in mind that this article looks at how religious Muslim individuals and groups in France and Turkey have been appropriating the human rights discourse and its national, regional and international legal channels to challenge state secular policies and redefine the relationship between religion and the state. By looking into two specific case studies – the work of the Collective Against Islamophobia in France (CCIF) and the Merve Kavakci case v. Turkey presented at the Strasbourg European Court of Human Rights (ECHR) – I investigate if groups and individuals have found through the use of this 'authorized narrative' a space where they can propose a new plural ethos that can better co-exist with their piety. This is a space where they can offer a more

plural and de-centralized vision of secularism. To complement this analysis, I also highlight some of the possible paradoxes found within the human rights discourse – paradoxes that might enlighten us on the challenges of using such a discourse, particularly to ask for the right to display publicly one's religion. In other words, I attempt to shed some light on whether the use of a rights-based discourse by religious rights groups and individuals can help resolve democratically disputes between the religious and the secular – encouraging perhaps the democratization of secularism in specific contexts.

The problematic nature of religious autonomy to minorities in democracies – the case of India's Muslims
Ayelet Harel-Shalev
This article focuses on the ambivalent effect of religious autonomy in India and the outcome for democracy in the country. The Indian constitution guarantees autonomy to its religious minorities, and promises the minorities the freedom independently to manage their religious affairs in addition to a proportional share of the budget. At the same time, the constitution emphasizes the aspiration to legislate 'uniform personal laws' for all the citizens of India in accordance with the principles of secularism, equality and with India's self-definition as a civic nation. This recommendation has however remained a 'dead letter' until today. In this domain, the state has constituted a civic law for Hindus, which adjusts Hinduism to democratic principles. In this sense, the state has nationalized Hinduism, and the government has assumed authority and reformed Hindu civic and marriage laws. However, although they have tried, the state's legal and political institutions have not interfered thus far with Muslim marriage and religious laws. Muslims are committed to the Sharia while Hindus must obey the state's civic laws. By avoiding enforcement of affirmative action for Muslims in the spheres of political representation or public employment, while simultaneously prohibiting
Hindus' group rights, and providing religious autonomy to the Muslim minority, the Constitution, which stresses so-called secularism as well as minority protection, intensifies the conflict between these two governance principles. The conclusion is that this situation not only leads to ideological conflicts and resource competition but also, overall, threatens the stability of India's democracy.

Conclusion: religion, democratization and secularization
Jeffrey Haynes
The overarching theme of this special issue was the attempts by various religious actors – Christian, Muslim, and Jewish – to try to assert their values and pursue their goals in variable political circumstances. We saw that they sought to do this in contexts characterized not only by secularization and political changes, some of which emanate from within countries, but also as a result of external pressures, often a consequence of globalization.

Religion and democratizations: an introduction

Jeffrey Haynes

London Metropolitan University, London, UK

The question of how religious actors[1] might affect democratization has been a controversial issue for decades. Scholars stressed the importance of political culture in explaining success or failure of democratization after World War II in West Germany, Italy and Japan.[2] In addition, religious traditions – for example, Roman Catholicism in Italy and Christian Democracy in West Germany – were said to be important in the (re)making of a country's political culture after an experience of totalitarian regimes.[3] During the 'third wave of democracy' (mid-1970s–mid-1990s), a lot of attention was paid to the role of religion in democratization.[4] For example, it was widely noted that in Poland, the Roman Catholic Church played a key role in undermining the communist regime and helping to establish a post-communist, democratically accountable regime.[5] This had a wider political effect beyond Poland, extending to Latin America, Africa and parts of Asia. There was also the contemporaneous rise of the Christian Right in the United States of America, and its considerable impact on the electoral fortunes of both the Republican Party and the Democratic Party. Add to this widespread growth of Islamist movements across the Muslim world, with significant ramifications for electoral outcomes in various countries, including Algeria, Egypt, Morocco, electoral successes for the Hindu nationalist Bharatiya Janata Party in India, and substantial political influence over time for various 'Jewish fundamentalist' political parties in Israel, and we have clear and sustained evidence of religion's recent democratic importance.

Focusing upon the East European democratizing experience more generally, Juan Linz and Alfred Stepan argued more than a decade ago that religion was *not* generally a key explanatory factor explaining democratization outcomes.[6] In relation to Muslim countries, Fred Halliday has recently argued that apparent barriers to democracy in some such countries are primarily linked to certain social and political features that they share.[7] These include in many cases long histories of authoritarian rule and weak civil societies and, although some of those features tend to be legitimized in terms of 'Islamic doctrine', there is in fact nothing specifically 'Islamic' about them. On the other hand, for Huntington, religions have a crucial impact on democratization.[8] He claims that Christianity has a strong propensity to be supportive of democracy while other religions, such as Islam, Buddhist and Confucianism, do not.

This book seeks to build on such insights and arguments. Collectively, they examine key debates on religion and democratization from three main perspectives:

- religious traditions have core elements which are more or less conducive to democratization and democracy;
- religious traditions may be multi-vocal – but at any moment there may be dominant voices more or less receptive to and encouraging of democratization;
- religious actors rarely if ever *determine* democratization outcomes. However, they may in various ways and with a range of outcomes be of significance for democratization.

The book is divided into two sections: (1) Religion, democratization and democracy, and (2) Secularization, democratization and democracy. Overall, they examine the three assertions in the bullet points above. Our general starting point is that in general around the world, religions have left their assigned place in the private sphere. This means they have in many cases become recognizably politically active in various ways and with assorted outcomes. This re-emergence from political marginality dates back until at least the 1980s. At that time, Casanova notes, 'what was new and became "news" … was the widespread and simultaneous refusal of religions to be restricted to the private sphere'.[9] This involved a remodelling and re-assumption of public roles by religion, which theories of secularization had long condemned to social and political marginalization.

It was once believed to be axiomatic that modernization inevitably leads to religious privatization and secularization. As a result, there would be a fundamental, global decline in religion's social and political importance. This was believed to be the case, regardless of religious tradition or form of political power dominant in the context in which religion found itself. The 1979 revolution in Iran posed fundamental questions in relation to this conventional wisdom. Contemporaneously, the Roman Catholic Church began to play an increasingly important role in relation to democratization in Central and Eastern Europe, Africa, East Asia and Latin America. These two developments not only collectively emphasized that modernization does not always leads to secularization but also that religion can sometimes play a fundamental role in issues of political representation and legitimacy. Contrary to the secularization theory, there has been a widespread – some say, global – resurgence of religion, often as a political actor in numerous countries.[10] This has involved various religious traditions. Overall, it emphasizes not only that there is more than one relevant interpretation of modernization but also that religion can and does play a role in political changes, even in parts of the world, including Europe, that have been long regarded as inevitably secularizing.

This introduction follows the following format. In the next section, I examine how religious deprivatization has led to political changes in many parts of the world. After that, I define religion, in order to clarify how it can affect politics and political outcomes. The third section examines three important components of politics: political society, civil society and the state, with a view to identifying and discussing religion's influence in relation to each. The final section examines briefly each of the chapters, seeking to relate them to the key issues of the book: the variable roles of religious actors in relation to secularization, democratization and democracy.

Religious deprivatization and political change: a worldwide phenomenon

Globally, two phenomena are simultaneously taking place. First, there is said to be an *increase* in various forms of spirituality and religiosity, although this also implies in many cases both fragmentation and decline in societal clout of hitherto leading religious organizations in many countries.[11] The increase in spirituality and religiosity are manifested in various ways including 'new' religious and spiritual phenomena, including manifestations of 'New Age' spirituality; 'foreign', 'exotic' Eastern religions, including Hare Krishna; 'televangelism'; renewed interest in astrology, and 'new' sects, such as the Scientologists. Note, however, that such religious entities, as Casanova points out, are 'not particularly relevant for the social sciences or for the self-understanding of modernity', because they do not present 'major problems of interpretation. ... They fit within expectations and can be interpreted within the framework of established theories of secularization'.[12] The point is that they are *normal* phenomena. They are examples of *private* religion. They do not individually or collectively question or challenge the extant arrangements of society, including political and social structures. Indeed, such religious phenomena are *apolitical*; and 'all' they really show is that many people are interested in spiritual issues and sometimes they involve new expressions. In addition, in many European Catholic countries – for example, Italy, Poland and Spain – the Catholic Church is losing moral appeal for many people, especially among the young.[13] In sum, globally the multiplicity of existing and new religious phenomena belies the idea that religion will inevitably lose its appeal for many people, even in apparently highly secular countries, including France and Turkey, both of which are examined in detail in this collection. In addition, innovative religious forms appear to be increasing their appeal, often at the expense of traditional religions. But from a *political* perspective these new religions are rarely of political importance.

Secondly, not only Christian churches – especially the Roman Catholic church in both transnational and national contexts – but also Islamic religious actors in many countries, as well as Jewish entities in Israel, now openly seek to articulate viewpoints on a variety of political and social issues, more readily and openly than in the past. Such religious entities typically resist state attempts to sideline them.

Three questions are central in seeking to account for religion's current political impact in many countries. First, *why* should religious organizations seek to ecome actors with political goals? In this book, contributors contend that this occurs when religious entities feel that change is necessary and that the state is not well equipped to oversee and lead such changes, not least because the solutions it seeks are secular ones; and they do not chime well with religious interpretations. Secondly, how *widespread* is the phenomenon? Our starting assumption is that it is extensive, although the following chapters indicate that it is not uniform in its implications. Thirdly, what are the *political consequences* of religion's intervention? The short answer is that they are variable, as the following chapters explain. For example, sometimes religion appears to have a pivotal influence on political outcomes – for example, the role of the Roman Catholic Church in Poland in relation to democratization in the 1980s, a topic which Troy examines in his chapter. Elsewhere, however, as Jamal shows in relation to Islamists in Egypt, Gozaydin and Grigoriadis explain regarding Islamic movements in Turkey, and Baumgart-Ochse and Jamal underline when looking at Jewish fundamentalists in Israel, outcomes can be unexpected and variable, sometimes expressed at the level of what Ulrich Beck has called 'sub-politics', that is, political contestation played out not in political society but at the level of civil society.[14]

While differing in terms of specific issues that encourage them to act politically, religious actors commonly reject the secular ideals that have long dominated theories of political development in both developed and developing countries, appearing instead as champions of alternative, confessional outlooks, programmes and policies. Seeking to keep faith with what they interpret as divine decree, they typically refuse to render to secular power holders automatic material or moral support. Instead, they are concerned with various social, moral, and ethical issues, which are however nearly always political to some degree. Religious actors may challenge or undermine both the legitimacy and autonomy of the state's main secular spheres, including government and more widely political society. In addition, many churches and other comparable religious entities no longer restrict themselves to the pastoral care of individual souls. Now, they raise questions about, *inter alia*, interconnections of private and public morality, claims of states and markets to be exempt from extrinsic normative considerations, and modes and concerns of government. What religious actors also have in common is a shared concern for retaining and increasing their social importance. To this end, many religious entities now seek to bypass or elude what they regard as the cumbersome constraints of temporal authority and, as a result, threaten to undermine the latter's constituted political functions. In short, refusing to be condemned to the realm of privatized belief, religion has widely reappeared in the public sphere, thrusting itself into issues of social, moral and ethical – and in many places, political – contestation.

The overall aim of this book is to examine involvement of various religious actors in relation to democratization outcomes in a number of specific countries and contexts. The book assesses this issue in relation to: Egypt, France, Georgia, India, Indonesia, Israel, Mali, Turkey, Ukraine, West Germany and Zimbabwe. These accounts focus upon the following religions: Hinduism, Islam, Judaism, Orthodox Christianity, Charismatic Christianity, Roman Catholicism and Protestantism.

However, the key point is not from which religious tradition individual religious actors come. Instead, as the chapters collected here emphasize, religious entities are very often also political actors, wielding varying degrees of influence on political outcomes, while sharing a focus on a key issue: a desire to change their societies in directions where what they regard as religiously acceptable standards of behaviour are central to public life, including political life. Pursuing such objectives, they use a variety of tactics and methods, operating either at the level of civil society and/or political society.

Defining democratization and religion

Before turning to these issues in detail, it is useful to start by discussing two of the key terms used in this book: democratization and religion.

Democratization is a process. It can occur in four not necessarily discrete stages: (1) political liberalization, (2) collapse of authoritarian regime, (3) democratic transition, and (4) democratic consolidation. *Political liberalization* is the process of reforming authoritarian rule. *Collapse of the authoritarian regime* stage refers to the stage when a dictatorship falls apart. *Democratic transition* is the material shift to democracy, commonly marked by the democratic election of a new government. *Democratic consolidation* is the process of embedding both democratic institutions and perceptions among both elites and citizens that democracy is the best way of 'doing' politics.

The four stages are complementary and can overlap. For example, political liberalization and transition can happen simultaneously, while aspects of democratic consolidation can appear when certain elements of transition are barely in place or remain incomplete. Or they may even be showing signs of retreating. On the other hand, it is nearly always possible to observe a concluded transition to democracy. This is when a pattern of behaviour developed *ad hoc* during the stage of regime change becomes institutionalized, characterized by admittance of political actors into the system – as well as the process of political decision-making – according to previously established and legitimately coded procedures.

Until then, absence of or uncertainty about these accepted 'rules of the democratic game' make it difficult to be sure about the eventual outcome of political transitions. This is because the transition dynamics revolve around strategic interactions and tentative arrangements between actors with uncertain power resources. Key issues include: (1) defining who is legitimately entitled to play the political 'game', (2) the criteria determining who wins and who loses politically, and (3) the limits to be placed on the issues at stake. What chiefly differentiates the four stages of democratization is the degree of uncertainty prevailing at each moment. For example, during regime transition *all* political calculations and interactions are highly uncertain. This is because political actors find it difficult to know: (1) what their precise interests are and (2) which groups and individuals would most usefully be allies or opponents.

During transition, powerful, often inherently undemocratic, political players, such as the armed forces and/or elite civilian supporters of the exiting authoritarian regime, characteristically divide into what Huntington has identified as 'hard-line' and 'soft-line' factions.[15] 'Soft-liners' are relatively willing to achieve negotiated solutions to the political problems, while 'hard-liners' are unwilling to arrive at solutions reflecting compromise between polarized positions. Democratic transition is most likely when 'soft-liners' triumph because, unlike 'hard-liners', they are willing to find a compromise solution.

A consolidated democracy is often said to be in place when political elites, political groups and the mass of ordinary people accept the formal rules and informal understandings that determine political outcomes: that is, 'who gets what, where, when and how'. If achieved, it signifies that groups are settling into relatively predictable positions involving politically legitimate behaviour according to generally acceptable rules. More generally, a consolidated democracy is characterized by normative limits and established patterns of power distribution. Political parties emerge as privileged in this context because, despite their divisions over strategies and their uncertainties about partisan identities, the logic of electoral competition focuses public attention on them and compels them to appeal to the widest possible clientele. In addition, 'strong' civil societies are thought to be crucial for democratic consolidation, in part because they can help keep an eye on the state and what it does with its power. In sum, there is democratic consolidation when all major political actors take for granted the fact that democratic processes dictate governmental renewal.

Despite numerous relatively free and fair elections over the last two decades in many formerly authoritarian countries, in most cases ordinary people continue to lack ability to influence political outcomes. In many cases, this may be because small groups of elites – whether, civilians, military personnel, or a combination – not only control national political processes but also manage more widely to dictate political conditions. Under such conditions, because power is still held by relatively small groups of elites, political systems have narrow bases from which most ordinary people are, or feel, excluded. This can be problematic because, by definition, a democracy should not be run by and for the few, but should signify popularly elected government operating in the broad public interest.

In sum, during the third wave of democracy, increased numbers of governments came to power via the ballot box – yet not all of them have exhibited strong democratic credentials.[16]

Turning to the issue of defining religion, it has long been noted how extraordinarily difficult it is to reach a consensus on this issue. Sociologists have tended to use two main approaches in this regard. Religion is either: (1) a system of beliefs and practices related to an ultimate being, beings, or to the supernatural; or (2) that which is sacred in a society, including ultimate inviolate beliefs and practices. For purposes of wider social science analysis, religion can usefully be approached (1) from the perspective of a body of ideas and outlooks – that is, theology and ethical code; (2) as a type of formal organization – that is, ecclesiastical 'church' or comparable entity; or (3) as social group – that is, a religious organization, movement or party. Religion can affect the temporal world in one of two ways: by what it *says* and/or *does*. The former relates to religion's doctrine or theology, the latter to its importance as a social phenomenon and mark of identity, which can function through various modes of institutionalization, including civil society, political society and religion-state relations.

It is necessary to distinguish between religion expressed at the *individual* and *group* levels: only in the latter is it normally of importance for understanding related political outcomes. From an individualist perspective, we are contemplating religion's *private*, spiritual side, 'a set of symbolic forms and acts which relates man (sic) to the ultimate conditions of his existence'.[17] But to move into the realm of politics, as we do in this book, is necessarily to be concerned with *group* religiosity, whose claims and pretensions are *always* to some degree political. That is, there is no such thing as a religion without consequences for value systems, including those affecting politics and political outcomes. Group religiosity, like politics, is a matter of collective solidarities and, frequently, of inter-group tension, competition and conflict, with a focus on either shared or disputed images of the sacred or on cultural and/or class, in short, political, issues. To complicate matters, however, such influences may well operate differently and with 'different temporalities for the same theologically defined religion in different parts of the world'.[18]

To try to bring together the relationship between democratization and religious actors in all their varied aspects and then to discern significant patterns and trends is not a simple task. But, in attempting it three points are worth emphasizing. First, there is something of a distinction to be drawn between looking at the relationship in terms of the impact of religion on democratization, and that of democratization on religion. At the same time, they are interactive: one stimulates and is stimulated by the other. In other words, because we are concerned with the ways in which power is exercised in society, and the ways in which religion is involved, the relationship between religion and democratization is both dialectical and interactive. Both causal directions need to be held in view.

Secondly, religions are creative and constantly changing; consequently their relationships with democratization can also vary over time. In this book, the authors are all concerned to examine religious entities in democratization outcomes both currently and over the last few decades.

Finally, as political actors religious entities can only usefully be discussed in terms of specific contexts; in the chapters that comprise this book, it is the relationship with government which forms a common, although not the only, focal point. Yet, the model of responses, while derived from and influenced by specific aspects of particular religions, is not necessarily inherent to them.

Rather this is a theoretical construct suggested by much of the literature on state–society relations, built on the understanding that religion's specific role is largely determined by a broader context. The assumption is that there is an essential core element of religion shaping its behaviour in, for example, Christian, Islamic, or Jewish societies and communities. However, the contributions to this book explicitly or implicitly question this assumption. The focus of many earlier studies was to seek to analyse how existing religious beliefs or affiliations affect political outcomes, including those related to democratization. In this book, however, we are equally concerned with the reverse process: how do specific political contexts affect how and what selected religious entities do in relation to democratization?

Religion, political society, civil society, and the state

To understand the general political importance of religious actors, and by extension how they involve themselves in democratization, it is necessary first to comprehend what they say and do in their relationship with the state. I mean something more than 'mere' government when referring to the state. The state is the continuous administrative, legal, bureaucratic, and coercive system that attempts not only to manage the various state apparatuses, but in addition to 'structure relations between civil and public power and to structure many crucial relationships within civil and political society'.[19] As a result, almost everywhere in the world, apparently regardless of the nature of political systems and/or the level of economic development in a country, states have over time sought to reduce and control religion's political importance and involvement. That is, around the world states have sought to privatize religion, and thus considerably to reduce its political impact. Sometimes, for example in Poland and Italy (Catholicism) and Turkey (Sunni Islam), states have attempted to erect a 'civil religion' arrangement, whereby a certain designated religious format effectively 'functions as the cult of the political community'.[20] The declared purpose is to try to create and develop forms of consensual, corporate religion, claiming to be guided by general, culturally appropriate, specific religious beliefs of intrinsic societal significance. In short, when states seek to develop 'civil religions' it is an attempted strategy to try to avoid social conflicts and promote national coordination and cohesion.

This book illustrates that religious actors' relationships with the state are by no means limited to attempts by the latter to build civil religions. In fact, in many countries, relations between religious entities and the state are not only now more visible, but also increasingly problematic. Why is this the case? First, it may be that recent increases in religious challenges to the authority of the state are merely transitory reactions in the context of the onward march of secularization. Secondly, even if the modern state is particularly vulnerable to legitimation crises, it does not necessarily mean that religion is again becoming *automatically* relevant to state functioning. Thirdly, religion-based challenges to state hegemony have roots in endeavours by the latter to assert a monitoring role vis-à-vis religion, in effect to control it. We can see such a development at three levels: political society, civil society and at the level of the state itself.

This book underlines that in many countries religion is being liberated from providing sometimes slavish legitimacy to secular authority. Many religious actors are now willing routinely to criticize and challenge the state in various ways in relation to a variety of issues and themes. Yet, even if heightened concern about the state's policies can be held up as evidence of the regeneration of the socio-political power of religion, we still need to ask further questions. The issues are themselves secular and in so far as religious agencies are active in these areas, this is a radical shift of concern from the supernatural, from devotional acts, to what are largely secular goals pursued by secular means. However, a note of caution is in order: we need to bear in mind that when religious interests act as 'pressure groups' – rather than as 'prayer bodies' – they are not necessarily going to be effective in what they seek to achieve. This is because the more secularized a society, the less likely it is that religious actors will be able to play a politically significant role.[21]

Religion and political society

At the level of political society – that is, the arena in which the polity specifically arranges itself for political contestation to gain control over public power and the state apparatus – we can note a range of religious responses that are in part dependent upon the degree of secularization. These include (1) resistance to the disestablishment and the differentiation of the religious from the secular sphere; the goals of many so-called religious 'fundamentalist' groups; (2) religious groups and confessional political parties' mobilizations and counter-mobilizations against other religions or secular movements and parties; and (3) religious organizations' mobilization in defence of religious, social and political freedoms – that is, demanding the rule of law and the legal protection of human and civil rights, protecting mobilization of civil society and/or defending institutionalization of democratically elected governments. In recent times in pursuit of such goals, we can note Roman Catholic transnational political mobilization in and between various countries, as Troy does in his chapter in this book, as well as activities of Islamist groups in various countries, including Turkey (the chapters by Barras, Grigoriadis, Gozaydin and Jamal) Egypt (Jamal), Mali and Indonesia (Künkler and Leininger).

Religion and civil society

Civil society is the arena where various social movements – including, neighbourhood associations, women's groups, religious entities, and intellectual currents – join with civic organizations, including, lawyers', journalists', trade unions', and entrepreneurs' associations, to constitute themselves into an ensemble of arrangements to express themselves and seek to advance their interests. Sometimes, the concept of *civil* society is used in contrast to *political* society. Unlike the latter, civil society refers to organizations and movements – *not* political parties – formally uninvolved in both the business of government and overt political management. Note however that this does not necessarily prevent civil society organizations from sometimes seeking to or actually exerting political influence, on various matters, including democratic outcomes and the content of national constitutions. Regarding religion at the level of civil society, one can distinguish between hegemonic civil religions – such as Evangelical Protestantism in nineteenth century America – and the recent public intervention of religious entities, concerned either with single issues such as anti-abortion or with morally-determined views of wider societal development, for example, in relation to homosexual rights or appropriate days for shops to open (on the latter issue, see Jamal's chapter in this book for the current situation in Israel). In trying to influence public policy – without themselves seeking to become political office-holders – religious entities may employ a variety of tactics, including, in no particular order: (1) lobbying the executive apparatus of the state, (2) going to court, (3) building links with political parties, (4) forming alliances with like-minded groups, both secular and/or from other religious traditions, (5) mobilizing followers to lobby and/or protest, and (6) working to sensitize public opinion via mass media. The overall point is that religious actors may use a variety of methods to try to achieve their objectives. Chapters in this book that focus upon the role of religion in civil society include Baumgart-Ochse's account of Jewish fundamentalist groups in Israel and that of Ganiel, in her account of the importance of spiritual capital for church development in Zimbabwe.

Religion and the state

Interactions between the state and religious entities are often referred to as 'church–state' relations. It is useful to point out, however, that one of the difficulties in seeking to survey contemporary 'church–state relations' is that the very concept of *church* is a somewhat parochial, Anglo-American standpoint with direct relevance only to Christian traditions. It is derived primarily from the context of British establishmentarianism – that is, maintenance of the principle of 'establishment' whereby one church is legally recognized as the only established church. In other words, when we think of church–state relations we may assume a single relationship between two clearly distinct, unitary and solidly but separately institutionalized entities. In this implicit model built into the conceptualization of the religion–political nexus there is but *one* state and *one* church; both entities' jurisdictional boundaries need to be carefully delineated. Both separation and pluralism must be safeguarded, because it is assumed that the leading church – like the state – will seek institutionalized dominance over rival religious organizations. For its part, the state is expected to respect individual rights even though it is assumed to be inherently disposed toward aggrandizement at the expense of citizens' personal liberty. In sum, the conventional concept of state–church relations is rooted in prevailing Christian conceptions of the power of the state of necessity being constrained by forces in society – including those of religion. In her chapter Ganiel shows, through a focus upon a specific Charismatic church in Zimbabwe that churches can seek to pursue their objectives, even when the state is powerful and its orientation is not conventionally pro-democracy.

Expanding the problem of church–state relations to non-Christian contexts necessitates some preliminary conceptual clarifications – not least because the very idea of a prevailing state–church dichotomy is culture-bound. As already noted, *church* is a Christian institution, while the modern understanding of *state* is deeply rooted in the Post-Reformation European political experience. In their specific cultural setting and social significance, the tension and the debate over the church–state relationship are uniquely Western phenomena, present in the ambivalent dialectic of 'render therefore unto Caesar the things which be Caesar's and unto God the things which be God's' (Luke 21: 25). Overloaded with Western cultural history, these two concepts cannot easily be translated into non-Christian terminologies.

The differences between Christian conceptions of state and church and those of other world religions are well illustrated by reference to Islam. In the Muslim tradition, mosque is not church. The closest Islamic approximation to 'state' – *dawla* – means, as a concept, either a ruler's dynasty or his administration. Only with the specific Durkheimian stipulation of *church* as the generic concept for *moral community, priest* for the *custodians of the sacred law,* and *state* for *political community* can we comfortably use these concepts in Islamic and other non-Christian contexts. On the theological level, the command–obedience nexus that constitutes the Islamic definition of authority is not demarcated by conceptual categories of religion and politics. Life as a physical reality is an expression of divine will and authority (*qudrah'*). There is no validity in separating the matters of piety from those of the polity; both are divinely ordained. Yet, although both religious and political authorities are legitimated Islamically, they invariably constitute two independent social institutions. They do, however, regularly interact with each other. Yet, as Jamal shows in relation to Egypt and Grigoriadis, Gozaydin, Barras and Jamal explain regarding Turkey, there may be sometimes serious tensions between Islamist actors and the state in regard to democratization and political outcomes more generally

The overall point is that tensions widely exist between secular power holders and religious actors of various kinds in the modern world. It is often the case in some European countries, for example, that religious actors, apparently regardless of their religious persuasion, may work individually or collectively towards reducing the ability of the state to sideline them. Barras shows this in relation to France where recent years have seen a campaign by some Muslim women to wear Islamic dress. While they regard it as a fundamental human right to be allowed to dress as they wish, French secularists see things differently: Muslim women's efforts to dress as they wish is regarded by the secularists as a direct contravention of a core French post-revolutionary principle: subjugation of religion by the state. In effect, such religious challenges reflect a wider development: a wish on the part of some religious actors to reverse religious privatization, a course of action which impacts on a variety of political and social concerns.

This book is divided into two sections. The first section which focuses on 'religion, democratization and democracy' comprises five chapters, those by Künkler and Leininger; Troy; Baumgart-Ochse; Jamal; and Ganiel. The second section, made up of four chapters, examines the issue of 'secularization, democratization and democracy', with chapters by Grigoriadis; Gozaydin; Barras; and Harel-Shalev.

In their chapter, Künkler and Leininger comparatively investigate the role of religious actors in the democratization processes of five 'young' democracies from several different religious traditions: Catholic, Protestant, Christian-Orthodox and Muslim. Their case studies are: West Germany after World War II, Georgia and the Ukraine post-1987/9, Mali after 1987 and Indonesia from 1998. Their analysis provides an overview of the roles various religious actors played in the erosion of authoritarian power in each of these countries, the transition to democracy and subsequent democratic consolidation, as well as de-democratization processes that to varying degrees have accompanied democratization in the five countries. They conclude by noting that religious actors did not determine democratic outcomes in the countries they review. They were however important in serving to highlight institutional conditions which enabled them to wield influence in democratization outcomes.

Troy focuses upon what he refers to as '"Catholic waves" of democratization'. In his chapter he seeks to ascertain whether Catholicism is or can be a major force in democratization. If it is such a force, why is this the case? Does a pro-democratization focus reflect the Church's core values and motivations? To examine this issue, Troy seeks to evaluate democratization outcomes where the Church was *not* involved. He shows that to get to the bottom of this issue, it is necessary to take into account fundamental Christian and thus also Catholic values and doctrines which are – despite all 'earthly' constraints – demonstrably in favour of both liberal and democratic values. In the case of the Catholic Church this is primarily because many of its adherents perceive the social message of the gospels as both theory and as a guide to praxis. Troy contends that the Church underwent a sea change in this regard following the Second Vatican Council (1962–1965), which enabled the Church's adoption of a pronounced focus on not only democracy but also human rights, religious freedom, and economic and human development.

Turning to Africa, Ganiel is interested in another form of Christianity in the decidedly non-democratic African country of Zimbabwe. She begins by noting that throughout much of Africa, what she refers to as 'charismatic Christianity' is spreading fast. Yet this form of Christianity has often been portrayed as an inhibitor of democratization. This is because its adherents are said either to withdraw from the often bruising environment of politics ('pietism') or to preach a prosperity gospel that encourages believers to pour their resources into their churches in the hope that God will 'bless' them, taking away the necessity of engaging with the rough and tumble of politics in order to bring about personal and community life improvements. Together, both courses of action are said to encourage such Christians to be politically quietist, unlike many Catholics, with no interest in democratization or other forms of political activity.

Her chapter utilizes an ethnographic case study of a 'progressive' charismatic congregation in Harare, Zimbabwe, following field work conducted in 2007. She provides evidence that 'pietism' or 'prosperity' are not the only options for charismatic Christians. Informed by the concept of 'spiritual capital,' she argues that some varieties of charismatic Christianity have the resources to contribute to democratization. For example, she argues that the Harare congregation's self-styled 'de-institutionalization' process is opening up new avenues for people to learn democratic skills and develop worldviews that are relationship-centred, participatory, and anti-authoritarian. Her chapter concludes that spiritual capital can be a useful tool for analysing the role of religions in democratization, including in Zimbabwe.

Baumgart-Ochse examines why Israel has found it so difficult to advance the peace process with the Palestinians since the Oslo Agreement of 1993. She explains that there are often close and supportive links between democracies and peace, an idea conceptualized as the 'democratic peace thesis', a presumption now commonplace in international relations (IR) literature. On the other hand, she notes, there are possible dangers of democratization processes for international peace and security. Her chapter argues that some of the mechanisms prevalent in democratizing states' ambivalent conflict behaviour help to explain why the state of Israel initially entered into the peace process with the Palestinians, but soon reverted to former hostile policies. In the initial stages of the peace process in the early 1990s, the then Labour-led government based its efforts towards peace on the typical norms of democratic peace and thus explicitly stated the need to improve Israel's defective democratic regime. This involved amending the electoral system by ending the de facto control in the occupied territories of the Palestinians, who did not participate in Israeli democratic politics. However, the prospect of 'land for peace' threatened the politicized religious Jewish settler-elite in the territories who feared not only the destruction of the basic tenets of their religious identity, but also the loss of both power and resources in Israeli politics As a consequence, this threatened elite engaged in fierce religious-nationalist mobilization in order to derail the peace negotiations and at the same time subvert the process of improving Israel's democratic regime.

Jamal is also interested in Israel's democracy and the role within it of the Arab minority. His chapter argues that when it comes to issues of religion and state, then democratization can take two opposing directions. Whereas in some cases the public return of religion and the subsequent representation of religious groups reflect democratization, in other cases, where state and religion are tightly integrated, democratization means the decoupling of state and religion and the downgrading of religious control of public institutions and individual personal status. To pursue this argument, his chapter examines state–religion relations not only in Israel but also for comparative purposes in Turkey and Egypt.

These cases are chosen for several reasons. The first is to demonstrate that the policy of suppression of religion from the public sphere by the state as in Turkey or the policy of formally institutionalized religion as in Israel and Egypt do not necessarily facilitate democratization, despite the fact that they do not undermine the fundamental principles of equal citizenship. The second reason is that these cases demonstrate that democratization could take two opposite directions when it comes to state–religion relations. The Turkish case demonstrates that in that country democratization implies the downgrading in importance of laïcité, especially allowing religious parties to run for elections or respecting provision of religious education outside state control. (In the second section of this book, chapters by Grigoriadias, Gozaydin and Barras also examine this theme from various perspectives.)

In Israel, democratization implies the decoupling of state and religious identity and the equalization of different religious streams and faiths. In Egypt, decoupling of state and religion may *facilitate* democratization, although such a change has not been sufficient to democratize the whole political regime. Thirdly, religion in Middle Eastern countries, even when considered procedurally democratic, as in Israel, nevertheless can form a major challenge to democratic equality and justice. Lastly, examining the Egyptian and Turkish cases provides evidence that different Islamic countries can develop different trajectories of state–religion relations.

The second section of the book comprises four chapters which focus on the theme of secularization, democracy and democratization. Grigoriadis focuses upon the history of Turkish modernization, which has been inextricably linked to the question of secularization. From the advent of the Turkish republic in 1923, Islam was held responsible for the underdevelopment and eventual demise of the Ottoman Empire. Based on the laïcité of the Second French Republic, the secularization programme of modern Turkey's founder, Kemal Atatürk, entailed the full subjugation of Islam to the state, its eradication from the public sphere and its limitation into a very narrowly defined private sphere. The transition of Turkey to multiparty politics in 1946 was linked with a rising role of Islam in the public sphere. Islam became a crucial element in the political vocabulary of peripheral political forces which challenged the supremacy of the secularist, Kemalist bureaucratic elite. While a number of military coups aimed – among other things to control religion – Turkish political Islam showed remarkable resilience and adaptability. Most recently, the transformation of the Justice and Development Party (*Adalet ve Kalkınma Partisi* – AKP) into the strongest proponent of Turkey's European Union integration brought Turkey closer than ever to EU membership, challenged the monopoly which the Kemalist elite enjoyed as the representative of Western political values and suggested an alternative more liberal version of secularism. Yet Turkey has been embroiled since 2007 in successive political crises which had secularism as their focal point. This chapter argues that the transformation of Turkish political Islam has produced an alternative, liberal version of secularism yet has not resolved deep social divisions. Building a liberal consensus between religious conservatives and secularists is imperative for the resolution of deep social divisions in Turkey. The European Union as a guarantor and initiator of reform could play a major role in building trust between the secularist and the religious conservative segments of society.

Gözaydin's contribution also examines the issue of Turkey's interlinked democratization and secularization process. Her chapter is concerned with the democratic involvement of the Fethullah Gülen movement in recent democratization in Turkey. She begins by explaining that since 1923 the official ideology of republican Turkey has been strictly secular. However, religious networking has always been a very important component of the socio-structural system in the country. Over time, the republican regime sought to stifle development of such networking, while at the same time also promoting changes in this regard. For 50 years – between about 1930 and about 1980 – Islamic networks in Turkey developed market relations that promoted strategies to improve the economic position of their members. In this context, several 'new' religious groups emerged, including the Fethullah Gülen movement.

Barras continues the theme of secularization in Turkey. She is however interested in comparing the situation in Turkey with that in France, another country that has had a long programme and policy of secularization. She relates this issue to the global human rights discourse which since the 1980s has been increasingly referred to by those seeking to develop their religious rights. She explains that this discourse has also been intrinsically linked to positivism, enlightenment and secularization. It is with these issues in mind that her chapter examines religious Muslim individuals and groups in both France and Turkey. In both cases, they have referred to the existing human rights discourse and its national, regional and international legal channels. The objective has been to try to challenge state secularization policies and redefine the relationship between Islam and the state.

She examines two specific case studies. The first is the work of the Collective against Islamophobia in France. The second is the Merve Kavakci *versus* Turkey case recently presented at the Strasbourg European Court of Human Rights. Barras investigates if groups and individuals have found through the use of this 'authorized narrative' a space where they can propose a new plural ethos that can better co-exist with their piety. This is a space where they can offer a more plural and de-centralized vision of secularism. To complement this analysis, she also highlights some of the possible paradoxes found within the human rights discourse. These paradoxes might potentially enlighten us to the challenges of using such a discourse, particularly to ask for the right to display publicly one's religion. In other words, she attempts to shed some light on whether the use of a rights-based discourse by religious rights groups and individuals can help resolve democratically disputes between the religious and the secular – encouraging perhaps the democratization of secularism in specific contexts.

The final chapter in this book focuses on the ambivalent effect of religious autonomy in India and the outcome for democracy in that country. The Indian constitution guarantees autonomy to its religious minorities, and promises the minorities the freedom independently to manage their religious affairs in addition to a proportional share of the budget. At the same time, the constitution emphasizes the aspiration to legislate 'uniform personal laws' for all the citizens of India in accordance with the principles of secularism, equality and with India's self-definition as a civic nation. This recommendation has however remained a 'dead letter' until today. In this domain, the state has constituted a civic law for Hindus, which adjusts Hinduism to democratic principles. In this sense, the state has nationalized Hinduism, and the government has assumed authority and reformed Hindu civic and marriage laws. However, although they have tried, the state's legal and political institutions have not interfered thus far with Muslim marriage and religious laws. Muslims are committed to Islamic (*Sharia*) law, while Hindus must obey the state's civic laws. By avoiding enforcement of affirmative action for Muslims in the spheres of political representation or public employment, while simultaneously prohibiting Hindus' group rights, and providing religious autonomy to the Muslim minority, the Constitution, which stresses the state's commitment to secularism as well as minority protection, intensifies the conflict between these two governance principles. The conclusion is that this situation not only leads to ideological conflicts and resource competition but also, overall, threatens the stability and health of India's democracy.

Notes

1. Religious faith encourages a religious actor to undertake action. Such actors include: churches and comparable religious organizations in non-Christian religions; social movements whose main motivating factor is members' religious beliefs; and political parties, whose ideology identifiably also has its roots in religious beliefs and traditions.
2. Linz and Stepan, *Problems of Democratic Transition and Consolidation*; Stepan, 'Religion, Democracy, and the "Twin Tolerations"'; Huntington, *The Third Wave*.
3. Casanova, *Public Religions in the Modern World;* Madeley, '*E unum pluribus*'.
4. Huntington, *The Third Wave*.
5. Weigel, *Witness to Hope*; Weigel, *Faith, Reason, and the War Against Jihadism*.
6. Linz and Stepan, *Problems of Democratic Transition and Consolidation*.
7. Halliday, *The Middle East in International Relations*.
8. Huntington, *The Clash of Civilizations*.
9. Casanova, *Public Religions in the Modern World*, 6.
10. Casanova, *ibid.*; Davie, *Religion in Modern Europe*; Stepan, 'Religion, Democracy, and the "Twin Tolerations"'.
11. Davie, *ibid.*
12. Casanova, *Public Religions in the Modern World*, 5.
13. Ceccarini, 'The Church in Opposition'; Hennig, 'Morality Politics in a Catholic Democracy.
14. Beck, 'Subpolitics',
15. Huntington, *The Third Wave*.
16. Carothers, 'End of Transition Paradigm'.
17. Bellah, 'Religious Evolution', 359.

18. Moyser, 'Politics and Religion in the Modern World an Overview', 11.
19. Stepan, *Rethinking Military Politics. Brazil and the Southern Cone*, 3.
20. Casanova, *Public Religions in the Modern World*, 58.
21. Wilson, 'Reflections on a Many Sided Controversy', 202–3.

References

Beck, Ulrich. 'Subpolitics'. *Organization & Environment* 10, no. 1 (1997): 52–65.
Bellah, Robert. 'Religious Evolution'. *American Sociological Review* no. 29 (1964): 358–74.
Carothers, Thomas. 'The End of the Transition Paradigm'. *Journal of Democracy* 13, no. 1 (2002): 5–21.
Casanova, Jose. *Public Religions in the Modern World*. Chicago and London: University of Chicago Press, 1994.
Ceccarini, Luigi. 'The Church in Opposition. Religious Actors, Lobbying and Catholic Voters in Italy'. In *Religion and Politics in Europe, the Middle East and North Africa*, ed. Jeffrey Haynes, 177–201. London: Routledge, 2009.
Davie, Grace. *Religion in Modern Europe: A Memory Mutates*. Oxford: Oxford University Press, 2000.
Halliday, Fred. *The Middle East in International Relations: Power, Politics and Ideology*. Cambridge: Cambridge University Press, 2005.
Hennig, Anja. 'Morality Politics in a Catholic Democracy. A Hard Road Towards Liberalisation of Gay Rights in Poland'. In *Religion and Politics in Europe, the Middle East and North Africa*, ed. Jeffrey Haynes, 202–26. London: Routledge, 2009.
Huntington, Samuel. *The Third Wave. Democratization in the Late Twentieth Century*. Norman: University of Oklahoma Press, 1991.
Huntington, Samuel. *The Clash of Civilizations and the Remaking of World Order*. New York: Free Press, 1996.
Linz, Juan, and Alfred Stepan. *Problems of Democratic Transition and Consolidation. Southern Europe, South America, and Post-Communist Europe*. Baltimore and London: John Hopkins University Press, 1996.
Madeley, John T.S. '*E unum pluribus*. The Role of Religion in the Project of European Integration'. In *Religion and Politics in Europe, the Middle East and North Africa*, ed. Jeffrey Haynes, 114–35. London: Routledge, 2009.
Moyser, George. 'Politics and Religion in the Modern World an Overview'. In *Politics and Religion in the Modern World*, ed. George Moyser, 1–27. London: Routledge, 1991.
Stepan, Alfred. *Rethinking Military Politics. Brazil and the Southern Cone*. Princeton, NJ: Princeton University Press, 1988.
Stepan, Alfred. 'Religion, Democracy, and the "Twin Tolerations"', *Journal of Democracy* 11, no. 4 (2000): 37–57.
Weigel, George. *Witness to Hope: The Biography of Pope John Paul II, 1920–2005*. New York: HarperCollins, 2005.
Weigel, George. *Faith, Reason, and the War against Jihadism: A Call to Action*. New York: Doubleday, 2007.
Wilson, Bryan. 'Reflections on a Many Sided Controversy'. In *Religion and Modernization*, ed. Steve Bruce, 195–210. Oxford: Clarendon Press, 1992.

The multi-faceted role of religious actors in democratization processes: empirical evidence from five young democracies

Mirjam Künkler[a] and Julia Leininger[b]

[a]*Princeton University, NJ, USA;* [b]*Deutsches Institut für Entwicklungspolitik (DIE), Bonn, Germany*

The article comparatively investigates the role of religious actors in the democratization processes of five 'young' democracies from the Catholic, Protestant, Christian-Orthodox and Muslim world: West Germany after World War II (1945–1969), Georgia and Ukraine post-1987/9, Mali (post-1987), and Indonesia from 1998. The analysis provides an overview of the roles religious actors played in the erosion of authoritarian rule, the transition to democracy and subsequent democratic consolidation processes, as well as de-democratization processes. Our three paired comparisons, including one in-country comparison, show that the condition which most affected the role of religious actors in all three phases of democratic transitions was the de facto autonomy they enjoyed vis-à-vis the political regime as well as the organizational form these actors took. Their aims, means, and the political significance of their theology were highly dependent on the extent to which they benefitted from de facto autonomy within the state.

Introduction

Little systematic research has been undertaken that examines the influence of religious authorities and organizations on the erosion of authoritarian regimes and on the success of transitions to democracy. Despite the fact that transition theorists also speak of the Third Wave of Democracy as 'The Catholic Wave',[1] few attempts have been made to systematize the factors that determine the contributions of religious actors to democratization processes and de-democratization processes.[2]

An important large-N study that addresses this lacuna is the Harvard Research Project on Religion and Global Affairs.[3] The research project examined all democratic transitions that occurred between 1972 and 2000, and discovered that in about a third of all 82 identified cases, religious actors played a significant and constructive role towards democratization. In contrast to what one might expect, crucial factors that appeared to facilitate a largely constructive impact of religious actors were not particular liberal theologies, gender-egalitarian values or the existence of democratic internal organizational structures of religious organizations. Rather, the research project concluded that religious actors and institutions exerted a positive role towards the erosion of authoritarian power and a democratic transition, when they enjoyed substantial freedom from state control and possibilities to avert state co-optation. This was particularly the case where they benefited from: (1) some legal autonomy which allowed them to become a platform for dissent somewhat immune to state intervention, and (2) transnational linkages which made them financially less dependent on domestic sources of income.[4]

In this article, we comparatively present the findings of six case studies that investigate the role of religious actors in the democratization processes of five 'young' democracies: West Germany (1945–1969), Georgia (1987–2007), Ukraine (1989–2007), Mali (1987–2007), and Indonesia (1991–2007). Each case study examines the role of religious actors in all three phases of democratization: the opening of the authoritarian regime, the democratic transition, and the processes of democratization and de-democratization once the formal-institutional transition to democratic rule had been achieved. The case studies are contributions to a volume we recently edited that presents in three paired comparisons evidence from the Catholic, Protestant, Christian-Orthodox and Muslim world.[5]

How did religious actors in these five societies support or impede the erosion of authoritarian rule, the transition to a democratic order and the consolidation of democratic politics? Did the extent to which they could politically influence these processes hinge primarily on their legal and financial independence from the state, as the Harvard research project found to be the case in its studies? If not, what were other factors conditioning the influence of religious actors on processes of (de-)democratization?[6] And finally, through which means did religious actors exert their influence?

By investigating the role of religious actors in democratization processes, we assume religious actors exert an impact on such processes. While we show that religious actors did not determine democratic outcomes, we illustrate the variation with which they have affected processes of regime change and elucidate the political, legal and institutional conditions under which their role has been significant. Finally, the article revisits the democratic compatibility debate – that suggests Protestantism is more conducive to democratization than other religious dominations – and clarifies whether our case studies render credence to arguments about Christian-Orthodox and Muslim exceptionalism.

In the following, we will first give a brief overview of the analysed cases, preceded by a note on methodology. In the subsequent empirical section, we showcase the variety of influences exerted by religious actors on democratization processes. In the third analytical section, we examine the reasons behind these different influences. This will lead to concluding reflections on common patterns that have prompted religious actors to support or obstruct democratization across the six cases.

1. Case selection and methodology

In our case selection we prioritized three criteria. First, we looked for overall variance in religious denomination and therefore chose cases that involve churches from Western Christianity, churches from Eastern Christianity, and organizations and authorities from the Muslim world. Secondly, we designed the comparison to show variance within each of the three sets: from the Western Christian world we chose the Protestant and Catholic Church in West Germany, from the Christian-Orthodox world we chose Orthodox churches in Ukraine and Georgia, and from the Muslim-majority world we chose Islamic actors in Indonesia and Mali. Thirdly, we selected countries that have undergone a transition to democratic rule and have experienced at least a decade of consolidation without reversal to autocracy – countries which, in the words of Freedom House, can be considered free or at least partly free (see Table 1).

1.1 Democratization

Democratization processes are classically thought of as a three-stage process, divided into the phase of 'the opening' during which authoritarian rule is sufficiently eroded so as to make way for a sustainable oppositional challenge; the phase of the transition itself, during which a fundamental change in the nature of power takes place; and the phase of consolidation, during which democracy becomes the 'only game in town'.[7] In *Problems of Democratic Transition and Consolidation*, Juan Linz and Alfred Stepan (1996) conceive of a transition as 'complete' when four requirements are met: there is sufficient agreement about political procedures to produce an elected government; the government is a direct result of universal, free and fair elections; the government has the *de facto* authority to generate new policies; and there is no *de jure* power-sharing outside the executive, legislative, and judicial branches.[8]

A democracy is consolidated when, *behaviourally*, 'no significant political groups attempt to overthrow the democratic regime or secede from the state'; *attitudinally*, the overwhelming majority of the people believe that any further change should take place within the perimeters of 'democratic formulas', even in the face of severe economic and political crises; and *constitutionally*, all 'governmental and non-governmental forces' become both subjected and habituated to the resolution of conflict within specific laws, procedures and institutions sanctioned by the new democratic regime.[9] Consolidated democracies need to have in place five interacting and mutually reinforcing arenas, each with its own organizing principle: a state apparatus (rational-legal bureaucratic norms), rule of law (constitutionalism), political society (free and inclusive electoral contestation), civil society (freedom of association and communication), and economic society (an institutionalized market).

Finally, in the spirit of Charles Tilly, we fully acknowledge that democratization processes may be accompanied by simultaneous de-democratization processes and that democratization processes are always reversible, although over time that possibility decreases.[10]

Table 1. Countries of the 'fourth wave of democratization' by their majority religion and the development of their Freedom House status (1989–2009).[a]

Majority religion	Freedom House status[b]	
	'Free' in 2009	'Partly free' in 2009
Predominantly Catholic/Protestant	Benin (10), Chile (5), Croatia (5), Czech Republic (11), German Democratic Republic (10), Estonia (9), Guyana (4), Hungary (5), Latvia (8), Lesotho (6), Lithuania (9), Marshall Islands (0), Mexico (2), Micronesia (0), Namibia (3), Panama (10), Poland (5), Slovenia (7), Slovakia (11), South Africa (7)	Burundi (4), Kenya (5), Liberia (4), Madagascar[c] (2), Malawi (5), Mozambique (7), Nicaragua (3), Zambia (5)
Predominantly Christian-Orthodox	Bulgaria (10), Romania (10), Serbia (4), Ukraine (6)	Georgia (3), Moldova (3), Montenegro (3), Macedonia (3)
Predominantly Muslim	Indonesia (5), Mali (7)	Albania (8), Bangladesh (0), Bosnia-Herzegovina (2), Burkina Faso (3), Gambia (-5), Guinea-Bissau (4), Niger (6), Nigeria[d] (2), Senegal (1), Sierra Leone (5)[e]
Predominantly Hindu		Nepal (1)
Predominantly Buddhist	Mongolia (10) Taiwan[f] (4)	Thailand (-4)

[a] Following Schmidt, *Demokratietheorien. Eine Einführung*, the 'Fourth Wave' comprises countries that started democratic transitions after 1989. McFaul similarly dates the beginning of the Fourth Wave in the early 1990s. See McFaul, *The Fourth Wave of Democracy and Dictatorship*. Only countries with a minimum population of 1 million are included.
[b] Since 1972, Freedom House has annually classified the status of political rights and civil liberties in most countries around the world on a scale between 1 (free) and 7 (unfree). We replicate the methodology of Schmidt 2008 and indicate in brackets the points countries improved in their Freedom House Status since the beginning of the fourth wave in 1989. For instance, '5' indicates a country has improved five points on the freedom scale (i.e. has become 'more free') between 14 (most unfree: 7 on the political rights scale plus 7 on the civil liberties scale) and 2 (most free: 1 on the political rights scale plus 1 on the civil liberties scale). As the table indicates, between 1989 and 2009, out of all the countries that started a transition towards democracy, only in Gambia and Thailand did the degree of freedom citizens enjoy substantially deteriorate.
[c] In Madagascar, 41% of the population is Christian, whereas the majority of 52% adheres to local religions.
[d] In Nigeria, 50% of the population is Muslim, 40% is Christian.
[e] For the Muslim-majority set, it should be noted that beside Indonesia and Mali listed as 'free' here, Albania, Senegal and Turkey are all scored as democracies in other authoritative indices, such as Polity IV and the Bertelsmann Transformation Index, at least since the mid-2000s. On a scale between -10 (authoritarian) and +10 (democratic), the last issue of Polity IV has scored Albania at 9, Indonesia and Senegal at 8, and Mali and Turkey at 7.
[f] In Taiwan, 93% of the population is Buddhist/Taoist.
Source: Schmidt, *Demokratietheorien. Eine Einführung*, World Fact Book (2009), and Freedom House (2009). For the CIA World Factbook 2009, see https://www.cia.gov/library/publications/the-world-factbook. For Freedom House ratings, see www.freedomhouse.org

We conceptualize the nature of the influence religious actors exert on democratization processes with three attributes: religious actors play a *constructive* role, where they directly or indirectly contribute to one or several of the three phases of democratization: the erosion of authoritarian rule, ensuring the democratic outcome of the transition, or the consolidation of democratic norms, modes of behaviour and attitudes. Examples of direct constructive influence include mass mobilization by Islamic actors against the continued reign of President Suharto in New Order (authoritarian) Indonesia, while the willingness to subject one's religious schools to state oversight and cooperate in curriculum development with a young democratic administration, for instance, would be an indirect constructive influence.

Secondly, religious actors play an *obstructive* role, where they directly or indirectly obstruct the erosion of an authoritarian regime, the democratic outcome of a transition or the consolidation of democratic norms, modes of behaviour and attitudes. Thirdly, religious actors play a *destructive* role, when they pro-actively and directly inhibit the internalization of democratic norms, modes of behaviour or attitudes. As will be seen below, religious actors may simultaneously render legitimacy to new democratic governments and thereby decrease the likelihood of authoritarian reversal, while also preventing the diffusion of egalitarian norms due to their incompatibility with certain tenets of their creed. There may be cases, in other words, where religious actors (like other actors) contribute directly and indirectly to both democratization and de-democratization processes at the same time. As we will see below, whatever is the majority religion may be reluctant to support an expansion of equal rights to religious minorities and agnostics and to give up state-endowed privileges enjoyed during the previous authoritarian regime. Similarly, religious actors may overall exert a positive role in one phase of democratization, while their actions may have adverse effects to democratization in another phase. Finally, one should note that while religious actors may contribute to the erosion of an authoritarian regime in the opening phase, this need not imply that they share democratic convictions or advocate a democratic (as opposed to a theocratic or otherwise authoritarian) alternative.

1.2 *Religious actors, secularism, and religion–state relations*

Drawing on Peter Berger's classic, *The Sacred Canopy* (1969), we think of religion as a 'set of beliefs that connects the individual to a community, and in turn to a sense of being or purpose that transcends the individual and the mundane'.[11] In the following, we use the phrase 'religious actors' as encompassing, on the individual level, religious authorities and intellectuals, and on the societal level, institutions and associations. On the individual level, religious authorities are those who have acquired the theological qualifications that prevail in a given religion or denomination. This usually involves several years of theological training with the subsequent licence to interpret the religious sources and to express normative and behavioural recommendations on the basis of these sources.

Religious institutions are those that address the spiritual, social, economic and/or political needs and interests of a religious group. These institutions vary with regard to their: (1) level of *organization* (how many of the potentially religious are *de facto* organized?); (2) level of *institutionalization* (how regularized is the protocol, how regulated are the competencies within the organization?); and (3) their *political function* (which function does the institution perform vis-à-vis society, beyond its core constituency?).[12]

Who are the religious actors in our five 'young' democracies and which organizational form did they take? In West Germany, the units of analysis are: the Catholic Church and the Protestant Church (*Evangelische Kirche Deutschland*, EKD), which in 1950 'organized' 44% and 51% of all German citizens respectively.[13] In our Christian-Orthodox set, we are dealing with the Autocephalous Orthodox Church of Georgia, several autocephalous Orthodox churches in Ukraine as well as several other organized religious groups in Ukraine. In Georgia, between 1996 and 2007, 70%–86% self-identified as nominally Christian Orthodox.[14] In Ukraine, about 60% of the population are Christian-Orthodox, but less than 20% were declared members of churches in 2006.[15] Finally, which religious organizations are we dealing with in the case studies from the Muslim world? Many analysts make a point of underscoring the extent to which religion in Muslim-majority countries is much less organized than is the case in most Christian-majority countries. This is however only partially true and varies from country to country. The religious landscapes of both Mali and Indonesia are dominated by well-structured institutionalized religious organizations. In the case of Mali, these are local and decentralized Sufi orders[16] as well as strong administrative mosque committees, which in total organize about 40% of the population.[17] In the case of Indonesia, they are multi-million member Islamic organizations, of which about 35% of the 206 million Indonesian Muslims are members.[18] The large Islamic organizations of Indonesian also have their own training institutions in place (mosque and school networks) to educate and certify new generations of theologians who reflect the same school of thought and law (*mazhab*). Besides theological training, they run about 13% of Indonesia's primary and secondary schools and administer a significant part of the health system by providing hospitals, clinics and health centres adjacent to their schools.

To sum up, in our case studies of West Germany, Ukraine and Georgia, the churches are the primary religious actors under review, while in Mali and Indonesia it is Islamic organizations and individual religious authorities which are our focus.

1.2.1 Secularization and religion-state-relations

In the study of democratization, institutional secularism (understood as strict separation between religion and state) has been widely seen as a precondition for democracy.[19] Recent research clearly challenges this assumption.[20] Although we cannot go into the details of this academic debate here, we will shortly introduce our understanding of key concepts, as the question of (secular) religion–state relations is important to the behaviour of religious actors in the transition phase, in particular with regard to which normative understanding of democracy they would support in constitutional drafting or reform processes.

The debate around the concepts of secularism and secularization has involved a myriad of different notions of these terms. While we agree with José Casanova (1994) that secularization is best understood as a process of differentiation of the secular spheres (state, law, economy, science) from religious institutions and norms, i.e. the transfer of persons, things, meanings, etc., from ecclesiastical or religious to civil or lay use, possession or control,[21] we believe that for the purposes of this article, the descriptive-institutional notion of 'religion–state relations' is sufficient to provide the background to the legal and political environment in which religious actors operate vis-à-vis the state.[22] Therefore, the following analysis is based on the assumption that democracy needs the 'twin tolerations',[23] but does not require secularity in the sense of a strict separation of state and religion. Recent research has shown that such a separation can rarely be found *de jure*, and is *de facto* nowhere present in contemporary democracies.[24] In his examination of comparative institutional religion–state relations, Jonathan Fox concludes that:

> only one state in the study [of 152 countries surveyed], the US, has absolute SRAS [separation of religion and state]. The explanation for this cannot be found in any uniqueness in the US constitutional structure. Of the 128 states in this study for which I was able to obtain an English-language copy of their constitution, 50 of them (including the US) have constitutional clauses or the equivalent that declare SRAS. Yet the majority of these states do not have SRAS. What seems to differentiate the US from other states with constitutional SRAS clauses is not the clauses themselves but, rather, the enforcement of those clauses. The US court system traditionally strictly interprets the establishment clause of the US Constitution. Based on these results, this policy appears to be the exception rather than the rule.[25]

1.3 Presentation of the cases

Our first paired comparison examines the role of the Catholic and the Protestant Church in the democratic consolidation process of West Germany 1945–1969 (compare overview in Table 2).[26] West German democracy, as the most longstanding democracy in our set, and one often referred to as a 'success story' of democratization in light of the pervasiveness of its totalitarian past,[27] generates insights into broader patterns and forms of interaction between the state and religious actors. Given the nature of West Germany's democratization process as based on an *intervention* where the erosion of the previous authoritarian regime was achieved primarily from outside rather than within (as opposed to Huntington's *replacements, transplacements* and *transformations*), our discussion of the German case focuses on the phases of transition and consolidation.[28]

The second paired comparison analyses the role of the Christian Orthodox churches in the stagnating transitions before and after the Orange Revolution in

Ukraine[29] and before and after the Rose Revolution in Georgia.[30] In these two states, the transition to democracy involved cooperation between incumbents and the opposition at the beginning of the 1990s and thus took the form of a *transplacement*. Our third paired comparison examines the role of Islamic leaders and organizations in the erosion of authoritarianism, transition to democracy and its consolidation in Mali after 1987[31] and Indonesia after 1991, two cases of democratization from below (*replacement*).[32]

2. The constructive, obstructive and destructive influences of religious actors in democratization processes

In all six case studies, religious actors did not effect the democratic outcome of political transformation processes. However, with variation in the context, the constructive impact of certain religious actors outweighed the obstructive or destructive influences of the same or other religious actors. Religious actors buttressed existing democratic developments and tendencies through their engagement in public life, for instance through civil society activism, social movements, lobby organizations, or political parties.[33]

While it is not possible to summarize the findings of all six case studies in a way that would do all justice, we will highlight the defining characteristics of the processes under review in the following sections of the article, examining the influence of religious actors in each of the three phases of democratization. We provide additional findings in the tables in order to generate a more complete picture of the cases under review (see Tables 3–5).

2.1 Opening phase: the role of religious actors in the erosion of authoritarianism

In four of our six case studies (Indonesia, Ukraine, Mali, and Georgia), religious actors had a constructive role to play in the opening phase, particularly so in Ukraine and in Indonesia (see Table 3).[34] In Indonesia, the two largest Islamic organizations in the country, the modernist Muhammadiyah and the traditionalist Nahdlatul Ulama (NU), contributed to the erosion of authoritarian power in the 1990s and more importantly, to the acceptance – among grassroots as well as elites – of a democratic alternative.[35] Significantly, the NU, the largest organization in the country, had argued as early as 1984 that Islam was compatible with the equality of non-Muslim citizens and that Indonesia, the largest Muslim-majority state in the world, would not need to adopt Islam as the official state religion or expand the jurisdiction of religious law in order to protect or promote the Muslim identity of its citizens. According to the NU position, the protection of religious diversity on part of the government was legitimate (or perhaps even warranted) from the viewpoint of Islam. Amien Rais, the chairman of the *Muhammadiyah*, furthermore, played a crucial role in holding together anti-regime coalitions between pro-democratic and anti-democratic students groups, whose demonstrations

Table 2. Overview of case studies: democratic assessment and regime types.

	Pre-democratic regime type[a]	Type of transition[b]	Transition-phase	Freedom House (2009)[c]				Polity IV (2008)[d]		BTI (2008)[e]		
					Political rights	Civil liberties	Degree of freedom			Democracy Index (rank)	Management Index (rank)	Status Index (rank)
Germany	Totalitarian regime	Intervention	1945–1949	1949 2009	n.a. 1	n.a. 1	n.a. free	1949 2007	10 10			
Georgia	Post-totalitarian regime	Transplacement	1991–1995	1995 2009	4 4	5 4	partly free partly free	1995 2007	4 6	6,9 (42)	6,63 (23)	6,6 (38)
Ukraine	Post-totalitarian regime	Transplacement	1990–2004	2004 2009	4 3	4 2	partly free free	2004 2007	6 7	7,4 (35)	5,21 (55)	6,93 (35)
Indonesia	Authoritarian regime	Replacement	1998–2004	2004 2009	3 2	4 3	partly free free	2004 2007	8 8	6,5 (54)	5,27 (53)	6,17 (48)
Mali	Authoritarian regime	Replacement	1991–1992	1992 2009	2 2	3 3	free free	1992 2007	7 7	7,3 (36)	6,25 (26)	6,16 (49)

[a] Typology based on Linz and Stepan, *Problems of Democratic Transition and Consolidation: Southern Europe, South America, and Post-Communist Europe*, 5–6, see endnote 9.
[b] Transition type as defined by Huntington, *The Third Wave: Democratization in the Late Twentieth Century*, Chapter 3. see endnote 29.
[c] The first year refers to the end of the transition phase in each country. Since 1972, Freedom House has classified the status of political rights and civil liberties in most countries around the world on a scale between 1 (free) and 7 (unfree). Countries with an average score of political rights and civil liberties between 1 and 2.5 are considered 'free', those with an average score between 3 and 5 'partly free'.
[d] Polity classifies countries on a scale between −10 to +10 annually. Ratings capture the degree of contestation and transparency of political systems. Countries with a score of +7 and above are generally considered to be democratic.
[e] The Bertelsmann-Transformation-Index comprises a Status-Index (which captures the status of the transformation towards both democracy (in the Democracy-Index) and a market economy (in the Market Index)) and a Management-Index (which captures the success of political elites to manage the transformation considering varying levels of difficulty). The Status-Index is the mean of the Democracy-Index and the Market-Index (the latter is not shown here). The Democracy-Index measures the progress towards democracy along five criteria (stateness, political participation, rule of law, stability of democratic institutions, political and social integration) and 20 indicators. The Management-Index measures management performance along four criteria (steering capability, resource efficiency, consensus building and international cooperation). Scores given along each of the 18 indicators range from a minimum 1 to a maximum 10. 'Rank' reflects a given country's rank among the 125 countries covered in the index, with 1 being the most successful, 125 being the least successful.
Sources: Freedom in the World Country Ratings 1972–2007 (www.freedomhouse.org); Polity IV Project (http://www.systemicpeace.org); Transitionphase: Germany: Wolfrum, Wolfrum, *Die geglückte Demokratie*; Georgia: Jawad, *Democratic Consolidation in Georgia after the 'Rose Revolution'?*; Ukraine: Birch, *Elections and Democratization in Ukraine*; Indonesia: Liddle and Mujani, *Indonesian Democracy. From Transition to Consolidation*; Mali: Leininger, *Die ambivalente Rolle islamischer Akteure im malischen Demokratisierungsprozess*.

Table 3. The role of religious actors in the erosion of the authoritarian regime.[a]

	Constructive	Obstructive
Georgia (1987–1991)	Religious actors play virtually no role, and have an indirect influence, if any. They give tacit support for anti-regime demonstrations in April 1989. Emphasis is placed on subversive potential of Georgian nationalism against Soviet state.	
Ukraine (1989–1990)	Religious actors appeal to the state to expand civil liberties (specifically freedom of association and press) and thereby contribute indirectly to opening of regime.	The Russian Orthodox Church functions as the only official church of the country and serves as an arm of Soviet influence in Ukraine.
Indonesia (1991–1998)	NU formulates democratic alternative from Islamic perspectives in 1980s; Abdurrahman Wahid founds *Forum Demokrasi* in 1991. *Muhammadiyah* mobilizes thousands of members for demonstrations against Suharto in 1997 and 1998. Islamist student movement KAMMI meets with military generals who implicitly advocate non-democratic future regime.[b,c]	ICMI founded in 1991, represents sectarian interests and channels potential opposition activists into regime-sponsored organization. UN chair Abdurrahman Wahid calls for end to anti-system demonstrations.
Mali (1987–1991)	*Salafiyya* groups and Imams support idea of a multi-party system through public statements and newspapers. *Hizboulla al Islamiya* members participate in anti-regime demonstrations but do not support democratization.[c]	Bala Kalé, Imam of the *Grande Mosque* in Bamako and head of AMUPI prompts Muslims to support the authoritarian regime.

[a] Since Germany's totalitarian regime ended abruptly with the country's defeat in World War II, the role of religious actors in the erosion of Nazi Germany is not considered here. Generally, it must be said that the churches were *gleichgeschaltet* during the Nazi regime, and except for very small pockets of resistance such as the Protestant 'Bekennende Kirche' (Confessing Church), supported, legitimized, or at least did not actively oppose, Nazi rule.
[b] Although the Indonesian KAMMI and the Malian *Hizboulla al Islamiya* did not favour a democratic alternative, they contributed to the erosion of the authoritarian regime.
[c] Eroding an authoritarian regime is distinct from participating in the construction of a democratic alternative. Whether the democratic option prevails over theocratic and authoritarian alternatives, is a question settled in the transition period, and therefore dealt with in the section below.

and street protests ultimately induced President Suharto to resign.[36] The actions of some religious leaders and organizations contributed to the erosion of this authoritarian regime, even though they did not necessarily fully endorse a democratic alternative at the time. The Islamist student movement, Kesatuan Aksi Mahasiswa

Islam Indonesia (KAMMI), met several times with certain military generals who likely envisioned a non-democratic future regime. If this alliance had prevailed over other groups, it would have likely replaced the New Order[37] by another kind of authoritarianism.[38] The prevailing of democratically-minded Islamic leaders and groups over movements like KAMMI was therefore crucial.

In Ukraine, many anti-communist activists were themselves religious authorities in the lower ranks of the ecclesiastic hierarchy or had been socialized in a highly religious environment. They were motivated by the desire both to resist state suppression (all indigenous religious organizations were prohibited; only the Russian Orthodox Church that was locally installed by the Soviet Union was legal), as well as to create a common Ukrainian national church. Especially the illegal Greek-Catholic Church in West Ukraine, which operated in the underground, indirectly rendered support to the emerging democratic opposition with its calls for the legalization of alternative sources of information and the toleration of discursive spaces insulated from state intervention.[39]

Although partly constructive, the role of religious actors in the opening phase remained minor in both Mali and in Georgia. During the authoritarian regime of Moussa Traoré (1961–1990) only one Islamic organization was legally recognized, the *Association Malien pour l'Unité et Progrés d'Islam* (AMUPI), which predominantly consisted of Sufi orders. Being mostly co-opted by the state and financially dependent upon the regime, AMUPI remained largely apolitical. Only the *Salafiyya* fringe groups (with which about 5.5% Malians identify) openly criticized the Traoré regime and called for a multi-party system and a secular order[40] that would guarantee an independent space for religious actors.[41] Although the Salafiyya were able to contribute to the opposition's democratic debate and gathered support particularly in rural areas, unlike Indonesian religious actors they lacked the mass support and capacity to mobilize that would have permitted them to have a significant role to play in the ousting of President Moussa Traoré.[42] Only a small, anti-democratic group, the *Hizboulla al Islamiya*, is known to have participated in the mass demonstrations in late March 1991, which finally led to the overthrow of the Traoré regime.

In Georgia, the Orthodox Church decided to sanctify national hero Ilja Tschawtschawadse in the midst of *glasnost* and thereby bolstered Georgian nationalism against the Soviet regime.[43] The Orthodox Church generally, however, shied away from taking explicit oppositional stances. The political significance of its actions was tacit at best.

Some religious actors also exerted an obstructive effect on the erosion of the New Order in Indonesia, the pre-democratic regime in Mali, and Soviet rule in Ukraine. An Association of Islamic Intellectuals (ICMI) was founded in Indonesia in 1991 which became an important vehicle for Muslim sectarian interests. Although internally diverse in its ideological orientations, ICMI took the wind out of the sails of that part of the anti-Suharto opposition that felt Muslims were not adequately represented in the army and state bureaucracy. By giving Muslim elites the sense that Suharto's New Order was now more responsive to their interests, the establishment of ICMI co-opted parts of the opposition and obstructed the democratic opening. The leaders of the two largest Islamic organizations, *Muhammadiyah* and NU, also played ambiguous roles during the breakdown of the New Order. The disdain of NU's chairman Abdurrahman Wahid for street protests and demonstrations and his (unheeded) public call for an end to the seizure of the national legislature could have put an end to the public uprising. In Mali, Bala Kalé, the Imam of the *Grande Mosque* in the capital city, Bamako, and the head of the only legalized Islamic organization at that time, called for members to support the authoritarian regime rather than join the emerging democracy movement.[44] In Ukraine, the engagement of religious actors in the underground was outperformed by the strong involvement in authoritarian politics of the Russian Orthodox Church – itself a major pillar to Soviet rule.[45]

Overall, the influence of religious actors in contributing to the erosion of the authoritarian order remained minor in Mali, Ukraine and Georgia, in contrast to Indonesia. These findings reflect the results of the Harvard Research Project on Religion and Global Politics, in that religious actors in the former three countries were far less independent financially and legally from the regime. While NU and the *Muhammadiyah* in Indonesia functioned as relatively autonomous civil society organizations that could to some extent resist the meddling of the regime into its internal affairs and its activities, the Ukrainian illegal churches' political involvement was by far outweighed by that of the Russian Orthodox Church. The more independent religious actors were in organizational terms – such as the Greek-Catholic Church in West Ukraine and the lower-ranking clergy of the underground autocephalous churches – the more significant was their contribution to the erosion of authoritarian rule. The autocephalous Orthodox Church of Georgia and the only legally recognized Muslim organization in Mali, AMUPI, were tightly intertwined with politics. They were both effectively co-opted by the state.

2.2 Transition phase: the role of religious actors in the establishment of democratic rule

As a result of the democratic transition, all five countries under review either passed new constitutions, or substantively revised their extant one (see Table 4).[46] The contribution of religious actors to these processes varied, depending on their organizational form and the legal space in which they could operate.[47] In all cases, the nature of religion–state relations during the preceding regime exerted a strong impact on the design of religion–state relations in new or revised constitutions.

The German Basic Law of 1949 in many respects reflects provisions from the Constitution of the Weimar Republic, including those of church–state law and the cooperative nature of religion–state relations.[48] Article 4 of the Basic Law corresponds to the guarantees of positive religious freedom as defined in the Weimar Reichsverfassung (WRV) of 1919. Article 140 of the Basic Law explicitly incorporates articles 136–9 and 141 of the WRV into the new constitution. While religious freedom is guaranteed, churches enjoy a privileged position in

Table 4. The role of religious actors in the transition phase.

	Constructive	Obstructive	Destructive
West Germany/ Catholic Church (1945–1949)	Catholic Church influences constitution-building through Christian politicians, particularly of the CDU.		Catholic Bishops and lay councils threaten not to recognize the Basic Law.
West Germany/ Protestant Church (1945–1949)	EKD legitimizes the young democracy's first democratic elections by explicitly asking members to vote.		
Georgia (1991–1995)		The Orthodox Church of Georgia nearly succeeds in negotiating for itself the status of an established church.	The Orthodox Church of Georgia retains the connection of ethnicity to religion, thereby exacerbating ethnic conflict.
Ukraine (1990–2004)	Religious organizations actively lobby during the constitutional drafting process for the non-establishment of any church and the legal equality of all religious organizations in the country. Religious authorities run for elections. Religious organizations endorse newly founded religious parties.	The Russian Orthodox Church increasingly becomes a tool for Russia to secure its interests in Ukraine and maintain its influence in both civil and political society.	
Indonesia (1998–2004)	Amien Rais (*Muhammadiyah*) leads four rounds of constitutional revisions. Abdurrahman Wahid (NU) abandons prohibitions against Confucian practices.	Religious parties (unsuccessfully) advocate the establishment of a religious quota system in the public administration and government, and a stronger role for Islamic law.	Religious leaders, including Amien Rais, incite inter-religious and anti-Chinese violence.
Mali (1991–1992)	Islamic associations contribute to constitution-making in National Conference (NC). Parts of *Salafiyya* and others who favoured an Islamic order accept results of NC and submit to democratic rule.	Some Islamic associations, under the leadership of *Hizboullah*, create an umbrella organization to counter democratic order, but fail due to lack of popular support.	

comparison to other civil society organizations by virtue of being recognized as public corporations that may collect taxes. Accordingly, the churches strongly advocated the preservation of their privileges granted in the Weimar Constitution and ultimately succeeded in having their pre-1933 legal status restored. Yet substantive disagreement ensued over the role of religious instruction in public education. Catholic Bishops and Catholic lay councils threatened not to recognize the new constitution, unless parents were granted the right to instruct their children in religious matters.[49] Eventually, voluntary religious instruction in public education was agreed upon.[50]

The Georgian Constitution of 1995 provides for religious freedom in article 19 (1); and article 19 (2) prohibits persecution and discrimination based on speech, thought, conviction and belief. Article 9 grants freedom of belief and religion, but also acknowledges the Apostolic Autocephalous Orthodox Church of Georgia for its historic role in the struggle for independence and self-determination of the Georgian people. Article 9, and in particular this acknowledgement, was a compromise between those advocating an established state church, on the one hand, and those insisting on the separation of church and state, on the other. While the Orthodox Church of Georgia failed to negotiate for itself the status of an established church, it was granted extraordinary privileges and exclusive access to material and immaterial resources of the state: Only the Apostolic Autocephalous Orthodox Church of Georgia and no other church/religious organization is recognized as a public corporation and is exempt from paying taxes. Only its priests are exempted from military service and only they qualify to serve as chaplains in hospitals and the military.

The Ukrainian Constitution of 1996 explicitly stipulates the separation of religion and state, and emphasizes that no religion may be imposed by the state (Article 35). Religious communities maintain their own houses of worship and organize the training of the clergy in their own private institutions of higher learning. Religious organizations collect their own dues and receive no financial support from the state. However, religious non-devotional instruction is provided as an obligatory school subject in all public schools from grades 1–12 under the rubric of 'Christian ethics'. All major holidays that are celebrated by the Orthodox and the Greek-Catholic Churches are recognized as public holidays by the state. Religious organizations other than the Russian Orthodox Church had a strong incentive to actively lobby during the constitutional drafting process before 1996 for the non-establishment of any church and the legal equality of all religious organizations in the country.[51]

Simultaneously, the Russian Orthodox Church increasingly became a tool used by Russia to effect certain Russian influences in civil society, and in political society through the association of religious parties with particular churches and the (unsuccessful) public calls on part of Russian Orthodox clergy to elect a Russia-friendly presidential candidate in 2004.[52]

In Indonesia, the most defining characteristics of religion–state relations were not changed when the 1945 constitution (with the pan-religious, neither Islamist nor secularist national ideology of *pancasila*) underwent four rounds of revision between 1999 and 2001. Beside the recognized official religions of Islam, Christianity, Hinduism and Buddhism, the country officially recognized Confucianism as one additional 'religion', but did not allow for the disconnection of citizenship and religion. Indonesians continue to need to identify themselves as members of one of the official religions on identity cards and state documents, and those who profess none or other religions (such as Judaism or local religions), need to falsely declare themselves adherents to one of the official creeds.

Remarkably, the most important product of the transition, the reformed constitution, was heavily shaped by the involvement of leading Muslim politicians and representatives of Islamic interests, who steered the country through renewed discussions about the expansion of Islamic law and the introduction of a quota system in parliament and the public service based on religion. However, none of these proposals won majority support. The constitutional revisions were started during the presidency of Abdurrahman Wahid, the former chairman of the largest traditional Islamic organization, *Nahdlatul Ulama* (NU), and were undertaken under the leadership of the then parliamentary speaker Amien Rais who until 1999 had been the chairman of the country's largest modernist Islamic organization (the *Muhammadiyah*). The two leaders of the most important Muslim organizations in the country were therefore centrally involved in the constitutional reforms, and it was under Wahid in 2001 that Confucianism was recognized as an official religion by reversing earlier restrictions against its recognition.

Finally, in Mali, the post-transition constitution of 25 February 1992 reaffirmed the laicist character of the state and stipulated the latter's immutability. There is no religious instruction in public schools in Mali, and no state funding for private religious schools. Citizenship is not tied to religious affiliation. Through Article 128 religious parties are prohibited. Out of the five countries studied here, Mali maintains the strongest formal institutional separation of religion and the state.[53] This result did not suit the interests of all of the ten Islamic organizations that had actively participated in the constitution-drafting process as official members of the National Conference (August 1992).[54] With the exception of the largest organization, AMUPI, the small and ad-hoc organizations advocated two chief demands: the abolition of the laicist orientation of the state, its replacement by Islam as an established religion, and the right to found Islamic political parties. However, these demands remained unheeded when the National Conference voted for a laicist constitution. Justifications against the religious party ban were twofold: Democracy-minded organizations such as the *Association Islamique pour le Salut au Mali* (AISLAM) viewed religious parties (just as any type of party) as part of liberal democracy. Others, the so-called *intégristes*, to which the *Hizboullah* and dissenters of AMUPI belonged, advocated Islamic law as providing a blueprint for a just social order and believed religious parties to be the natural vehicle for an Islamic agenda. When the National Conference ratified the new constitution in August 1992, most Islamic organizations accepted their defeat and ultimately consented to the document. Even though nine Islamic organizations founded the umbrella *Comité de Coordination des Associations Islamiques du Mali* to promote an Islamic model of society, the *Comité* was never able to exert noteworthy influence on politics due to a lack of popular support and mobilizational capacity.

Comparing the six cases, the following observations stand out: Considering the output of the examined constitution-drafting processes, all five countries exhibit historical continuities with the previous order of religion–state relations. Everywhere, the democratic transition led to constitutional guarantees of the positive right to religious freedom, and everywhere, the majority religion could gain certain privileges not afforded to smaller religions.[55] Whereas the role of religious actors is relatively similar within each paired comparison, their role differed amongst the three religions: unlike the majority religions in our other cases, the officially recognized Orthodox churches contributed little to the democratic content of the emerging normative consensus. In Germany, the role of the Catholic and the Protestant Churches was more varied once they had achieved guarantees for the preservation of their privileges granted under Weimar, and the churches' ambitions to influence the constitutional process focused on matters of education rather than religious freedom. In the two Muslim-majority countries, religious actors decisively legitimized new or reformed political institutions, and sometimes were even pivotal in safeguarding and expanding legal bases for religious pluralism and diversity.[56]

2.3 Consolidation phase: the role of religious actors in (de-)democratization

2.3.1 The reorganization of the religious sphere

Liberalized politics that accompany democratic transitions typically involve the deregulation of civil society as a result of the expansion of civil liberties. This deregulation may bring to light all sorts of societal groups previously suppressed by the authoritarian regime, including those of a shady nature. We observed the phenomenon of a reorganization of the religious sphere in all our case studies, where the transition period initially witnessed the mushrooming of religious organizations. In Ukraine, Mali and Indonesia, this included illiberal ones, which, however, remain until today politically marginal.

Overall, religious organizations became more diverse and multi-vocal after the democratic transition (see Table 5). In Ukraine, the national (Ukrainian) autocephalous Orthodox Church, prohibited during Soviet rule, was revived, and the Orthodox establishment split in two, with the majority re-entering the national church and a minority remaining under the Moscow patriarchate.[57] Since then the creation of one single Ukrainian Orthodox Church is a highly politicized topic that dominates the public discourse. The politically influential Greek-Catholic community re-emerged as a vocal actor, and numerous other religious organizations have since taken hold in the country, to the effect that Ukraine is recognized today among sociologists of religion as the most religiously diverse country in Europe.[58] By contrast, the religious landscape of Georgia has hardly changed as a result of

Table 5. Role of religious actors in consolidation phase.

	Constructive	Obstructive	Destructive
West Germany/ Catholic Church (1949–1969)	Largest centrist party CDU founded predominantly by Catholics. In civil society, church fulfils important social functions and services (schools, hospitals, etc.). Mobilization of constituents in political demonstrations against re-militarization and against diplomatic alliances that would make German unification less likely and involve Germany in East–West polarization.	It is only at the Second Vatican Council in 1964–1967 that the Catholic Church officially recognizes the principles of religious freedom and a democratic state based on the rule of law. However, the anti-democratic stance of the church translates into anti-democratic action in Germany only in terms of the controversy over religious instruction in public schools.	
West Germany/ Protestant Church (1949–1969)	In civil society, church fulfils important social functions and services (schools, hospitals, etc.). Mobilization of constituents in political demonstrations against re-militarization and against diplomatic alliances that would make German unification less likely and involve Germany in East–West polarization.	Leading theologians are sceptical of liberal democracy and publicly oppose multi-party democracy.	

(*Continued*)

Table 5. Continued.

	Constructive	Obstructive	Destructive
Georgia (1995–2003/2003–)			Church contributes to polarization along ethnic lines and the promotion of particularist over national identities.
Ukraine (2004–)		Russian Orthodox Church is perceived as a tool used by Russia to meddle in Ukrainian domestic affairs.	
Indonesia (2004–)	The mainstream Islamic organizations speak out against domestic terrorist attacks and are generally supportive of inter-faith toleration and democracy.	State Ulama Council issues *fatwa* in 2005 against secularism, liberalism, pluralism.	Terrorist Islamist groups repeatedly bomb targets in the capital and major tourist destinations in 2002–2005.
Mali (1992–)	Most Islamic actors respect democratic rule and support it through their democratic behaviour. HCIM is democratically organized. Islamic actors are the most accepted mediators in local conflicts and contribute to social peace.	Islamic associations are veto players in specific policy fields, especially family law and the abolition of the death penalty. They succeed in hindering the passing of a new, more liberal family law.	

democratization. The Orthodox Church of Georgia continues to be the dominant religious force in the country with the highest – and since the early 1990s even increasing – share of members (1993: 65%; 2007: 87.7% of the population).[59] Moreover, on the national question, the Orthodox Church of Georgia retained its implicit connection of ethnicity and religion and did nothing to alleviate the country's conflict with Abchasia. If anything, the church's ethno-nationalist rhetoric exacerbated the exclusionary character of Georgian Orthodox identity.

In Mali, Islam was for the most part organized either in Sufi orders or in marginal *Salafiyya* groups before the opening phase. After the opening, these two groups disintegrated and numerous offshoots emerged. Today, between 135 and 190 Islamic organizations are registered in the country.[60] Although Indonesia has always been quite diverse, radical groups suppressed under the New Order and exiled into neighbouring Malaysia emerged into the open after the transition. Protestant congregations, especially those of American origin, have also mushroomed in the capitals of Java and the Eastern parts of the country.[61]

2.3.2 The religious politics of consolidation

In our two Muslim-majority societies, religious actors supported and strengthened civil society activities as well as a more democratic political society (behavioural dimension). At the same time, they normatively hindered the expansion of certain liberties, especially in the realm of family law, and more generally, gender equality (Linz and Stepan's attitudinal dimension). Certain religious actors have exerted an illiberal influence on legal reform in the realm of personal status and morality laws (which in Mali and Indonesia they feel should be regulated according to some notion of Islamic law). In Mali, rights advocacy groups have striven since the late 1990s to liberalize the family law of 1962. Various civil society actors, including religious authorities, participated in *Concertations Regionales* (regional consultation meetings) to deliberate over counter-drafts to the law, none of which have passed the legislature. Islamic organizations and authorities adhere to the democratic procedures, but take positions that are consistent neither with the notion of liberal democracy as laid out in the 1992 constitution, nor with the international conventions that Mali has signed and ratified. Parliamentarians are reluctant to pass a more egalitarian family law, in light of probable resistance from Islamic organizations and authorities, who beyond their mosque network have immediate access to believers by way of radio and television shows, as well as the 'prayer economy'.[62] Despite these efforts, Islamic actors have failed so far to influence various political decisions concerning morality laws. For instance, bars remain open during Ramadan despite protests from Islamic organizations, and the national lottery remains legal. Recently, Mahmoud Dicko, chairman of the *Haut Conseil Islamique* (HCIM) has publicly argued against the abolition of the death penalty.

While the two large Islamic organizations of Indonesia (and their chairmen) had pivotal roles to play towards the erosion of the New Order and the success of the transition, their direct political impact on consolidation processes is harder to identify. Internally, the organizations have diversified normatively, and differing – and often contradictory – voices emanate from their debates about religious freedom, family and morality laws. Both organizations initially founded political parties, which however have remained small and on the political margins (with 4–6%). At the same time, the state *ulama* council (MUI) has become one of the most important religious actors in the democratizing polity, with statements and *fatwas* on all major issues discussed in the legislature. As a council founded in 1975 primarily to rubberstamp the New Order's developmental policies, the council should have been abolished with the end of the Suharto era. However, fearing that such an act might strengthen critics of the newly emerging polity, the council was left intact and has since been able to consolidate its role as the authority on questions of Islamic law. In 2005, the council published a statement against secularism, liberalism and pluralism which seemed to bode ill for intra-Islamic debates on democracy and human rights norms, because it declared the three values as essentially un-Islamic. One of the two Islamic organizations eventually spoke out against the MUI statement, but it was a half-hearted affair.

In Ukraine, religious actors maintained their political influence through informal and public channels such as the media. Religious parties founded during the early transition period in the 1990s did not gain ground among voters. Instead, individual religious leaders were more socially and politically influential. In November 2004 shortly after the Orange Revolution, the representatives of the six largest religious groups wrote an open letter to President Kutschma to remind him of his duty to protect the constitution. In a standoff between the prime minister and the president, the letter tipped the balance in favour of the prime minister and thereby helped prevent a political escalation and possible slippage back into authoritarian politics.

The Orthodox Church of Georgia impeded consolidation by contributing to a further polarization along ethnic lines and the promotion of particularist over national identities. Sermons and speeches by the Katholikos-Patriarch Ilia II during the fighting in separatist regions emphasized ethnic affiliations rather than the common faith as a marker of national identity.[63] Particularly in Abchasia, this contributed to the ethnicization of the conflict between 1991 and 1995, and the later territorial disintegration of the Georgian state. Moreover, the Autocephalous Orthodox Church of Georgia is the most trusted institution of the country. Surveys from 2006 showed that 93% of the population approve of the work of the church, followed by the military (86%) and the media (83%). Although the church has a limited political function so far, it has an extraordinary potential to mobilize the population for or against the deepening of democratic norms and attitudes.

In Germany, similar to the Ukrainian case, some religious groups were highly involved in founding political parties and ran for political office. Both the Catholic and the Protestant Church periodically intervened into politics by functioning as a 'public conscience', and by encouraging citizens to participate in the electoral processes. Most important was perhaps the contribution of the religious academies that held public conferences and workshops designed by the occupying forces to strengthen civic and liberal norms.[64] It is interesting to note, however, how much theologically-motivated resistance existed at the time even within the Protestant Church against a governmental system many perceived to be imposed from abroad and not a home-grown product reflecting German cultural, social and political norms.

The most outstanding insight that emanates from the comparison is that religious actors became more diverse and multi-vocal after the democratic transition and their actions harder to identify as constructive, destructive or obstructive with regard to democratizing processes. Where theological reservations against the nascent democracy existed, their invocation became less and less frequent over time, suggesting a cautionary note against over-interpreting the political significance of theology. As Asef Bayat articulates,

> Resorting to mere literal readings of scripture to determine the democratic thrust of a religion will not take us very far, not only because ambiguity, multiple meanings and disagreement are embedded in many religious scriptures, but because individuals and groups with diverse interests and orientations may find their own, often conflicting truths in the very same scriptures. ... We need to examine the conditions that allow social forces to make a particular reading of the sacred texts hegemonic. And this is closely linked to groups' capacity to mobilize consensus around their 'truth'. ... The challenge is to give democratic interpretation material power, to infuse them with popular consciousness.[65]

In light of the above quote, we feel that the Christian-Orthodox Church of Georgia has been quite successful in linking an ethnic reading to the religious text and the history of Christianity in Georgia. In Mali, religious actors based their anti-liberal public discourse against the reform of the family law on religious texts. By contrast, the NU of Indonesia was able during the 1980s to link inter-faith tolerance to the reading of their text, even if not democratic or liberal values *per se*.

In some contexts, the actions of certain religious actors had a destructive impact on democratic consolidation, but where the state enjoyed autonomy and capacity, and the society had behaviourally and attitudinally accepted democratic norms, the state was generally able to deal with such actors and their societal influence in ways not different from other (non-religious) radical opponents to the regime.

3. Factors conditioning the role of religious actors

Two factors stand out in explaining the variation of religious actors' influences across our cases and in the different phases of transformation. The first is the organizational form of religious actors, the second the extent to which they enjoyed *de facto* autonomy from interference by the state.

3.1 Organizational form of religious actors

In Germany and Indonesia, where religious organizations are mass-based, religious actors had a high mobilizational capacity,[66] which in the latter case became a crucial vehicle in sustaining high levels of public contestation to effect regime change.[67] In Germany, the churches mobilized their constituents in political demonstrations during the consolidation phase, against re-militarization as well as against diplomatic alliances that would make German unification less likely and involve Germany in East–West polarization.

In Mali, where, like in Indonesia, a Huntingtonian replacement of power took place, Islamic actors had only a small role to play during the opening of President Traoré's authoritarian regime. While religious organizations other than AMUPI had been prohibited before 1991, a heterogeneous landscape of Islamic organizations developed in the early 1990s. In particular, small associations and non-governmental organizations (NGOs) with socio-political aims lobbied for particular interests in policy fields such as social security and family law. They also supported – and in the rural areas very often formed a substitute for – the state's welfare security system, for instance in regards to maternal healthcare and health education. Highly dependent on funding from abroad, these organizations function as small-scale enterprises.[68] Overall, Mali's heterogeneous religious actors possess low mobilizational capacity.

In Ukraine, where all indigenous religious organizations were prohibited before 1989 and the Russian Orthodox Church installed in their place, religious actors could hardly influence the political process. Their impact depended largely on the personal influence of individuals. After 1989, the religious landscape changed dramatically: it was revived and it spectacularly diversified. But this had little effect on the capacity of religious actors to exert political influence, as religious organizations became fragmented and their mobilizational capacity limited. Attempts to create one unified Autocephalous Orthodox Church of Ukraine were highly politicized and have thus far been unsuccessful.

The Georgian Orthodox Church retains its monopolistic hold on the 'religious market', which endows it with remarkable ideational power. With its high levels of legitimacy in the eyes of Georgian citizens, it could easily mobilize members for political causes. So far, it has limited itself to rhetoric from the pulpit.

Religious organizations in all six cases function as important providers of social welfare, running schools, kindergartens, hospitals, retirement homes, and the like, and thereby remain closely in contact with the grass roots. As such, they are invaluable to the state and thus enjoy an important bargaining chip they can use to influence certain policy-making.

3.2 The legal position of religious actors vis-à-vis political regimes

Our case studies showed that religious actors' legal position vis-à-vis the state is one of the main factors that influences their impact and the scope of their political and social engagement towards (de-)democratization. We identified the following areas that could be found in almost all of our paired comparisons and are thus relevant independent from specific religious denominations (see Table 6).

Table 6. Organizational forms of religious actors and their significance for their roles in political processes.

	Organizational form	Political significance
West Germany/ Catholic Church	Homogeneous, large organization, rooted in political and civil society Network of Catholic academies for adult education; Mass-based church fairs ('*Katholikentag*').	Close connection to political elite and established lobby organizations; institutionally part of social security system; civic education programmes foster 'responsible citizens'; high capacity to mobilize.
West Germany/ Protestant Church	Homogeneous, large organization, rooted in political and civil society; Network of Protestant academies for adult education; Mass-based church fairs ('*Kirchentag*').	Close connection to political elite and established lobby organizations; institutionally part of social security system; civic education programmes foster 'responsible citizens'; high mobilizational capacity.
Georgia/ Georgian Orthodox Church	Homogeneous organization with extraordinarily high level of legitimacy in population.	Potentially high capacity to mobilize.
Ukraine/ Ukrainian Orthodox Church	Fragmented organizations.	Diverse political positions result in low level of political influence; low capacity to mobilize.
Indonesia/Islamic Organizations	De-centralized and mass-based organizations, close connections to grass roots.	High capacity to mobilize.
Mali/Islamic Organizations	Heterogeneous 'landscape' of Islamic organizations: De-centralized and specialized associations and NGOs with close connections to grass roots in specific areas; Sufi centres with low level of formal institutionalization; administrative committees of mosques. Individual charismatic Muslim leaders.	Overall low capacity to mobilize; influential in specific policy areas (social and family policies) and social security function. Indirect political influence through consultations of national politicians with individual authorities (Sufi centres). Usually, no political aims (religious authorities are charismatic more than political).

Special status of majority religion. In most cases, majority religions were able to negotiate during the democratic transition a special status or at least no deterioration of their position as compared to the pre-democratic regime. For example, the Autocephalous Orthodox Church in Georgia enjoys substantive privileges that are not granted to minority religions and, thus limit religious freedom and the scope of manoeuvre of other religious groups in the country. The German churches were able to secure their place as major officially recognized providers of social welfare and succeeded in their insistence on Christian (voluntary and non-devotional) instruction in public schools.

Formally institutionalized dialogue between state and religion. In all cases, the special status of the majority religion is reflected in the establishment of formal institutional arrangements, initiated by the state in order to enhance relations between state and religion. These institutions give the religious actors space to manoeuvre and make them an institutionalized part of national politics. Examples include the *Haut Conseil Islamique* in Mali; the state-instituted *ulama* council in Indonesia; and the Commission on Relations between State and Religion in Ukraine. These institutional provisions foster the self-organization and strengthen the formal influence of Muslim organizations beyond their diverse informal alliances with political and civil society.

Formal intermediary institutions: religious political parties. Only in one case was a religious party, the German Christian Democratic Union (CDU), successful in becoming a long-standing majority party. Whereas the party disassociated from its religious social base over time, it constituted a platform for the German Catholic Church to influence German democratization on the level of the political elite. In Ukraine, Georgia and Indonesia, where religious actors founded political parties shortly before the first post-transition legislative elections, these parties remained at the margins of politics and slowly dissociated from the religious institutions and core constituencies. Comparatively, the Malian case stands out because the constitutional ban of religious parties led to a strong channelling of political interests into a social organization in the first half of the 1990s. Today, the overall weakness of the party system in Mali, and thus the absence of a formally institutionalized intermediary level, further strengthens the Islamic organizations' role in politics through informal and formal institutions such as consultations with national politicians or the *Haut Conseil Islamique*.

4. Conclusions

We have summarized the major findings of a research project that examined the role of religious actors in democratization processes in five countries and six case studies: the Catholic and the Protestant Churches in West Germany after 1945, the Orthodox Churches in Ukraine and Georgia shortly before and after the fall of the Iron Curtain, and Islamic organizations in Mali before and after 1987 and Indonesia before and after 1998.

Overall, our comparison across religious, geographic and temporal variance showed that the role of religious actors in all three phases of democratic transitions was most influenced by the *de facto* autonomy they enjoyed vis-à-vis the political regime as well as the organizational form these actors took. Their aims, means, and the political significance of their theology were highly dependent on their legal status within the state.

If we consider the means through which religious actors influenced (de-)democratization in our case studies, they made foremost use of *ideational* means (in the constitution-drafting processes of the transition; also in granting or withholding legitimation of political elites in all phases) and *institutional* means (as important providers of social welfare in the transition and consolidation phases). Large-scale anti-system *mobilization* was only possible in Indonesia, where the Islamic organizations enjoyed popular support among communities to call for participation in anti-system protests and benefited from the legal space to engage in sustained anti-regime activities.

With respect to the opening phase, our case studies confirmed a previous large-N research project,[69] which found that religious actors can only contribute to the erosion of an authoritarian regime where they enjoy some legal independence from the regime and a legal space in which to manoeuvre. This was the case in particular in Indonesia.

In the phase of transition, the newly emerging normative consensus was often reflected in a new or substantively revised constitution. We have summarized the findings regarding the involvement of religious actors in the constitution-drafting and ratification processes. Here religious actors' advocacy for special privileges was usually contingent upon the nature of previously extant constitutional or legislative clauses regarding religion–state relations. In all six cases, religious actors could secure certain privileges, while having to compromise on the question of religious freedom and non-establishment. In none of the five countries was the majority religion officially established as a state religion after democratization, and in all protection of religious pluralism and positive religious freedom became new constitutional norms, or were retained as such.

Finally, in the consolidation phase, a restructuring of the religious sphere took place in all five countries, with the consequence that fringe groups were able to emerge and claim space for themselves where civil society was less regulated by the state than it had been before. Some established religious actors founded political parties and thereby attempted to institutionalize their access to the legislature and important policy debates. Over time, however, the connections between these political parties and the religious actors severed and religious political parties, not unlike non-religious parties, emancipated themselves from their original social base. Equally important, religious radical groups over time presented a challenge to state authority not unlike other radical or anti-constitutional groups and a state that managed to democratically consolidate found ways to deal with such groups through conventional instruments of the rule of law. Post-transition developments in our cases studies indicate that the extent to which religion presents the exception to politics dramatically decreases over time in democratized systems of government, and religious politics (so often portrayed as inherently dangerous to democracy) became not unlike regular politics.

In the context of the debate on the compatibility of religion and democracy, it is noteworthy that leading Protestant theologians – like their Catholic counterparts – opposed democracy during the West German democratic consolidation process on theological as well as attitudinal grounds, arguing that the system prioritized individual rights over duties (which did not cohere with 'Christian values'), that it was a foreign imposition, and that corporatist representative institutions were much closer to 'German culture' with its strong history of corporatist arrangements than the newly established liberal parliamentary system. This sheds a different light on the long cultivated view of Protestantism as the denomination most inclined of all towards liberal democratic norms. More importantly, it underscores once more the contextual nature of the 'democratic compatibility' debate.

Against the background of our findings, three questions in particular merit closer attention in academic research on religious actors in democratization. First, there is a need for systematic, both large-N and case-based, comparative research on the influence of religious actors in (de-)democratization processes, so as to improve our understanding of the conditions that shape their engagement with political and social actors and, through the latter, their impact on democratization and de-democratization processes. Second, future research should examine more closely the effect on regime legitimacy where religious actors provide crucial social services. How does the fact that religious organizations perform important welfare functions *in lieu* of the state affect the state's legitimacy in all three phases of the transition, in particular in contexts of sheer lack of state capacity (such as Mali)? Third, the role religious actors play in the formation and reform of religion–state relations, either at constitutional moments, or in times of 'normal politics' when pertinent legislation is being passed, merits closer research. When and when not are religious actors able to define the agenda, to protect particularist interests, to safeguard ecclesiastical privileges? This is of interest especially in democratizing Muslim-majority countries (such as Indonesia, Mali, Senegal) when legislative proposals of personal status law are on the agenda that may qualify liberal rights and equal citizenship.

Acknowledgements

We thank Ipek Gencel Sezgin, Alfred Stepan and Jeff Haynes for their close readings and invaluable comments, as well as Maryam Rutner and Allison Wood for their research assistance.

Notes

1. Casanova, 'Civil Society and Religion: Retrospective Reflections on Catholicism and Prospective Reflections on Islam', 1041; Philpott. 'The Catholic Wave'.
2. Actor-centred analyses, which are popular in the study of democratization, pay little or no attention to religious actors, see e.g. O'Donnell, Schmitter and Whitehead, *Transitions from Authoritarian Rule*. Also Linz and Stepan, *Problems of Democratic Transition and Consolidation: Southern Europe, South America, and Post-Communist*

Europe. Exceptions for individual case studies include Mainwaring, *The Catholic Church and Politics in Brazil, 1916–1985*; Kalyvas, *The Rise of Christian Democracy in Europe*; Cheng and Brown, *Religious Organizations and Democratization: Case Studies From Contemporary Asia*; Maser, Peter, *Kirchen in der DDR*.

3. While the Harvard research project focuses on the opening and transition phases of democratization, it does not, however, examine the role of religious actors in deepening and consolidating democratic rule. More detailed findings of the Harvard research project are forthcoming in Philpott, Toft and Shah, *God's Century: Religion and the Future of Global Politics*. For an audio summary, listen to the podcast http://www.cfr.org/content/publications/media/2007/6-21-07.mp3 (accessed March 26, 2009).

4. Examples of condition (2) can be found in numerous (pre-dominantly Latin American) countries as well as Poland and the Philippines, where the Catholic Church played a constructive role towards democratization. An example of condition (1) is, for instance, East Germany, where due to a Soviet-imposed 1953 regulation, inter-church communication could not be intercepted by the state security (STASI) and where, as a consequence, dissidents in the 1980s who otherwise were little concerned with religion and the church used church communication channels to plan protests and demonstrations. See Peter Maser, *Kirchen in der DDR*.

5. Künkler and Leininger, *Zur Rolle religiöser Akteure in Demokratisierungsprozessen*.

6. The forms and means of exercising influence are also captured in our research. For the results, see Künkler and Leininger; *Zur Rolle religiöser Akteure in Demokratisierungsprozessen*.

7. Phases of democratization were introduced by O'Donnell, Schmitter and Whitehead, *Transitions from Authoritarian Rule*. For a discussion of democracy as 'the only game in town', see Linz and Stepan, *Problems of Democratic Transition and Consolidation: Southern Europe, South America, and Post-Communist Europe*, 5.

8. Linz and Stepan, *Problems of Democratic Transition and Consolidation: Southern Europe, South America, and Post-Communist Europe*, 3.

9. Ibid., 5–6.

10. In the words of Charles Tilly: '... democratization and de-democratization occur continuously, with no guarantee of an end point in either direction'. See Tilly, *Democracy*, 24; also Linz and Stepan, *Problems of Democratic Transition and Consolidation: Southern Europe, South America, and Post-Communist Europe*, 6; Svolik, 'Authoritarian Reversals and Democratic Consolidation'.

11. Lundskow, *The Sociology of Religion. A Substantive and Transdisciplinary Approach*. Peter Berger, in his *The Sacred Canopy*, identifies four questions that drive all 'religions': Who am I? Why am I here? How should I live? What happens when I die? Berger, *The Sacred Canopy. Elements of a Sociology of Religion*.

12. Religious actors are usually part of civil society, which we understand, in the spirit of Thomas Janoski, as '... a sphere of dynamic and responsive public discourse between the state, the public sphere consisting of voluntary organizations, and the market sphere concerning private firms and unions'. Compare Janoski, *Citizenship and Civil Society*. Janoski's concept is based on Jürgen Habermas, *Strukturwandel der Öffentlichkeit. Untersuchungen zu einer Kategorie der bürgerlichen Gesellschaft*, where he divides social entities into four areas: state, private sphere, market and the public.

13. See the homepage of the German Federal Office of Statistics (Statistisches Bundesamt) www.destatis.de (accessed June 14, 2009).

14. See Boeckh, 'Orthodoxie und demokratische Transformation in der Ukraine'.

15. Ukraine. International Religious Freedom Report 2007, http://www.state.gov/g/drl/rls/irf/2007/90205.htm (accessed February 18, 2009); World Values Survey 2006 (compare www.worldvaluessurvey.org).

16. Sufi orders, also 'brotherhoods' or *tariqas*, are groups of students of Islam who gather around a spiritual leader ('cheick' or 'sheikh'). In Mali, the Sunni *Qadiriyya* and *Tijaniyya* are the two main orders. They associate themselves to the Maliki School of Islamic jurisprudence (*mazhab*). In contrast to neighbouring Senegal, Malian Sufi orders are loosely organized.
17. Afrobarometer, *Summary of Results. Round 3 of Afrobarometer Survey in Mali*, 13.
18. van Bruinessen, 'Islamic State or State Islam? Fifty Years of State–Islam Relations in Indonesia'.
19. The most prominent and representative work for this argument is Samuel Huntington's *The Clash of Civilizations and the Remaking of World Order*.
20. For instance see Fox, *A World Survey of Religion and the State*. For a summary of the academic debate and its political implications see Elshtain, 'Religion and Democracy'.
21. Casanova, *Public Religions in the Modern World*, see in particular pp. 211–15. Casanova distinguishes three different notions of secularization (differentiation of secular spheres; decline of religious beliefs in modern societies, and privatization of religion). See also Künkler and Leininger 'Säkularisierung' in Dieter Nohlen and Rainer-Olaf Schultze (eds), *Lexikon der Politikwissenschaft, Theorien, Methoden, Begriffe*.
22. The case studies summarized here aim to capture the role of religious actors in democratization processes, that is, their empirical contribution or obstruction to the dissemination and realization of democratic values and modes of behaviour.
23. The concept of the 'twin tolerations' was developed by Stepan, 'The World's Religious Systems and Democracy: Crafting The 'Twin Tolerations'. Stepan argues that state and religion are *de facto* not strictly separate in most long-standing democracies, but instead are institutionally intertwined in a system of mutual toleration. What is important from the viewpoint of democratic theory is that the two spheres ought not infringe on each other's competencies. The 'twin tolerations' model only works in a democratic state that upholds the separation of religious and political authority, and strives to take an equidistant approach towards different religious communities as well as towards religious vis-à-vis non-religious citizens.
24. Fox, *A World Survey of Religion and the State*. Also Künkler and Meyer-Resende, *A Missing Link: Why Europe Should Talk about Religion when Promoting Democracy Abroad*.
25. Fox, *Do Democracies Have Separation of Religion and State?*, 12.
26. Based on the articles by Klein, 'Die Rolle der evangelischen Kirche Deutschlands im Demokratisierungsprozess nach 1945', and Liedhegener, 'Der deutsche Katholizismus und seine konstitutive Rolle im Demokratisierungsprozess Westdeutschlands nach 1945'. When we refer to (West) Germany in the following, we always refer to Germany in the confines of the case study, i.e. West Germany 1945–1969.
27. Wolfrum, *Die geglückte Demokratie: Geschichte der Bundesrepublik Deutschland von ihren Anfängen bis zur Gegenwart*.
28. Samuel Huntington (1991) distinguishes between democratic transitions from below (which he calls *replacements*), from above (*transformations*), through cooperation between incumbents and the democratic opposition (*transplacements*) and through foreign *intervention*. Huntington, *The Third Wave: Democratization in the Late Twentieth Century*, Chapter 3.
29. Boeckh, 'Orthodoxie und demokratische Transformation in der Ukraine'.
30. Jawad and Reisner, 'Die Nationalisierung der Religion in der Orthodoxen Apostolischen Kirche Georgiens – Begünstigung oder Hindernis im Demokratisierungsprozess?'.
31. Leininger, 'Die ambivalente Rolle islamischer Akteure im Demokratisierungsprozess Malis',
32. Indonesia and Mali are two of five Muslim-majority countries that according to major political science indices qualify as democracies today (Freedom House: <3 in civil and

political rights score; and >7 on Polity IV). Senegal experienced a transition to democracy in 1990, Mali in 1991, Albania in 1989/2005, Indonesia in 1998, Turkey gradually since 1961, and has been classified as a democracy without interruption since 1989.

33. For a discussion of three different types of 'public religions' see Casanova, *Public Religions in the Modern World*; and Casanova, 'Rethinking Public Religions'.
34. Since West German democratization occurred not as a result of an opening but foreign intervention, the West German case is not considered in this phase.
35. The *Nahdlatul Ulama* claims a membership of about 35 million, the modernist *Muhammadiyah* about 30 million members.
36. Künkler, 'Zum Verhältnis Staat-Religion und der Rolle islamischer Intellektueller in der indonesischen Reformasi', 'Politische Theologie und Soziale Bewegungen: Die Roll Islamischer Organisationen in der indonesischen Reformasi'.
37. The 'New Order' was the presidency of General Suharto (1965–1998) that defined itself against what later became known as the 'Old Order' under Indonesia's first post-independence president Sukarno (1945–1965).
38. Scott, 'Indonesia Reborn?'. Similarly, *Muhammadiyah*'s chairman Amien Rais' occasional use of sectarian rhetoric to unify Muslims against alleged Christian and Chinese conspiracies in politics and business could have easily tipped support towards a sectarian rather than democratic future.
39. Boeckh, 'Orthodoxie und demokratische Transformation in der Ukraine'; Bociurkiw, 'Politics and Religion in the Ukraine: Orthodox and Greek Catholics in Ukraine', 136. The Greek Catholic Church accepts the authority of the Pope in Rome and therefore is not part of the Christian-Orthodox denomination. The exception Rome made for the Greek Catholic Church (one made to only very few religious congregations, such as several Oriental Christian communities), is to allow it to submit itself to the authority of the Pope while maintaining much of the Orthodox liturgy.
40. Salafiyya (or Wahabiyya) are context-specific terms for a Malian Islamic minority that appeared in the 1950s as a countermovement to Sufism. They refer to themselves as 'reformists' and are not as exclusionary as Salafi groups in most other countries.
41. This turn towards pro-democratic arguments occurred only in the third generation of the Salafiyya in Mali.
42. Soares, *Islam and the Prayer Economy*.
43. Ilia Tschawtschawadses was a leading figure of the national 'Tergdaleulebi' *intelligenzia* who advocated a modernization of the Georgian nation in the late nineteenth century. He was killed in 1907. In 1987, the Georgian Autocephalous Orthodox Church acknowledged his efforts by beatifying him. In doing so, the Orthodox Church connected the Georgian dissidents' movement to intellectual elites to work jointly towards the erosion of Soviet rule.
44. Leininger, 'Die ambivalente Rolle islamischer Akteure im Demokratisierungsprozess Malis'; Hock, *Fliegen die Seelen der Heiligen? Muslimische Reform und staatliche Autorität in der Republik Mali seit 1960*, 145.
45. Boeckh, 'Orthodoxie und demokratische Transformation in der Ukraine'. Sysyn, 'The Third Rebirth of the Ukrainian Autocephalous Orthodox Church and the Religious Situation in Ukraine, 1989–1991', 192.
46. In the following we focus on constitution-drafting processes and their output, because a constitution establishes the basis for the legal-formal[0] relations between state and religion in a democracy.
47. The effect of *de jure* and *de facto* autonomy on the capacity of religious actors to exert an impact on political transformation processes differs from phase to phase in the following manner. In the opening phase *de facto* autonomy is decisive: even where *de jure* religious organizations may be relatively independent, authoritarian regimes usually find extra-legal ways to incapacitate and/or co-opt them, like other civil

society organizations. In the transition phase, *de facto* autonomy increases the likelihood that religious actors can use their legal status during constitutional drafting and reform processes to bargain for *de jure* autonomy. In the consolidation phase, *de jure* autonomy is only extant where no religion is officially established as the state religion.

48. The West German constitution of 23 May 1949 was called 'Basic Law' rather than 'constitution', because only a document regulating all of Germany (beyond West Germany) was to function as a constitution. For the sake of comprehensibility, we use the term constitution here, even though it would be more accurate to speak of it only as the 'Basic Law'.
49. Catholic interests were well-represented in the 'Parlamentarischer Rat' (constitutional drafting committee) through delegates of the Christian Democratic Union (CDU).
50. The Protestant Church of Germany (EKD), its representatives and politicians closely associated with it, did not exert a unified and identifiable influence on the constitution-drafting process. Rather, the EKD played an important role in legitimizing the young democracy's first democratic elections by explicitly asking members to vote with the slogan: 'A Christian citizen supports parliaments'. See Klein, 'Die Rolle der evangelischen Kirche Deutschlands im Demokratisierungsprozess nach 1945'; *Rundschreiben*, July 16, 1949; Evangelisches Zentralarchiv Berlin 2/278.
51. Moreover, during the 1990s, Christian-Orthodox groups founded political parties such as the *Ukrainska christjansko-demokratitschna partija* (Ukrainian Christian Democratic Party, UCDP) or *Respublikanska christjanska partija* (RCP, Republikanische Christliche Partei) and religious authorities ran in elections, thereby endowing the nascent democracy with some degree of legitimacy.
52. Boeckh, 'Orthodoxie und demokratische Transformation in der Ukraine'.
53. Mali's strong separation of religion and state is a legacy of French colonial rule (1883–1960). A political culture of publicly emphasizing the laicist character of the state, created during colonial rule, carried on in the First (1960–1968) and Second Malian Republic (1968–1992). The Constitution of 1992 is based on the Constitution of the Fifth French Republic of 4 October, 1958.
54. The Malian National Conference is considered to be one of the most participatory constitution-building processes in West Africa. More than 1,800 participants from politics, civil society, and the military took part.
55. *Georgia*: article 9 (1) and article 19 (1) of the Constitution of 1995; *Ukraine*: article 35 of the Constitution of 1996; *Indonesia*: Article 29 of the revised 1945 Constitution of Indonesia; *Mali*: article 4 and article 12 of the Constitution of 1992; *Germany*: article 4 of the Constitution of 1949.
56. Although the positions of some Malian Islamic organizations during the National Conference were likely to be interpreted as 'obstructive', one must note that they behaviourally followed democratic rules during the transition and accepted the democratic outcome of the National Conference. Moreover, due to their small size and *ad hoc* character, they were by far outweighed by the traditional and strong AMUPI. Anti-democratic thought did not emerge as a significant element in the public discourse on the new democratic order.
57. Today there are three Orthodox churches with different leadership in the Ukraine: one that responds to the Moscow Patriarchate (this was the only legal Orthodox Church during Soviet rule), one that responds to the Kiev Patriarchate, and also the Ukrainian Autocephalous Orthodox Church, which was founded in 1918, prohibited by the Soviets in the early 1930s and revived after 1989. Both the Orthodox Church of the Kiev Patriarchate and the Ukrainian Autocephalous Orthodox Church tended to support the Orange Revolution whereas the Moscow Patriarchate did not.
58. Casanova, 'Between Nation and Civil Society: Ethnolinguistic and Religious Pluralism in Independent Ukraine', 203–28, 215.

59. International Republican Institute, 'Georgian National Voter Survey (21 August–10 September 2007)', http://www.iri.org/eurasia/georgia/pdfs/2007-11-08-georgia.pdf (accessed March 26, 2009).
60. Le Vine, 'Mali: Accommodation or Coexistence'.
61. Examples include the Christian Evangelical Church in Minahasa (GMIM), the Protestant Church in the Moluccas (GPM), the Protestant Evangelical Church in Timor (GMIT), the Protestant Church in Western Indonesia (GPIB), the Indonesian Protestant Church Gorontalo (GPIG), the Indonesian Protestant Church Donggala (GPID), the Indonesian Protestant Church Baggai Kepulawan (GPIBK), the Indonesian Protestant Church Papua (GPI-Papua), the Indonesian Protestant Church Buol Tolitili, the Christian Church Luwuk Banggai (GKLB), the Evangelical Christian Church Talaud (GERMITA), and the Indonesian Ecumenical Christian Church.
62. Through this prayer economy politicians seek purchased advice from religious authorities on particular policy questions. Soares, *Islam and the Prayer Economy*.
63. For instance, the patriarch declared that every single murderer of a Georgian would be decried as a traitor to the Georgian nation and would be noted in a special register and damned forever, see Jawad and Reisner, 'Die Nationalisierung der Religion in der Orthodoxen Apostolischen Kirche Georgiens – Begünstigung oder Hindernis im Demokratisierungsprozess?'.
64. Compare Springhart, *Aufbrüche Zu Neuen Ufern: Der Beitrag Von Religion Und Kirche Für Demokratisierung Und Reeducation Im Westen Deutschlands Nach 1945*.
65. Bayat, *Making Islam Democratic. Social Movements and the Post-Islamist Turn*, 5.
66. Mobilizational capacity encompasses the degree of organization of the society (how many of the citizens are mobilizable by the organization?) and the organization's ability to mobilize (whether organizations do decide to call for mobilization or not, how intensively, for how long, etc.).
67. In Germany this was not the case, because the country's democratization after World War II was initiated from the outside.
68. Recent developments in mass media (especially radio, internet and to a limited extent also television) have fostered the emergence of individual *charismatic* Islamic authorities as Cheick Soufi Bilal or Chérif Haïdara. Mostly they have no political aims.
69. See endnote 3.

Note on contributors

Mirjam Künkler is Assistant Professor in Near Eastern Studies at Princeton University.

Julia Leininger is Researcher at the German Development Institute/Deutsches Institut für Entwicklungspolitik (DIE).

Bibliography

Afrobarometer. *Summary of Results*. Round 3 of Afrobarometer Survey in Mali, 2005.
Bayat, Asef. *Making Islam Democratic. Social Movements and the Post-Islamist Turn*. Stanford, CA: Stanford University Press, 2007.
Berger, Peter L. *The Sacred Canopy. Elements of a Sociology of Religion*. New York: Random House, 1990 [1967].
Birch, Sarah. *Elections and Democratization in Ukraine*. Basingstoke: Palgrave Macmillan, 2000.
Bociurkiw, Bohdan. 'Politics and Religion in the Ukraine: Orthodox and Greek Catholics in Ukraine'. In *The Politics of Religion in Russia and the New States of Eurasia*, ed. Michael Bourdeaux, 131–62. Armonk/London: M.E. Sharpe, 1995.

Boeckh, Kathrin. 'Orthodoxie und demokratische Transformation in der Ukraine' ['Orthodoxy and Democratic Transformation in the Ukraine']. In *Zur Rolle religiöser Akteure in Demokratisierungsprozessen*, ed. Mirjam Künkler and Julia Leininger. Wiesbaden: VS Verlag, 2009.

Casanova, José. *Public Religions in the Modern World*. Chicago, IL: University of Chicago Press, 1994.

Casanova, José. 'Between Nation and Civil Society: Ethnolinguistic and Religious Pluralism in Independent Ukraine'. In *Democratic Civility: The History and Cross-Cultural Possibility of a Modern Political Ideal*, ed. Robert W. Hefner. New Brunswick, NJ: Transactions Publications, 1998.

Casanova, José. 'Civil Society and Religion: Retrospective Reflections on Catholicism and Prospective Reflections on Islam'. *Social Research* 68, no. 4 (2001): 1041–80.

Casanova, José. 'Rethinking Public Religions'. In *SSRC Handbook on Religion and World Affairs*, ed. Tim Shah, Alfred C. Stepan, Monica Duffy Toft, 203–28. New York: The Social Science Research Council, forthcoming 2010.

Cheng, Tun-Jen, and Deborah Brown, eds. Religious Organizations and Democratization: Case Studies from Contemporary Asia. Armonk, NY: Sharpe, 2005.

Elshtain, Jean Bethke. 'Religion and Democracy'. *Journal of Democracy* 20, no. 22 (2009): 5–17.

Fox, Jonathan. *A World Survey of Religion and the State*. Cambridge: Cambridge University Press, 2007.

Fox, Jonathan. 'Do Democracies Have Separation of Religion and State?'. *Canadian Journal of Political Science* 40, no. 1 (2007): 2–25.

Habermas, Jürgen. *Strukturwandel der Öffentlichkeit. Untersuchungen zu einer Kategorie der bürgerlichen Gesellschaft* [*The Structural Transformation of the Public Sphere. An Inquiry into a Category of Bourgeois Society*]. Frankfurt: Suhrkamp Verlag, 2006.

Hock, Carsten. *Fliegen die Seelen der Heiligen? Muslimische Reform und staatliche Autorität in der Republik Mali seit 1960* [*Do the Souls of the Saints Fly? Muslim Reform and State Authority in the Republic of Mali since 1960*]. Berlin: Klaus Schwarz Verlag, 1999.

Huntington, Samuel P. *The Third Wave: Democratization in the Late Twentieth Century*. Norman: University of Oklahoma Press, 1991.

Huntington, Samuel. *The Clash of Civilizations and the Remaking of World Order*. New York: Simon & Schuster, 1996.

Janoski, Thomas. *Citizenship and Civil Society*. Cambridge: Cambridge University Press, 1998.

Jawad, Pamela. *Democratic Consolidation in Georgia after the 'Rose Revolution'?* PRIF Reports No. 73. Frankfurt: Peace Research Institute Frankfurt, 2005.

Jawad, Pamela, and Oliver Reisner. 'Die Nationalisierung der Religion in der Orthodoxen Apostolischen Kirche Georgiens – Begünstigung oder Hindernis im Demokratisierungsprozess?' ['The Nationalization of Religion in the Orthodox Church of Georgia – Fostering or Hindering Democratization?']. In *Zur Rolle religiöser Akteure in Demokratisierungsprozessen*, ed. Mirjam Künkler and Julia Leininger. Wiesbaden: VS Verlag, forthcoming 2009.

Kalyvas, Stathis. *The Rise of Christian Democracy in Europe*. Ithaca, NY: Cornell University Press, 1996.

Klein, Michael. 'Die Rolle der evangelischen Kirche Deutschlands im Demokratisierungsprozess nach 1945' ['The Role of the German Protestant Church in the Process of Democratization after 1945']. In *Zur Rolle Religiöser Akteure in Demokratisierungsprozessen*, ed. Mirjam Künkler and Julia Leininger. Wiesbaden: VS Verlag, forthcoming 2009.

Künkler, Mirjam. 'Zum Verhältnis Staat-Religion und der Rolle islamischer Intellektueller in der indonesischen Reformasi' ['On Religion-State Relations and the Role of Muslim Intellectuals in the Indonesian Reformasi']. In *Religion in Diktatur und Demokratie – Zur Bedeutung von religiösen Werten, Praktiken und Institutionen in politischen Transformationsprozessen* [*Religion in Dictarorship and Democracy – On the Relevance of Religious Values, Practices, and Institutions in Political Transformation Processes*], ed. Stephanie Garling and Simon W. Fuchs, 84–102. Villigster Profile. Wuppertal. 2007.

Künkler, Mirjam. 'Politische Theologie und Soziale Bewegungen: Die Rolle Islamischer Organisationen in der indonesischen Reformasi' ['Ideas and Social Movements: The Role of Islamic Organizations in the Indonesian Reformasi']. In *Zur Rolle religiöser Akteure in Demokratisierungsprozessen*, ed. Mirjam Künkler and Julia Leininger. Wiesbaden: VS Verlag, forthcoming 2009.

Künkler, Mirjam, and Julia Leininger. 'Säkularisierung' ['Secularization']. In *Lexikon der Politikwissenschaft, Theorien, Methoden, Begriffe* [*Encyclopedia of Political Science. Theories, Methods and Concepts*], 3rd edn. ed. Dieter Nohlen and Rainer-Olaf Schultze. München: Beck Verlag, forthcoming 2009.

Künkler, Mirjam, and Julia Leininger, eds. *Zur Rolle religiöser Akteure in Demokratisierungsprozessen* [*On the Role of Religious Actors in Processes of Democratization*]. Wiesbaden: VS Verlag, 2009.

Künkler, Mirjam, and Michael Meyer-Resende. *A Missing Link: Why Europe Should Talk about Religion when Promoting Democracy Abroad*. Democracy Reporting International. Discussion Paper No.1, June 2009, revised 2nd edn. http://www.democracy-reporting.org/papers.html (accessed July 15, 2009).

Leininger, Julia. 'Die ambivalente Rolle islamischer Akteure im Demokratisierungsprozess Malis' ['The Ambivalent Role of Islamic Actors in Mali's Democratization']. In *Zur Rolle religiöser Akteure in Demokratisierungsprozessen*, ed. Mirjam Künkler and Julia Leininger. Wiesbaden: VS Verlag, forthcoming 2009.

Le Vine, Victor. 'Mali: Accommodation or Coexistence'. In *Political Islam in West Africa. State–Society Relations Transformed*, ed. William F.S. Miles, 73–99. London: Lynne Rienner Publishers, 2007.

Liddle, Bill, and Saiful Mujani. 'Indonesian Democracy. From Transition to Consolidation'. In *Indonesia, Islam and Democratic Consolidation: Comparative Perspectives*, ed. Mirjam Künkler, Azyumardi Azra, and Alfred Stepan. Columbia University Press, forthcoming 2010.

Liedhegener, Antonius. 'Der deutsche Katholizismus und seine konstitutive Rolle im Demokratisierungsprozess Westdeutschlands nach 1945' ['The German Catholicism and its Constitutive Role in the West German Democratization Process after 1945']. In *Zur Rolle religiöser Akteure in Demokratisierungsprozessen*, ed. Mirjam Künkler and Julia Leininger. Wiesbaden: VS Verlag, forthcoming 2009.

Linz, Juan J., and Alfred C. Stepan. *Problems of Democratic Transition and Consolidation: Southern Europe, South America, and Post-Communist Europe*. Baltimore, MD: Johns Hopkins University Press, 1996.

Lundskow, George. *The Sociology of Religion. A Substantive and Transdisciplinary Approach*. Thousand Oaks, CA: SAGE Publications, 2008.

Mainwaring, Scott. *The Catholic Church and Politics in Brazil, 1916–1985*. Stanford, CA: Stanford University Press, 1986.

Maser, Peter. *Kirchen in der DDR* [*Churches in the German Democratic Republic*]. Bonn: Bundeszentrale für Politische Bildung, 2000.

McFaul, Michael. 'The Fourth Wave of Democracy and Dictatorship. Non-Cooperative Transitions in the Post-communist World'. *World Politics* 54, (January 2002): 212–44.

O'Donnell, Guillermo, Philippe C. Schmitter and Laurence Whitehead, eds. *Transitions from Authoritarian Rule*. Baltimore, MD: Johns Hopkins University Press, 1986.

Philpott, Daniel. 'The Catholic Wave'. *Journal of Democracy* 15, no. 2 (2004): 32–46.

Philpott, Daniel, Monica Duffy Toft, and Tim Shah. *God's Century: Religion and the Future of Global Politics*. New York: Norton Press, forthcoming 2010.

Schmidt, Manfred G. *Demokratietheorien. Eine Einführung* [*Theories of Democracy*]. 4th edn. Wiesbaden: VS Verlag, 2009.

Scott, Margaret. 'Indonesia Reborn?'. *New York Review of Books* 45, no. 13 (1998).

Soares, Benjamin. *Islam and the Prayer Economy. History and Authority in a Malian Town*. Ann Arbor: University of Michigan Press, 2005.

Springhart, Heike. *Aufbrüche zu neuen Ufern: Der Beitrag von Religion und Kirche für Demokratisierung und Reeducation im Westen Deutschlands nach 1945* [*Departure to New Grounds. The Contribution of Religion and Church to Democratization and Re-Education in West Germany after 1945*]. Leipzig: Evangelische Verlagsanstalt, 2008.

Stepan, Alfred C. 'The World's Religious Systems and Democracy: Crafting the "Twin Tolerations"'. In *Arguing Comparative Politics*, 213–54. New York: Oxford University Press, 2001.

Svolik, Milan. 'Authoritarian Reversals and Democratic Consolidation'. *American Political Science Review* 102, no. 2 (2008): 153–68.

Sysyn, Frank E. 'The Third Rebirth of the Ukrainian Autocephalous Orthodox Church and the Religious Situation in Ukraine, 1989–1991'. In *Seeking God. The Recovery of Religious Identity in Orthodox Russia, Ukraine, and Georgia*, ed. Stephen K. Batalden, 191–219. DeKalb, IL: Northern Illinois University, 1993.

Tilly, Charles. *Democracy*. Cambridge: Cambridge University Press, 2007.

van Bruinessen, Martin. 'Islamic State or State Islam? Fifty Years of State-Islam Relations in Indonesia'. http://www.let.uu.nl/~Martin.vanBruinessen/personal/publications/State-Islam.htm (accessed February 18, 2009).

Wolfrum, Edgar. *Die geglückte Demokratie: Geschichte der Bundesrepublik Deutschland von ihren Anfängen bis zur Gegenwart* [*The Successful Democracy: The History of the Federal Republic of Germany from its Beginnings to the Present*]. Stuttgart: Klett-Cotta, 2006.

'Catholic waves' of democratization? Roman Catholicism and its potential for democratization

Jodok Troy

Department of Political Science, University of Innsbruck, Austria

The aim and scope of the article is to examine if Catholicism is or can be a major force in democratization. And if so, what are its core values and motivations? To examine this issue, it is also necessary to evaluate democratization outcomes where the church was not involved. We shall see that it is unavoidable to take into account fundamental Christian and thus also Catholic values and doctrines which are – despite all 'earthly' constraints – in *favour* of both liberal and democratic values. In the case of the Catholic Church this is primarily because it perceives the social message of the gospels not merely as theory but also as a call to action, followed by many of its adherents. The article argues that the main reason for this was the result of the church's changing political theology, following the Second Vatican Council (1962–1965), which enabled the church's adoption of a pronounced focus on: human rights, religious freedom, democracy, and economic development.

'The end of history' and the resurgence of religion

According to Samuel Huntington, the third wave of democratization (1974–1990) occurred as a result of five key developments: loss of legitimacy of authoritarian regimes, economic changes, regional contingency factors, external factors, *and* the – changed – role of the Roman Catholic Church.[1] Huntington observed that the third wave was overwhelmingly a 'Catholic' one. Out of the 30 countries that made a transition to democracy during this time, most were predominantly Catholic, including: Portugal and Spain, many Latin American countries, the Philippines, and Poland and other Eastern European countries. At first glance, then, Catholicism seems to be highly significant in this shift to democracy. It also raises two important questions: The first is to ask if the Roman Catholic

Church really had such a potential for democratization and if the answer is yes, then the second is: What were its origins?

Roman Catholic social teaching, as argued by some theologians, sociologists, and political scientists can have a significant impact on world politics, particularly on processes of democratization and conditions normally perceived as necessary for democracy such as political and religious freedom and enhanced economic development.[2] This is particularly because many leaders of the Roman Catholic Church (hereafter the church), including recent popes, have perceived the social message of the gospels not merely as theory but as a call to action. As often assumed, the main reason for the presumed positive effects of the church regarding democratization was the change in its political theology. Of particular importance here was the Second Vatican Council (known as Vatican II). The outcome of Vatican II reflected, among other things the Church's enhanced concern with human rights, religious freedom, and economic development, and enabled the church to incorporate these issues into its teaching. Thus, the question is: Can the church justifiably be characterized as a promoter of democracy, or, at least, for liberalization, from its post-Vatican II emphasis on human rights issues?[3]

The aim and scope of this contribution is to examine if Catholicism is or can be a major force in democratization. To do this, we need to assess the church's core values and motivations for action. Another issue to be examined is the evaluation of the cases where the church was not engaged in, or appeared overtly to support, democratization outcomes in various countries. In seeking to answer these questions, we shall see that it is unavoidable to take not only fundamental Christian but also Catholic values and doctrines into account. Overall, these are – despite all 'earthly' constraints – in *favour* of both liberal and democratic values.

Shortly after the Cold War and the breakup of the Soviet Union in the late 1980s, Fukuyama predicted in his book, *The End of History*, the victory of liberal democracy as the leading and best political system in the time to come.[4] Indeed, for Diamond, democracy – although not always, he admits, in its liberal form – now finds almost global acceptance.[5] In this context it seems reasonable to suppose that politics and, even more, democracy dealing with and taking religious values seriously, cannot bring civil peace and thus foster democratization. In liberal terms this is first of all because, one cannot bargain and therefore agree on fundamental and thus, even more, absolute religious values, as for example Fukuyama argues.[6] It is not possible to accept both, originally liberal values and absolute religious values at the same time. Absolute religious values and claims, it seems, directly contradict liberal values such as, for example, that the way of life, although within some limits, is up to us and not compromised by any other transcendental power. According to liberal ideas, secularism of any kind – that is, the outcome of a process of secularization, whereby church and state are formally and institutionally separate – must be the most obvious and logical consequence of democratization.[7]

This liberal assumption – that is, the continuing separation between religion and political order, particularly democracy – sees itself more and more confronted with the experience of a claimed global religious resurgence.[8] What is of general importance in this context is that a widespread and intensified public and political discourse concerning religion and politics is taking place in many countries around the world.[9] Within this discourse the issue of religion and violence is at the forefront. But nevertheless, the claimed religious resurgence and associated discourse also leads us to think about links between religion and peace as well as democracy.[10] As already noted, Huntington was one of the first to make a positive link between religion – in his particular case, Catholicism – and the third wave of democratization in the late twentieth century.[11] Others, for example José Casanova, argue that religion is per se compatible with democracy.[12] Overall, not only religions in general but also specific Christian denominations in particular are relatively under-analysed or even downplayed in the context of democratization. The most obvious example of one that has been extensively studied is the proclaimed link between *Protestantism* and capitalism. This is portrayed as a basic foundation for democratization and then democracy, a link that goes back to Max Weber's writings in the early twentieth century.[13] It is the task of the present article to try to evaluate the explicit *Catholic* possibilities and restraints regarding its effects on democratization.[14]

Religion and democracy: status quo vs. change

Although the links between both religion and democracy and religion and democratization have been overlooked or even ignored for a long time, various approaches to these issues have recently emerged.[15] Historically, the church was certainly one, if not the main actor opposing the modern sovereign territorial nation state, as it emerged after the Peace of Westphalia in 1648. This is mainly because the church itself dominated social life in much of Europe at that time as, an actor as well as a structure, perceiving the unity of the *Respublica Christiana* ('Christian Republic') in danger as the Peace of 'Westphalia replaced [religious] unity with segmentation. What triumphed there was a system of polities, defined by territory, within each of which a single authority ... was supreme, or sovereign'.[16] The supreme actor and structure – 'the Christian Republic' – which dominated both social and political life was henceforward significantly demoted. At least in Western Europe, first the 'rights of man', including political liberalization and then democratization, followed, and developed mainly in the context of the emerging sovereign territorial nation state. It is thus not surprising that the church also opposed the first attempts to establish the 'rights of man' and democracy as a political system as this very process threatened the church's unity and questioned its claim of holding absolute truths such as moral values as well as political convictions such as its claims of regulating political and social life.

Today, however, with the global establishment of the system of states and an emerging international society, the dissemination of ideas about democracy, and in some cases democratization itself, things are different.[17] One of the main scholarly as well as public arguments in the church focuses on decisions made at the

Second Vatican Council (1962–1965).[18] It is sometimes argued that Vatican II led the church into the twentieth century.[19] In doing so, it also acknowledged democracy as the 'best' political system, especially as it necessarily involves highlighting the importance of religious freedom for democratic freedoms more generally. Huntington was at the forefront of this argument, arguing that if it 'were not for the changes within the Catholic Church and the resulting actions of the church against authoritarianism, fewer Third Wave transitions to democracy would have occurred and many that did occur would have occurred later'.[20] Summarizing the effects of the third wave, Daniel Philpott argues that:

> It is a striking finding: why would countries the majority of whose population belong to a particular religious community, especially one that has historically distrusted democracy, compose the motor of a global trend in democratization. ... Behind the Catholic Wave was a sea change in the Catholic Church's political theology: the Second Vatican Council (1962–1965), where the Church adopted human rights, religious freedom, democracy, and economic development into its teaching and declared its withdrawal from temporal prerogatives – a definitive, doctrinal embrace of differentiation.[21]

Indeed, Catholic social teaching has had a significant impact on some dimensions of world politics. This is particularly because the church views the social message of the gospels not merely as theory but as a call to action:

> As far as the Church is concerned, the social message of the Gospel must not be considered a theory, but above all else a basis and a motivation for action. Inspired by this message, some of the first Christians distributed their goods to the poor, bearing witness to the fact that, despite different social origins, it was possible for people to live together in peace and harmony. Through the power of the Gospel, down the centuries monks tilled the land, men and women religious founded hospitals and shelters for the poor, Confraternities as well as individual men and women of all states of life devoted themselves to the needy and to those on the margins of society, convinced as they were that Christ's words 'as you did it to one of the least of these my brethren, you did it to me' (Mt 25:40) were not intended to remain a pious wish, but were meant to become a concrete life commitment.[22]

Some papal encyclicals have been serious and sensitive instruments in analysing certain issues in international affairs.[23] Their most noteworthy importance regarding Catholic social teaching is the aim to further social justice, with a key focus on the common good.[24] Even more, the Second Vatican Council provided the most important documents regarding today's interventionalist notion of the church in international affairs.[25] For example, *Lumen Gentium*, the Council's Dogmatic Constitution, describes the church as an evangelical movement with a global mission. *Dignitatis Humanae*, the Council's Declaration on Religious Freedom, made it possible for the church to arise as a proponent of human rights. *Gaudium et Spes*, the Council's Pastoral Constitution, stresses the importance of a free and virtuous society in pluralistic terms, especially regarding the notion of the church as the agent of culture, rather than a conventional political player.[26] More generally, the middle of the twentieth century marked many important shifts in the foreign policies of the Holy See.[27] For example, the Cuban missile crisis, in which Pope John XXIII played an important role, exposed the urgent need for peaceful coexistence between the ideologically opposed superpowers as the primary goal of the church.[28] Finally, in the middle of the 1960s, the Second Vatican Council marked the church's turn from a promoter of the status quo to an active liberation force including its support for basic human rights.[29]

Consequently, the church today seeks to encourage the creation and development of a cooperative world society that stresses individual rights rather than a balance of power in international affairs. This is clear from, for example, how the late Pope John Paul II vehemently opposed the second Gulf War in 1991, in part because he saw its purpose as the preservation of a balance of power. In terms of realist analysis, this was a war of 'necessity' not one of 'choice'.[30] It is obvious then that the Holy See, on a rather normative basis, seeks to encourage so-called global governance. This is particularly done through the United Nations, especially after the third Gulf War in 2003 which the church strongly opposed.[31] The concept of a law-based world society is an old and well documented one in Catholic teaching, found for example in the thoughts of St. Augustine and even more so in the teachings of Francisco de Vitoria and Francisco Suarez as well as in the newer official Catholic documents such as in the pastoral constitution *Gaudium et Spes* speaking about the achievement of peace via justice:

> Peace is not merely the absence of war; nor can it be reduced solely to the maintenance of a balance of power between enemies; nor is it brought about by dictatorship instead, it is rightly and appropriately called an enterprise of justice. Peace results from that order structured into human society by its divine Founder, and actualized by men as they thirst after ever greater justice. The common good of humanity finds its ultimate meaning in the eternal law. But since the concrete demands of this common good are constantly changing as time goes on, peace is never attained once and for all, but must be built up ceaselessly. Moreover, since the human will is unsteady and wounded by sin, the achievement of peace requires a constant mastering of passions and the vigilance of lawful authority.[32]

The problem, however, is that the argument for a sea change in Catholic political theology as a consequence of Vatican II, is on its own insufficient for a comprehensive explanation of the church's championing of democratization in the last quarter of the twentieth century. We can note that the church has not been a promoter of human rights and democracy everywhere, not even in states with a Catholic majority. The church exercised a relative successful and direct influence on democratization, for example in Poland, Spain, the Philippines but a weak one elsewhere, for example in Argentina. Philpott concludes that the church was most likely to be successful when the popular perception was to see the church as distinct from the state in various forms (governance, domestic alliances, in its identification with national identity, etc.). Even more important, despite their often close relationship with authoritarian governments, Catholic leaders such as bishops where seen as representative figures of a transnational organization that was not per se perceived in alliance with authoritarian governments. This was also important in enabling the church to have an impact on democratization outcomes in Catholic countries.[33]

However, to explain the shortcomings of exclusively theological explanations regarding religion and democratization such as the prominent place of social justice, Anderson draws attention to issues beyond that of the theological changes which characterized Vatican II. In addition, he points to the church's pursuit of religious hegemony and its concern to maintain 'market share'. Put crudely, where the 'Catholic Wave' occurred, it took place in part because most of Protestant-majority countries already were democracies, and most exhibited the middle income level which scholars since Lipset have claimed are a necessary starting point for democratization. As Jeffrey Haynes illustrated with examples from Africa, the church engaged in leadership roles in democratization processes not necessarily only in order to focus on progressive change but also to try to achieve or maintain hegemony.[34]

The second additional explanation why the church has supported democracy in some places and in others has not – and on occasion even supported incumbent authoritarian regimes – is based on a rational choice argument: trying to maintain market share. Using examples from South America, Anthony Gill points out that the common explanations concerning Catholicism and democratization are insufficient, involving, *inter alia*, growing awareness of social injustice and changes during the course of the Second Vatican Council. This is mainly because 'these ostensibly impacted upon the whole Catholic Church yet only some national hierarchies adopted a "progressive" position'.[35] Instead, Gill explains the differentiation between pro- and contra democracy with the rational element of competition: '[W]here the Church faces greater competition for members, bishops will be under pressure to defend the interests of the poor, thereby breaking their traditional alliance with the elite. Not doing so would lead to a greater loss of poorer parishioners to competing groups'. For Gill, if there is no competition, 'episcopacy can ignore parishioner complaints ... and continue an alliance with the political elite'.[36] On the other hand, the church has a regionally impressive role in conflict regulation and settlement in South America. As a result, it can be, at least to some degree, characterized as a role model in this regard for other regions. There are, however, especially in the case of South America a few concerns which have to be noted. In South America the church developed a high capability of adjustment to the local circumstances, for example in adopting liberation theology, which sought to address popular social grievances. Furthermore, the church itself, and particularly its followers, have often suffered significantly from violent political conflicts as victims of oppressive regimes, which make it, at least to a certain degree, no different to other sufferers who could identify themselves with the church.[37] Furthermore, and what Gill's analyses miss, is that there is acknowledgement of the impact of the role of ideas about justice and the power of movement in the church's shift. This does not only concern senior figures, such as bishops, but also religious orders, lower clerics, lays (movements), etc. who engaged in grass roots movements according to the new standards the Second Vatican Council set out.[38] Philpott, for example, points out that 'the more widely these ideas [about justice] were held among a nation's Catholics, the more likely their church was to take up oppositional democratic politics'.[39]

Secularism and the 'twin tolerations'

The Western social science notion of secularism leads to two fundamental notions of religion within politics: That religion either has to be completely banned from the public sphere (Laicism, as in Turkey or France. See Jamal's and Barras's contributions in this special issue)[40] or the notion of religion (particularly Christianity – a la Huntington – and Judaism) as a cultural foundation of democracy. For Hurd, as a result, the constructed political paradigm of secularism is 'one of the most important organizing principles of modern politics'.[41] The consequence is that secularism should thus be defined as 'a political negotiation over the accepted role of religion in public life rather than as an a priori category'.[42] As a result, we cannot regard the widely claimed resurgence of religion as a 'special atavistic anomaly'[43] but rather an integral and constitutive part of modern politics.[44] The two most obvious phenomena of religious resurgence are the widely noted Islamic movement, especially because it is often, yet erroneously, associated with violence, and dynamic Evangelical Protestantism (especially in the two Americas and Africa).[45]

What we can be sure about is that modernity has not necessarily brought secularization and is thus not equivalent to secularization but instead highlights the pluralizing character of society.[46] The notion of the pluralistic character of modernity with its open space for 'many Gods' represents not only a challenge for analysis and understanding of international affairs but also in relation to their scientific study. In this context, differentiation between church and state, as Philpott notes, 'may well foster the health of religion, giving it the very autonomy by which it flourishes'.[47] Sociological research indicates that religious competition – in a differentiated system – fosters religious participation and creates a 'religious freedom cycle'.[48] At the same time this is a counter argument to the rational choice explanation of the maintenance of a market share as well as to the hegemonic argument regarding the role of the church's participation in democratization.

In order to understand the church–state relationship better than only viewing it from the secularism paradigm, Alfred Stepan points to the widely noted notion of the 'twin tolerations'. This refers to 'the minimal boundaries of freedom of action that must somehow be crafted for political institutions vis-à-vis religious authorities, and for religious individuals and groups vis-à-vis political institutions'. Because no European country has a church–state relationship marked by overt or fundamental mutual hostility, then the 'European lesson' indicates that not separation (a mere radical differentiation), but rather the 'constant political construction and reconstruction of the "twin tolerations"'[49] must be the fundamental understanding of religion in the context of democracy. In this regard Stepan points to three fundamental misinterpretations regarding the interplay between religion and democracy: First, there is the assumption of the uni-vocality of religion. In reviewing the role of the Catholic Church during the third wave of democratization, Huntington seems to be aware of multi-vocality, that is, the possibility of change of religious doctrines regarding democratization and democracy. In *The Clash of Civilizations*, however, this awareness changes towards the assumption of the uni-vocality of religion.[50] Another misinterpretation in Stepan's view is the fallacy of 'unique founding conditions'. This refers to certain conditions (for example, capitalism) that do have to be present during democratization. This mainly applies to Max Weber's seminal study *The Protestant Ethic and the Spirit of Capitalism*.[51] Rather, the point is that each culture has found its own particular resources to meet the minimum criteria for democracy. Thus, the Protestant religion and the *Spirit of Capitalism* as a 'unique founding condition' gets relativized in some analyses, pointing out that the attempts for democratization in mainly Protestant countries were unintended and did not happen due to genuine religious causes.[52]

Third, Stepan points out the problematic issue of removing religion from the political agenda. In attempting to find an 'overlapping consensus' Rawls and other liberals try to discover arguments for (so-called freestanding) conceptions of political justice also including religion. Nevertheless, Rawls pays almost no attention as to how actual polities 'have consensually and democratically arrived at agreements to "take religion off the political agenda"'. Politics is about conflict. Often times, particularly in Western European countries, this conflict was just about the place of religion in politics and in the polity. Agreement about the role of religion in politics is often achieved by employing 'arguments that are *not* conceptually freestanding but deeply embedded in their own religious community's comprehensive doctrine'.[53] It is thus the task of religious leaders to convince their followers – with public arguments – of the legitimate multivocality of their religion although this contradicts Rawls' argument of freestanding public reasoning: 'Liberal arguing' as Stepan agreeably points out 'has a place in democracy, but would empty meaning and history out of political philosophy if we did not leave room for democratic bargaining and the nonliberal public argument within religious communities that it sometimes requires'.[54] Catholicism with its potential for clear cut political proposals and the hierarchical given consensus for effective action – particularly concerning (social) justice – has thus an advantage (unlike, for example, Protestantism)[55] when it comes to the necessity of the nonliberal argument wit in religious communities to bargain about the multivocality of religion and its place within the polity.

Religious traditions and political outcomes

To be sure, the basic argument here and elsewhere in the literature, with only a few exceptions,[56] is that religious traditions alone do not determine political outcomes, including those related to both democratization and democracy. Rather, the argument is that democratization is made possible the more actors are engaged in favour of democracy, rather than undermining it. This for example includes the pursuit of 'facilitating factors' (such as, for example, pacification, economic development, rule of law, civil society, etc.) as well as 'constituting factors' (such as, for example, protection of minority rights, low level of corruption, free and fair elections, etc.).[57] Religion, regarding political processes such as democratization, for example in pursuing social justice, is one factor among many.[58] One should thus not overestimate the impact of religion upon democratization as does, for example, George Weigel regarding the importance of the Catholic Church and Pope John Paul II in bringing down communism.[59] Moreover, one should not forget that certain democratic core values, including a certain degree of popular power, participation, competition, consent, and (in the case of liberal democracy) the protection of individual and minority rights and the emphasis on individuality as such, can be perceived as opposed to some religious values such as the emphasis on the importance of community and solidarity.

At any given time there are dominant discourses in any religion. Sometimes they are in favour of uni-vocality and sometimes they are in favour of multi-vocality, debating and accepting, for example, core democratic values.[60] This is, for instance, also clear in the contribution of Christian, mainly Catholic-dominated, democratic parties in Europe helping to consolidate democracy – mainly in drawing on the doctrine of subsidiarity – in the post Second World War era in Western Europe and which tried, often without much success, to help consolidate democracies in South America.[61] The concept of subsidiarity – which holds that government should undertake only those initiatives which exceed the capacity of relevant non-government groups – was most prominently formulated in the encyclica *Rerum Novarum* and shaped Catholic political understanding, especially concerning domestic political issues since then.[62]

So far we have noted several basic assumptions regarding the relationship between Christianity, Roman Catholicism and democracy. First of all, facing a claimed religious resurgence, there is a need to focus the interest of political science on religion.[63] Secondly, we need to view the paradigm of secularism differently, not as a political programme *tout court*. Rather, we should regard it as a constant dialogue between politics and the place of religion in the public realm. Thirdly, the church developed itself, crudely speaking, as a significant promoter of issues in favour of democracy, like human rights, rather than undermining it. Therefore it is important to accept the usefulness of the multi-vocality approach of every religion, that religion is not determined for or against democracy. In the Catholic case this was mainly the sea change in political theology introduced doctrinally by Vatican II. However, there were and still are cases in which these changes do not apply. Therefore we examined other explanations beyond the theological change, such as the hegemonic approach and the attempt to maintain market share.

Furthermore, as we saw above, it is obvious that religion is only one factor among others in democratization. Theological debates about religious doctrines and democracy thus reflect only a small part of the 'real world'. Rather, the nature of the church–state relationship reflects the 'real world' better in pointing out, for example, that this relationship is of greater importance than the level of belief or practice based on theological assumptions. It is the level of differentiation within the church–state relationship which fosters the 'health' of religion due to its autonomy. The level of the church–state relationship is, for example, illustrated in other cases of the church's democratization involvement in South America. There the third wave illustrated that democracy needs an ally. Religion – in South America mainly Catholicism – was sometimes this ally.[64] There, the church provided necessary resources such as, for example, education, or it acted as an originator of issues that engaged civil society, especially where civic institutions were weak. It is thus indeed the case that religious institutions can in some contexts act as a significant factor in a growing acceptance of democracy:

> Historically in Iberia, Latin America, and elsewhere, the Catholic Church has been associated with the local establishment, the land-owning oligarchy, and authoritarian government. In the 1960s, this changed. The repositioning of the Catholic Church from a bulwark of the status quo, usually authoritarian, to a force for change, usually democratic, brought a powerful social institution in opposition to dictatorial regimes. It deprived those regimes of the legitimacy claimed from religion and provided protection, support, organization, resources, and leadership to pro-democratic opposition movements.[65]

We should, however, note that various current trends in global political culture, such as transnational structures, subsidiarity, and devolution, are not new phenomena for the church. In Catholic history, these concepts have been familiar for a long time.[66] The strong participation of the church in international organizations (i.e. United Nations) and even lobbying activities (i.e. European Union) reflect that familiarity: '[The] Holy See's participation in such international legal instruments is empirical testimony to the distinctive place it occupies in the formal, legal aspects of international public life, and to the permanence of moral issue in world politics.'[67] The church can thus justifiably be characterized as a transnational religious actor, 'defined as any non-governmental actor which claims to represent a specific religious tradition which has relations with an actor in another state or within an international organization'[68] with considerable soft power. Particularly the internal transnational and hierarchical nature of the Catholic Church proved to be a promoter for democracy in several cases while providing material and doctrinal support to local churches.[69] Whereas Eastern Orthodox churches, which tend to be far more national rather than transnational, face a far more compromised situation when the state often plays a major role in the internal affairs of churches.[70] At least since the 1980s and 1990s the political aspect of the transnational element in Roman Catholicism increased significantly, starting with the influence of the Polish pope, John Paul II, and his involvement with bringing down communism in Poland, in particular his support of the solidarity movement. On the global level during this time several other indicators can be identified which promoted transnationalism: the beginning of socialist states' collapse, the defeat of national security doctrines, the questioning of the non interference principle, and, particularly the rise of – also religiously motivated – civil society as a source of soft power.[71]

At least since Vatican II the church developed into a global transnational religious actor.[72] First of all, the general political as well as social shift from North to South indicates the slow but steady downgrading of the once exclusively Roman or European institution. Secondly, at least at the elite level, the church developed towards a homogenized and globalized Catholic culture.[73] There are three main expressions which characterize this homogenized and globalized Catholicism. First of all, the widening and growing importance of papal encyclicals addressing not only religious but also secular issues such as human rights. Secondly, the growing active role of the papacy in international relations which is, third, mainly due to its increased public visibility. It is thus indeed the case that the church and global Catholicism represent a transnational religious actor with considerable influence in international affairs, particularly in terms of soft power.[74] As Casanova puts it,

> the ongoing process of globalization offers a transnational religious regime like Catholicism, which never felt fully at home in a system of sovereign territorial nation-states, unique opportunities to expand, to adapt rapidly to the newly emerging global system, and perhaps even assume a proactive role in shaping some aspects of the new system.[75]

No end of history: Catholicism in international affairs

The church has always stressed the importance of addressing faith and reason at the same time. In the words of the current pope, Benedict XIV, from 'God's standpoint, faith liberates reason from its blind spots and therefore helps it to be ever more fully itself'.[76] The specific Catholic concept of comparative justice is destined to work against secular dogmatic temptations and in favour of democracy. As the American National Conference of Catholic Bishops put it in 1983:

> The category of comparative justice is destined to emphasize the presumption against war which stands at the beginning of just-war teaching. In a world of sovereign states recognizing neither a common moral authority nor a central political authority, comparative justice stresses that no state should act on the basis that it has 'absolute justice' on its side. Every party to a conflict should acknowledge the limits of its 'just cause' and the consequent requirement to use only limited means in pursuit of its objectives. Far from legitimizing a crusade mentality, comparative justice is designed to relativize absolute claims and to restrain the use of force even in a 'justified' conflict.[77]

In an age of a declared 'clash of civilizations' the Holy See and the pope, viewed from the perspective of an 'ethic reservoir', have the chance to use its institutional and moral capabilities. The late pope, John Paul II, who died in 2005, had a sense for geopolitical trends and left well established and extended diplomatic processes. Even though it seems that Benedict XVI's papacy focuses not so much on world politics but predominantly on ethical and moral issues, as his encyclicals indicate,[78] it is the current pope's aim to recognize and address the new political, cultural, and religious trends in world politics.[79] We live in a very complex world, where outcomes often seem strongly affected by religious and cultural circumstances and differences. The chance is thus that the focus of the current pope will be on ethical and social issues, addressing faith and reason equally, rather than addressing only 'hard' political issues.[80] In other words, the Holy See now seeks to use its soft power to achieve its objectives in current international affairs.[81] This especially applies to questions of justice. With emphasis upon social and comparative justice, the church and its leaders have played a remarkable role in transnational justice.[82] Pope John Paul II famously pointed out the importance of justice as the foundation of peace as well as the importance of forgiveness for justice in his formula 'No Peace without Justice. No Justice without Forgiveness.'[83] Social and political peace, based on justice – for example provided by religious processes such as truth commissions which seek for truth, forgiveness, and reconciliation – is without doubt a condition both for democracy as a kind of political order and for democratization more generally.

Due to its universalistic claim, Catholicism as a monotheistic religion does not represent a dualistic point of view. Rather Roman Catholicism can be characterized as a negative universalistic approach. This means 'negative' in the sense that the foundation of its universalism is difference – the acknowledgement of difference(s) between humans. Catholic universalism therefore is an iterative universalism: Every human and every people can repeat the experience of the fundamental claims. Based on this assumption it becomes clear what 'the political' means in the Catholic context: an aggregate state stressing the importance of the dignity of difference.[84] Catholicism, in this sense, also addresses the post-political age which ignores the agonistic foundation of politics and society. It is one, if not the major, task of democracy to transform the genuine antagonistic character (the struggle between enemies) of human relations into an agonistic (the struggle between adversaries) one. This requires a conflictual consensus and the acceptance of the pluralist and antagonist characteristics of 'the political'.[85] And this is what democracy and particularly democratization are about: an aggregate state of the political order which is in a constant process of discussion with an open, not predetermined, end state.

In reviewing the relationship between Catholicism and democratization, one has to think simultaneously about two fundamental issues. First of all, the hegemonic approach characterizing every kind of social order.[86] This is true both for Roman Catholicism and its vision of social order and for democracy as a form of political and social order. Even democracy unfolds itself hegemonically and makes universal claims which affect not only political but also social and other issues.[87] Even democracy calls for some absolute truths which can be questioned when it comes, for example, to the issue of seeking to impose Western style (liberal) democracy around the world, as the American government has recently discovered in, for example, Iraq. At the same time one should also recall the constant 'earthly' struggle of politics: an ongoing and un-finishable process of discussion about the shaping of the political, social and economic order. The political institution of democracy with its ongoing process of discussion and deliberation prevents this constant struggle from becoming ideological and seeking to realize a certain set of goals right away, even perhaps through violent means. At first glance, Catholicism seems to be just this: A political and social order with clear goals. But still, as the examination above indicates, Catholicism also offers an ongoing discussion concerning the 'earthly' political and social order in both current and historical terms.[88]

Political parties are an essential part of political systems, including democratic ones, as they are engaged in the above-mentioned continuing struggle of trying to shape the political, social, and economic order. In terms of ideal types, political parties should comprise three key elements and fulfil three major tasks: First, they are organizations which reflect their traditional political heritage and foundations (for example conservative, social democratic, liberal, etc.). Secondly, they are forums of discussion, drawing on their political heritage and discussing it within civil society. Thirdly, they seek to be political problem solvers. In a certain – not theological – way these characteristics also apply to religions and their assumed role in politics and the public sphere. In this regard the church sometimes points more to its traditional and cultural heritage, sometimes to its potential as a discussion forum and sometimes to its capacity as a problem solver. All of these three elements are not fully understandable without having a closer look at the church's theology and its claims for absolute truths. Over time, the church has shown a considerable potential to become a promoter for democracy in offering itself as a forum of discussion in civil society and as a problem solver in sometimes even violent political conflicts.[89]

As the present article illustrates, one must consider the multi-vocality of religion and the dominant discourses at any given point of time when considering the issue of democratization. This is particularly obvious when having a closer look at the different conceptions of the transcendental and its two main occurrences: identity-based and interest-based. A narrow and identity-based one fosters ideological and exclusive attempts whereas a wide one fosters a tolerant one based on interest-driven actions.[90] Still, interest-driven actions are always based – at least to a certain degree – on identity. Identity represents the ground on which interests are formed and preformed.[91] In this regard the church is not that much different from other actors and institutions which follow identity-based aims. A solely multi-vocal understanding of religion thus 'overlooks constraints for political action imposed by particular religious traditions'.[92] It is thus a key question whether the church will encourage a more identity-based or a more interest-based policy in certain democratization processes.

Just because the church and Christianity in general hold fast to absolute spiritual truths, its adherents may become more flexible towards subordinate 'earthly' values. As Butterfield, the English School of International Relations scholar put it, this is 'because he [the Christian] can hold fast to spiritual truth – not turning any mundane programme or temporal ideal into the absolute of absolutes – the Christian has it in his power to be more flexible in respect of all subordinate matters, and to ally himself with whatever may be the best for the world at a given moment'.[93] Christian teaching and Christianity itself with its compassion even for the enemy is indeed a 'risky' religion which is able to think outside the ordinate framework and is therefore a constant threat to the status quo as, for example, an established political order.[94] The institutionalized church sometimes aims to uphold the status quo due to its rational aims (for example, to maintain a market share or hegemony). Still, Christian and therefore also Catholic religious insights are certainly in favour of liberal and even democratic values. Especially the theological doctrines of the dignity of the person, the dignity of difference as such and the church's emphasis upon social justice are the church's main contributions to foster liberal and democratic values.

Finally, to engage critically in the debate of the role of religion in politics and thus also religion in the context of democratization it is necessary to overcome the quasi-liberal understanding of secularism which sees religious belief as private, equalizing 'personal' and 'subjective'.[95] In *Democracy in America* Alexis de Tocqueville famously stressed, in the example of the USA, the importance of Christianity to democracy. But this necessarily implies and indeed requires public debates about religious values and their place in politics as well. In this respect, Catholicism offers an ongoing magisterium pointing in its recent history particularly towards the importance of pluralism, difference, and social justice. These are fundamental virtues without which democracy cannot exist.

Acknowledgements

The author would like to thank Lucian N. Leuestan, Jeffrey Haynes, and the panel participants of the *Religion and Democratizations. Friend or Enemy?* Conference at London Metropolitan University, 17–18 April 2009 for comments and suggestions on earlier versions of this article.

Notes

1. Huntington, *The Third Wave*.
2. See, for example, Weigel and Royal, *Building the Free Society*.
3. Hertzke, 'Roman Catholicism and the Faith-Based Movement for Global Human Rights'.
4. Fukuyama, *The End of History and the Last Man*.
5. Diamond, 'The State of Democratization at the Beginning of the 21st Century'; Diamond et al., *Consolidating the Third Wave Democracies*.
6. Fukuyama, 'History and September 11', 30.
7. For a critical discussion of this aspect see particularly Dacey, *The Secular Conscience*.
8. See especially Thomas, *The Global Resurgence of Religion and the Transformation of International Relations*.

9. See, for example, Norris and Ingelhart, *Sacred and Secular*; Thomas, *The Global Resurgence of Religion*; Fox, *A World Survey of Religion and the State*.
10. Even more, for some, religion is 'a missing dimension of statecraft', involving 'faith-based diplomacy'. Johnston, and Sampson, *Religion. The Missing Dimension of Statecraft*; Johnston, ed., *Faith-Based Diplomacy*.
11. Huntington, *The Third Wave*, 73–85.
12. Casanova, *Public Religions in the Modern World*; Bader, 'Religious Pluralism: Secularism or Priority for Democracy?'; Bader, *Secularism or Democracy?*; Walzer, *Über Toleranz*.
13. Weber, *The Protestant Ethic*.
14. For a more comprehensive introduction to the issue of Christianity and democracy see Anderson, *Christianity and Democratization*.
15. The link between religion and democracy refers, first of all, to the issue of secularism and secularization. On the other hand the link between religion and democratization refers to the issue of whether religious insights and values can promote or demote democratization as a process and, even more, stabilize or destabilize an established democracy.
16. Philpott, 'The Catholic Wave', 33.
17. Clark, 'Democracy in International Society'; Mayall 'Democracy and International Society'.
18. See, for example, Grasso and Hunt, *Catholicism and Religious Freedom*.
19. Hastings, *Modern Catholicism*.
20. Huntington, *The Third Wave*, 85.
21. Philpott, 'Explaining the Political Ambivalence of Religion', 510.
22. John Paul and Pham, *Centesimus Annus*, para. 57.
23. Already before the Second Vatican Council, encyclicals addressed political questions. *Divini Redemptoris*, for example, addressed the challenges of communism long before George Kennan did, and *Mit brennender Sorge* addressed the evil of Nazism in an era of appeasement.
24. Paulhus, 'Uses and Misuses of the Term "Social Justice"'.
25. Hehir, 'Papal Foreign Policy'.
26. Rahner and Vorgrimler, *Kleines Konzilskompendium*, 123–200, 655–75, 423–552.
27. Hehir, 'Papal Foreign Policy'.
28. Zizola, *The Utopia of Pope John XXIII*. The encyclical *Pacem in Terris*, published only a few months after, reflected the experiences of the Cuban Missile Crisis.
29. Vander Stichele et al., *Disciples and Discipline*.
30. Haas, *War of Necessity, War of Choice*.
31. Ryall, 'How many Divisions?', 28–31; Johnstone, 'Pope John Paul II and the War in Iraq'.
32. *Gaudium et Spes*, para. 78.
33. Philpott, 'The Catholic Wave', 42–3.
34. Haynes, *Religion in Third World Politics*; Haynes, 'Religion and Democratization in Africa'.
35. Anderson, 'Religion, Politics and International Relations', 394.
36. Gill, *Rendering Unto Caesar*, 7, 48.
37. Ibid.
38. For the 'power in movement' see particularly Tarrow, *Power in Movement*.
39. Philpott, 'Has the Study of Global Politics found Religion?', 194; Philpott, 'Explaining the Political Ambivalence of Religion'.
40. Jamal, 'Democratizing State–Religion Relations: A Comparative Study of Turkey, Egypt and Israel'; Barras, 'A Rights-Based Discourse to Contest the Boundaries of State Secularism? The Case of the Headscarf Bans in France and Turkey'.

41. Hurd, *The Politics of Secularism in International Relations*, 23. 'It [secularism] is a discursive tradition defined and infused by power. The social construction of secularism has taken two distinct paths in international relations: a laicist trajectory, in which religion is seen as an adversary and an impediment to modern politics, and a Judeo-Christian secularist trajectory, in which religion is seen as a source of unity and identity that generates conflict in modern international politics' (*ibid.*). Bruce argues that the secularization paradigm is primarily an explanation for the past of the 'First World'. Bruce, *God is Dead*.
42. Hallward, 'Situating the "Secular"', 1.
43. Lausten and Waever, 'In Defense of Religion', 149.
44. Peter Berger called secularization 'falsified'. Berger, 'Secularization Falsified'.
45. Still, as Peter Berger notes, '[r]eligious dynamism is not confined to Islam and Pentecostalism. The Catholic Church, in trouble in Europe, has been doing well in the Global South. There is a revival of the Orthodox Church in Russia. Orthodox Judaism has been rapidly growing in America and in Israel. Both Hinduism and Buddhism have experienced revivals, and the latter has had some successes in proselytizing in America and Europe'. Berger, 'Secularization Falsified', 24.
46. 'Modernity is not characterized by the absence of God but by the presence of many gods.' Berger, 'Secularization Falsified', 23–4.
47. Philpott, 'The Catholic Wave', 41.
48. Grim and Finke, 'Religious Persecution in Cross-National Context'; Stark and Finke, *Acts of Faith*.
49. Stepan, 'Religion, Democracy, and the "Twin Tolerations"', 37, 42.
50. Huntington, *The Clash of Civilizations*.
51. Weber, *The Protestant Ethic*.
52. Bruce, 'Did Protestantism Create Democracy?'.
53. Stepan, 'Religion, Democracy, and the "Twin Tolerations"', 45. See also, for example, Rawls, *A Theory of Justice*; Rawls, *Political Liberalism*.
54. Stepan, 'Religion, Democracy, and the "Twin Tolerations"', 45–6.
55. Freston, 'Protestantism', 43.
56. The most obvious exception is probably the work of George Weigel. See below, note 59.
57. Etzioni, *Security First*, 43.
58. 'Religious tradition cannot determine outcomes, but when the factors working for or against democratization are finely balanced, then whose God is prevalent may just make a difference.' Anderson, 'Does God Matter, and If So Whose God?', 214.
59. Weigel, *The Final Revolution*. Weigel rejects the common interpretations regarding the causes of the end of communism in Eastern Europe such as, for example, the role of Ronald Reagan or Mikhail Gorbachev because, in his view, they miss the main point: that communism represented not simply a political system but rather a claim for human omnipotence in establishing heaven on earth. It is thus that the Catholic Church and especially Pope John Paul II inspired, prepared and mobilized the Polish people to resist communism. The 'martyr cardinals', for example, became symbols of resistance to the communist oppression.
60. Anderson, 'Does God Matter, and If So Whose God?', 205–6.
61. Kalyvas, *The Rise of Christian Democracy in Europe*; Papini, *The Christian Democrat International*.
62. Leo XIII, *Rerum Novarum*; John Paul and Pham, *Centesimus Annus*, para. 48.
63. See also Philpott, 'Has the Study of Global Politics Found Religion?'.
64. For a basic overview over the peacebuilding activities of the (predominantly Catholic) Churches in South America see, for example, Kurtenbach, 'Die Rolle der Kirchen bei der Konfliktregulierung in Zentralamerika'.

65. Xenias, 'Can Global Peace Last Even if Achieved? Huntington and the Democratic Peace', 368.
66. Ryall, 'The Catholic Church as a Transnational Actor', 46.
67. Weigel, 'Roman Catholicism in the Age of John Paul II', 21.
68. Shani, 'Transnational Religious Actors and International Relations', 308.
69. Stepan, 'Religion, Democracy, and the "Twin Tolerations"', 53.
70. Others, for example Evangelicals, seem to be worried that the structural transformation weakens the personal one mainly because the Evangelical denomination developed itself steadily from a standpoint on certain special rights toward a more general approach. Wallis, *The Great Awakening*; Haynes, 'Religion and a Human Rights Culture in America'; Hertzke, *Freeing Gods Children*.
71. Haynes, *An Introduction to International Relations and Religion*, 142–3.
72. Shani, 'Transnational Religious Actors and International Relations', 312–15.
73. Haynes, 'Transnational Religious Actors and International Politics', 150.
74. Haynes, *An Introduction to International Relations and Religion*, 142–3.
75. Casanova, 'Globalizing Catholicism and the Return to a "Universal" Church', 121–2.
76. Benedict, *God is Love*, para. 28a.
77. National Conference of Catholic Bishops, *The Challenge of Peace*, no. 93.
78. Pope Benedict XVI, *God is Love*; *Love in Truth*; *Saved in Hope*.
79. See, for example, Benedict's address at the United Nations in 2008. Pope Benedict XVI, *Meeting with the Members of the General Assembly of the United Nations Organization*.
80. Weigel, *Faith, Reason, and the War against Jihadism*, 64.
81. See, for example, Nye, *Soft Power*.
82. See, for example, Philpott, 'When Faith meets Reason'; Philpott, *The Politics of Past Evil*.
83. Pope John Paul II, *No Peace without Justice*.
84. Manemann, 'Monotheismus und Demokratie', 64–9.
85. Mouffe, *On the Political*; Mouffe, 'Democracy in a Multipolar World'.
86. Laclau and Mouffe, *Hegemony and the Socialist Strategy*.
87. It is thus only logical recalling Winston Churchill's famous saying that 'Democracy is the worst form of government, except for all those other forms that have been tried from time to time.' Sir Winston Churchill, Speech, House of Commons (November 11, 1947).
88. See, for example, Ratzinger, *Theologische Prinzipienlehre*, 136–9, 159–99.
89. One practiced and successful method in the church's peace building efforts is, for example, third party mediation in conflicts in which there is no particular religious dimension present. These faith-based initiatives have been successful primarily because they are altruistic or carried out as a matter of charity, as the lay Catholic community of St. Egidio in Mozambique demonstrated. Another example is the Pope's visit in Cuba 1998, which had both religious and political ramifications. Douglas Johnston and Brian Cox, 'Faith-Based Diplomacy and Preventive Engagement', 22.
90. Schäfer, 'The Janus Face of Religion'.
91. Lebow, *A Cultural Theory of International Relations*, 562–70.
92. Minkenberg, 'Democracy and Religion', 904.
93. Butterfield, *Christianity, Diplomacy and War*, 3.
94. Ibid., 1–13.
95. Dacey, *The Secular Conscience*. See also the encyclica of John Paul II, *Fides et Ratio*, challenging post-modern thought asserting that faith and reason are not incompatible. Pope John Paul II, *Encyclical Letter, Fides et Ratio*; Foster and Koterski, *The Two Wings of Catholic Thought*.

Notes on contributor

Dr Jodok Troy studied political science, history and Catholic theology at the University of Innsbruck in Austria. Since 2005 he has been a scientific collaborator at the department of political science of the University of Innsbruck, and in 2007 he was a research fellow at the Center for Peace and Security Studies at Georgetown University in Washington, DC. The main research areas are religion in international relations, faith-based diplomacy, and international relations theories.

Bibliography

Anderson, John. 'Does God Matter, and If So Whose God? Religion and Democratization'. *Democratization* 11, no. 4 (2004), 192–217.
Anderson, John. 'Religion, Politics and International Relations. The Catholic Contribution to Democratization's "Third Wave": Altruism, Hegemony or Self-Interest?'. *Cambridge Review of International Affairs* 20, no. 3 (2007): 383–99.
Anderson, John. *Christianity and Democratization. From Pious Subjcects to Critical Participants*. Manchester: Manchester University Press, 2009.
Bader, Veit. 'Religious Pluralism: Secularism or Priority for Democracy?'. *Political Theory* 27, no. 5 (1999): 597–633.
Bader, Veit. *Secularism or Democracy? Associational Governance of Religious Diversity*. Amsterdam: University of Amsterdam Press, 2007.
Barras, Amélie. 'A Rights-Based Discourse to Contest the Boundaries of State Secularism? The Case of the Headscarf Bans in France and Turkey'. Democratization 16, no. 6 (2009): 1235–58.
Berger, Peter L. 'The Desecularization of the World: A Global Overview'. In *The Desecularization of the World. Resurgent Religion and World Politics*, ed. Peter L. Berger, 1–18. Washington, DC: Ethics and Public Policy Center, 1999.
Berger, Peter L. 'Secularization Falsified'. *First Things* (2008): 23–7.
Bruce, Steve. *God is Dead. Secularization in the West*. Malden, MA: Blackwell Pub., 2002.
Bruce, Steve. 'Did Protestantism Create Democracy?'. *Democratization* 11, no. 4 (2004) 3–20.
Butterfield, Herbert. *Christianity, Diplomacy and War*. New York and Nashville: Abingdon-Cokesbury Press, 1954.
Casanova, José. *Public Religions in the Modern World*. Chicago: University of Chicago Press, 1994.
Casanova, José. 'Globalizing Catholizism and the Return to a "Universal" Church'. In *Transnational Religion and Fading States*, ed. Susann Hoeber Rudolph, 121–43. Boulder, CO: Westview Press, 1997.
Clark, Ian. 'Democracy in International Society: Promotion or Exclusion?'. *Millennium – Journal of International Studies* 37, no. 3 (2009): 563–81.
Dacey, Austin. *The Secular Conscience: Why Belief Belongs in Public Life*. Amherst, NY: Prometheus Books, 2008.
Diamond, Larry. 'The State of Democratization at the Beginning of the 21st Century'. *The Whitehead Journal of Diplomacy and International Relations* (Winter/Spring 2005): 13–18.
Diamond, Larry, et al., eds. *Consolidating the Third Wave Democracies*. London: John Hopkings University Press, 1997.
Etzioni, Amitai. *Security First: For a Muscular, Moral Foreign Policy*. New Haven, CT: Yale University Press, 2007.
Foster, David Ruel, and Joseph W. Koterski, eds. *The Two Wings of Catholic Thought: Essays on Fides et Ratio*. Washington, DC: Catholic University of America Press, 2003.

Fox, Jonathan. *A World Survey of Religion and the State*. Cambridge: Cambridge University Press, 2008.
Freston, Paul. 'Protestantism'. In *Routledge Handbook of Religion and Politics*, ed. Jeffrey Haynes, 26–47. London: Routledge, 2009.
Fukuyama, Francis. 'History and September 11'. In *Worlds in Collision. Terror and the Future of Global Order*, ed. Ken Booth and Timothy Dunne, 27–36. Basingstoke: Palgrave Macmillan, 2004.
Fukuyama, Francis. *The End of History and the Last Man* [New ed.]. New York and London: Free Press, 2006.
Gill, Anthony. *Rendering Unto Caesar: The Catholic Church and the State in Latin America*. Chicago, IL: University of Chicago Press, 1998.
Grasso, Kenneth L., and Robert P. Hunt, eds. *Catholicism and Religious Freedom: Contemporary Reflections on Vatican II's Declaration on Religious Liberty*. Lanham, MD: Sheed & Ward, 2007.
Grim, Brian J., and Rodger Finke. 'Religious Persecution in Cross-National Context: Clashing Civilizations or Regulated Religious Economies'. *American Sociological Review* 72, no. 4 (2007): 633–58.
Hallward, Maia Carter. 'Situating the "Secular": Negotiating the Boundary between Religion and Politics'. *International Political Sociology* 2, no. 1 (2008): 1–16.
Haass, Richard N. *War of Necessity, War of Choice: A Memory of Two Iraq Wars*. New York: Simon & Schuster, 2009.
Hastings, Adrian. *Modern Catholicism: Vatican II and After*. London: Society for Promoting Christian Knowledge, 1991.
Haynes, Jeffrey. *Religion in Third World Politics*. Boulder, CO: Rienner, 1994.
Haynes, Jeffrey. 'Transnational Religious Actors and International Politics'. *Third World Quarterly* 22, no. 1 (2001): 143–58.
Haynes, Jeffrey. 'Religion and Democratization in Africa'. *Democratization* 11, no. 4 (2004) 66–89.
Haynes, Jeffrey. *An Introduction to International Relations and Religion*. Harlow: Pearson, 2007.
Haynes, Jeffrey. 'Religion and a Human Rights Culture in America'. *The Review of Faith & International Affairs* 6, no. 2 (2008) 73–82.
Hehir, Bryan. 'Papal Foreign Policy'. *Foreign Policy* 78, no. Spring (1990): 26–48.
Hertzke, Allen. 'Roman Catholicism and the Faith-Based Movement for Global Human Rights'. *The Review of Faith and International Affairs* 3, no. 3 (2005/2006) 19–24.
Hertzke, Allen. *Freeing Gods Children. The Unlikely Alliance for Global Human Rights*. Lanham, MD: Rowman & Littlefield, 2006.
Huntington, Samuel P. *The Third Wave: Democratization in the Late Twentieth Century*. London: University of Oklahoma Press, 1993.
Huntington, Samuel P. *The Clash of Civilizations and the Remaking of World Order*. New York: Simon & Schuster, 2003.
Hurd, Elizabeth Shakman. *The Politics of Secularism in International Relations*. Princeton, NJ: Princeton University Press, 2008.
Jamal, Amal. 'Democratizing State–Religion Relations: A Comparative Study of Turkey, Egypt and Israel'. *Democratization* 16, no. 6 (2009): 1142–69.
Johnston, Douglas, ed. *Faith-Based Diplomacy. Trumping Realpolitik*. Oxford: Oxford University Press, 2003.
Johnston, Douglas, and Brian Cox. 'Faith-Based Diplomacy and Preventive Engagement'. In *Faith-Based Diplomacy: Trumping Realpolitik*, ed. Douglas Johnston, 11–29. Oxford: Oxford University Press, 2003.
Johnston, Douglas M., and Cynthia Sampson, eds. *Religion. The Missing Dimension of Statecraft*. New York: Oxford University Press, 1995.

Johnstone, Brian V. 'Pope John Paul II and the War in Iraq'. *Studia Moralia* 41, no. 2 (2003): 309–30.

Kalyvas, Stathis N. *The Rise of Christian Democracy in Europe*. Ithaca, NY: Cornell Univ. Press, 1996.

Kurtenbach, Sabine. 'Die Rolle der Kirchen bei der Konfliktregulierung in Zentralamerika – Modell für andere Regionen?'. In *Friedensstiftende Religionen?: Religion und die Deeskalation politischer Konflikte*, ed. Manfred Brocker and Mathias Hildebrandt, 269–83. Wiesbaden: VS Verlag für Sozialwissenschaften | GWV Fachverlage GmbH, 2008.

Kurth, James. 'The Vatican's Foreign Policy'. *The National Interest* 32 (Summer 1993): 30–52.

Laclau, Ernesto, and Chantal Mouffe. *Hegemony and the Socialist Strategy: Towards a Radical Politics*. London: Verso, 2001.

Lausten, Carsten Bagge, and Ole Waever. 'In Defense of Religion. Sacred Referent Objects for Securitization'. In *Religion in International Relations. The Return from Exile*, ed. Fabio Pavlos and Petito Hatzopoulos, 147–80. New York: Palgrave Macmillan, 2003.

Lebow, Richard Ned. *A Cultural Theory of International Relations*. Cambridge and New York: Cambridge University Press, 2008.

Manemann, Jürgen. 'Monotheismus und Demokratie. Eine Standortbestimmung'. In *Westliche Moderne, Christentum und Islam. Gewalt als Anfrage an monotheistische Religionen*, ed. Wolfgang Palaver, Roman Siebenrock, and Dietmar Regensburger, 59–76. Innsbruck: Innsbruck University Press, 2008.

Mayall, James. 'Democracy and International Society'. *International Affairs* 76, no. 1 (2000): 61–75.

Minkenberg, Michael. 'Democracy and Religion: Theoretical and Empirical Observations on the Relationship between Christianity, Islam and Liberal Democracy'. *Journal of Ethnic and Migration Studies* 33, no. 6 (2007): 887–909.

Mouffe, Chantal. *On the Political*. London: Routledge, 2006.

Mouffe, Chantal. 'Democracy in a Multipolar World'. *Millennium – Journal of International Studies* 37, 3 (2009): 549–61.

National Conference of Catholic Bishops. *The Challenge of Peace: God's Promise and Our Response. A Pastoral Letter on War and Peace by the National Conference of Catholic Bishops*. Washington DC: National Conference of Catholic Bishops, 1983.

Norris, Pippa, and Ronald Ingelhart. *Sacred and Secular: Religion and Politics Worldwide*. Cambridge: Cambridge University Press, 2004.

Nye, Joseph S. *Soft Power: The Means to Success in World Politics*. New York: Public Affairs, 2004.

Papini, Roberto. *The Christian Democrat International*. Lanham, MD: Rowman & Littlefield Publishers, 1997.

Paulhus, Normand J. 'Uses and Misuses of the Term "Social Justice" in the Roman Catholic Tradition'. *Journal of Religious Ethics* 15, no. 2 (1987) 261–83.

Philpott, Daniel. 'The Catholic Wave'. *Journal of Democracy* 15, no. 2 (2004): 32–46.

Philpott, Daniel, ed. *The Politics of Past Evil: Religion, Reconciliation, and the Dilemmas of Transitional Justice*, Notre Dame, IN: University of Notre Dame Press, 2006.

Philpott, Daniel. 'Explaining the Political Ambivalence of Religion'. *American Political Science Review* 101, no. 3 (2007) 505–25.

Philpott, Daniel. 'Has the Study of Global Politics Found Religion?'. *Annual Review of Political Science* 12 (2009): 183–202.

Philpott, Daniel. 'When Faith Meets History: The Influence of Religion on Transitional Justice'. In *The Religious in Response to Mass Atrocity: Interdisciplinary Perspectives*, ed. Thomas Brudholm and Thomas Cushman, 174–212. Cambridge: Cambridge University Press, 2009.

Pope, Leo XIII. *Rerum Novarum: Encyclical of Pope Leo XIII on Capital and Labour*, Vatican, 1892. http://www.vatican.va/holy_father/leo_xiii/encyclicals/documents/ hf_l-xiii_enc_15051891_rerum-novarum_en.html (accessed March 1, 2009).
Pope Pius XI. *Divini Redemptoris*. http://www.vatican.va/holy_father/pius_xi/encyc licals/documents/hf_p-xi_enc_19031937_divini-redemptoris_en.html.
Pope, Pius XI. *Mit brennender Sorge*. http://www.vatican.va/holy_father/pius_xi/ encyclica ls/documents/hf_p-xi_enc_14031937_mit-brennender-sorge_en.html.
Pope, Benedict XVI. *Love in Truth: Caritas in veritate*. San Francisco, CA: Ignatius Press, 2008.
Pope, Benedict XVI. *Saved in Hope: Encyclical Letter of the Supreme Pontiff Benedict XVI*. San Francisco and Vatican City: Ignatius Press? Libreria Editrice Vaticana, 2008, 2007.
Pope, Benedict XVI. *God is Love: Deus caritas est, Encyclical letter of the Supreme Pontiff Benedict XVI to the Bishops, Priests, and Deacons, Men and Women Religious, and all the Lay Faithful, on Christian Love*. San Francisco: Ignatius Press; Libreria Editrice Vaticana, 2006.
Pope, Benedict XVI. *Meeting with the Members of the General Assembly of the United Nations Organization: Address of His Holiness Benedict XVI*, April 18, 2008. http:// www.vatican.va/holy_father/benedict_xvi/speeches/2008/april/documents/hf_ben-xvi_spe_20080418_un-visit_en.html (accessed March 1, 2009).
Pope, John Paul, II, and Pham John-Peter. *Centesimus Annus: Assessment and Perspectives for the Future Catholic Social Doctrine Proceedings of the International Congress on the Fifth Anniversary of the Promulgation of the Encyclical Letter Centesimus Annus, Rome, April 29–30, 1997*. Città del Vaticano: Libreria Editrice Vaticana, 1998.
Pope, John Paul, II. *No Peace without Justice: No Justice without Forgiveness*. Message for the Celebration of the World Day of Peace Vatican, January 1, 2002. http:// www.vatican.va/holy_father/john_paul_ii/messages/peace/documents/hf_jp-ii_mes_ 20011211_xxxv-world-day-for-peace_en.html (accessed March 1, 2009).
Pope, John Paul, II. *Encyclical Letter, Fides et Ratio, of the Supreme Pontiff John Paul II: To the Bishops of the Catholic Church on the Relationship between Faith and Reason*. Washington, DC: United States Catholic Conference, 1998.
Rahner, Karl, and Herbert Vorgrimler, eds. *Kleines Konzilskompendium: Sämtliche Texte des Zweiten Vatikanums; allgemeine Einleitung – 16 spezielle Einführungen – ausführliches Sachregister; mit einem Nachtrag vom Oktober 1968: Die nachkonziliare Arbeit der römischen Kirchenleitung*. 28. Aufl. Freiburg im Breisgau: Concilium Vaticanum: Herder, 2000.
Ratzinger, Joseph. *Theologische Prinzipienlehre: Bausteine zur Fundamentaltheologie*. 2., unveränd. Aufl. Donauwörth: Wewel, 2005.
Rawls, John. *A Theory of Justice*. Cambridge, MA: Belknap Press, 2005a.
Rawls, John. *Political Liberalism*, Exp. ed. New York: Columbia University Press, 2005b.
Ryall, David. 'The Catholic Church as a Transnational Actor'. In *Non-State Actors in World Politics*, ed. Daphne Wallace and William Josselin, 41–58. New York: Palgrave, 2001.
Ryall, David. 'How Many Divisions?: The Modern Development of Catholic International Relations'. *International Relations* 14, no. 2 (1998) 21–34.
Schäfer, Heinrich. 'The Janus Face of Religion: On the Religious Factor in "New Wars"'. *Numen: International Review for the History of Religions* 51, no. 4 (2004): 407–31.
Shani, Giorgio. 'Transnational Religious Actors and International Relations'. In *Routledge Handbook of Religion and Politics*, ed. Jeffrey Haynes, 308–322. London: Routledge, 2009.
Stark, Rodney, and Roger Finke. *Acts of Faith. Explaining the Human Side of Religion*. Berkeley, CA: University of California Press, 2002.

Stepan, Alfred. 'Religion, Democracy, and the "Twin Tolerations"'. *Journal of Democracy* 11, no. 4 (2000) 37–57.
Tarrow, Sidney. *Power in Movement: Social Movements and Contentious Politics.* New York: Cambridge University Press, 1994.
Thomas, Scott M. *The Global Resurgence of Religion and the Transformation of International Relations. The Struggle for the Soul of the Twenty-first Century.* New York: Palgrave Macmillan, 2005.
Vander, Stichele, Carolineet, *et al. Disciples and Discipline. European Debate on Human Rights in the Roman Catholic Church.* Leuven: Peeters, 1993.
Wallis, Jim. *The Great Awakening. Reviving Faith & Politics in a Post-Religious Right America.* New York: HarperOne, 2008.
Walzer, Michael. *Über Toleranz. Von der Zivilisierung der Differenz.* Hamburg: Rotbuch Verlag, 1998.
Weber, Max. *The Protestant Ethic and the 'Spirit' of Capitalism and Other Writings.* New York: Penguin Books, 2002.
Weigel, George. *The Final Revolution. The Resistance Church and the Collapse of Communism.* New York: Oxford University Press, 1992.
Weigel, George. 'Roman Catholicism in the Age of John Paul II'. In *The Desecularization of the World. Resurgent Religion and World Politics*, ed. Peter L. Berger, 19–35. Washington, DC: Ethics and Public Policy Center, 1999.
Weigel, George. *Faith, Reason, and the War against Jihadism. A Call to Action.* New York: Doubleday, 2007.
Weigel, George, and Robert Royal, eds. *Building the Free Society: Democracy, Capitalism, and Catholic Social Teaching.* Grand Rapids, MI and Washington, DC: Eerdmans? Ethics and Public Policy Center, 1993.
Xenias, Anastasia. 'Can Global Peace Last Even if Achieved? Huntington and the Democratic Peace'. *International Studies Review* 7 (2005): 357–86.
Zizola, Giancarola. *The Utopia of Pope John XXIII.* New York: Orbis, 1978.

Democratization in Israel, politicized religion and the failure of the Oslo peace process

Claudia Baumgart-Ochse

Peace Research Institute, Frankfurt, Germany

While the positive relationship between democracies and peace is by now a commonplace of international relations (IR) literature, the possible dangers of democratization processes for international peace and security have only recently become a focus of IR research. This article argues that some of the mechanisms prevalent in democratizing states' ambivalent conflict behaviour help to explain why the state of Israel initially entered into the peace process with the Palestinians, but soon reverted to former hostile policies. In the initial stages of the peace process in the early 1990s, the Labour-led government based its efforts towards peace on the typical norms of democratic peace and thus explicitly stated the need to improve Israel's defective democratic regime. This involved amending the electoral system by ending the de facto control of the Palestinians in the territories, who did not participate in Israeli democratic politics. However, the prospect of 'land for peace' threatened the politicized religious Jewish settler-elite in the territories who feared not only the destruction of the basic tenets of their religious identity, but also the loss of both power and resources in Israeli politics. As a consequence, this threatened elite engaged in fierce religious-nationalist mobilization in order to derail the peace negotiations and at the same time subvert the process of improving Israel's democratic regime.

Introduction

When Yitzhak Rabin and Yasser Arafat shook hands on the lawn of the White House in September 1993, the world had great expectations of the Oslo Accords that were designed to initiate and structure a peace process between Israel and the Palestinians in order to resolve their longstanding conflict. However, by the mid-1990s, the Oslo process seemed to be trapped in a renewed cycle of violence, mutual mistrust and power politics. With the outbreak of the Al Aqsa Intifada a mere seven years after the signing of the Oslo Accords, the peace process finally collapsed and violence returned with unprecedented severity.

In retrospective, the peace process stands out as a short period of calm and rapprochement between Israel and the Palestinians in an otherwise hostile and violent history of conflict. This article maintains that insights from research on the democratic peace, democratization, and the role of religious actors in violent conflicts can help to advance a comprehensive understanding of Israel's decisive role in the rise and fall of the peace process. In addition to important external factors that helped to pave the way to direct negotiations between Israel and the Palestinians, the peace process was closely intertwined with a process of improving democratic governance in Israel. The political leadership of the early 1990s embarked on a journey to transform the Israeli regime from a defective illiberal and exclusive democracy to a full-fledged liberal democracy. This policy was explained with the need to adapt to the requirements of peace with the Palestinians and the Arab states. In its public statements, the Labour-Meretz government (1992–1996) explicitly linked democracy and peace and justified its commitment to the peace process by drawing on the typical normative liberal and democratic arguments as proposed by democratic peace theory.[1]

But the prospect of giving back the territory occupied in 1967 threatened the religious-Zionist settler elites who had become the main proponents and close allies of the state in the settlement project. The settler movement not only positioned itself as the most fervent opponent of the peace process but also championed the nationalist mobilization against the government's policy to transform Israel into a liberal, pluralistic democracy, because it feared the loss of resources and privileges. The low degree of institutional differentiation between religion and state in Israel as well as the settler's political theology and mobilization skills turned the religious Zionist settlers into effective spoilers of both democratization and peace. But their success can only be explained in full by looking at the ideological opportunity structure in which their political theology resonated. When Palestinian suicide terrorism shook the peace process in the mid-1990s, Israel's secular political elite stuck to the ambivalent rhetoric of the democratic peace, yet later used its arguments and preferences in order to justify the policy of halting the peace process as well as the use of military force against the Palestinians, made solely responsible for the recurrence of violence. This changed use of democratic peace arguments served as a gateway for the religious settler movement's framing of the peace process as existentially threatening not only their own community but the Jewish state as a whole. The religious Zionists' image of the Palestinian enemy found its correspondence in the secular political elite's depiction of the Palestinians as diametrically opposed to peace and reconciliation. This concurrence of enemy images severely impaired the chances for a peaceful resolution of the Israeli–Palestinian conflict in the 1990s.

The promise of the democratic peace

Democratic peace research essentially deals with democracies' ability to handle their international conflicts in a non-violent, peaceful manner. The most robust empirical finding of democratic peace research is the so-called 'separate peace': the observation that democracies do not fight each other whereas their conflict behaviour does not differ from that of other regime types when the opponent is a non-democracy.[2] Yet some studies also find evidence for a general tendency of democracies to pursue non-violent conflict resolution, though this finding is statistically weaker.[3] Drawing on Kant's treatise on the 'Perpetual Peace', democratic peace researchers see the main cause for this pacifying tendency in the liberal normative and utilitarian preferences of citizens in democratic states. First, citizens have internalized non-violent or lawful ways of conflict resolution, respect for human rights and the rule of law. And, secondly, they rationally calculate the risks of war and want to avoid the casualties as well as the material costs. These liberal norms and preferences are deeply rooted in democratic culture. Transmitted through democratic institutions, they ideally shape the foreign policy of democracies which consequently display a strong tendency towards peaceful conflict resolution. In the monadic version of democratic peace theory, citizens' preferences suffice to produce the peaceful behaviour expected; in the dyadic version, the preferences' impact on decisions about the use of force depends on the regime type of the adversary. The merits of democratic government and liberal norms for inner and outer peace seem to be so irresistibly persuading that the promotion of democracy has become a major pillar of Western democracies' foreign policy.

Democratic peace, democratic wars

The basic finding that liberal democracies do not fight each other is still widely thought to be beyond criticism. But the democratic peace has its 'dark sides', as recent research has convincingly shown. First, the empirical evidence of the last decades casts serious doubts on the claim that liberal preferences always promote peace except when the adversary is a non-democracy. The democratic interventionism since the 1990s suggests a more complex pattern. Since the end of the Cold War, Western liberalism lacks a powerful ideological opponent in international politics and feels more than ever entitled to make the world safe for democracy – if necessary, by way of war. The threat of international terrorism, heightened by the attacks of 9/11, appears to give this task an even greater urgency.[4] But at the same time, there is a noticeable variance in democracies' behaviour towards non-democratic states: Some are ready to intervene, be part of a coalition and start wars against non-democratic states whenever they think it is necessary for regime change, for humanitarian or security reasons; others refrain from such action. This variance suggests that it is not necessarily the regime type of the adversary which determines a democracy's willingness to use military force; rather, there is ample reason to give renewed attention to the monadic level of democratic peace. The state of Israel, a democratic country which acceded to a peace process with the Palestinians in the early 1990s but returned to the use of military force when that process was disrupted by violent societal spoilers, therefore makes a highly interesting case study.

In the democratic peace literature, two explanations for warring democracies can be found. First, a new generation of critical democratic peace researchers has begun to look into the ambivalences and contradictions of liberalism and democratic rule itself which might come in the way of peace.[5] The same liberal normative and utilitarian reasons that cause some democracies to abstain from the use of military force might in other cases be referred to as legitimization for going to war.[6] For example, the respect for human life might result in the decision not to risk the lives of one's own soldiers as well as to avoid casualties on the side of the opponent. Yet the same respect for human life can be cited in order to justify a military intervention which aims to remove a cruel authoritarian ruler or to halt a genocide. In order to wrap democracies' wars in genuinely liberal justifications, it is necessary to stigmatize the opponent as being diametrically opposed to all that is constitutive for the European Enlightenment project: human rights, peace, constitutionalism, and justice. Kant wrote about the possibility of such a type of opponent, calling it an 'unjust enemy'. In a securitization move,[7] the liberal-democratic elites define the nation's security, its way of life or the liberal international order as being existentially threatened by rogue states, warlords or terrorists, the 'unjust enemies' of our days.[8] This speech act of securitization which is based on the perception of an existential threat is, of course, susceptible to misjudgement and exaggeration and therefore need not necessarily reflect the actual degree of danger. It might have to do more with domestic politics than with external menace, diverting the public's attention from internal struggles.

Secondly, while mature democracies usually refrain from waging war, this is not always true for very young democracies or states which are still in the process of becoming democratic. Generally, democratization reduces the risk of violent conflict. But uneven, rocky transitions or reversals on the path to democracy can increase the war-proneness significantly.[9] Mansfield and Snyder have argued that the proper sequence of the different phases in transitions is pivotal not only for the stability but also for the peacefulness of the democratizing regime's foreign policy. If a state lacks strong political institutions such as an effective bureaucracy, the rule of law, organized parties or professional news media, then it is not sufficiently equipped to manage the rapid increase of popular political participation. Elites threatened by democratization are tempted to play the nationalist card in order to mobilize the newly empowered constituencies in the unguarded competition for power and resources. Therefore, democratizing states that initiate wars are often characterized by an exclusionary nationalism that builds on the designation of domestic and international opponents as 'enemies' and 'traitors' who jeopardize the nation and need to be fought against; such states are torn by 'pressure-group politics by military, ethnic, or economic groups that seek a parochial benefit from policies that raise international tensions'.[10] This 'dark side of democracy' which surfaces regularly in uneven, rocky transitions has its historical roots in the emergence of democratic rule in modern Europe when the *demos*, the citizens, soon came to be equated with the *nation* or the *ethnos*, an exclusionary imagined community with a shared history and culture.[11] This 'ethnic flesh of nationalism' needs to be 'tamed' by institutions[12] and transformed into a civic national identity;[13] otherwise, it may nourish hatred and violence.

Democratization and the ambivalence of religion

In recent years, politicized religion has in many cases superseded ethnicity as a primary source for this kind of nationalist mobilization. Mann has pointed out that many politicized fundamentalist movements within the great religious traditions have wrapped their political ambitions in democratic language: '... contemporary religious violence results primarily from the rise of claims to *theo-democracy* – claims to political rule by "we, the religious people"',[14] thereby justifying to deprive those of their civic rights who do not belong to that specific religious community.

Whether and to what extent religions in general affect democratization is a highly controversial issue. Some scholars describe religious traditions as a defining element of political culture which they see as a major causal factor for the success or failure of democratization; others stress economic and institutional factors as determining the outcome of transitions. In the latter scholars' view, religion is multi-vocal and may provide resources for both supporters and opponents of democracy – but it is only secondary to the main drivers: institutions and economy.[15] Anderson, in his review of these debates, draws the conclusion that religions may be multi-vocal, but that 'at any point in time the dominant voices within them may prove more or less receptive to pluralistic development'.[16] And although religion is only one factor out of many, it may alter the balance between supportive and disruptive influences. In the same vein, Philpott argues that religions are indeed ambivalent in their attitude towards democratization as well as towards political violence. In his view, this variance is best explained by looking at two causal factors: First, the actual degree of mutual autonomy between religious bodies and state institutions which ranges from differentiated to integrationist; and secondly, the dominant political theology of the religious group which can be understood as a set of ideas about legitimate political authority. For example, a political theology that endorses religious freedom and the separation of spiritual and temporal authority nurtures a positive stance towards democracy. Such a political theology will flourish if the religious body already enjoys institutional differentiation from the state.[17] In contrast, politicized fundamentalist groups[18] are characterized by integrationist political theologies that seek to remodel the social and political order according to a religious utopian ideal which religious leaders construct by selecting and reinterpreting parts of the religious tradition. Philpott stresses that both postures are conceptually linked: '... the sorts of differentiation and political theology that lead religious actors to encourage democracy are the same ones whose absence tends to result in religious support for political violence, and vice versa'.[19]

Politicized fundamentalist groups are, as Eisenstadt has shown, genuinely modern movements. In the context of modernity, the task to organize social and political life in the absence of an overarching, transcendental legitimization of order can only be fulfilled through political action. Politicized fundamentalist actors do just that: they seek to replace modernity's pluralism and existential uncertainty by re-establishing the transcendental realm as the only legitimate source for political authority. Yet, they do it by way of distinctively modern political action which at times even utilizes democratic procedures.[20] Great importance in this respect is attached to the role of religious-political elites. Hasenclever and de Juan have alluded to the crucial influence of religious elites on the posture of politicized religious groups towards violent conflict. If the religious leadership finds it useful and possible to use religious traditions for the mobilization of believers for political ends, then they will engage in the process of framing the situation accordingly.[21] In analogy to the securitization moves which fuel liberal-democratic justifications of the use of military force, religious elites, too, engage in securitization. Religion is an especially vulnerable referent object to securitization: It has to do with the existential, sacred and absolute. Consequently, threats against religious referent objects are perceived as existential threats 'demanding immediate and effective action'.[22]

But Hasenclever and de Juan caution against an overestimation of religion's impact on armed conflicts: according to most quantitative studies, although religion rarely is the cause of conflicts, it often influences how existing conflicts are managed.[23] In the course of democratization, politicized fundamentalist elites who pursue an integrationist political theology and entertain a close relationship with the state may well feel threatened by the prospect of pluralism, the expansion of civil rights and broad political participation. If they manage to successfully mobilize their constituency by effective securitization of religious referent objects such as a sacred territory or the holy nation, they may not only jeopardize the transition process but also drag their state into an international war. Mansfield and Snyder have highlighted the problematic role of competitive old or new elites in democratization processes; if these elites adhere to politicized fundamentalist worldviews, their securitization moves might prove even more dangerous.[24] In order to analyse Israel's role in the rise and failure of the peace process, it is therefore highly instructive to examine the ideology and the actions of the politicized fundamentalist elite in Israel.

The historical evolution of politicized religion in Israel

The most fervent opposition to the Oslo peace process in the 1990s in Israel came from the Jewish settler community and the broader religious Zionist camp.[25] The settlers raged against the government's policy to return parts of the territories occupied by Israel in 1967 to the Palestinians. For them, the slogan 'land for peace' meant that the Labour-led government was ready to relinquish the holy land which God himself had promised to the Jewish people. Radical religious Zionism discerned signs of the beginning redemption in the sequence of historical events in the twentieth century: Zionist mass immigration, the founding of the state in 1948, and then the miraculous 'liberation' of the heartland of Jewish civilization (in their terminology, Judea, Samaria and East-Jerusalem with the Temple Mount) in the 1967 war. Therefore, they vehemently opposed a peace process which seemingly aimed to reverse this redemptive process.

The idea that religiously orthodox Jews would interpret Zionism and the secular Jewish state as signs of redemption were unimaginable just a century earlier.[26] When Zionism emerged in Europe in the late nineteenth century, the traditional rabbinical authorities rejected this overtly secular national movement on religious grounds. Over the centuries of Jewish diaspora in Europe, they had developed a theology that kept alive the longing for Zion and the Land of Israel in liturgy and prayer. But they adopted a passive stance, prohibiting any action by Jews that tried to 'force the end'. God imposed the exile on the Jews – and only he would redeem his people and bring them back to the Land of Israel under the rule of the coming Messiah. The only way to hasten redemption was by prayer and strict observation of Jewish law. When the secular, assimilated leaders of Zionism in Europe set out to emigrate to Israel and settle the land, the majority of orthodox rabbis condemned this movement as false messianism. Only a few sought to cooperate with Zionism in a pragmatic way in order to escape the deteriorating situation for the Jews in Europe due to rising anti-Semitism. Zionism itself, despite its being a secular nationalist movement in line with the European nationalisms of the time, was nevertheless reliant on the rich cultural fabric of stories, motifs and symbols offered by the Jewish religious tradition in order to construct a national narrative that would attract and mobilize the Jewish communities scattered all over Europe and beyond.[27] Not least of these motifs is the Land of Israel itself which served as a focal point for the Zionist efforts to forge a modern Jewish nation that would leave behind the humiliating state of exile.

The first orthodox scholar who found an innovative, systematic theological answer to the challenge of modern secular Zionism was Abraham Isaac HaCohen Kook (1865–1935), the first Chief Rabbi of the Jewish community in Palestine, the yishuv. While traditional rabbinic theology believed that the holiness of the Land of Israel was conditioned on the observation of the commandments, Kook conceived of holiness as a quality inherent to the land because of God's presence. He therefore concluded that 'the real and organic holiness of Jewry can become manifest only by the return of the people to its land, the only path that can lead to its renascence'.[28] Only in the Land of Israel could the Jewish people be a vessel for God's eternal light. Combining mystical and kabbalistic thought with European dialectical philosophy, Kook argued that the secular Zionists were in fact fulfilling God's plan without being aware of it. But he believed that the secular rebellion against traditional religion was just a temporary phenomenon which would gradually be transcended into a religious reawakening of the secularists upon the return of the Jewish people to the Land of Israel.[29]

Despite its originality, Kook's theology remained largely marginal during the following decades that saw the establishment of the State of Israel in 1949 and the subsequent process of state- and nation-building as well as the absorption of mass immigration under the leadership of the secular-socialist elite. The religious Zionist movement, embodied in the Mizrachi party (later National Religious Party – NRP), maintained a moderate outlook and supportive relationship with the state, but did not engage in a mystical-theological interpretation of history. The ultraorthodox parties rejected the secular state and its policies, but nevertheless opted for pragmatic coexistence in a consociational setting.[30]

The integrationist political theology of the settler movement

It was only after the 1967 war that Kook's theology re-emerged. By that time, Kook's son Zvi Yehuda HaCohen Kook was head of the yeshiva which his father had founded in Jerusalem, Merkaz haRav. His few disciples considered him to be the authoritative interpreter of the late Kook's works. When the Israeli army achieved a sweeping victory and grabbed former Arab territories in the 1967 war, it took most Israelis by surprise. The governing Labour Party favoured giving back parts of the land in exchange for peace while keeping others for security reasons. But there was more to the 1967 victory than questions of security and territorial adjustment: 'The war reconnected the State with the Land ... The return to cherished landmarks and longed-for vistas, pregnant with rich cultural associations, reawakened a long dormant impulse associated with the mystique of the land.'[31]

Kook and his students not only offered a theological-messianic reading of the political events which acquired a sacred, transcendental quality, but began to invest all their energy and missionary zeal into the 'liberation' and settlement of the territories.[32] The Jewish radicals set out to establish the first settlements in the occupied territories, presenting themselves as the new *avant garde* pioneers of Zionism, albeit in a religious version. At this time, the leadership of the NRP was taken over by a new generation of young politicians who came from the settler community. In the situation of crisis after the Yom Kippur war which had cast serious doubts on the invincibility of the Israeli army, the radicalized religious Zionist camp offered an alternative raison d'être for the State of Israel: to be a Jewish state in the sacred Jewish land which fulfils biblical prophecy, not only a state of Jews on any given territory. In 1974, the settler organization that became the most important non-parliamentarian political movement in Israel in the 1970s and 1980s, Gush Emunim, was founded. Many graduates from Merkaz HaRav were found in Gush's top ranks.

Although Israeli society as a whole did not endorse the radical political theology of the settlers, the general mood was in favour of a reformulation of Israeli politics that would strengthen the Jewish character of the state, deepen the bond with the land, and adopt more hawkish policies towards the Arabs and the Palestinians. Gush Emunim was the tip of the iceberg: radical, innovative, daring, messianic. Yet beneath floated the broader iceberg of the religious Zionist, traditionally Jewish camp in Israeli society.[33] Consequently, in the 1977 elections, the Likud came into power under the leadership of Menachem Begin. The new government supported the settlement drive in the occupied territories on a grand scale, cooperating with the religiously motivated settlers of Gush Emunim as well as establishing large settlements for non-ideological Israelis who were offered comfortable, state-subsidized housing across the Green Line.[34]

The religious settler movement, epitomized by Gush Emunim, meets the criteria of a politicized fundamentalist religion as stipulated above. First, the settlers adhered to an integrationist political theology. They aimed for the reconstitution of the Israeli social and political order according to their selective reading of Jewish religious tradition. At the top of their religious-normative priorities ranged the Land of Israel, its appropriation and settlement; then followed their idea of a truly Jewish state which would function according to Jewish law. In order to realize this integrationist political theology, the activists of the settlement movement and religious Zionism engaged in political action which took on the quality of religious ritual.[35]

The settlers and the Jewish State

The enormous influence of the settlement movement on Israeli politics in the 1970s and 1980s, which resulted in the rapid growth of the settlements in the occupied territories, stemmed from a double strategy. One the one hand, the settlers formed a very active and well organized non-parliamentarian network that established itself as the ideological mouthpiece of the broader Land of Israel-movement. They were very successful in mobilizing their supporters to take part in mostly illegal settlement activities, mass demonstrations and political lobbying. On the other hand, the settlement movement worked to lower the degree of differentiation between religion and state with the aim to promote the settlement project – a process which Oded Haklai has termed 'state penetration'.[36] The settlers were well-represented in the party system by the NRP and exploited their position as power-brokers in coalitional politics. They regularly filled ministerial posts in coalitional governments such as Housing and Construction and Education which were crucial for promoting their cause. Activists from the settlement movement played the card of communal politics, getting on the state's payroll as teachers, rabbis or mayors in the settlements. Moreover, they infiltrated arms of the civil and military bureaucracies: settler leaders such as Schilo Gal,[37] Schimon Einstein[38] or Avi Maoz[39] managed to acquire strategically important positions in governmental agencies such as the department for rural development in the Ministry for Housing and Construction or the Civil Administration as well as in government-funded organizations such as the Jewish Agency or the World Zionist Organization which were involved in the administration of the territories and the planning, development and funding of the settlements. From these positions, they built alliances with people in the state apparatus, thereby undermining the latter's loyalty to the state and the rule of law. Talya Sason, the state attorney who was assigned to examine the establishment of illegal outposts, stated that

> the engine behind a decision to establish outposts are probably regional councils in Judea, Samaria and Gaza, settlers and activists, imbued with ideology and motivation to increase Israeli settlement in the Judea, Samaria and Gaza territories. Some of the officials working in the Settlement Division of the World Zionist Organization, and in the Ministry of Housing & Construction, cooperated with them . . . .[40]

In the 1970s, the settlement movement began to establish religious colleges (*yeshivot*) which in contrast to the traditional Ultraorthodox yeshivot combined religious learning and army service. Students from these colleges soon began to fill the ranks of the army, preferring elite units which served in the occupied territories. This new generation of officers was ideologically close to the settlers and increasingly critical towards the secular state and its institutions.

In sum, the settlement movement succeeded in positioning itself as an influential factor in society, politics and administration in order to promote the settlement project in the occupied territories as well as to realize its integrationist political theology of a truly Jewish State of Israel according to a selective reading of the biblical tradition.[41]

Israel: a defective democracy

In commonly used democracy indices, Israel for decades has been ranked among the group of Western liberal-democratic states which achieve the highest scores.[42] But these indices are based on theoretically and normatively undemanding concepts of democracy which are even narrower than Dahl's classic formulation of polyarchy.[43] McHenry Jr and Mady have strongly criticized the accuracy and meaningfulness of the quantitative measure of the degree of democracy in Israel on grounds of empirical and conceptual problems. Not only do the indices differ in their definitions of democracy, they also fail to account for major empirical problems of the Israeli political system such as status of Israel's largest minority group, the Arab citizens of Israel.[44] Therefore, it is not surprising that many qualitative researchers came to deviating results when assessing the democratic character of Israel's political system, yet again depending on the concept of democracy which they apply, ranging from formal minimalist to normatively demanding definitions.

Although Israel's democratic character was not seriously questioned until the 1990s, researchers had begun to examine various problems regarding the electoral regime 20 years earlier. The proportional representation electoral arrangement and the highly fragmented party system were frequently criticized for hampering the political process, especially when in the 1980s these features led to serious government crises. But the consensus was that Israel 'suffered not so much from structural deficiencies, but rather from operational "imperfections"'.[45] Against the background of Israel's hostile security environment and its having to cope with mass migration from different cultural backgrounds, many researchers in fact regarded Israel's political system as surprisingly democratic.[46]

This overall positive evaluation was only challenged in a vibrant debate in the 1990s which addressed three fundamental shortcomings. First, there is the status of the Arab citizens of Israel who enjoy political rights but who are severely disadvantaged when it comes to civil rights. The second issue is the occupation of the Palestinian territories by which Israel controls a large Palestinian population which does not participate in Israel's electoral regime. Third, there is the low degree of differentiation between religion and state in Israel.[47] For example, religious authorities are endowed with jurisdiction in personal status matters and the state allocates huge funds for religious education and institutions,[48] with a clear preference for Jewish institutions over other religions' institutions.[49] Against this background, an increasing number of scholars doubted that Israel qualified as a fully-fledged liberal democracy, but due to its uniqueness should be categorized as an 'ethnic democracy',[50] 'ethnocracy',[51] or 'Jewish zealotocracy'.[52] This was because the political system privileged the Jewish population over the country's Arab citizens, while neither its territorial borders nor its boundaries of citizenship were clear cut.[53]

Democratization in the 1990s and the Oslo peace process

The debate on the substance and quality of Israel's democratic governance did not accidentally take place in the 1990s. Rather, it was the academic reflection of a growing dissatisfaction with the norms and processes of Israeli democracy mounted ever since severe government crises in the 1980s and increased by an intensive soul searching in Israeli society concerning the moral and political justification of military occupation during the first Palestinian Intifada (1987–1993). The critical voices against the settlement project and its proponents grew, both from within Israel as well as from the international community. In fact, the academic debate was itself part of a process of democratization in Israel in the 1990s which was closely intertwined with the peace process between Israel and the Palestinians. The so-called Oslo process, to be sure, had many causes. The end of the Cold War released the Israeli–Palestinian conflict from superpower rivalry; the Iraq War in 1991 implied a restructuring of the regional power balance in the Middle East and, pushed by the United States, resulted in the multilateral Madrid peace conference; the oil crisis in the Arab states – caused by low and falling oil process – weakened the economy in the Palestinian territories, encouraging the Palestine Liberation Organization (PLO) to seek a way out of the stalemate. But without Israel's readiness to rethink some of the basic norms and principles underlying its political system, the peace process would not have been possible. Of course, Israel did not undergo a transition from autocracy; but certainly its leadership in the early 1990s recognized a strong interrelation of the scope and quality of Israeli democracy on the one hand and peace on the other hand. Thus, the government embarked on a process of improving the above-mentioned defects of its only partially democratic governance, thereby paving the way – at least theoretically – for peaceful conflict resolution with the Palestinians.

Most importantly, Israel took important steps to amend its electoral regime by working towards an end of military occupation of the West Bank and Gaza. In 1993, it recognized the PLO as the legitimate representative of the Palestinian people and negotiated the Oslo Accords that encompassed the establishment of an independent Palestinian national authority, with representatives elected democratically by the Palestinian people, which was meant to successively take over governing responsibility in the Palestinian territories. Thus, Israel sought to end its factual control of millions of people who did not partake in its electoral and political participation regimes. Not least of the motives guiding this policy was to secure a Jewish majority in the state of Israel in order to maintain the character of Israel as a Jewish and democratic state, even if that goal entailed territorial compromise. Yet despite this ethno-national motive, the projected end of occupation certainly promised an improvement of the defective electoral regime of Israeli democracy.

Secondly, the status of the Arab citizens of Israel was gradually ameliorated. 'From an initial situation of overwhelming suspicion and de facto domination on one side, against overwhelming alienation and demoralization on the other, the overall trend was toward gradual, if halting and incomplete, liberalization.'[54] By the 1990s, there was visible representation of Arabs in some fields of public life – for example the appointment of the first Arab ambassador representing Israel to Finland. The Rabin government, which came into office in 1992, was more active in the Arab sector and increased the budgets for education, culture and child allowances, though it did not invite the Arab parties into the coalition. Dowty detected a trend towards consociational power-sharing arrangements within the framework of law between the Jewish majority and the Arab population, who were increasingly achieving the status of a recognized, autonomous minority. Progress towards Palestinian self-rule in the territories strengthened that trend by de-linking the situation of the Arab citizens of Israel from developments in the West Bank and in Gaza. It was hoped that the peaceful resolution of the Israeli–Palestinian conflict would improve the security situation, reduce ethnic tensions within Israel, and help expand civil rights to all citizens. Instead of prioritizing Arab-Palestinian nationalism, the Arabs in Israel now concentrated on civic issues and integration into Israeli society. Some scholars even spoke of the 'Israelization' of the Arab minority in the period after the Oslo Accords, fuelled by the hope for full and just equality between the Arab minority and the Jewish majority.[55]

Thirdly, the new government made efforts to advance the differentiation between religion and state in Israel. Since the founding of Israel, the relationship of religion and state had been regulated by a de facto status quo which had strong consociational elements. The political leadership ensured cooperation from the religious parties by guaranteeing that Jewish religious holidays would be official state holidays, that Jewish dietary law would be kept in public institutions, that the religious courts would be responsible for personal status law, and that the independent ultraorthodox education system would be recognized by the state in addition to the official secular and national-religious branches of education.[56] Moreover, the leading parties, Labour and Likud, consistently invited the smaller religious parties into government coalitions although it was not necessary arithmetically. In 1992, the centre-left government led by Yitzhak Rabin for the first time in Israeli history broke with this tradition. Rabin instead negotiated with the relatively new religious Sephardic party Shas which joined the government but left after just a year. As a consequence, the religious parties did not have the chance to fill ministerial posts which in former governments usually were assigned to them. For example, the education ministry, a traditional turf of the religious parties, was now headed by Shulamit Aloni from the leftist Meretz party. As a vocal opponent of the religious establishment she actively worked to diminish the influence of religion on public affairs. Even more important for peace, the Ministry of Housing and Construction was no longer in the hands of the national-religious parties who had used this post to channel funds into the settlements in the occupied territories. This change in coalition politics was accompanied by a general trend towards a higher degree of differentiation between religion and state: For example, some aspects of religious legislation were less and less enforced, such as the prohibition to open shops on Saturday. Over time, the Supreme Court has 'legislated on numerous occasions in a clear liberal direction',[57] thereby diminishing religious authorities' influence.

The leading political elite of the Labour-Meretz coalition explicitly reverted to the universalistic, liberal and secular part of the Zionist heritage in order to back up its aim to strengthen the democratic, civil character of the State of Israel. They understood the peace process as 'part of an overall transformation of Israeli society from a Jewish-Zionist nation-state, based on the unique destiny and values of Judaism, into a liberal Western democracy'.[58] In speeches and statements, leading Israeli politicians brought forward arguments that exactly mirrored the utilitarian and normative liberal preferences proposed by democratic peace theory, namely to avoid the casualties and the material costs of war as well as to adhere to human rights and democratic norms of non-violent conflict resolution. Prime Minister Rabin, in a speech in the Knesset in 1993, defended the Oslo Accords by explicitly expressing the imperative to minimize the human and material costs of war: 'This Government has decided to try to put an end to hate, in order that our children and grandchildren will not again experience the painful price of wars, terror, and violence.'[59] He then went on to say that Israel needed to integrate itself into a changing world, making an argument which stresses liberal-democratic norms of peaceful conflict resolution: 'We must extricate ourselves from the sense of isolation that has gripped us for almost 50 years. We must join the campaign for peace, conciliation, and international cooperation that is currently sweeping the entire globe'.[60] Addressing the Knesset only a few weeks after the signing of the Oslo Accords in Washington, Rabin cited his own words towards the Palestinians on that occasion in which he based the quest for peace on human rights and human dignity: 'We, like you, are people who want to build a home, to plant a tree, to love, live side by side with you – in dignity, in empathy, as human beings, as free man. We are today giving peace a chance . . . .'[61]

De-democratization and re-escalation: the effect of religious spoilers and the ambivalence of liberalism

In the mid-1990s, the international and regional conditions for the peace process to accomplish its goals were still very promising. The United States as well as many of the Arab neighbours supported or at least tolerated Israeli–Palestinian negotiations. But from within both societies the peace-opponents voiced harsh criticism; and not only that, they engaged in violent protest against what seemed to them as a sell-out of their respective national ethos. On the Palestinian side, the opposition accused Arafat and his entourage of treachery and collaboration with the enemy. The Palestinian Authority (PA) was a direct product of the Oslo process and therefore the natural partner of Israel and the United States, but in the eyes of the critics not the legitimate representative of the Palestinian people. Arafat was torn between the demands of his constituency, the oppositional movements and the obligations of the Oslo agreements. The terrorist organizations such as Hamas and Jihad al-Islami tried to disrupt the peace process by launching several series of suicide terrorist attacks in Israel, the most terrible one in March 1996.[62]

The settlers began what has been called a 'Jewish Intifada' shortly after the signing of the Oslo accords, attacking Palestinians in the occupied territories and demolishing their property. In 1994, Baruch Goldstein, a Jewish extremist from Kiryat Arba, murdered 29 Muslim worshippers in Hebron. The tragic climax of Jewish violence against the Oslo process was the assassination of Prime Minister Yitzhak Rabin in November 1995. He was killed by a Jewish extremist from the radical religious Zionist camp. The months up to the assassination were characterized by a growing polarization of Israeli society concerning two overlapping issues: first, the future of the occupied territories and the peace process; and secondly, the identity of the Jewish state. The religious Zionist elite, who had successfully penetrated the state apparatus and benefited greatly from state resources for its settlement endeavour, now felt existentially threatened by the new government's policy of 'land for peace'. In analogy to old elites who are threatened by the newly empowered constituencies in democratizing states with weak institutions,[63] the radical religious Zionist elites were shocked by the prospect of territorial compromise and played the ethno-nationalist card in order to mobilize support for their struggle against Oslo.

Rabin and his foreign minister Shimon Peres had based their position in the peace process on a reformulation of Israeli identity which drew on the liberal, civil and secular heritage of Zionism. If Israel was to be a liberal democracy instead of an isolated, ethno-nationalist warrior state, they argued, then it had to abandon its undemocratic rule over the Palestinians in the occupied territories.[64] The nationalist and religious Zionist camp argued that the territories formed an integral part of the Land of Israel, given to the Jews by God himself, and therefore were constitutive for the Jewish identity of the state. Security issues and religion 'virtually merged into one new dimension, or continuum, which might be labelled as "Jewishness", that is, viewing defence issues and policies through a Jewish perspective'.[65] The settlers, led by a vocal elite of radical rabbis from the occupied territories, declared the Oslo accords to be against Jewish law and initiated a massive wave of protest against the government, including mass demonstrations, incitement, and calls by settler rabbis to soldiers to refuse evacuation orders of settlements.

The result was that the religious Jewish public was identified with hawkish, ultra-nationalist positions on the peace process; and the secular Israelis were reckoned to be leftist doves, ready and willing to make considerable concessions. Personal religious observance had become the most important socio-demographic factor for the prediction of voting behaviour in national elections.[66] But the clear polarization masked the fact that a majority of Israelis still favoured continuing the peace process, yet did not want to compromise on the Jewish character of the state.[67] In addition, suicide bombings by Hamas, only a few weeks before the elections in 1996, contributed to the election victory of the outspoken Oslo critic, Binyamin Netanyahu (at the time of writing, early July 2009, again prime minister of Israel), who set up a centre-right coalition which included the religious Zionist parties. Although Netanyahu claimed to be faithful to the Oslo accords, his government acted to the contrary and worked to halt the peace process and accelerate the expansion of Jewish settlements in the territories. Most of the efforts of the Rabin government at democratizing the defective Israeli democracy and pushing forward the peace process were thwarted by the recapture of political power by the national camp and its religious Zionist allies. The brief period, in which the Arab citizens of Israel had reason to hope for greater equality and full civil rights, ended rather abruptly: 'The Rabin assassination, the Likud party's rise to power, and the obstacles that plagued the negotiation process further resulted in an atmosphere of disorientation and hopelessness'[68] among the Arabs in Israel. The incorporation of the traditional religious-Zionist parties into the government re-established their hold on ministerial posts and government revenues, thereby lowering the degree of differentiation between religion and state significantly.[69] And, most importantly, the prospect of ending Israel's undemocratic control of the Palestinian territories seemed further off than in the immediate period after the signing of the Oslo Accords.

In Netanyahu's public statements in the mid-1990s, both the 'dark side' of democratic peace-arguments and the political theology of the religious Zionist camp were employed to justify his government's policy in the peace process. First and foremost, he sought to portray Arafat and the Palestinian Authority as notorious peace opponents who could not be trusted because they allowed and possibly even supported terrorism. '... all those mass suicide attacks, were not sporadic. ... Those were institutionalized attacks by Hamas and Islamic Jihad, and they were perpetuated with the knowledge and approval of the PA in order to obtain more areas and bring more pressure to bear on Israel'.[70] Therefore, slowing down the peace process and using military force in reaction to unguarded Palestinian violence were legitimate democratic reactions in his view. While Netanyahu claimed that Israel wanted to proceed with the peace process and preferred non-violent modes of conflict resolution, he conditioned this benevolent policy on the Palestinians' ability to halt terrorist attacks. Simultaneously, he doubted not only the PA's ability but also its serious intention to fight terrorism. Thereby, he indirectly qualified the PA as a terrorist or rogue state; or in Kant's words: as an 'unjust enemy'.[71]

Although the democratic peace arguments prevailed in his statements, the prime minister also used motifs and arguments which drew on the political theology of the settlement movement. He explicitly placed Zionism in the tradition of Jewish religion, called the settlers 'the real pioneers of our days' and Jerusalem 'the eternal capital of the Jewish people';[72] he spoke about the biblical idea of the 'ingathering of the exiles' and related that biblical prophesy had been fulfilled in the modern State of Israel; he called Hebron 'a Jewish town, with a Jewish history'[73] and said that the settlement of the Land of Israel was a basic right of the Jewish people. Although Netanyahu avoided the messianic, mystical rhetoric of Gush Emunim, he nonetheless integrated many of the arguments of religious Zionist political theology into his political statements.

Ehud Barak, the settlers, and the end of the peace process

At the end of the 1990s, the external circumstances were still in favour of peace. Moreover, the United States, the European Union and other states in the region and beyond pressed the conflict parties to overcome the stalemate of the peace process stemming from the Netanyahu era. When the Labour politician Ehud Barak took office in 1999, many hoped that this would bring a breakthrough in the peace process.

On the Palestinian side, the feeling of deep frustration with the peace process dominated the political mood. Nothing of what the Palestinians had hoped for when they signed the Oslo accords had come true. Instead of a Palestinian state, a growing economy and a free society, they had to cope with expanding settlements, confiscation and fragmentation of territory, high rates of unemployment, poverty and a crippled and corrupt PA.[74] The pressure on Arafat to bring about a substantial change of the Palestinian situation increased. The years of the Netanyahu government, which by 1999 had effectively stalemated the peace process by way of simple renegotiation of former agreements and simultaneous postponement of the implementation of these agreements, added to the Palestinian impasse.[75]

In the 1999 election campaign, a former chief of staff of the Israel Defence Force, Ehud Barak, succeeded in winning the support of voters from Israel's political centre. He was able to credibly deliver the message that he would not compromise on Israel's national security, but at the same time restart the peace process on a regional as well as on a bilateral level. He was successful in the run for the Prime Minister's office, but was then confronted with a highly fragmented Knesset due to the split vote for prime minister and parliament. His party list 'One Israel', a merger of the Labour party, the moderate religious Meimad party and the liberal Gesher, won 26 seats. Together with the other parties on the left, the progressive camp only got about 50 seats (out of 120) and therefore was not able to compose a governing coalition on its own. Barak chose not to invite Likud into the coalition because of its obstructive stance on the peace process. Instead he opted for a coalition that deliberately included the religious Zionist (NRP) and ultraorthodox parties (Shas) as well as other small nationalist parties (Israel b'Aliya) in order to gather broad support for his planned peace policies and reunite the polarized Israeli society.

After a failed attempt to initiate negotiations with the Syrians, Barak turned to the Israeli–Palestinian track. However, he was soon confronted with opposition from his coalition partners. Following violent clashes surrounding the commemoration of the 'Nakbah'[76] by the Palestinians, negotiations were again suspended. The United States tried to revive the peace process and accepted Barak's proposal to summon the conflict parties for end status negotiations in Camp David in July 2000. Given the fact that even smaller transfers of territory had caused major quarrels in Israeli politics, the plan conclusively to negotiate the end status issues seemed rather ambitious. Barak disclosed that he was ready to make concessions and offer the Palestinians over 90% of the West Bank.[77] But a few days before Barak eventually left Jerusalem for the United States, his coalition partners from the ultra-nationalist and religious Zionist camp left the coalition, leaving the Prime Minister without a majority in parliament. The Camp David negotiations collapsed, as did the negotiations in Taba a few months later which were held in the midst of the Al Aqsa Intifada.

The role of the politicized religious actors during this period was rather ambivalent. On the one hand, they had reluctantly come to terms with the fact that the peace process seemed irreversible. The absolute, maximalist idea of Greater Israel existed 'mostly as a theoretical ideology rather than as a potentially implemented policy'.[78] Not least the assassination of Rabin had yielded a reassessment of ideological positions and caused internal fighting over the legitimacy of the murder and its implications for religious Zionism's political ambitions. Instead of territorial maximalism, the religious Zionists now concentrated on protecting and enhancing the Jewish identity of the State of Israel. Yet despite this serious crisis at the end of the decade, the religious settlers were crucial for the failure of Camp David and the renewed escalation of violence in September 2000. First, religious Zionist political theology has become a legitimate part of Israeli discourse. Through their share in state education as well as through the Hesder Yeshivot, the religious Zionist elite had successfully spread their ideological views to the broader public. They had effectively linked their political theology with the security concerns of many Israelis, presenting the settlement project as vital to individual and national security. This securitization process augmented the provisos against possible territorial concessions and conclusive end status negotiations. In addition, the radical religious Zionists succeeded in lowering the degree of differentiation between state and religion and secured themselves crucial positions in the administrative governmental agencies which dealt with the infrastructure and expansion of settlements.[79] By the time of Camp David, the 'engine' of the settlement project had produced facts on the ground that fuelled Palestinian mistrust and were very difficult to reverse.

When it came to end status negotiations, the religious parties opted to leave the coalition and withdrew their support of Prime Minister Barak's policies. Without the Knesset majority, Barak had to conduct negotiations on very thin ice and ultimately failed. With hindsight it appears that a renewed outbreak of violence was just a question of time. When opposition leader Ariel Sharon visited the Temple Mount in East Jerusalem in September 2000, accompanied by hundreds of Israeli security personnel, this provocative gesture provided the spark that let the situation explode. The Palestinian demonstrations which started immediately after this visit expanded quickly and soon turned violent. Yet Prime Minister Barak did not revert to any of the arguments of religious Zionist political theology in his public statements in which he justified Israel's heavy use of military force in reaction to the violent protest. Instead, he almost exclusively relied on democratic peace rhetoric. Addressing the Knesset at the fifth anniversary of Rabin's assassination, he very clearly linked the issues of democracy and peace: 'If Israel wishes to attain peace and preserve its character as a democratic, Jewish state, Israel cannot retain all the territory it captured in 1967 and rule over another people'.[80] Barak sought to portray Israel as a just and peace-committed democratic state, 'a "model society" that affords its citizens social justice, economic prosperity, and safety; a state living in co-existence, cooperation, and amicable relations with all its neighbors'.[81] Furthermore, he stressed that Israel paid respect to the Palestinian right of self-determination and had the desire to 'reconcile our differences and achieve a historic compromise in which both sides will have to relinquish part of their dream on order to make room for the other to realize his most fervent desire'.[82] But from Barak's perspective, Arafat and the PA openly disregarded Israel's willingness to make peace and instead intentionally opted for violence. In another statement, shortly after the outbreak of the Al Aqsa-Intifada in September 2000, he ascribed the sole responsibility to Arafat and the PA, depicting the Palestinians as a sort of 'unjust enemy': 'We are witnessing an acute and violent escalation in our relations with the Palestinians. Responsibility for this rests with Chairman Arafat and the Palestinian Authority.'[83] Confronted with such an 'unjust enemy', Barak presented Israel's military reaction as legitimate and appropriate: 'With the same determination that we struggled to seek peace, we will know how to fight against violence.'[84]

Conclusions

When the State of Israel started the Oslo peace process with the Palestinians in the early 1990s, its political course almost appeared like a textbook example of democratic peace. The Rabin government, which took office in 1992, explicitly linked its peace policy to an improvement of Israeli democracy and a civil-secular reformulation of its hitherto mainly ethno-religiously defined identity. In particular, the new government worked to amend the disadvantaged status of the Arab citizens of Israel, enhance the differentiation of religion and state, and end the occupation of the territories and its factual control of millions of Palestinians who did not participate in its electoral regime. It appeared that Israel was about to move from an illiberal, partly exclusive democracy to a fully-fledged liberal democracy in order to enable the peace process with the Palestinians.

But the programme of 'land for peace' which guided the peace process was perceived as an existential threat to the religious Zionist settler movement. Since the 1967 war, the religious settlers had championed the settlement endeavour in the occupied territories and secured themselves support from large parts of Israeli society as well as massive financial, logistical and political backing from the state. They had successfully spread their integrationist political theology as well as lowered the degree of differentiation between religion and state in order to realize their ethno-religious vision of the Jewish state. After the Oslo Accords became public in 1993, the settler movement therefore engaged in a sustained campaign against the peace process as well as against the broader course of democratization. They effectively securitized the territorial issue by presenting the peace process as an existential threat not only to the settlements, but to the whole state of Israel. But this securitization only proved to be effective after Palestinian spoilers undermined the peace process with an outbreak of suicide bombing in the mid-1990s. Successive Israeli governments argued that Israel as a democracy was still interested in negotiations and peaceful conflict-resolution, but did not have a partner for peace on the other side. They utilized the ambivalent language of the democratic peace in order to describe the Palestinian Authority as a sort of 'rogue state' against which military force was legitimate and appropriate. This ambivalent use of the liberal-democratic peace arguments served as an opportunity structure for the politicized fundamentalist framing of the conflict brought forward by the religious Zionists; taken together, it proved to be destructive for the peace process as well as for the democratization of the Israeli democracy.

Acknowledgements

This article draws on my doctoral dissertation (Baumgart-Ochse, *Demokratie und Gewalt im Heiligen Land*) conducted at the Peace Research Institute Frankfurt (PRIF) and supported by the Deutsche Stiftung Friedensforschung (DSF). The support of PRIF and DSF as well as of the Internationale Promotions-Centrum (IPC) at the University of Frankfurt is gratefully acknowledged. The author would like to thank Jeff Haynes, Harald Müller, Guy Ben-Porat, Jonas Wolff, Dirk Peters, and the participants of the workshop 'Religion and Democratisations: Friend or Enemy?' at London Metropolitan University for valuable comments.

Notes

1. In addition to the structural constraints on democratic leaders' actions, democratic peace theory puts forward the cultural or normative explanation that liberal and democratic values foster peaceful foreign policy. For the classical formulation, see Maoz and Russett, 'Normative and Structural Causes of Democratic Peace, 1946–1986'.
2. See the introductory literature: Chan, 'In Search of Democratic Peace: Problems and Promise'; Doyle, 'Kant, Liberal Legacies, and Foreign Affairs'; Fendius Elman, *Paths to Peace: Is Democracy the Answer*; Geis, 'Diagnose: Doppelbefund, Ursache: ungeklärt?'; Levy, 'War and Peace'; Ray, 'The Democratic Path to Peace'; Russett, *Grasping the Democratic Peace: Principles for a Post-Cold War World*; Russett and Oneal, *Triangulating Peace. Democracy, Interdependence, and International Organizations.*
3. Discussions of the monadic version can be found in Benoit, 'Democracies Really Are More Pacific (in General)'; Czempiel, 'Kants Theorem. Oder: Warum sind die Demokratien (noch immer) nicht friedlich?'; Hasenclever and Wagner, 'From the Analysis of a Separate Democratic Peace to the Liberal Study of International Conflict'; MacMillan, 'Beyond the Separate Democratic Peace'; Müller, 'The Antinomy of the Democratic Peace'; Müller and Wolff, 'Democratic Peace: Many Date, Little Explanation?'.
4. Freedman, 'The Age of Liberal Wars'.
5. Brock, Geis and Müller, *Democratic Wars. Looking at the Dark Side of Democratic Peace;* Geis, Brock and Müller, Demokratische Kriege als Antinomien des Demokratischen Friedens: Eine komplementäre Forschungsagenda'.
6. Müller, 'The Antinomy of the Democratic Peace', 503–7.
7. For the theory of securitization as proposed by the Copenhagen School, see Buzan, Wæver and de Wilde, *Security – A New Framework for Analysis.*
8. Müller, 'Kants Schurkenstaat: Der "ungerechte Feind' und die Selbstermächtigung zum Kriege'; Desch, 'America's Liberal Illiberalism. The Ideological Origins of Overreaction in U.S. Foreign Policy'.
9. Ward and Gleditsch, 'Democratizing for Peace'; Gleditsch and Ward, 'War and Peace in Space and Time: The Role of Democratization'.
10. Mansfield and Snyder, *Electing to Fight. Why Emerging Democracies go to War.* For an excellent review of the literature on democratization and war, see Cederman, Hug and Wenger, 'Democratization and War in Political Science'.
11. Mann, *The Dark Side of Democracy. Explaining Ethnic Cleansing*, 3; Anderson, *Imagined Communities. Reflections on the Origin and Spread of Nationalism.*
12. Nodia, 'Nationalism and Democracy', 7.
13. Mansfield and Snyder, *Electing to Fight. Why Emerging Democracies go to War*, 172–3.
14. Mann, *The Dark Side of Democracy. Explaining Ethnic Cleansing*, 513; Juergensmeyer, *The New Cold War? Religious Nationalism Confronts the Secular State.*
15. Stepan, 'Religion, Democracy, and the "Twin Tolerations"'.
16. Anderson, 'Does God Matter, and If So Whose God? Religion and Democratization', 207.
17. Philpott, 'Explaining the Political Ambivalence of Religion'. A similar argument has been made in Rueschemeyer, Huber Stephens and Stephens, *Capitalist Development & Democracy*, 275.
18. Fundamentalism in a broad sense also encompasses conservative, quietist groups that reject any entanglement with politics; therefore, the term 'politicized fundamentalism' better captures those groups who might turn into dangerous opponents of democratization because of their intention to remodel state and society according to their political theology. See Brocker, 'Politisierte Religion: Die Herausforderung des Fundamentalismus in vergleichender Perspektive'.

19. Philpott, 'Explaining the Political Ambivalence of Religion', 506.
20. Eisenstadt, 'Fundamentalism, Phenomenology, and Comparative Dimensions', 264ff.
21. Hasenclever and de Juan, 'Grasping the Impact of Religious Traditions on Political Conflicts: Empirical Findings and Theoretical Perspectives'.
22. Laustsen and Waever, 'In Defense of Religion: Sacred Referent Objects for Securitization', 159; see also Almond, Sivan and Appleby, 'Fundamentalism: Genus and Species', 94.
23. Hasenclever and de Juan, 'Grasping the Impact of Religious Traditions on Political Conflicts: Empirical Findings and Theoretical Perspectives'; Hasenclever and Rittberger, 'Does Religion Make a Difference? Theoretical Approaches to the Impact of Faith on Political Conflict'.
24. Juergensmeyer, *The New Cold War. Religious Nationalism Confronts the Secular State*, 173–8; Laustsen and Waever, 'In Defense of Religion: Sacred Referent Objects for Securitization'.
25. Religious Zionism denotes a stream in Judaism which bases its supportive stance towards the Zionist efforts to establish a Jewish state in the 'Land of Israel' on Jewish religious tradition and Jewish law. It is therefore a unique combination of religion and nationalism. In general, religious Zionism is associated with modern orthodoxy which allows for the participation of believers in modern life. Religious Zionists are also called the 'knitted skullcap community', referring to the colourful kippot worn by the men. In contrast, ultraorthodoxy traditionally rejects the idea of a secular state of Israel and advocates retreat from modern life. Yet in recent years, there has also emerged a stream which merges ultraorthodox religious observance and nationalism (*Hardal*).
26. For the historical dimension of Jewish reactions to Zionism see among others Salmon, *Religion and Zionism. First Encounters*; Eisenstadt, *Die Transformation der israelischen Gesellschaft*; Hertzberg, *The Zionist Idea. A Historical Analysis and Reader*.
27. Zuckermann, 'State and Religion: An Aporetic Relationship in Zionism'.
28. Quoted in Hertzberg, *The Zionist Idea. A Historical Analysis and Reader*, 429.
29. On Kook's theology, compare amongst others Ravitzky, *Messianism, Zionism, and Jewish Religious Radicalism*; Aran, 'Jewish Zionist Fundamentalism: The Bloc of the Faithful in Israel (Gush Emunim)'; Aran, 'The Father, the Son, and the Holy Land'; Gruenwald, 'Mysticism and Politics in the State of Israel'.
30. Cohen and Susser, *Israel and the Politics of Jewish Identity. The Secular-Religious Impasse*.
31. Aran, 'The Father, the Son, and the Holy Land', 273; see also Sandler, *The State of Israel, the Land of Israel. The Statist and Ethnonational Dimensions of Foreign Policy*.
32. Ravitzky, *Messianism, Zionism, and Jewish Religious Radicalism*, 81ff.
33. Sprinzak, 'The Iceberg Model of Political Extremism'.
34. The 'Green Line' stands for the de facto borders of Israel until 1967, determined by the armistice agreements of 1949 between Israel and the neighbouring Arab states.
35. Aran, 'The Father, the Son, and the Holy Land', 296.
36. Haklai, 'Religious-Nationalist Mobilization and State Penetration'.
37. Chairman of the Gusch Etzion Regional Council in the 1990s, then personal advisor to Prime Minister Ehud Barak.
38. Head of the department for rural development at the Ministry for Housing and Construction in the 1990s.
39. General Director of the Ministry for Housing and Construction. See Haklai, 'Religious-Nationalist Mobilization and State Penetration', 730ff; and Zertal and Eldar, *Lords of the Land. The War Over Israel's Settlement Policy in the West Bank*, Chapter 6.
40. Sason, *Summary of the Opinion Concerning Unauthorized Outposts*. See also Newman, 'From Hitnachalut to Hitnatkut. The Impact of Gush Emunim and the

Settlement Movement on Israeli Politics and Society'; Lein and Weizman, *Land Grab. Israel's Settlement Policy in the West Bank.*
41. For a detailed analysis see Baumgart-Ochse, *Demokratie und Gewalt im Heiligen Land.*
42. See Marshall and Jaggers, *Polity IV Project. Political Regime Characteristics and Transitions, 1800–2000*; Freedom House, *Freedom in the World.*
43. Dahl, *Polyarchy: Participation and Opposition.*
44. McHenry Jr and Mady, 'A Critique of Quantitative Measures of the Degree of Democracy in Israel'.
45. Sheffer, 'Political Change and Party System Transformation', 149.
46. Lijphart, 'Israeli Democracy and Democratic Reform in Comparative Perspective'; Diamond and Sprinzak, 'Israeli Democracy Under Stress'; Horowitz and Lissak, *Trouble in Utopia. The Overburdened Polity of Israel.*
47. According to Merkel's ('Embedded and Defective Democracies') model of 'embedded democracy', the Israeli regime therefore features several defects in the electoral regime, the political participation regime and the civil rights regime. Thus it does not qualify as a fully-fledged liberal democracy, but should be categorized as a defective democracy.
48. For example, in 2005–2006 18.2% of Israeli students were enrolled in religious state primary schools which are generally affiliated with religious Zionism, another 26.2% in ultraorthodox schools, and 55.5% in secular state primary schools. See Maoz, 'Religious Education in Israel'. The ultraorthodox population in Israel receives further financial support through the Ministry of Housing and Construction and the Ministry for Religious Affairs.
49. For a discussion of the religious–state relations in Israel and their implications for democracy, compare Fox and Rynhold, 'A Jewish and Democratic State? Comparing Government Involvement in Religion in Israel with other Democracies'.
50. Smooha, 'Ethnic Democracy: Israel as an Archetype'; Smooha, 'The Model of Ethnic Democracy: Israel as a Jewish and Democratic State'; Shafir and Peled, 'Citizenship and Stratification in an Ethnic Democracy'.
51. Yiftachel, *Ethnocracy. Land and Identity Politics in Israel/Palestine.*
52. Pappé, 'Israel at a Crossroads Between Civic Democracy and Jewish Zealotocracy'.
53. Yet other scholars defended the democratic character of the Israeli political system. See for example Neuberger, 'Israel – A Liberal Democracy With Four Flaws'; Gavison, 'Jewish and Democratic? A Rejoinder to the "Ethnic Democracy" Debate'; Dowty, 'Is Israel Democratic? Substance and Semantics in the "Ethnic Democracy" Debate'.
54. Dowty, *The Jewish State. A Century Later*, 207.
55. See Rekhess, 'The Arabs of Israel After Oslo: Localization of the National Struggle'. Most notable, there has been a remarkable rise of Arab NGOs in Israel, providing services in education, health or planning, but also advocating civil rights and equality vis á vis the Israeli state. See Jamal, 'The Counter-Hegemonic Role of Civil Society: Palestinian-Arab NGOs in Israel'.
56. Cohen and Susser, *Israel and the Politics of Jewish Identity. The Secular-Religious Impasse*, 18ff.
57. Fox and Rynhold, 'A Jewish and Democratic State? Comparing Government Involvement in Religion in Israel with Other Democracies'.
58. Goldberg, 'The Electoral Fall of the Israeli Left', 57; see Barnett, 'The Israeli Identity and the Peace Process'; Ben-Porat, *Global Liberalism, Local Populism. Peace and Conflict in Israel/Palestine and Northern Ireland.*
59. Rabin, 'Statement in the Knesset on the Israel-PLO Declaration of Principles, 21 September 1993'.
60. Ibid.
61. Ibid.

62. Parsons, *The Politics of the Palestinian Authority. From Oslo to al-Aqsa*.
63. Mansfield and Snyder, *Electing to Fight. Why Emerging Democracies go to War*, 9.
64. Barnett, 'The Israeli Identity and the Peace Process'.
65. Goldberg, 'The Electoral Fall of the Israeli Left', 57; see also Elazar and Sandler, 'Introduction: The Battle over Jewishness and Zionism in the Post-Modern Era'.
66. Shamir and Arian, 'Collective Identity and Electoral Competition in Israel'.
67. An ultraorthodox party supported Netanyahu in the direct elections for Prime Minister with the slogan 'Netanyahu is good for the Jews'. The National Religious Party featured the election slogan 'Zionism with a Soul'.
68. Rekhess, 'The Arabs of Israel After Oslo: Localization of the National Struggle', 33.
69. This reversal of democratizing trends is mainly situated in the political realm; in the legal realm, the Supreme Court by and large kept its liberal course throughout the 1990s and 2000s, enhancing the civil rights of Arab citizens as well as aiming towards greater differentiation between religion and state. Yet the court did not intervene in the Israeli bureaucracy's uneven allocation of public resources based on allegedly neutral reasons such as place of residence or different religious and cultural needs and interests; therefore, Benvenisti and Shaham, ('Facially Neutral Discrimination and the Israel Supreme Court') speak of facially neutral discrimination.
70. Netanyahu, 'Address to the Likud Central Committee'.
71. See Ish-Shalom's ('Theory as a Hermeneutical Mechanism: The Democratic-Peace Thesis and the Politics of Democratization') excellent analysis of Netanyahu's use of democratic peace arguments.
72. Netanyahu, 'Speech on the Presentation of the Government to the Knesset'.
73. Netanyahu, 'Address to the Likud Central Committee'.
74. Hammami and Tamari, 'The Second Uprising: End or New Beginning?'.
75. Boyle Mahle, 'A Political-Security Analysis of the Failed Oslo Process'.
76. The Palestinians call the first Arab-Israeli war 1948–1949 'Nakbah' (Arabic for catastrophe), because it resulted in the flight and expulsion of 750,000 Palestinians from their homes in former Mandate Palestine and shattered their national aspirations. For data on the refugees, see www.un.org/unrwa/refugees/index.html.
77. The exact proposals are subject of contestation, see Pressman, 'Visions in Collision'.
78. Pedahzur, 'The Downfall of the National Camp?', 40.
79. This is also the conclusion of Talya Sason, the attorney who was commissioned by Prime Minister Ehud Olmert to research the ways in which illegal outposts are established and funded. See her very interesting and revealing report, Sason, *Summary of the Opinion Concerning Unauthorized Outposts*.
80. Barak, 'Address on the Fifth Anniversary of Rabin's Assassination'.
81. Ibid.
82. Ibid.
83. Barak, 'Statement to the Israeli People'.
84. Ibid.

Notes on contributor

Dr Claudia Baumgart-Ochse is Research Fellow at the Peace Institute Frankfurt (PRIF), Germany.

Bibliography

Almond, Gabriel A., Emmanuel Sivan, and Scott R. Appleby. 'Fundamentalism: Genus and Species'. In *Fundamentalisms Comprehended*, ed. Martin E. Marty and Scott R. Appleby, 399–424. Chicago, London: The University of Chicago Press, 1995.

Anderson, Benedict R. *Imagined Communities.* London: Verso, 1983.
Anderson, John. 'Does God Matter, and If So Whose God? Religion and Democratization'. *Democratization* 11, no. 4 (2004): 192–217.
Aran, Gideon. 'The Father, the Son, and the Holy Land'. In *Spokesmen for the Despised. Fundamentalist Leaders of the Middle East,* ed. Scott R. Appleby, 294–327. Chicago, London: The University of Chicago Press, 1997.
Aran, Gideon. 'Jewish Zionist Fundamentalism: The Bloc of the Faithful in Israel (Gush Emunim)'. In *Fundamentalism Observed,* ed. Martin E. Marty and Scott R. Appleby, 265–344. Chicago: University of Chicago Press, 1991.
Barak, Ehud. 'Address by Prime Minister Barak on the Fifth Anniversary of Rabin's Assassination, November 8, 2000'. www.mfa.gov.il/MFA (accessed February 14, 2007).
Barak, Ehud. 'Statement to the Israeli People by Prime Minister Ehud Barak, October 7, 2000'. www.mfa.gov.il/MFA (accessed February 13, 2007).
Barnett, Michael. 'The Israeli Identity and the Peace Process'. In *Identity and Foreign Policy in the Middle East,* ed. Michael Barnett and Shibley Telhami, 58–87. Ithaca, NY: Cornell University Press, 2002.
Baumgart-Ochse, Claudia. *Demokratie und Gewalt im Heiligen Land. Politisierte Religion in Israel und das Scheitern des Osloer Friedensprozesses* [*Democracy and Violence in the Holy Land. Politicized Religion in Israel and the Failure of the Oslo Peace Process*]. Baden-Baden: Nomos, 2008.
Benoit, Kenneth. 'Democracies Really Are More Pacific (in General)'. *Journal of Conflict Resolution* 40, no. 4 (1996): 636–57.
Ben-Porat, Guy. *Global Liberalism, Local Populism. Peace and Conflict in Israel/Palestine and Northern Ireland.* Syracuse, NY: Syracuse University Press, 2006.
Benvenisti, Eyal, and Dahlia Shaham. 'Facially Neutral Discrimination and the Israeli Supreme Court'. *New York University Journal of International Law and Politics* 36, no. 4 (2004): 677–716.
Boyle Mahle, Melissa. 'A Political-Security Analysis of the Failed Oslo Process'. *Middle East Policy* 12, no. 1 (2005): 79–96.
Brock, Lothar, Anna Gies, and Harald Müller, eds., *Democratic Wars. Looking at the Dark Side of Democratic Peace.* New York, Basingstoke: Palgrave Macmillan.
Brocker, Manfred. 'Politisierte Religion: Die Herausforderung des Fundamentalismus in vergleichender Perspektive' ['Politicized Religion: The Challenge of Fundamentalism in Comparative Perspective']. *Zeitschrift für Politikwissenschaft* [*Journal of Political Science*] 13, no. 1 (2003): 23–52.
Buzan, Barry, Ole Wæver, and Jaap de Wilde. *Security – A New Framework for Analysis.* Boulder, CO: Rienner, 1998.
Cederman, Lars-Erik, Simon Hug, and Andreas Wenger. 'Democratization and War in Political Science'. *Democratization* 15, no. 3 (2008): 509–24.
Chan, Steve. 'In Search of Democratic Peace: Problems and Promise'. *Mershon International Studies Review* 41 (1997): 59–91.
Cohen Asher, and Bernard Susser. *Israel and the Politics of Jewish Identity. The Secular-Religious Impasse.* Baltimore, MD: The Johns Hopkins University Press, 2000.
Czempiel, Ernst-Otto. 'Kants Theorem. Oder: Warum sind die Demokratien (noch immer) nicht friedlich?' ['Kant's Theory. Or: Why are Democracies (still) not Peaceful?']. *Zeitschrift für Internationale Beziehungen* [*Journal of International Relations*] 1996 no. 1 (1996): 79–101.
Dahl, Robert. *Polyarchy: Participation and Opposition.* New Haven, CT: Yale University Press, 1971.
Desch, Michael C. 'America's Liberal Illiberalism. The Ideological Origins of Overreaction in U.S. Foreign Policy'. *International Security* 32, no. 3 (2007/08): 7–43.

Diamond, Larry, and Ehud Sprinzak. 'Israeli Democracy Under Stress'. In *Israeli Democracy Under Stress*, ed. Ehud Sprinzak, 1–12. Boulder, CO: Rienner, 1993.
Dowty, Alan. 'Is Israel Democratic? Substance and Semantics in the "Ethnic Democracy" Debate'. *Israel Studies* 4, no. 2 (1999): 1–15.
Dowty, Alan. *The Jewish State. A Century Later*. Berkeley: University of California Press, 1998.
Doyle, Michael W. 'Kant, Liberal Legacies and Foreign Affairs'. In *Debating the Democratic Peace*, ed. Michael E. Brown, 3–57. Cambridge, MA: MIT Press, 2001.
Eisenstadt, S.N. 'Fundamentalism, Phenomenology, and Comparative Dimensions'. In *Fundamentalisms Comprehended*, ed. Martin Marty E., Scott R. Appleby, 259–76. Chicago, IL: The University of Chicago Press, 1995.
Eisenstadt, Shmuel N. *Die Transformation der israelischen Gesellschaft* [*The Transformation of Israeli Society*]. Frankfurt: Suhrkamp, 1992.
Elazar, Daniel J., and Shmuel Sandler. 'Introduction: The Battle over Jewishness and Zionism in the Post-Modern Era'. In *Israel at the Polls, 1996*, ed. Daniel J. Elazar and Shmuel Sandler, 1–32. London: Frank Cass, 1998.
Fendius Elman, Miriam, ed. *Paths to Peace: Is Democracy the Answer?*, Cambridge, MA: MIT Press, 1997.
Fox, Jonathan, and Jonathan Rynhold. 'A Jewish and Democratic State? Comparing Government Involvement in Religion in Israel with other Democracies'. *Totalitarian Movements and Political Religions* 9, no. 4 (2008): 507–31.
Freedman, Lawrence. 'The Age of Liberal Wars'. In *Force and Legitimacy in World Politics*, ed. David Armstrong, Theo Farrell, and Bice Maiguashca, 93–107. Cambridge: Cambridge University Press, 2005.
Freedom House. *Freedom in the world 2009*. www.freedomhouse.org/template.cfm?page=22&year=2009 (accessed September 30, 2009).
Gavison, Ruth. 'Jewish and Democratic? A Rejoinder to the "Ethnic Democracy" Debate'. *Israel Studies* 4, no. 1 (1999): 44–72.
Geis, Anna. 'Diagnose: Doppelbefund, Ursache: ungeklärt?' ['Diagnosis: Separate Peace, Cause: Unknown?']. *Politische Vierteljahresschrift* [*Political Quarterly*] 42 (2001): 282–98.
Geis, Anna, Lothar Brock, and Harald Müller. "Demokratische Kriege als Antinomien des Demokratischen Friedens: Eine Komplementäre Forschungsagenda' ['Democratic Wars as Antinomies of Democratic Peace: A Complimentary Research Agenda']'. In *Schattenseiten des Demokratischen Friedens. Zur Kritik einer Theorie liberaler Außen- und Sicherheitspolitik* [*Dark Sides of Democratic Peace. Critique of a Theory of Liberal Foreign and Security Policy*], ed. Anna Geis, Lothar Brock, and Harald Müller, 69–92. Frankfurt, New York: Campus, 2007.
Gleditsch, Kristian S., and Michael D. Ward. 'War and Peace in Space and Time: The Role of Democratization'. *International Studies Quarterly* 44 (2000): 1–29.
Goldberg, Giora. 'The Electoral Fall of the Israeli Left'. In *Israel at the Polls, 1996*, ed. Daniel J. Elazar and Shmuel Sandler, 53–72. London: Frank Cass, 1998.
Gruenwald, Ithamar. 'Mysticism and Politics in the State of Israel'. In *Religion and the Political Order. Politics in Classical and Contemporary Christianity, Islam, and Judaism*, ed. Jacob Neusner, 95–108. Saint Louis, MO: Scholars Press, 1996.
Haklai, Oded. 'Religious-Nationalist Mobilization and State Penetration'. *Comparative Political Studies* 40, no. 6 (2007): 713–39.
Hammami, Rema, and Salim Tamari. 'The Second Uprising: End or New Beginning?'. *Journal of Palestine Studies* 15, no. 2 (2001): 5–25.
Hasenclever, Andreas, and Alexander De Juan. 'Grasping the Impact of Religious Traditions on Political Conflicts: Empirical Findings and Theoretical Perspectives'. *Die Friedens-Warte* 82, no. 2/3 (2007): 19–47.

Hasenclever, Andreas, and Volker Rittberger. 'Does Religion Make a Difference? Theoretical Approaches to the Impact of Faith on Political Conflict'. In *Religion in International Relations: The Return from Exile*, ed. Pavlos Hatzopoulos and Fabio Petito, 107–47. New York: Palgrave Macmillan, 2003.

Hasenclever, Andreas, and Wolfgang Wagner. 'From the Analysis of a Separate Democratic Peace to the Liberal Study of International Conflict'. *International Politics* 41, no. 4 (2004): 465–71.

Hertzberg, Arthur. *The Zionist Idea. A Historical Analysis and Reader.* Philadelphia, Jerusalem: The Jewish Publication Society, 1997.

Horowitz, Dan, and Moshe Lissak. *Trouble in Utopia. The Overburdened Polity of Israel.* Albany: State University of New York Press, 1989.

Ish-Shalom, Piki. 'Theory as a Hermeneutical Mechanism: The Democratic-Peace Thesis and the Politics of Democratization'. *European Journal of International Relations* 12, no. 4 (2006): 565–98.

Jamal, Amal. 'The Counter-Hegemonic Role of Civil Society: Palestinian-Arab NGOs in Israel'. *Citizenship Studies* 12, no. 3 (2008): 283–306.

Juergensmeyer, Mark. *The New Cold War? Religious Nationalism Confronts the Secular State.* Berkeley: University of California Press, 1993.

Laustsen, Carsten Bagge, and Ole Waever. 'In Defense of Religion: Sacred Referent Objects for Securitization'. In *Religion in International Relations: The Return from Exile*, ed. Pavlos Hatzopoulos and Fabio Petito, 147–80. New York: Palgrave Macmillan, 2003.

Lein, Yehezkel, and Eyal Weizman. *Land Grab. Israel's Settlement Policy in the West Bank.* B'Tselem: The Israeli Information Center for Human Rights in the Occupied Territories, 2002.

Levy, Jack. 'War and Peace'. In *Handbook of International Relations*, ed. Walter Carlsnaes, Thomas Risse, and Beth A. Simmons, 350–68. London: Sage, 2002.

Lijphart, Arend. 'Israeli Democracy and Democratic Reform in Comparative Perspective'. In *Israeli Democracy Under Stress*, ed. Ehud Sprinzak, 107–23. Boulder, CO: Rienner, 1993.

MacMillan, John. 'Beyond the Separate Democratic Peace'. *Journal of Peace Research* 40, no. 2 (2003): 233–43.

Mann, Michael. *The Dark Side of Democracy. Explaining Ethnic Cleansing.* Cambridge: Cambridge University Press, 2005.

Mansfield, Edward D., and Jack L. Snyder. *Electing to Fight. Why Emerging Democracies go to War.* Cambridge, MA: MIT Press, 2005.

Maoz, Asher. 'Religious Education in Israel'. *Tel Aviv University Legal Working Paper Series* no. 44 (2007).

Maoz, Zeev, and Bruce Russett. 'Normative and Structural Causes of Democratic Peace, 1946–1986'. *American Political Science Review* 87, no. 3 (1993): 624–38.

Marshall, Monty G., and Keith Jaggers. 'Polity IV Project. Political Regime Characteristics and Transitions, 1800–2000'. www.cidcm.umd.edu/inscr/polity (accessed March 12, 2005).

McHenry Jr., Dean and Abdel-Fattah Mady. 'A Critique of Quantitative Measures of the Degree of Democracy in Israel'. *Democratization* 13, no. 2 (2006): 256–82.

Merkel, Wolfgang. 'Embedded and Defective Democracies'. *Democratization* 11, no. 5 (2004): 33–58.

Müller, Harald. 'The Antinomy of the Democratic Peace'. *International Politics* 41, no. 4 (2004): 494–520.

Müller, Harald. 'Kants Schurkenstaat: Der "ungerechte Feind" und die Selbstermächtigung zum Kriege' ['Kant's Rogue State: The "Unjust Enemy" and the Self-Entitlement to War']. In *Den Krieg überdenken. Kriegsbegriffe und Kriegstheorien in der*

Kontroverse [*War Revisited. Debating Concepts and Theories of War*], ed. Anna Geis, 229–49. Baden-Baden: Nomos Verlagsgesellschaft, 2006.
Müller, Harald, and Jonas Wolff. 'Democratic Peace: Many Data, Little Explanation?'. In *Democratic Wars. Looking at the Dark Side of Democratic Peace*, ed. Anna Geis, Lothar Brock, and Harald Müller, 41–73. New York: Palgrave Macmillan, 2006.
Netanyahu, Benjamin. 'Prime Minister Netanyahu, Address to the Likud Central Committee, Tel Aviv, 5 September 1996 (Excerpts)'. *Journal of Palestine Studies* 26, no. 2 (1996): 162–4.
Netanyahu, Benjamin. 'Speech by Prime Minister Benjamin Netanyahu on the Presentation of the Government to the Knesset, June 18, 1996'. www.mfa.gov.il/MFA (accessed January 12, 2007).
Neuberger, Benyamin. 'Israel – A Liberal Democracy With Four Flaws'. In *The State of Israel: Between Judaism and Democracy*, ed. Joseph E. David, 361–70. Jerusalem: The Israel Democracy Institute, 2002.
Newman, David. 'From Hitnachalut to Hitnatkut. The Impact of Gush Emunim and the Settlement Movement on Israeli Politics and Society'. *Israel Studies* 10, no. 3 (2005): 192–224.
Nodia, Ghia. 'Nationalism and Democracy'. In *Nationalism, Ethnic Conflict, and Democracy*, ed. Larry Diamond and Marc F. Plattner, 3–22. Baltimore, MD: The Johns Hopkins University Press, 1994.
Pappé, Ilan. 'Israel at a Crossroads Between Civic Democracy and Jewish Zealotocracy'. *Journal of Palestine Studies* XXIX, no. 3 (2000): 33–44.
Parsons, Nigel. *The Politics of the Palestinian Authority. From Oslo to al-Aqsa*. Boston, MA: Routledge, 2005.
Pedahzur, Ami. 'The Downfall of the National Camp?'. In *Israel at the Polls, 1999*, ed. Daniel J. Elazar and Ben M. Mollov, 37–54. London: Frank Cass, 2001.
Philpott, Daniel. 'Explaining the Political Ambivalence of Religion'. *American Political Science Review* 101, no. 3 (2007): 505–25.
Pressman, Jeremy. 'Visions in Collision'. *International Security* 28, no. 2 (2003): 5–43.
Rabin, Jitzhak. 'Statement in the Knesset by Prime Minister Rabin on the Israel-PLO Declaration of Principles, 21 September 1993'. http://www.mfa.gov.il/MFA (accessed January 12, 2007).
Ravitzky, Aviezer. *Messianism, Zionism, and Jewish Religious Radicalism*. Chicago, IL: University of Chicago Press, 1996.
Ray, James Lee. 'The Democratic Path to Peace'. *Journal of Democracy* 8, no. 2 (1997): 49–64.
Rekhess, Elie. 'The Arabs of Israel After Oslo: Localization of the National Struggle'. *Israel Studies* 7, no. 3 (2002): 1–44.
Rueschemeyer, Dietrich, Evelyne Huber Stephens, and John D. Stephens. *Capitalist Development & Democracy*. Tokyo: University of Chicago Press, 1992.
Russett, Bruce. *Grasping the Democratic Peace: Principles for a Post-Cold War World*. Princeton, NJ: Princeton University Press, 1993.
Russett, Bruce, and John Oneal. *Triangulating Peace. Democracy, Interdependence, and International Organizations*. New York: W.W. Norton & Company, 2001.
Salmon, Yosef. *Religion and Zionism. First Encounters*. Jerusalem: Hebrew University Magnes Press, 2002.
Sandler, Shmuel. *The State of Israel, the Land of Israel. The Statist and Ethnonational Dimensions of Foreign Policy*. Westport: Greenwood Press, 1993.
Sason, Talya. *Summary of the Opinion Concerning Unauthorized Outposts*. Jerusalem: The Government of the State of Israel, The Prime Minister's Office, 2005.
Shafir, Gershon, and Yoav Peled. 'Citizenship and Stratification in an Ethnic Democracy'. *Ethnic and Racial Studies* 21, no. 3 (1998): 408–27.

Shamir, Michal, and Asher Arian. 'Collective Identity and Electoral Competition in Israel'. *American Political Science Review* 93, no. 2 (1999): 265–77.

Sheffer, Gabriel. 'Political Change and Party System Transformation'. In *Parties, Elections, and Cleavages. Israel in Comparative and Theoretical Perspective*, ed. Reuven Y. Hazan and Moshe Maor, 148–71. London: Frank Cass, 2000.

Smooha, Sammy. 'Ethnic Democracy: Israel as an Archetype'. *Israel Studies* 2, no. 2 (1997): 198–241.

Smooha, Sammy. 'The Model of Ethnic Democracy: Israel as a Jewish and Democratic State'. *Nations and Nationalism* 8, no. 4 (2002): 475–503.

Sprinzak, Ehud. 'The Iceberg Model of Political Extremism'. In *The Impact of Gush Emunim. Politics and Settlement in the West Bank*, ed. David Newman, 27–45. Bockenham, Sydney: Croom Held Ltd, 1985.

Stepan, Alfred. 'Religion, Democracy, and the "Twin Tolerations"'. *Journal of Democracy* 11, no. 4 (2000): 37–57.

Ward, Michal D., and Kristian S. Gleditsch. 'Democratizing for Peace'. *American Political Science Review* 92, no. 1 (March 1998): 51–61.

Yiftachel, Oren. *Ethnocracy. Land and Identity Politics in Israel/Palestine*. Philadelphia: University of Pennsylvania Press, 2006.

Zertal, Idith, and Akiva Eldar. *Lords of the Land. The War Over Israel's Settlements in the Occupied Territories, 1967–2007*. New York: Nation Books, 2007.

Zuckermann, Moshe. 'State and Religion: An Aporetic Relationship in Zionism'. In *Politik und Religion im Judentum [Politics and Religion in Judaism]*, ed. Christoph Miething, 199–208. Tübingen: Niemeyer, 1999.

Democratizing state–religion relations: a comparative study of Turkey, Egypt and Israel

Amal Jamal

Tel Aviv University, Israel

This article examines the complex relationship between state, religion and democratization in Turkey, Egypt and Israel. It demonstrates that binary and static models of separation and integration between state and religion are not sufficient to understanding the complex relationship between them and chances of democratization. Based on examining the democratization processes in the three Middle Eastern countries, the article argues that separation or integration between state and religion, although different, does not precondition democratic transformation and democratization. It is the form, the measure and the direction of separation or integration that makes the difference. The article demonstrates that democratization is not a one dimensional linear model, but rather can take two opposing directions when it comes to religion and state relations. Whereas in some cases the public return of religion and the subsequent representation of religious groups reflect democratization, in other cases, where state and religion are tightly integrated, democratization means the decoupling of state and religion and the downgrading of religious control of public institutions and individual personal status. Moreover, the examination of the three Middle Eastern countries demonstrates that democratization could involve the return of religion to the public sphere, as part of the basic democratic right of social groups to be represented and their right to participate in determining their cultural and ideological environment. It could also involve the deinstitutionalization of religion as exclusive authority and identity in the public sphere and in the private life of individuals. Based on such understanding the article claims that dynamic models of state–religion relations are necessary in order to anticipate the chances of democratization and consolidation.

The generalization that religion and democracy are incompatible and that religiosity is antagonistic to democratization is problematic. Religiosity as such is not necessarily undemocratic. This is true as long as religion is a popular social belief and a component of societal culture, submissive to the freedom of choice. Religion and religiosity are sociological constructs before being theological and spiritual identity. The social construction of religious identity is a dynamic process in which the state plays an important role. This role is central to understanding the chances of democratization. State–religion relations become a serious challenge to democratic authority and regimes when religious belief is either institutionalized by state structures as exclusive authority in personal affairs or on the other hand suppressed by the state.

The separation or the integration between state and religion, although different, does not precondition democratic transformation and democratization. It is the form and the measure of separation or integration that makes the difference. Democratization could involve the return of religion to the public sphere, as part of the basic democratic right of social groups to be represented and their right to participate in determining their cultural and ideological environment. It could also involve the deinstitutionalization of religion as exclusive authority and identity in the public sphere and in the private life of individuals. When it comes to state–religion relations, democratization is a process that aims at an end result, namely the ability of people to practise their beliefs and have them fairly represented in the public sphere, without demanding exclusive control of public institutions.

This article argues that when it comes to issues of religion and state, then democratization can take two opposing directions. Whereas in some cases the public return of religion and the subsequent representation of religious groups reflect democratization, in other cases, where state and religion are tightly integrated, democratization means the decoupling of state and religion and the downgrading of religious control of public institutions and individual personal status. To pursue this argument, this paper examines state–religion relations in three Middle Eastern states, namely Turkey, Egypt and Israel.

These cases were chosen for three main reasons. The first is to demonstrate that the policy of suppression of religion from the public sphere by the state as in Turkey or the policy of formally institutionalized religion as in Israel and Egypt do not necessarily facilitate democratization, despite the fact that they do not undermine the fundamental principles of equal citizenship. The second reason is that these cases demonstrate that democratization could take two opposite directions when it comes to state–religion relations. The Turkish case demonstrates that in that country democratization implies the downgrading in importance of laicism (see Grigoriadias's article in this special issue),[1] especially allowing religious parties to run for elections or respecting provision of religious education outside state control. In Israel, democratization implies the decoupling of state and religious identity and the equalization of different religious streams and faiths. In Egypt, decoupling of state and religion may *facilitate* democratization, although such a change has not been sufficient to democratize the whole political regime. Thirdly, religion in Middle Eastern countries, even when considered procedurally democratic, as in Israel (see Baumgart-Ochse's article in this special issue),[2] nevertheless can form a major challenge to democratic equality and justice. Fourthly, examining the Egyptian and Turkish cases provides evidence that different Islamic countries can develop different trajectories of state–religion relations.[3]

This article also argues that the relationship between state, religion and democratization should be viewed in dynamic rather than static terms. Democratization is a non-unitary and contingent political process as well as a context-dependent variable that may include various and sometimes even contradictory processes. In some cases, the de-institutionalization of religion as exclusive authority over the spiritual and personal life of individuals facilitates freedom of religion and from religion, thereby representing democratization. This is true as long as the decoupling of state and religion does not lead to dismantling of religious rights, such as the case in France (see Barras's article in this special issue).[4] However, sometimes the return of religion to the public sphere, the access of religious groups and integration of religious values into the public sphere and freedom of conscience, and expanding the realm of social and cultural pluralism in the public sphere together represent a democratization process. In addition, if the political system is to become or remain democratic, then the return of religion to the public sphere and the onset of a representative political system should not lead to exclusive domination of political authority by religious groups nor infringe on individuals' basic rights of choice, especially freedom of religion and from religion.

The politicization of religious belief as the major or sole source of social and political authority based on the divinity of the faith could become a major hurdle for democratization, undermining two major principles of democratic power structures. These are, first, limited power, that makes political authority submissive to the rule of law and, secondly, transitive power that makes political power submissive to change according to the will of the people.[5] Nonetheless, religiosity does not have to be secularized, privatized or suppressed in order to be compatible with democratic forms of government. Ensuring that religious belief does not translate into the state blocking freedom of conscience or dismissing public reasoning and deliberation is theoretically sufficient for the reconciliation of state and religion in one democratic regime.[6]

The direction of the democratic process depends to a significant degree on the extent to which religious affiliation and belief is focused in institutionalized structures, and exclusive or open and plural. The relationship between democratization and religion does not necessarily stem from an essential characteristic of the latter. It is rather related to the dominant forms of its construction and politicization, something that can change with time. One has to differentiate between self-critical, tolerant and pluralistic forms of religious affiliation, where the community of faith is conceived as a wilful community of affiliation subordinated to the freedom of conscience, on the one hand, and intolerant and chauvinist forms of religious affiliation, where the community of faith is conceived in organic and trans-historical terms, on the other. Whereas the first form of religiosity can coexist with democratic forms of government in the public sphere, the other tends to be rigid and identified with absolute forms of public reason and government. One has also to differentiate between popular religion – that is, forms of religion not controlled by institutional structures and where individuals have complete freedom of choice and the state neither endorses nor suppresses religion – and forms of state religion where freedom of and from religion is suppressed to variable degrees. The examination of the three cases focuses on the nature of the dynamics of state–religion relations in the last few decades and the form and pattern of democratization in each country. Comparisons between them will enable us to draw both empirical and theoretical conclusions that may help us understand chances of democratization in the Middle East region more widely.

Institutionalizing popular religion and democratization

The enduring role of religion and its place in the daily life of different societies make it necessary to escape judgmental assertions and look for analytical tools that help in understanding its impact on the chances of democratization. On the one hand, dismissing the political importance of religiosity or adopting dichotomous models that view democracy and religion as two antagonistic world views and authority systems is reductive.[7] On the other hand, adopting one hegemonic state religion is counter-democratic not only in pluralistic and multi-religious societies, but also in homogenous religious ones. In many democracies, such as the United States, the United Kingdom, Germany, Sweden, Denmark and others, religion and religious institutions still play major roles without clashing with democratic freedoms.[8] As some Orthodox Christian and Islamic states have demonstrated, including, Greece and Indonesia, no religion has proved itself to be absolutely immune to democracy and the changes that it brings.[9] In addition, processes of democratization have taken place in many states where religion has a central influence and role in the public sphere. In some such countries, 'illiberal democracy' has developed. Indonesia is sometimes given as an example in this regard.[10]

Based on these understandings and changes in various countries of the world, it is more than appropriate to follow Stepan's claim that it is the institutional analysis of democratization, rather than the essentialist cultural paradigm[11] that is more adequate to analyse and understand the place and role that religion can play in democratization process.[12] As long as religious or other groups do not use violence, do not violate the rights of other citizens, and stay within the rules of the democratic game, normatively they should be granted the right to advance their interests, both in civil and political society. On the other hand, social groups should be constitutionally prohibited from utilizing state institutions to determine the hegemonic public good, belief system and personal status of citizens. Religiosity may clash with the liberal worldview, but as long as it is a matter of free choice, it does not contradict democracy.

Stepan's 'twin tolerations' and differentiation have become very central concepts in any treatment of the place of religion in democratic political structure.

Stepan has made clear that civilizational or cultural analysis of the relationship between democracy and religion lead to essentialization and inaccurate generalizations that do not help in understanding the complexities of this relationship and the hurdles of democratization.[13] Any generalization, claiming that there is incompatibility between certain religions and democracy, is not only inaccurate, but also not historical and therefore, does not help in our understanding of the circumstances and conditions in which democracy can develop and flourish.[14] Historical evidence demonstrates that there is nothing deterministic about a religion's relationship to democracy.[15] This view should not be understood as underestimating the challenges that religion has introduced to democratic politics in many states in the world, even after periods in which some scholars declared 'the end of history'.

Following the above mentioned observations, one could generalize that religion plays an ambivalent role in politics. The influence of religion is not one dimensional and while it can lead to authoritarianism, it can also contribute to tolerance and democratization.[16] In other words, religion as such is not necessarily a democratic or non-democratic factor of political regimes.

Philpott has demonstrated that the relationship between religious and political authority depends on two major factors; namely differentiation and political theology.[17] Whereas the first describes how religious and political authority are related, the second deals with the shared ideas about legitimate political authority contained in religious bodies. Philpott claims that the interaction between these two factors explains whether religion would support democratization or political violence. Based on this interaction, he speaks of four models of relationship between religious and political authority. The first model is conflictual integrationism, where a regime with an integrationist political theology suppresses religion, denying the autonomy and political participation of religious institutions. The second model is consensual integrationism, where the institutional authority of religion and state is intertwined. The third model is conflictual differentiation, where religion and the state contest for political authority. The fourth model is consensual differentiation, where religious freedom is guaranteed and religious institutions are free to participate in the political game and promote their views.[18]

Philpott's four models are helpful in pinpointing the variety of relationships between state and religion, something that is manifested in different states. They highlight the various forms of separation and collaboration between political and religious authorities and shed light on their institutional manifestations. However, when examining religious and political authority relations or the differentiation between state and religion, one has to remain attuned to the empirical fact that neither state nor religion should be treated as unitary and homogenous actors. As has been demonstrated by scholars of the modern state, it is far more than one dimensional.[19] On the other hand, religion cannot also be treated as a homogenous set of beliefs and practices. It is important to pay attention to the institutional differentiation between various religious streams within the same faith as well as the differences between various groups of faith in the same state. Recent developments in the Islamic world demonstrate the gap that can develop between 'moderate' and 'radical' interpretations of religion and its role in society and state.[20] Notwithstanding, Philpott's analysis is of great importance in helping us to examine the complexity of state–religion relations from a standpoint that pays attention to the internal differentiations within each of these categories. Furthermore, it is crucial to view state–religion relations as a dynamic process that could change from conflictual to reconciliatory and vice versa rather than in rigid and inflexible categories. The three cases of this study demonstrate the major changes that can take place over time between state and religion. Moreover, different state organs can develop different relationships with various religious groups within a state. Thus, the dynamic, multiple and changing characters of state and religion and the numerous models of interaction between them together demand cautious and thoughtful analysis.

In this regard, one has to pay attention to the differences between institutionalized religion, which intends that religion should play a prominent, *institutionalized* role in the public sphere and in the state, and popular religion, which refers to the basic beliefs of people that are manifested in their daily life, beliefs that are not institutionalized in the same way. Institutionalized religion either takes or aspires to take a formal form and can play either a political instrument in the hands of political regimes to promote state authority, such as the case in Egypt, or a legitimate competitor over state authority, such as the case in Israel. Popular religion is usually an informal belief system that may not have aspirations to political power but nevertheless forms a very basic trait of people's identity that demands respect and representation in the political culture of the state. The politicization of popular religion, as we shall see in our case studies, may turn 'innocent' belief systems into an essential identity trait and establish new differentiations between various citizens based on their primordial affiliation, based on their citizenship status, such as the differentiations between Muslims and Coptic Christians in Egypt or Jews and Muslims, Christians and Druzes in Israel. The politicization of religious belief and its institutionalization in state identity, as two of the cases analysed here demonstrate, can lead not only to compromising individual autonomy vis-à-vis community, but also to the exclusion of religious minorities from equal access to state identity and resources, thereby undermining one of the basic principles of democratic regime, namely freedom of conscience and equality.

Based on such understanding, one can differentiate between four different models of state–religion dynamics that are closely related to Philpott's models, but focus more on the transitive nature of state–religion relations. The first model is found in cases where the state has an institutionalized religion, yet is tolerant of other religious groups, as well as non-religious ones. The second model is in cases where the state has an intolerant and exclusivist state religion, where religious minorities or non-religious groups are excluded from state power or discriminated against. Conceiving these two models in dynamic terms has to be cognizant of shifts from the second model to the first and vice versa. Shifts from the second to the first model, reflect democratization processes that may end up with plural and tolerant political cultures, an important characteristic of some modern democracies. Shifts from the first to the second reflect the decay of democracy. The third model is when the state has no institutionalized religion but is sensitive to religious beliefs and tolerant of religious manifestations in the public sphere, including organized democratic religious parties. The fourth model encompasses states that do not have an institutionalized religion and are intolerant or even repressive and disrespectful towards manifestations of religious belief in the public sphere. The democratization process between these two models is when a shift starts taking place from the fourth towards the third, where the state respects religious belief and even participation in the political system, while guaranteeing not sliding toward the second model. In order to demonstrate the dynamics of such shifts, we turn now to three different Middle Eastern states, in which state–religion relations are undergoing dynamic changes that may elaborate the centrality of the dynamic nature of state–religions relations and its contribution to the chances of democratization.

Turkey

Turkey is well known for its efforts to suppress religion and religiosity from the public sphere and establish a rigid separation between state affairs and religious affairs, without giving up its control of religious institutions and education. Following the decline of the Ottoman Empire after World War I, modern Turkey was instituted from the start as a secular state, in which religion was separated from politics, yet simultaneously controlled by the state. The state was constructed according to the French model, where the republic was instituted in modern secular terms based on citizenship (see both Grigoriadis' and Gozaydin's articles in this special issue).[21] However, whereas in France religion was privatized, the Kemalist state did not leave religion in the free hands of social actors.[22] It invested vast amounts of resources in socialization, seeking to control religious education and practices.

The state established a Directorate of Religious Affairs in order to keep under its control the basic religious services of the population.[23] The state sought objective secularization by separating state from religion on the formal and constitutional level. On the other hand, the state suppressed religion on the societal level and controlled religious socialization, seeking subjective secularization of society. As Keyman puts it: 'If we employ Michel Foucault's concept of governmentality, secularism [was] used by the state as an "effective technology of the government of the self" by creating a boundary between the public sphere and the private sphere, in which religious claims to identity are confined as private, individualistic and particular'.[24]

The Turkish state has claimed that it sought the dissemination of secular reason and the imposition of scientific rationality in its traditional, 'backward' Islamic society, in an attempt speedily to transform and modernize society. However, this claim did not square with reality. The state took upon itself a top-down engineering project that aimed to lift society from its religiosity, which was conceived to be the main factor of its backwardness. The goal was a secular state, equated with western civilization and modernity.[25] For Serif Mardin, the transformation of Turkish society involved 'several changes, including: (1) transition of the political system from the authority of personal rule to impersonal rules and regulations; (2) shift in understanding the order of the universe from divine law to positivist and rational thinking; (3) change from a community founded upon the "elite-people cleavage" to a "populist-based community"; and (4) a move from a religion-based community to a secular nation-state.'[26]

These major institutional and cultural changes were undertaken by the state as perceived indispensable steps in processes of modernization and subjective secularization of society. In order to guarantee this result the state took absolute institutional and constitutional control of religious affairs. It sought official disestablishment of religion from the state, while keeping the constitutional control of religious affairs, aiming at the dissemination of a particular type of Turkish identity in society.

However, as has been demonstrated by Casanova, Onis, Yilmaz, Keyman, Kadioglu and others, state efforts to suppress religion leading to subjective secularization did not succeed, and the 1980s and 1990s were marked by the resurgence of Islamist parties.[27] The efforts made by the Kemalist state to impose rigid solutions for complex cultural and political problems did not succeed. As Keyman puts it: 'The Turkish state did not aim to act "impartially" towards different Muslim and non-Muslim religious communities. Instead its main aim was to control and regulate religious activities through constitutional and institutional means, in order to establish a strict separation between the state and religion.'[28] In this context, claims Casanova, 'ultimately the project of constructing such a (secular) nation-state from above is likely to fail because it is too secular for the Islamists, too Sunni for the Alevis and too Turkish for the Kurds'.[29] He adds that 'a Turkish state in which the collective identities and interests of these groups cannot find public representation cannot be truly representative democratic state, even if it is founded on modern secular constitutional principles'.[30]

The imposition of laicist identity formation has been a clear marker of the authoritarianism of the Turkish state since the early twentieth century. Therefore, it was the resurgence of religion as a potent political force manifested in the rise of the Welfare Party and later the Justice and Development Party (AKP), which entered the democratic political game in the early 2000s, that reflected developing democratization in Turkey. These parties, which represented widening and emerging commercial and new middle class segments of society, also reflected the public resurgence of Islam.[31] In addition, they claimed to represent a new cultural Turkish identity that sought to combine authentic cultural and religious identity and modernism.

As Nilufer Gole puts it, the new Muslim subject in Turkey seeks not a total submission to modernism, as the secular elite of the state sought, but rather a merger of modernity with Islamic values.[32] Yilmaz, following Gole, asserts the difference between political Islam of the 1980s and the 1990s. In his view, in the 1980s, 'the adherents of political Islam set for themselves the task of Islamic revolution' by 'conquering the state apparatus and transforming the society in line with the precepts of Islam'.[33] In this regard, claims Yilmaz, 'the Islamist revolutionaries of the 1980s were no different from the socialist revolutionaries of the 1970s'.[34] In his view, the Muslim individual of the 1990s did not submit to oppressive tendencies embedded in imposing collective communal religious identity. Instead, Islamists sought a constructive combination between private life and the collective public sphere. This new religious identity was at the centre of the AKP's political programme in the 2000s, which sought to integrate modern Islamic identity into the public sphere, despite the secularist elite's continued, intense suspicion. As a result, the AKP unexpectedly and purposefully sought to liberalize rather than Islamize. The liberalization of the state opened new avenues for ideological and political pluralism, where minorities – religious and national – had growing access to the public sphere. It legitimated the existence of religious parties in the political system and the freedom of consciousness when this freedom meant adherence to religious beliefs and practices. The liberalization policies promoted by the AKP can so far be viewed in pragmatic terms that seek to expand its space for manoeuvre in Turkey's political system.

This trend in Turkish politics seems to reflect the rise of popular religion and its integration in the electoral political game, seeking representation in state authority, without demanding its institutionalization. This process takes place while emphasizing the search for new formulas that may lead to integrating Turkey into the European Union, based on the Helsinki decision of 1999. For that purpose, the AKP, which won a healthy majority in the elections of 2002 and of 2007, is leading a process of democratization, not only in the sense of representing growing segments of Turkish Islamic society, but also by de-nationalizing Turkish citizenship in order to make it inclusive for Turkish-Kurds, who were excluded from Turkish politics by the secular nationalist for decades. Politics represented by the AKP appears to be aimed at empowering citizenship, and active participation and substantial representation of all segments of Turkish society in the state and the public sphere. However, some observers of Turkish politics warn that the AKP's politics seeks to bypass constitutional constraints and aims to utilize democratic politics in order to promote an Islamic religious worldview.[35]

Kadioglu claims in this regard that denationalization refers 'to processes that enable those legal Turkish citizens who are non-Muslims and who are not of Turkish descent to make legitimate claims about their different religious, linguistic, and cultural existence in the public realm within the territorial boundaries of the Turkish state'.[36] In her view the fact that Turkish citizenship has religious (Sunni sect of Islam) and linguistic (Turkish) dimensions, its denationalization legitimates the political and social participation on the part of Greeks, Armenians, Jews, Kurds, Arabs, Alevis, Circassians, Georgians, Lazes, and others. This change in Turkish politics reflects the liberalization process that has characterized Turkey in the last few years, where various national, social and cultural groups can seek to retain and claim their differences without being suppressed by state authorities, as used to be the case.

The combination of the resurgence of a particular type of political Islam and the denationalization of Turkish citizenship seem to feed off each other and promote a new political culture and civic identity that is more inclusive and democratic. Since the new Islamic identity fostered by the AKP is relatively inclusive and open, it seems that deterministic formulas regarding state–religion relations are not able to understand easily the recent political trends taking place in Turkey. As Murat Somer puts it,

> The Turkish experience shows that free and fair elections coupled with a guided democracy and economic development can generate incentives for political Islam to moderate and to adopt democracy. But it also suggests that sustainable moderation by Islam coupled with democratic consolidation may require strong secularist democrats as much as it requires Muslim democrats.[37]

A careful balance between these two main camps – religious and secular – may be necessary to guarantee the consolidation of democracy and block any future radicalization of Islamic forces. Based on experience of democratization in other countries of the world, it seems that the new balance of power between a liberalizing Islamic party, involving increasing economic ties with the European Union, and suspicious secular elites, especially in the army, is a fundamental and necessary condition in the given circumstances of Turkey to guarantee continuous democratization and the rise of consensual differentiation.[38] So far, religious freedom seems to be guaranteed and religious institutions are free to participate in the political game. As long as no attempts are made to re-institutionalize religion, as an official and exclusive set of public values or practices, it seems that the Turkish case demonstrates gradual and cautious transition to democracy.

Egypt

Egypt is constitutionally defined as an Islamic state. Islam is institutionalized as the state religion, controlled by the country's religious institutions. Chapter one, article 2 of the Egyptian constitution declares that 'Islam is the religion of the state and Arabic its official language. Principles of Islamic law (*Shari'a*) are the principal source of legislation.' This article has immediate implications for the civic status of non-Muslims, especially the country's main religious minority, Coptic Christians, who form 5–10% of the Egyptian population, as well as on secular Muslims and on other social groups, especially women, whose rights, it is argued, are negatively affected by *Shari'a* law.[39] Accordingly, religious affiliation is prioritized over civic equality and adherence to religious rules is elevated over principles of civic freedom and equality. The state is heavily involved in maintaining religious belief as the hegemonic social and cultural ideology in society.

The constitutionalization of Islam and making the state responsible for applying *Shari'a* law undermines the basic principles of freedom of religion and freedom from religion. Public institutions have to adhere to religious rules, especially in personal status and family law, despite the fact that Egypt is not a radical *Shari'a* state. The Egyptian state is constitutionally and legally based on Western models, where the state has strong autonomous institutions. The Egyptian government considers the state as democratic, despite the fact that according to long-term Freedom House judgements, it is not.[40] Egypt has a centralized authoritarian regime that is able to maintain social and political stability through establishing institutional balances between various segments of Egyptian society and promoting a traditional national ideology based on a moderate model of political Islam. The religious role of the state is a clear continuation of a strong tradition in Islamic Arab culture, where the state integrates political and social tasks and blurs the differences between the private and the public.[41] The state conceives itself as the agent that is responsible for removing world views and practices from the public sphere that may contradict with what is conceived as acceptable in Islamic *Shari'a* law. To fulfil this task the state does not have to be controlled by religious leaders. It is enough to have an official institution to fulfil this role, namely the Al-Azhar University, directly related to the presidency, considered the highest authority in religious studies in the state.[42] Another orthodox Islamic and state institution, namely the grand Mufti of the republic, determines the religious norms accepted officially and followed by state institutions including the courts. The grand Mufti is a state official and a religious authority, head of Dar al-Ifta',[43] a government agency charged with issuing religious legal opinions on any question to Muslims who ask for them. This state agency plays a major political and judicial role in legitimating and even confirming decisions of the government and the courts in cases that have to do with religious affairs in the broadest sense. In other words, not only does the parliament have its own obligations to religious law, but also its legislation and regulations are scrutinized by an appointed religious authority that has the constitutional right for 'judicial review'.

Simultaneously, oppositional Islamic movements are heavily scrutinized by the government in order to prevent them from challenging the religious status quo and as a consequence the political authority of the hegemonic elite. Although the Muslim Brotherhood Movement (MB) was allowed to participate in the parliamentary elections and even won 88 seats out of 454 in the 2005 elections, the movement does not enjoy much freedom and does not really influence policy making. As Mustafa and Norton claim

> The political elite in Egypt today is restricted to those who are well connected to the bureaucratic-security apparatus. This elite excludes almost all genuine liberals, almost all women, and Coptic Christians (who account for 5 to 10% of the population). Egypt exhibits no more than a superficial multiparty system. Outside the hegemonic National Democratic Party (NDP), the 19 approved political parties are small, docile, and not influential. The regime permits them to play no more than cosmetic role.[44]

Elections for the parliament and for the presidency fulfil the requirement, Steven Heydemann claims, of 'upgrading authoritarianism'.[45] Elections are heavily dominated by the president and the hegemonic National Democratic Party (NDP) ruling party which has an absolute majority in the parliament. As a result, elections are largely symbolic. The constitutional revisions that were introduced in May 2005 and permitted contested elections are very restrictive and may lead oppositional forces to give up participation in the next elections.[46] The Egyptian parliament has recently been engaged in amending its own laws in order to ensure that there is the appearance of real competition for power.[47] But competition is not real and does not have serious impact on the matrix of power. Since meaningful democratization might well lead to the taking over of the state by the MB movement, which has a different view of state–religion relations, then the regime remains preoccupied with detaining its rivals for political power. As a result, it seeks to block Islamic candidates from winning seats in the parliament. If democratization means Islamization, then the ruling elite has to provide a counter-discourse to the radical Islamic groups that have managed to penetrate wide segments of Egyptian society. The incremental Islamization of the Egyptian society in the past three decades, manifested in the rising influence of Islamic forces in social and cultural affairs, has led to serious tension between the hegemonic authoritarian elite and the oppositional liberal elite which demands genuine democratization, but finds itself aligned with the former in trying to prevent radical Islamization of Egyptian society.[48] The ruling elite has exploited the rise of Islamic forces to curb any democratization and maintain a tight grip on the electoral system, as the parliamentary elections in the recent two decades demonstrate.[49] The fear of the rising power of the MB has led to opening the way for secular forces to enter the political scene, which in turn eased the critique on the authoritarian regime.[50] The common interests of the ruling and liberal elites reflect the deep crisis in the latter and the schizophrenic position it has to take in the given conditions and more crucially the complexity of the relationship between state and religion, on the one hand, and democratization, on the other.

This complexity is also reflected in the question of why the MB participates in elections, despite the fact that they are only symbolic. It is hard to give a definite answer to this question. However, one is able to speak about a dual strategy of the Islamic movement in Egypt. The MB movement has long been active on the social level, seeking Islamization through popular education. The movement is also active in civil society, seeking to establish networks of social and political connections that answer basic social and economic needs and encourage political loyalty or at least commitment to the state.[51]

The other strategy of the movement is to participate in the electoral game as a tactic of self-defence. Hamzawi and Brown claim that the participation of the MB movement in elections come 'to protect [them] from the authoritarian impulses of ruling elites'.[52] In their view, 'The Brotherhood's foothold in the formal political system was among its best tools for self-defense: It could rely on the few privileges that its legislators enjoy to reduce the effects of the official restraints that the state was placing upon it.'[53]

When it comes to the commitment of Islamic movements to democratic power structures, scholars tend to agree that these movements, especially in the case of the MB, are somewhat ambivalent. Bahgat Korany emphasizes the rise of moderate Islamist thinking in the last decades that diverts from radical conservative reading of Islam. He claims that

> [t]wo basic points should be reiterated from this cursory analysis of some of the basic readings of neo-Islamists. First, the relationship between Islam and democracy is not one of mutual exclusiveness but rather of adaptation and accommodation because at the level of basic principles of tolerance and respect for freedom of choice they do converge. Second, Islam does impose limits beyond which accommodation and adaptation cannot go: respect for the basic pillars of religion and obedience to *Shari'a*. It is the function of ijtihad and the work of reason to show where accommodation and compromises can or cannot be established.[54]

Nevertheless, Korany agrees with some leading neo-Islamist leaders who are characterized by their conservative Islamist view and still view democracy, political parties and pluralism as western tools of colonization that should be either abolished or reinterpreted under Islamic rule. Haqqani and Fradkin claim that 'Islamism's original conception of a healthy Islamic political life made no room for – indeed rejected – any role for parties of any sort.'[55] Islamist groups present themselves as the precursor of Islamic revival. They claim to represent the essence of Islam and reflect the aspiration of the *umma* (community of believers) for an Islamic state. As Haqqani and Fradkin demonstrate, most Islamist political thinkers reject pluralism, as a foreign idea. When it comes to the state, Haqqani an Fradkin claim that '[t]he Brotherhood and its offshoots ... took a further step by insisting that the state take the lead in applying *Shari'a*, thereby making the political act of establishing an Islamic state central to their ideology'.[56]

The political dynamics between the authoritarian regime, which utilizes institutionalized Islam for its own purposes and the institutionalized oppositional Islamic movements, demonstrate that neither is really committed to democratic power structures.[57] It seems that in contradiction to the Turkish case, Egypt is characterized by a stalemate situation based on an anti-democratic balance of power that renders democratization difficult. As Hamzawi and Brown demonstrate, political tolerance of Islamist participation in the elections on the side of the regime and the participation of Islamist movements in the elections come to promote goals that are beyond their declared goals and even contradictory and do not necessarily promote democracy.[58] The regime seeks to institutionalize Islam in order to curb the power of the radical and even moderate Islamists. It promotes Islamic rulings and facilitates the application of some Islamic *Shari'a* laws in order to compete with the Islamic movement for public legitimacy. On the other hand, Islamic movements use modern state institutions, especially the participation in parliamentary elections, to protect themselves and use the system for their own purposes.[59] Notwithstanding this negative evaluation and despite the fact that these interests, although contradictory, may open a window for a constructive process of mutual trust building, where each of the two parties – the ruling elite and the moderate Islamists, especially the Wasat Party, which is a moderate Islamist party first established in the mid-1990s[60] – will be willing to reach compromises that promote mutual interests.[61] Such compromises could lead to some democratization of the political system and open the way for new forms of power sharing that maintain the grip of the current ruling elite over the democratization process.

The differences that have appeared within the MB movement and the tension between conservatives and moderates that began surfacing in the past decade have led to new instrumental coalitions between Islamists and secular parties.[62] President Mubarak's regime has long suppressed radicals, marginalizing their voice, a policy that aimed to facilitate the rise of the moderates. However, the regime has also been interested in establishing a better relationship with the MB in order to facilitate the transfer of power following Mubarak.[63] Therefore, informal relations were developed between the MB and governmental officials, something that strengthened the collaboration between the authoritarian regime and Islamist forces. This trend has made liberalization even more challenging. Also, as a result of the change of article 76 of the 1971 constitution, elections for the presidency were pluralized and nine candidates competed with Mubarak in the 2005 election, leading to his winning with 88% of the vote.[64]

This situation keeps liberal political forces, such as the New Wafd Party, the Liberal Party and the Progressive Unionist Party, marginal, lacking any serious influence in the public sphere and in decision making circles. The claimed liberalization policies of the regime and the symbolic democratization of the political system are therefore emptied of any meaning. The regime sought some economic and political reforms that aimed to deal with increasingly critical voices and growing levels of dissatisfaction among the middle and lower classes, including low ranking officials of the state.[65] Not only did these reforms not bring any significant changes, they did not in addition contribute to democratization. In this regard Egypt differs from Turkey, where the economic reforms in the last few years have led to relative and widening prosperity and the rise of new middle classes. Poverty in Egypt and the inability of the regime to lead a serious transformation in the economy with an impact on the wellbeing of the average citizens still forms a fruitful ground for radical Islamization that counters moderate trends, manifested in the Wasat Party and its supporters.

The rapprochement between the regime and the neo-Islamists has some negative implications for Coptic Christians and liberal Muslims. The current situation is such that non-Muslims and liberal and secular Muslims face very harsh state policies, as a result of the need of the ruling elite to compete with Islamist movements for the loyalty of the Egyptian population. To that one should add the slowing down of reforms in the family law that were propagated by the feminist movement and received positive attention in the past, such as issues of inheritance, divorce and citizenship status of children.[66]

In conclusion, it seems that despite some agreed shifts in the relationship between the state and religious movements, their relationship is still mainly conflictual. The minor liberalization of the state at the political level has to be balanced with illiberal measures on the religious front in order to strengthen the legitimacy of the regime. The strengthening of authoritarianism has put liberal social forces in a deadlock. The perceived extremism of the Islamic parties, such as the MB, and the fear of their eventual grip over the state and consequently on the legislative and judicial systems, push liberals to adopt a cautious position towards democratization, something welcomed by the ruling elite. This leaves the Islamist parties as the main force pushing for democratization, but suspected by the authoritarian and the liberal elites who seem intent on a gradual upgrading of authoritarianism without significant democratization.

Israel

The relationship between state and religion in Israel is symbiotic. It was explicated by Eliezer Don-Yehiya as a consociational relationship, based on politics of accommodation.[67] It was explained by others as dominated by civil religion agreed on by all Jewish parties in the Israeli state, but excluding Arab citizens.[68] Still others have used Daniel Elazar's idea of covenantalism to highlight the mutual toleration between secularists and religious communities in the Jewish state.[69] All agree that religion is deeply institutionalized in the Israeli state on the symbolic-cultural, institutional, functional and programmatic levels. Israel was established based on the idea of the divine home of the Jewish people. The establishment of the state in the given circumstances was considered by many a 'miracle'. Until today, many parts of Israeli Jewish society still attribute to Israel mythical terms.

The declaration of Israel as a Jewish state in 1948 has undermined the universality and generality of citizenship. Ethno-religious affiliation, rather than civic membership was established as the main principle of citizenship. The exact meaning of Jewishness was purposely not defined. Nonetheless, it was conditioned by the historical bond between biblical religiosity and modern nationalism. The ambiguity and generality of the definition came to avoid direct clashes between the religious establishment and the hegemonic secular elite. This ambiguity led to major tensions and even clashes between the secularized elites, the population and the religious orthodox establishment that still reaches periodic new peaks. The growing secularizing trends that began in the 1980s and the eagerness of orthodox and ultra-orthodox communities to maintain their grip on religious affairs and keep the Israeli state and public sphere loaded with religious meaning led to what has been called a 'culture war'.[70]

In order to understand the roots of this war and grasp its dynamics and impact on democratic values and democratization, one has to look at the implications of the various meanings of Jewishness and the relationship between them. The first meaning of Jewishness that has a clearly negative implication on democratization in Israel is the modern national meaning of Judaism. Zionism has led to the development of a modern Jewish national identity that aspired for self-determination as an independent state, realized with the establishment of the state of Israel in 1948. As Ottolenghi puts it, 'Zionism used tradition as a source of legitimacy for its national claims and could not disentangle its argument for Jewish self determination from religious identity. This apparent contradiction meant that most secular Zionists could not do away with religion, and actually needed it, lest the very justification for their movement's existence be weakened.'[71] Ben Gurion, the 'secular' founding father of the state admired the bible, viewed it as holy historical book and aspired to follow its stories, as if they were historical facts.[72] In the Israeli declaration of independence the bible is mentioned and the prophets of the Jewish people are portrayed as prolific figures to be followed. Despite the fact that Zionism forms a break with religious theology and breaks away from an eschatological vision of Judaism, it remains confined within the Jewish historical narrative.[73]

This national meaning of Jewishness, as ethno-cultural community, has immediate implications for non-Jews in Israel. The first group of non-Jews is the indigenous Arab population, whose status is institutionalized as second class citizens.[74] The second group of non-Jews is those who emigrated to Israel based on the law of return, but who did not meet the official definition of a Jew and therefore had to convert to Judaism, living as second class citizens or even in some cases, deported.[75] The third group of non-Jews is the guest workers, who were imported to Israel, established the country as their home and brought children into the world in Israel. Yet, neither they nor their children can become citizens or permanent residents of the country.[76] All three groups, despite fundamental differences, are influenced by the national meaning of Jewishness and have to live with either a downgraded citizenship or as foreign aliens with no civic status.

The second meaning of Jewishness in the state of Israel is a religious one. In June 1947, Ben Gurion, the founding father of the Israeli state, reached an agreement with the ultra-orthodox Jewish establishment, led by Agudath Israel party, that they would not oppose the establishment of a Jewish state in exchange for a written promise – the status quo document – that the Jewish state would respect the dominant situation of religious affairs that existed in the Jewish community in Palestine before 1948. The letter, sent by the Jewish agency to the ultra-orthodox leadership has conditioned state–religion relations since the inception of the state, despite the changes that took place since.[77]

The letter referred to four different topics of central importance that until today have direct implications on democratic values, such as freedom of movement, personal status, personal autonomy and equality. The first topic is the institutionalization of religious jurisprudence over the personal status and family law. Marriage, divorce, alimony, inheritance, and burial and all related issues, including the definition of who is a Jew that is crucial for the right of immigration, were to be regulated by religious law enacted by rabbinical courts, monitored by the highest religious authority, namely the Rabanut Rashit, which is exclusively controlled by the ultra-orthodox community.

The hegemony of the ultra-orthodox establishment over personal status and family law has had major implications on the status of at least three major Jewish communities. The first group is the secular Jews, who have been forced to follow religious codes and regulations in personal affairs. This means that civil marriage is not legalized and therefore not possible in Israel, also for those who are fully secular and view religious belief as contradictory to their freedom of conscience. As a result, many Jewish citizens, either marry in accordance with traditional rules or leave the country in order to get a civil marriage in a foreign state. This reality, which is still hegemonic in all Jewish communities in Israel, overrules the spirit of liberal democratic laws such as the 1992 Basic Law of Human Dignity and Freedom. This law was declared to have a constitutional status by the Israeli Supreme Court of Justice, but is still suspended when it clashes with laws regulating the personal status and family issues, such as in the case of the judicial rulings of the Law of Rabbinical Courts (Marriage and Divorce) from 1953.[78] Despite the fact that in some cases the Supreme Court issued verdicts declaring the Rabbinical Court subordinate to the civil courts, this decision was specific and limited for certain areas, such as division of property in divorce proceedings.[79] Various efforts were made to bypass liberal decisions of the Supreme Court and establish the exclusive authority of the Rabbinical courts in personal status affairs, the last of which was led by the current Minister of Justice, Yaacov Ne'eman, who is religious himself.[80]

The second community influenced by this first clause of the agreement is the conservative and reform Jewish congregations, which include hundreds of thousands of Jews that have adopted different and more liberal interpretations of the holy book and as a result developed their own religious practices in Israel and abroad. The exclusive recognition of one stream of Judaism has led to major tensions, especially when it comes to the application of the Law of Return that entitles every Jew to emigrate to Israel and become an Israeli citizen. The hegemony of ultra-orthodox Jews over religious affairs, including the population register, makes it difficult for Jews from non-orthodox streams or those newly converted to get an official recognition of their religious practices. In recent decades, especially the 1980s and 1990s, ultra-orthodox religious parties have sought to institutionalize the orthodox conversion to Judaism as the only recognized method acceptable in Israel.[81] Although this attempt did not succeed, it characterized the implications for civic equality of the monopoly of ultra-orthodox Jews over the religious affairs in Israel.[82] Until today, thousands of new immigrants face difficulties getting married, divorced or buried as Jews as a result of not being recognized as 'proper' Jews by the Interior Ministry controlled by ultra-orthodox bureaucrats. Only recently the High Rabbinical Court dismissed thousands of conversions facilitated by state rabbis.[83] Such a decision demonstrates the strong hold that the ultra-orthodox establishment has over state agencies, which leads to the imposition of a very limited interpretation of Jewishness. Arguably, this practice violates basic human rights, especially the freedom of conscience and the liberty to practice family life.[84] Even political parties of secular orientation, such as Kadima and the Likud, have not made serious efforts to promote state-led liberalization of the conversion process, fearing loss of support of religious parties that normally guarantee the stability of any governing coalition.[85]

The third group of Israelis that are directly affected by the first clause of the status quo agreement are women. The ultra-orthodox monopoly on personal status immediately translates into privileges for males in all family affairs. In matters of divorce, inheritance and division of property Jewish orthodoxy favours men over women. Therefore, despite major changes in the last decade, women are still discriminated against in these matters. The establishment of the family civic court in 1995, which specializes in all matters of family law, was able to change positively the status of women in Israeli society. However, in matters of divorce, the rabbinical court maintains a parallel authority.[86] One of the most tragic implications in this regard is what has been called 'misoravot get'[87] – wives whose husbands refuse to divorce them – and 'Agonot' – abandoned wives. Such cases keep women bonded to the men, since religious law does not give women the right to leave a marriage, regardless of its nature. The phenomenon of separation between men and women in some public transportation vehicles is another manifestation of the dominancy of religion in public life.[88]

The second central topic in the status quo document has to do with religious education. Based on this clause, since 1948 the ultra-orthodox educational system has been granted full autonomy from state control. It was not merged with the official educational system, despite the fact that it is fully financed by the state. This situation was even expanded in the last few years. The state finances the educational system of the entire ultra-orthodox community – Ashkenazi and Mizrahi – without having any access to its contents and materials. The attempts to reform this system in 2003 and enforce 'core subjects' in all educational subsystems in Israel did not succeed.[89] The ministry managed to impose its programme on all secular, national-religious and Arab schools, but not on ultra-orthodox schools, thereby deviating from the principle of equality claimed to be the basic value of the entire state-financed educational system. One can add that ultra-orthodox education is based on a very conservative conception of social organization, where patriarchal hierarchy is worshiped and the subordination of women to male dominancy is the rule. When such education is financed by the state one cannot but wonder how can the state claim democratic authority and establish the rule of law in the entire Israeli society, while supporting counter-democratic social groups and granting them authority not only over their life, but also over the personal lives of millions of secular Jews.

The third topic that came up in the status quo document was religious holidays, which became the official holidays of the state, establishing a serious gap between civic and religious affiliation and identification with the state. The state is thereby fully identified with the Jewish community and enacts Jewish cultural and religious customs. One of the major implications of such universality of religious holidays is public services, especially public transportation, which do not function on holidays. In the past decades, secular social groups tried to challenge this situation.

There was a well known attempt to change the decision enforced in August 1982 on the main Israeli airline, El Al that prevented it from flying on Saturdays and Jewish holidays. This attempt was blocked by religious parties and the religious establishment even after the company was privatized in the 1990s.[90] The dominance of religious affairs in the Israeli public sphere is also translated in the enforced shutting down of malls and shopping places on holidays. Although important changes took place in this field in the past two decades, it is still the exception to open shopping places on Saturdays and holidays. In cases, where owners opened despite restrictions, the interior ministry, controlled by religious parties or municipalities in which the religious establishment has power, issues penalty fines, such as in Kfar Saba or Tel Aviv.[91]

The fourth topic of attention in the status quo agreement is that Jewish dietary laws would be enforced in all public government catering. Although this may sound a minor issue, it has become a very central topic in the Israeli public sphere. Two examples are sufficient to illustrate the contradiction of this clause and democratic values. The first has to do with the freedom of persons not to follow religious practices and second, the freedom to sell non-kosher food. Attempts to change these rulings in individual municipalities were blocked by municipally-funded religious councils.[92] The second example has to do with the clash between the Basic Law: Freedom of Occupation, which allows importation of non-kosher meat, and the priority given to Jewish dietary laws in the status quo document. Ultra-orthodox parties, which represent almost 20% of the Israeli population managed to amend the Basic Law: Freedom of Occupation, which has a constitutional status, and submit it to regular legislation in 1994, preventing Israeli companies from importing non-Kosher meat, despite the fact that a high percentage of the Israeli secular population eats non-kosher.

Gideon Levi from *Ha'aretz* daily newspaper summed up this situation on 12 April 2009 saying:

> We must admit that this society has rather dark religious aspects. Foreigners landing in Israel might ask themselves what country they're in: Iran, Afghanistan or Saudi Arabia? In any case, it's not the liberal, secular and enlightened society it purports to be. Thieves' hands do not have to be hacked off or women's faces covered to be a religious country. Just as an occupying state, which controls 3.5 million people lacking basic civil rights, cannot call itself 'the only democracy in the Middle East', so a country that has no bread for a week because of its religion cannot call itself secular and liberal.[93]

Levi admits that Israel has experienced increased political and social openness in recent years. However, he still claims that one should not delude oneself. In his view, almost everything in Israel is religious, from the cradle to the grave, from marriage to divorce. He mentions the fact that until this very day there are streets without buses and tracks without trains on the Sabbath. El Al, the largest Israeli airline sits idle one day a week. He also mentions the fact that various road projects are cancelled or delayed for years because they are planned on ancient burial sites. Levi mentions the increasing phenomenon of separation of men and women in certain buses.[94] In his view, 'religion has never been separate from the state here; hand in hand they oversee our way of life'.[95]

A very important implication of state–religion relations in Israel on democratization has to do with the hegemony of Jewish religion in state affairs and the fact that one fifth of the Israeli citizenry is not Jewish. The Arab community in Israel is composed of three different religious groups that are not related to the Jewish faith. The hegemony of the latter has led to discrimination of the former on symbolic and material levels. The allocation of resources by the state is very influenced by the hegemony of the Jewish religious establishment, leading to institutionalized discrimination against Muslims, Christians and Druzes.[96] Furthermore, the relationship between state and religion in the Jewish society becomes the model adopted for the treatment of the other religious groups, something that leads to violating basic human rights of individual secular members of these communities, such as in cases of civil marriage and divorce procedures.[97]

In contrast to the two other country cases analysed in this article, in Israel the issue of religion has another dimension. Religious parties and movements have been heavily engaged in the promotion of settlements in the Occupied Palestinian Territories (OPTs). Although we cannot delve deeply into this topic here due to space limitations, religious agents have been very active in legitimizing the historical bond between the OPTs and the historical right of Jewish people to settle these territories (see Baumgart-Ochse in this special issue).[98] Religious parties are very involved in utilizing state resources to promote illegal settlements, violating state and international laws. Any peace negotiations with the Palestinians regarding settling the Israeli–Palestinian conflict that entailed withdrawal from the OPTs has been faced with violent eruptions and theological arguments that made such an option very difficult to pursue. The settler movement establishes its reasoning on religious terms, deeply tied with the logic of the Jewish state.[99]

Conclusions

Our discussion suggests several important conclusions. The first, based on the three cases analysed here, is that any deterministic relationship between state, religion and democracy is not only inaccurate but also misleading. There is no religion that is immune to change and democratization, as the 'clash of civilizations' argument, made by the late Samuel Huntington, has claimed.[100] The Turkish and Egyptian cases, where Islam is the dominant religion, demonstrate that whereas in Turkey one can speak of a clear democratization process in which Islamic parties are taking a leading role, in Egypt the state elite, which is mainly secular, utilizes religion in order to block democratization. The forms of political participation of religious agents in the state are very crucial factors to look at when evaluating the chances for democratization. Whereas in Egypt and Israel the state has institutionalized religion, giving priority to a particular communal and individual identity over others, in Turkey recent years demonstrate that the state is becoming an arena in which religious, as well as secular, parties are welcomed to compete for power. It seems that the secular military elite, which still holds the 'right' to intervene in the political process, is showing greater tolerance, something that is facilitating the gradual and cautious democratization of state–religion relations. The Turkish state does not have an institutionalized religion, despite the fact that the state plays a role in controlling religious institutions and education. So far, the religious parties that entered the political system through democratic elections do not seek to capture state power in order to institutionalize religious identity as the exclusive or dominant identity of the state. The institutionalization of religion may take different forms and have as a result different consequences on the chances of democratic reforms.

As indicated in the article's introduction, in order to understand it, one has to view the state–religion relationship in dynamic terms. The processes taking place in the three countries, demonstrate that democratization in state–religion relations could take different forms. In states that have institutionalized religion, such as in Egypt and Israel, democratization does not have to mean deinstitutionalizing religion, as much as the transformation from intolerant state–religion relations to tolerant ones. The Israeli case is a good example of some changes in this direction, whereas the Egyptian case demonstrates that in some situations changes taking place in state–religion relations appears to make the authoritarian system more secure. The Turkish experience, where there has been an intolerant separation of state and religion, shows that there has been some positive movement. In particular, it is possible to argue that key institutions of the state, for example, the armed forces, are – albeit reluctantly – becoming more tolerant to a religious presence both in the public sphere in general and in the political system in particular. In short, acceptance of religious parties in the political system reflects a gradual process of democratization in the country.

Another conclusion is that, whereas popular religion does not necessarily clash with democratization, institutionalized religion may well do so, by virtue of the fact that it may seek to turn religious belief into a foundational identity of the state, determining the nature of the public culture and significantly influencing personal status, as in Israel. Institutionalized religion may seek to control state power in order to penetrate the public and the private spheres and determine their content. Although the three cases do not establish the liberal claim that religion clashes with public reason, our discussion demonstrates that institutionalized religion may carry the propensity to do so. The Israeli example demonstrates what Elazar has called covenantalism, which is a constructive way to avoid religious authoritarianism and reach both accommodations and compromises that respect basic human rights and democratic procedures based on a common moral identity.[101] However, this may be possible only to a limited extent. It is true within Jewish society in Israel only. It demonstrates the case that religion may not clash with democratization or liberalization processes, but when institutionalized, it may limit basic civic rights and liberal values. There is a fundamental agreement in Israel within Jewish society regarding the Jewishness of the Israeli state.

There is also an agreement that: (1) there is no single interpretation of Judaism, and (2) the competition between the parties concerning the dominant Jewish worldview is open for free contestation, as well as for those who conceive Judaism as a cultural rather than a religious identity. This reality in Israel demonstrates that state–religion relations have to be generally viewed in dynamic and flexible terms.

These three cases also illustrate that religion offers legitimate popular norms and values but is compatible with democratization only when left as a matter of choice, neither manipulated by the state, nor completely excluded by it. When religion is an imposed system of values or perceived as a primordial identity, promoted by the state or oppositional political parties, it directly clashes with democratization. The changes in the worldview of the Islamic movement in Turkey, which came to accept that religious belief cannot compromise private autonomy, is a good example in this context. Also the willingness of the religious parties or at least some of them in Israel to accept the priority of the civic code when it clashes with rabbinical judgment is another example that religion can be tolerant and accommodate democratic and pluralist political culture. Egypt remains the example most remote from democratic rule, although religion is actually not the main hurdle against democratization. The ruling elite utilizes religion in order to compete with radicalized Islamic movements that are no longer willing to accept their exclusion from state power. The changes in the Islamic movement in Egypt and the rise of the moderates and the Wasat party illustrate that the Turkish model could be repeated if the ruling elite is willing to liberalize and democratize the state.

In conclusion, one could generalize that the process of democratization may take different forms and directions when it comes to state–religion relations. Whereas in Turkey democratization means the involvement and participation of religious parties in the democratic system, in Israel and more forcefully Egypt, despite the differences, democratization obliges the easing of the integration of religion and state and the deinstitutionalization of the official religion of the state. In other words, democratization is not a one dimensional linear process, but rather a complex process of compromises and checks and balances between various social and political forces that seek participation and representation in the political system. Democratization is best served when the 'twin tolerations' is established as a very basic value of the political culture of any state.

Notes

1. Grigoriadis, 'Islam and Democratization in Turkey: Secularism and Trust in a Divided Society'.
2. Baumgart-Ochse, 'Democratization in Israel, Politicized Religion and the Failure of the Oslo Peace Process'.
3. Brumberg and Diamond, 'Introduction'.
4. Barras, 'A Rights-Based Discourse to Contest the Boundaries of State Secularism? The Case of the Headscarf Bans in France and Turkey'.

5. Sartori, *The Theory of Democracy*; Locke, *Two Treatise of Government*.
6. Yates, 'Rawls and Habermas'.
7. Al-Azmeh, *Secularism*.
8. Diamond, Plattner and Costopoulos, *World Religions*; Marquand and Nettler, *Religion and Democracy*.
9. Philpott, 'Explaining the Political Ambivalence of Religion'; Stepan, 'Religion'; Zubaida, 'Trajectories'; Hadiz, 'The Rise of Neo-Third Worldism'.
10. Hadiz, 'The Rise of Neo-Third Worldism?'.
11. The paradigm was instigated by Huntington's theory of clash of civilizations. See: Huntington, *The Clash of Civilizations*.
12. Stepan, 'Religion'.
13. Ibid.
14. Linz and Stepan, *Problems of Democratic Transition*; Diamond, Plattner and Costopoulos, *World Religions*.
15. Mikenberg, 'Democracy and Religion'.
16. Philpott, 'Explaining the Political Ambivalence of Religion'.
17. Ibid.
18. Ibid., 522.
19. Cudworth, Hall and McGovern, *The Modern State*; Giddens, *The Nation State*; Tilly, *Coercion*.
20. Al-Azmeh, *Islams and Modernities*.
21. Grigoriadis, 'Islam and Democratization in Turkey: Secularism and Trust in a Divided Society'; Gozaydin, 'The Fethullah Gülen Movement and Politics in Turkey: A Chance for Democratization or a Trojan Horse?'.
22. Keyman, 'Modernity, Secularism and Islam'.
23. Yilmaz, 'Islam'.
24. Keyman, 'Modernity, Secularism and Islam', 219.
25. Kazancigil and Ozbudun, eds., *Ataturk, Founder of a Modern State*.
26. Mardin, *The Genesis of Young Ottoman Thought*, 10–80.
27. Casanova, *Public Religions in the Modern World*; Yilmaz, 'Islam'; Keyman, 'Modernity, Secularism and Islam'; Kadioglu, 'The Pathologies of Turkish Republican Laicism'.
28. Keyman, 'Modernity, Secularism and Islam', 225.
29. Casanova, 'Civil Society and Religion', 1064.
30. Ibid., 1065.
31. Gole, *The New Public Faces of Islam*.
32. Yilmaz, 'Islam', 491.
33. Ibid.
34. Ibid.
35. Keyman, 'Modernity, Secularism and Islam'.
36. Kadioglu, 'Denationalization of Citizenship?', 284.
37. Somer, 'Moderate Islam and Secularist Opposition in Turkey', 1286.
38. Mousseau, 'Democracy, Human Rights and Market Development in Turkey'.
39. El-Safty, 'Women in Egypt'.
40. http://www.freedomhouse.org/template.cfm?page=363&year=2008 (accessed July 3, 2009).
41. Balqis, *The State*.
42. Gasper, *The Power of Representation*.
43. Dar al-Ifta', is the official agency that issues fatwas, which is a committing religious decision, issued by the Mufti, which means religious preacher.
44. Mustafa and Norton, 'Stalled Reform', 40.
45. Hedeymann, *Upgrading Authoritarianism*.

46. http://www.freedomhouse.org/template.cfm?page=363&year=2008 (accessed July 3, 2009).
47. Mustafa and Norton, 'Stalled Reform'.
48. Hala, 'Egyptian Parliamentary Elections'.
49. Dillman, 'Parliamentary Elections'.
50. Hala, 'Egyptian Parliamentary Elections'.
51. Al-Awadi, *In Pursuit of Legitimacy*.
52. Hamzawy and Brown, 'A Boon or a Bane for Democracy?', 53.
53. Ibid., 53.
54. Korany, 'Egypt's Overdue Reform', 88.
55. Haqqani and Fradkin, 'Going Back to the Origins', 15.
56. Ibid., 14.
57. Jamal, 'Reassessing Support for Islam and Democracy'; Hala, 'Egyptian Parliamentary Elections'.
58. Hamzawy and Brown, 'A Boon or a Bane for Democracy?'.
59. Dillman, 'Parliamentary Elections'.
60. Abdelhadi, 'Egypt May Allow First Islamist Party'.
61. Stacher, 'Post-Islamist Rumblings in Egypt'.
62. Stark, 'Beyond "Terrorism" and "State Hegemony"'.
63. Ibid.
64. Hamzawi, 'Opposition in Egypt'.
65. Korany, 'Egypt's Overdue Reform'.
66. Mashhour, 'Islamic Law and Gender Equality'; El-Safty, 'Women in Egypt'.
67. Don-Yehiya, 'Conflict Management of Religious Issues'.
68. Liebman and Don-Yehiya, 'The Dilemma of Reconciling Traditional'.
69. Cohen and Rynhold, 'Social Covenants'; Elazar, *Israel*.
70. Cohen, 'Changes in the Orthodox Camp'; Cohen and Liebman, 'The Struggle Among Religious Zionists'.
71. Ottolenghi, 'Religion and Democracy in Israel', 39–40.
72. Masalha, *The Bible and Zionism*.
73. Jamal, 'The Hardships of Racialized Time'; Chowers, 'Time in Zionism'; Eisenstadt and Lissak, *Zionism and the Return to History*.
74. Jamal, 'Contradictions of State-Minority Relations in Israel'; Jamal, 'Nationalizing State'; Ghanem, *The Palestinian-Arab Minority in Israel*; Rouhana, *Palestinian Citizens in an Ethnic Jewish State*.
75. There are around 300,000 Israeli residents that are not Jews according to the state and there is deep political controversy concerning their future status. Many of them are not willing to convert according to religious law and therefore face problems when they decide to get married or divorced.
76. The Israeli government established a new emigration unit in the Population Registrar Office of the Ministry of Interior in order to discover non-Jewish illegal emigrants, whose number is estimated to reach 300,000 people and deport them. See: Azoulai, 'MKs Criticized Emigration Agency'; Wieler-Folk and Koshrek, 'The New Unit of the Emigration Authority Began Operating'; Camp and Reichman, *Foreigner Workers*.
77. Boaz, *Status Quo*.
78. Corinaldi, 'Protecting Minority Cultures'.
79. See, HCJ 1000/92, *Bavli v. Supreme Rabbinical Courts*.
80. Aloni, *Democracy in Chains*; *Haaretz*, May 21, 2009, 4.
81. Boaz, *Status Quo*.
82. Shafir and Peled, *Being Israeli*.
83. http://www.ynet.co.il/articles/0,7340,L-3735607,00.html (accessed July 3, 2009).

84. Ravitzky, *Religion and State*.
85. http://www.ynet.co.il/articles/0,7340,L-3537893,00.html (accessed July 3, 2009).
86. Corinaldi, 'Protecting Minority Cultures'.
87. Whereas scholars of the phenomenon indicate that there are thousands of women, who are misuravot get, official sources from the rabbinical courts claim that there are about 200 women only. For more information see: Lutan, 'Misuravot Get in Israel'.
88. In some buses that connect major cities in Israel there is a clear separation between men and women. The women are asked to sit at the back side of the bus and wear 'decent' clothing. Fisher, 'Fully Kosher Busses'.
89. Yona, *In Virtue of Difference*.
90. See, HCJ 721/94, *El Al v. Denilovitz*.
91. See the discussion of this issue in the Knesset: http://portal.knesset.gov.il/Com10bikoret/he-IL/Messages/H260208.htm (accessed July 10, 2009); see also examples of municipalities that issued fines: http://local1.gns.co.il/kfar-saba/45480/article.htm (accessed July 10, 2009); http://www.globes.co.il/news/article.aspx?did=1000434696&fid=821 (accessed July 3, 2009); see the policy of the Ministry of Industry, Commerce and Employment: http://news.walla.co.il/?w=/1/1244833 (accessed July 10, 2009).
92. http://www.haaretz.co.il/hasite/spages/973423.html (accessed July 3, 2009); on the public debate on this topic and its implications for the stability of the governmental coalition in 2008, see: http://www.ynet.co.il/articles/1,7340,L-3530966,00.html (accessed July 3, 2009).
93. Levi, 'The Dark Religious'.
94. See on the struggle against this separation led by the well-known non-governmental organization Kolech: http://www.kolech.org (accessed July 3, 2009).
95. Levi, 'The Dark Religious'.
96. See, HCJ 240/98, *Adalah and others v. Minister of Religion and others*.
97. Karayanni, 'Living in a Group of Ones Own'.
98. Baumgart-Ochse, 'Democratization in Israel, Politicized Religion and the Failure of the Oslo Peace Process'; Zertal and Eldar, *Lords of the Land*.
99. Ibid.; Taub, *The Settlers: The Struggle on the Meaning of Zionism*.
100. Huntington, *The Clash of Civilizations*.
101. Elazar, *Israel*; Cohen and Rynhold, 'Social Covenants'.

Notes on contributor

Dr Amal Jamal is a senior lecturer at the Political Science Department at Tel Aviv University and chair of The Walter Lebach Center for Arab–Jewish Coexistence. His research fields include political theory and communication, nationalism and democracy, civil society and social movements, indigenous minority politics and civic equality. He has published extensively on Palestinian and Israeli politics and society. Three of his recent books are: *Arab Politic Sphere in Israel* (Indiana University Press); *The Palestinian National Movement: Politics of Contention, 1967–2005* (Indiana University Press); and *Media Politics and Democracy in Palestine* (Sussex Academic Press).

Bibliography

Abdelhadi, Magdi. 'Egypt May Allow First Islamist Party'. http://news.bbc.co.uk/2/hi/middle_east/4316258.stm (accessed July 10, 2009).

Al-Awadi, Hesham. *In Pursuit of Legitimacy: The Muslim Brothers and Mubarak, 1982–2000*. London: Tauris Academic Press, 2004.

Al-Azmeh, Aziz. *Secularism from a Different Perspective*. Beirut: Center for the Study of Arab Unity, 1992.
Al-Azmeh, Aziz. *Islams and Modernities*. New York: Verso, 1993.
Aloni, Sholamit. *Democracy in Chains*. Tel Aviv: Am Oved, 2008.
Azoulai, Yuval. 'MKs Criticized Emigration Agency'. *Haaretz* 4, July 9, 2009.
Balqis, Abdel Illah. *The State in Modern Islamic Thinking*. Beirut: Center for Arab Unity Studies, 2004.
Barras, Amélie. 'A Rights-Based Discourse to Contest the Boundaries of State Secularism? The Case of the Headscarf Bans in France and Turkey'. *Democratization* 16, no. 6 (2009): 1237–60.
Baumgart-Ochse, Claudia. 'Democratization in Israel, Politicized Religion and the Failure of the Oslo Peace Process'. *Democratization* 16, no. 6 (2009): 1115–42.
Boaz, Chagai. *Status Quo: Culture, Politics and Society in Religion-State Relations in Israel*. Tel Aviv: Hamol, 2001.
Brumberg, Daniel, and Larry Diamond. 'Introduction'. In *Islam and Democracy in the Middle East*, ed. Diamond Larry, Marc Plattner, and Daniel Brumberg, ix–xxvi. Baltimore, MD: Johns Hopkins University Press, 2003.
Camp, Adriana, and Rivka Reichman. *Foreign Workers: The Political Economy of Guest Workers in Israel*. Jerusalem: Van Leer and Hakkibutz Hameuchad, 2008.
Casanova, Jose. *Public Religions in the Modern World*. Chicago, IL: University of Chicago Press, 1994.
Casanova, Jose. 'Civil Society and Religion'. *Social Research* 68, no. 4 (2001): 1041–80.
Chowers, Eyal. 'Time in Zionism: The Life and Afterlife of Temporal Revolution'. *Political Theory* 26, no. 5 (1998): 652–86.
Cohen, Asher. 'Changes in the Orthodox Camp and their Influence on the Deepening Religious-Secular Schism at the Outset of the Twenty-First Century'. In *Critical Issues in Israeli Society*, ed. Alan Dowty, 71–94. Westport and London: Greenwood, 2004.
Cohen, Asher, and Jonathan Rynhold. 'Social Covenants: The Solution to the Crisis of Religion and State in Israel?'. *Journal of Church and State* 47, no. 7: 725–46.
Cohen, Asher, and Charles S. Liebman. 'The Struggle Among Religious Zionists over the Issue of a Religious State'. In *Religion, Democracy and Israeli Society*, ed. Charles S. Liebman, 37–55. London: Harwood Academic Publishers, 1997.
Corinaldi, Michael. 'Protecting Minority Cultures and Religions in Matters of Personal Status both within State Boundaries and beyond State Frontiers – the Israeli System'. In *Families Across Frontiers*, ed. Nigel Lowe and Douglas Gillian, 385–94. The Haugue: Martinus Nijhoff Publishers, 1996.
Cudworth, Erika, Tim Hall, and John McGovern. *The Modern State: Theories and Ideologies*. Edinburgh: Edinburgh University Press, 2007.
Diamond, Larry, March Plattner, and Philip Costopoulos, eds. *World Religions and Democracy*. Baltimore, MD: Johns Hopkins University Press, 2005.
Dillman, Bradford. 'Parliamentary Elections and the Prospects of Political Pluralism in North Africa'. *Government and Opposition* 35, no. 2 (2000): 211–36.
Don-Yehiya, Eliezer. 'Conflict Management of Religious Issues: The Israeli Case in Comparative Perspective'. In *Parties, Elections and Cleavages*, ed. Reuven Hazan and Moshe Maor, 85–108. London: Frank Cass, 2000.
Eisenstadt, Shmuel Noah, and Moshe Lissak. *Zionism and the Return to History: A New Appraisal*. Jerusalem: Yad Yitzhak Ben Zvi, 1999.
Elazar, Daniel. *Israel: Building a New Society*. Bloomington: Indiana University Press, 1986.
El-Safty, Madiha. 'Women in Egypt: Islamic Rights versus Cultural Practices'. *Sex Roles* 51, no. 5/6 (September 2004): 273–81.
Fisher, Zahava. 'Fully Kosher Busses'. http://www.kolech.org/show.asp?id=25486 (accessed July 10, 2009).

Gasper, Michael Ezekiel. *The Power of Representation: Publics, Peasants, and Islam in Egypt*. Stanford, CA: Stanford University Press, 2009.
Ghanem, As'ad. *The Palestinian-Arab Minority in Israel, 1948–2000: A Political Study*. New York: State University of New York Press, 2001.
Giddens, Anthony. *The Nation State and Violence*. Cambridge: Polity Press, 1985.
Gole, Nilufer. *The New Public Faces of Islam*. Istanbul: Metis, 2000.
Gözaydin, İştar B. 'The Fethullah Gülen Movement and Politics in Turkey: A Chance for Democratization or a Trojan Horse?' *Democratization* 16, no. 6 (2009): 1214–36.
Grigoriadis, Ioannis N. 'Islam, and Democratization in Turkey: Secularism and Trust in a Divided Society'. *Democratization* 16, no. 6 (2009): 1194–213.
Hadiz, Vedi. 'The Rise of Neo-Third Worldism? The Indonesian Trajectory and the Consolidation of Illiberal Democracy'. *Third World Quarterly* 25, no. 1 (2004): 55–71.
Hala, Thabet. 'Egyptian Parliamentary Elections: Between Democratization and Autocracy'. *Africa Development* 31, no. 3 (2006): 11–24.
Hamzawi, Amr. 'Opposition in Egypt: Performance in the Presidential Elections and Prospects for the Parliamentary Elections'. *Policy Outlook: Carnegie Endowment* 22 (2005): 1–6.
Hamzawy, Amr, and Nathan Brown. 'A Boon or a Bane for Democracy?' *Journal of Democracy* 19, no. 3 (July 2008): 49–54.
Haqqani, Husain, and Hillel Fradkin. 'Going Back to the Origins'. *Journal of Democracy* 19, no. 3 (July 2008): 13–18.
Heydemann, Steven. *Upgrading Authoritarianism in the Arab World*. Washington, DC: United States Institute of Peace, 2007.
Huntington, Samuel. *The Clash of Civilizations and the remaking of World Order*. New York: Simon and Schuster, 1996.
Jamal, Amal. 'Contradictions of State-Minority Relations in Israel: The Search for Clarifications'. *Constellations* 16, no. 3 (2009): 493–508.
Jamal, Amal. 'The Hardships of Racialized Time'. In *Racism in Israel*, ed. Yehouda Shenhav and Yossi Yona, 348–80. Jerusalem: Van Leer Institute and Hakibutz Hamyohad, 2008.
Jamal, Amal. 'Nationalizing State and the Constitution of "Hollow" Citizenship: Israel and its Palestinian Citizens'. *Ethnopolitics* 6, no. 4 (November 2007): 471–93.
Jamal, Amaney. 'Reassessing Support for Islam and Democracy in the Arab World? Evidence from Egypt and Jordan'. *World Affairs* 169, no. 2 (Fall 2006): 51–63.
Kadioglu, Ayse. 'Denationalization of Citizenship? The Turkish Experience'. *Citizenship Studies* 11, no. 3 (July 2007): 283–99.
Kadioglu, Ayse. 'The Pathologies of Turkish Republican Laicism'. Unpublished paper presented at a conference on Republicanism and Empire at Columbia University, April 3–4, 2009.
Karayanni, Michael. 'Living in a Group of One's Own: Normative Implications Related to the Private Nature of the Religious Accommodation for The Palestinian-Arab Minority in Israel'. *UCLA Journal of Islamic and Near Eastern Law* 6, no. 1 (2006–2007): 1–45.
Kazancigil, A., and Ozbudun Egun, eds. *Ataturk, Founder of a Modern State*. London: C. Hurst, 1981.
Keyman, Faut. 'Modernity, Secularism and Islam: The Case of Turkey'. *Theory, Culture and Society* 24, no. 2 (2007): 215–34.
Korany, Bahgat. 'Egypt's Overdue Reform: A Prototype of the Middle East to Come?' *Mediterranean Politics* 11, no. 1 (March 2006): 83–9.
Kubba, Laith. 'Institutions Make the Difference'. *Journal of Democracy* 19, no. 3 (July 2008): 37–42.
Levi, Gideon. 'The Dark Religious Side of Israel'. *Haaretz*, April 12, 2009.

Liebman, Charles. *Religion, Democracy and Israeli Society*. Amsterdam: Harwood Academic, 1997.
Liebman, Charles, and Eliezer Don-Yehiya. 'The Dilemma of Reconciling Traditional Culture and Political Needs'. *Civil Religion in Israel: Traditional Judaism and Political Culture in the Jewish State* 53–66. Los Angeles, CA: University of California Press, 1983.
Linz, Juan, and Alfred Stepan. *Problems of Democratic Transition and Consolidation: Southern Europe, South America and Post-Communist Europe*. Baltimore, MD: Johns Hopkins University Press, 1996.
Locke, John. *Two Treatise of Government*. Cambridge: Cambridge University Press, 1988.
Lutan, Orli. 'Misuravot Get in Israel', document of the Israeli Knesset. http://www.knesset.gov.il/MMM/data/docs/m01242.doc (accessed July 10, 2009).
Mardin, Serif. *The Genesis of Young Ottoman Thought: A Study in the Modernization of Turkish Political Ideas*. Syracuse, NY: Syracuse University Press, 2000.
Marquand, David, and Ronald Nettler, eds. *Religion and Democracy*. London: Blackwell Publishers, 2000.
Masalha, Nur. *The Bible and Zionism: Invented Tradition, Archeology and Postcolonialism in Palestine-Israel*. London: Zed Books, 2006.
Mashhour, Amira. 'Islamic Law and Gender Equality: Could be there a Common Ground?'. *Human Rights Quarterly* 27, no. 2 (2005): 562–96.
Minkenberg, Michael. 'Democracy and Religion: Theoretical and Empirical Observations on the Relationship between Christianity, Islam and Liberal Democracy'. *Journal of Ethnic and Migration Studies* 33, no. 6 (August 2007): 887–909.
Mousseau, Demet Yalcin. 'Democracy, Human Rights and Market Development in Turkey: Are They Related?'. *Government and Opposition* 41, no. 2 (2006): 298–326.
Mustafa, Hala, and Augustus Richard Norton. 'Stalled Reform: The Case of Egypt'. *Current History* 106 (January 2007): 39–41.
Ottolenghi, Emanuele. 'Religion and Democracy in Israel'. In *Religion and Democracy*, ed. David Marquand and Ronald Nettler, 39–49. London: Blackwell Publishers, 2000.
Philpott, Daniel. 'Explaining the Political Ambivalence of Religion'. *American Political Science Review* 101, no. 3 (August 2007): 505–26.
Ravitzky, Aviezer. *Religion and State in Jewish Philosophy: Models of Unity, Division, Collision and Subordination*. Jerusalem: Israel Democracy Institute, 2002.
Rouhana, Nadim. *Palestinian Citizens in an Ethnic Jewish State: Identities in Conflict*. New Heaven, CT: Yale University Press, 1997.
Sartori, Giovani. *The Theory of Democracy Revisited*. Chatham, NJ: Chatham House, 1987.
Shafir, Gershon, and Yoav Peled. *Being Israeli: The Dynamic of Multiple Citizenship*. Cambridge: Cambridge University Press, 2002.
Somer, Murat. 'Moderate Islam and Secularist Opposition in Turkey: Implications for the World, Muslims and Secular Democracy'. *Third World Quarterly* 28, no. 7 (2007): 1271–89.
Stacher, Joshua. 'Post-Islamist Rumblings in Egypt: The Emergence of the Wasat Party'. *The Middle East Journal* 56, no. 3 (Summer 2002): 415–32.
Stark, Jan. 'Beyond "Terrorism" and "State Hegemony": Assessing the Islamist Mainstream in Egypt and Malaysia'. *Third World Quarterly* 26, no. 2 (2005): 307–27.
Stepan, Alfred. 'Religion, Democracy and the "Twin Tolerations"'. In *World Religions and Democracy*, ed. Diamond Larry, March Plattner, and Philip Costopoulos, 3–26. Baltimore, MD: Johns Hopkins University Press, 2005.
Taub, Gadi. *The Settlers: The Struggle over the Meaning of Zionism*. Tel Aviv: Sephre Hemed, 2007.
Tilly, Charles. *Coercion, Capital and European States: AD 990–1992*. Cambridge, MA: Blackwell, 1992.

Wieler-Folk, Dana, and Koshrek Noa. 'The New Unit of the Emigration Authority Began Operating'. *Haaretz* (July 2 2009): 4.
Yates, Melissa. 'Rawls and Habermas on Religion in the Public Sphere'. *Philosophy and Social Criticism* 33, no. 7 (2007): 880–91.
Yilmaz, Hakan. 'Islam, Sovereignty and Democracy: A Turkish View'. *The Middle East Journal* 61, no. 3 (Summer 2007): 477–93.
Yona, Yossi. *In Virtue of Difference: The Multicultural Project in Israel*. Jerusalem: Van Leer and Hakkibutz Hameuchad, 2004.
Zertal, Idith, and Akiva Eldar. *Lords of the Land: The Settlers and the State of Israel, 1967–2004*. Tel Aviv: Kinneret, Zmora-Bitan, Dvir, 2004.
Zubaida, Sami. 'Trajectories of Political Islam: Egypt, Iran and Turkey'. In *Religion and Democracy*, ed. Marquand David and Ronald Nettler, 60–77. London: Blackwell Publishers, 2000.

Spiritual capital and democratization in Zimbabwe: a case study of a progressive charismatic congregation

Gladys Ganiel

Irish School of Ecumenics, Trinity College, Dublin, Ireland

Throughout Africa, charismatic Christianity has been caricatured as an inhibitor of democratization. Its adherents are said either to withdraw from the rough and tumble of politics ('pietism') or to preach a prosperity gospel that encourages believers to pour their resources into their churches in the hope that God will 'bless' them. Both courses of action are said to encourage such people to be politically quietist, with no interest in democratization or other forms of political activity. This is said to thwart democratization. This article utilizes an ethnographic case study of a 'progressive' charismatic congregation in Harare, Zimbabwe, in 2007, to provide evidence that 'pietism' and 'prosperity' are not the only options for charismatic Christianity. Drawing on the concept of 'spiritual capital', it argues that some varieties of charismatic Christianity have the resources to contribute to democratization. For example, this congregation's self-styled 'de-institutionalization' process is opening up new avenues for people to learn democratic skills and develop a worldview that is relationship-centred, participatory, and anti-authoritarian. The article concludes that spiritual capital can be a useful tool for analysing the role of religions in democratizations. It notes, however, that analysts should take care to identify and understand what variety of spiritual capital is generated in particular situations, focusing on the worldviews it produces and the consequences of those worldviews for democratization.

Introduction: democratization in Zimbabwe

There has been considerable debate about how democratization in Africa should be evaluated.[1] There is an emerging realization that African democracies cannot be judged against Western standards and conceptions, which are contextually rooted in the West's own historical development. So Salih, drawing on Merkel and Dahl, develops a 'polyarchical' evaluation which assesses democracy according to these criteria[2]:

(1) freedom to form and join organizations;
(2) freedom of expression and alternative sources of information; and
(3) eligibility for public office and the right of political leaders to compete for support and votes in free and fair elections.

Koelble and Lipuma push the debate further, claiming that most standards used to evaluate democratization are 'EuroAmerican' and therefore inappropriate for assessing post-colonial political developments in Africa.[3] They argue that 'the real measure of democracy is the extent to which governance conforms to the visions of democracy worked out by the governed'.[4] The task of the political analyst, then, becomes one of determining the values and standards of the host population. Consequently, analysts should seek to evaluate political institutions and practices according to the extent to which they meet the population's expectations – not the extent to which they conform to EuroAmerican ideal types.

Disagreements about how analysts should evaluate democracy are a key aspect of a debate between various scholars – including, Bratton, Chikwana and Sithole[5] and Moore[6] – about how Zimbabweans *really* think about democratization in their country. Bratton, Chikwana and Sithole draw on recent Afrobarometer survey results to argue that Zimbabweans' enthusiasm for democracy is waning. On the other hand, Moore interprets these results to mean that Zimbabweans simply realize that what passes for democracy in their country does not meet their own standards for good governance.

However, these debates are interesting but inconclusive. One thing that does seem beyond dispute is that democratization in Zimbabwe – whether evaluated by external EuroAmerican or by contextual Zimbabwean standards – has been thwarted.[7] This is surprising. After Zimbabwe won its independence from white-run Rhodesia in 1980, there were signs that it would become a democratic success story. The new prime minister, Robert Mugabe, promised 'reconciliation' with the whites. The agricultural sector, dominated by whites, was initially left largely untouched and food production soared. Mugabe's Zimbabwe African National Union-Popular Front (ZANU-PF) government initially undertook much needed reforms in health and education, and a substantial, well-educated black middle class developed. But these successes masked other tensions and political intrigues.[8] Ndebele people in the Matabeleland region of Zimbabwe faced violence and killings on a massive scale during the Gukurahundi massacres following independence.[9] Raftopoulos has interpreted this as an attempt by Mugabe to subordinate his rivals in the name of national 'unity'.[10] ZANU-PF inherited economic problems from the Rhodesian regime, including a large foreign debt. ZANU-PF's land reform and redistribution policies progressed at a slow but steady pace in the first decade after independence, but stalled dramatically during the

1990s.[11] While these policies were initially supported financially by the British government, it eventually withdrew its support.[12] Over time, Zimbabwe's foreign debt became 'unpayable', and far-reaching Structural Adjustment Programmes were imposed by the International Monetary Fund, as a condition of further financial assistance.[13] Over time, economic concerns were reflected in political developments. Significant rumblings of discontent among citizens were heard in 2000, when Zimbabweans rejected a referendum to amend the constitution, which would have given Mugabe more powers as president. Mugabe claimed he would accept this result.[14] But within days, violent and haphazard 'invasions' of white-run farms began.[15]

At the same time, censorship of the media and the oppression of a newly established political party the Movement for Democratic Change (MDC, formed in 1999) and civil society groups increased.[16] The MDC's efforts to secure political change were repeatedly foiled by rigged elections, violent intimidation, and internal divisions. Similarly, the National Constitutional Assembly (NCA) was established to pressurize the government to reform the constitution. In addition, Women of Zimbabwe Arise (WOZA) was formed to publicize state repression through demonstrations. Both NCA and WOZA were violently suppressed by security forces. It was difficult to access independent media and education, especially in rural areas. ZANU-PF instituted a thorough propaganda campaign via both the media and the teaching of 'patriotic history'.[17]

Following elections in 2008, ZANU-PF eventually agreed to a power sharing government with the MDC. However, ZANU-PF retained control of the police and security forces, which involved a difficult compromise for the MDC. Questions remain about Mugabe and ZANU-PF's sincerity in accepting the coalition. While this power-sharing experiment might be considered a step towards democratization, the workability of the coalition is uncertain. Some schools have re-opened, there is more food in shops, and prices of some basic goods have decreased.[18] But the political climate remains strained and there appears to have been few other improvements in the everyday lives of citizens.[19] For Inglehart and Welzel, socio-economic development is the crucial variable that leads to conditions that allow people to develop 'self-expression values', which in turn forms the basis of 'effective democracy'.[20] These conditions are clearly absent in Zimbabwe today, where the main concern of most citizens is no doubt everyday survival. At the time of my fieldwork in February–April 2007, 80% of Zimbabweans lived below the poverty line and the annual inflation rate was 2,200%.[21] By July 2008 annual inflation was calculated at 231,000,000% – the last figure that was released. In an attempt to curb inflation, in January 2009 the government allowed trading in foreign currencies.[22]

Despite the challenges such difficult economic circumstances pose to everyday activities, Raftopoulos and Alexander provide evidence of increased activism amongst groups in Zimbabwe's public sphere.[23] Although groups such as the NCA, the trade unions and some of the churches initially focused on regime change, Raftopoulos and Alexander identify a recent shift towards human rights discourses, constitutional reform, and publicizing injustices. For example, such groups (especially networks of churches) played a role in publicizing Operation Murumbatsvina in 2005. This was a large-scale demolition of houses in high density suburbs of Harare, areas that mainly supported the MDC.[24] In 2006, WOZA conducted nationwide consultations and produced a 'People's Charter' that outlined an alternative vision of Zimbabwean society and politics. In Koelble and Lipuma's terms, these groups mobilized largely because the Zimbabwean state was failing 'miserably to meet the standards of the Zimbabwean citizenry'.[25] Koelble and Lipuma claim:

> There is a growing chasm between the visions of democracy circulating in the Zimbabwean public sphere and the political practices of the Mugabe government. In the eyes of Zimbabwe's democrats, Mugabe's razing of the shanty settlements surrounding Harare in mid-2005 is anti-democratic less because it violates their [Zimbabweans] version of individual rights than because it violates their [Zimbabweans] sense of community and the right to have a place of belonging.[26]

The Christian churches were prominent in publicizing the injustice of Operation Murambatsvina. Three-quarters of Zimbabweans are practising Christianity and, as a result, churches and related organizations play a significant role in the social lives of many citizens.[27] Given that in many rural areas the church and the school are the only public institutions, Christian organizations are probably the most high-profile throughout Zimbabwean civil society as a whole.[28] This made such organizations well-placed to respond to the poor economic and political conditions in the country. But the roles of these different churches and organizations are diverse, with some choosing to address the difficult circumstances directly, and others judging that it is not their place to do so. Thinking of churches and organizations in terms of the variety of 'spiritual capital' which they produce may be helpful in analyzing their role in responding to Zimbabwe's poor political and economic context, including their ability to contribute to democratization.

Spiritual capital and democratization

'Spiritual capital' has its roots in the development of the concept of 'social capital'. Putnam is the major figure in this field, defining social capital in terms of networks of relationships within (bonding social capital) and between (bridging social capital) groups and individuals.[29] These relationships are said to nurture trust, laying foundations not only for the flourishing of society and the economy but also a better quality of democracy. Writing from and within an American context, Putnam observes that nearly half of all volunteering and personal philanthropy in the USA is church-related. He argues that religious attachment enhances participation in secular civic activity. Norris and Inglehart note that participation in religious *worship services* does not correlate with greater civic activity, but that participation in religious *organizations* does correlate with greater civic activity.[30]

Scholars have also begun referring to 'religious capital' and 'spiritual capital'.[31] Yet, the ways these terms are used in the literature is often confusing. At times they are conflated and seem to mean the same thing, while at other times scholars draw distinctions between them. Carkoglu has distinguished between religious and spiritual capital, differentiating between them by drawing an analogous relationship with bonding and bridging social capital.[32] For him, religious capital produces exclusivist 'bonding' identities, while spiritual capital is a 'bridging' resource that inspires people to act to help others beyond their immediate comfort zone. While this is an interesting distinction, it is not widespread in the literature. Rather, the trend seems to be to abandon use of the term religious capital (which was common in the early 1990s)[33] in favour of spiritual capital. Conceptions of spiritual capital retain the emphasis on the individual that is present in earlier discussions of religious capital,[34] while at the same time exploring how religious ideas and activities can have wider social and political impacts. For example, Berger and Hefner argue that there are *varieties* of spiritual capital within the world religions. These varieties promote different values, producing different worldviews about a number of issues, including democratization and development.[35] For Haynes, spiritual capital introduces an extra dimension to development. Development then is not just about material progress but also about 'redemptive hopes and expectations'.[36] Following this convention, from here I will use the term spiritual capital in this article.

In order to develop the analytical worth of the term 'spiritual capital' in relation to democratization, it is necessary to focus on both empirical and comparative research, which note that there are *varieties* of spiritual capital. At the same time, we need to analyse both religious actors' *ideas* and *practices* and *networks*. Following the argument put forward by Weber in *The Protestant Ethic and the Spirit of Capitalism*, this article suggests that religious ideas can have a wide, diffuse cultural impact, including an impact on democratization.[37]

Spiritual capital, democratization and charismatic Christianity in Africa

Considerable scholarly attention has been devoted to the role of religion in democratization in Africa.[38] For example, Haynes analyses the role of both elite level leaders and popular religious movements across the continent, concluding that while there have been important examples in which religion has played a democratizing role (such as South Africa), on the whole 'religious actors have not been able to help advance democracy beyond a stage often characterized by cosmetic rather than substantial changes'.[39] Ranger's recent edited volume updates and at times challenges this conclusion.[40] Ranger divides Africa's democratic history into three phases, and explores the role of the churches during each era or 'revolution'. He says that across the continent mainline churches, such as the Catholic and established Protestant mission churches, took centre stage during the 'first democratic revolution' anti-colonial struggles. Yet, their role was ambiguous, with some churches legitimating and supporting white-led minority regimes, and others challenging them. Charismatic[41] churches were conspicuously absent from politics in the 1950s and 1960s. Charismatic churches include both mission churches and home-grown churches, and can be characterized by their belief in the bible as an infallible guide to faith, their imperative to evangelize, and their emphasis on deep-felt religious experiences such as conversion, speaking in tongues, and belief in miracles. Over time, these churches either withdrew altogether from politics or offered repressive regimes their tacit support. This was a dominant pattern in Kenya, South Africa and Zimbabwe.[42]

Ranger dates the next phase of African democratic history, the 'second democratic revolution', from the late 1980s. This was concerned with addressing the injustices perpetrated by the post-colonial governments. Ranger claims that the mainline churches retained enough independence and moral authority to speak out against violence, militarism and one-party rule. However, as Haynes has noted, their authority and influence were often limited.[43] As in the first anti-colonial democratic revolution, Ranger does not consider the role of charismatic churches during this era to be substantial. Ranger's depiction of the 'third democratic revolution', which he dates from the early 1990s to the present, ascribes a different role altogether to charismatic churches. No longer on the margins of mainline Christianity, they are growing rapidly in many African countries. Using South African charismatic churches as an example, Ranger claims that by virtue of their numbers and their promotion of a 'moral opposition to the new nationalist order',[44] they are now crucial to ensuring 'the sustainability of democracy' in Africa.[45]

This conclusion echoes an earlier, 'cultural potentiality argument' about charismatic Christianity.[46] Advocates of this view, including Maxwell, claim that people involved in highly participatory charismatic churches would learn skills necessary to become democratic citizens.[47] Freston noted, however, that such arguments were not rooted in much empirical evidence.[48] But Ranger's volume, featuring country-by-country case studies, provides examples of charismatic and evangelical Christians in Africa who have become purveyors of moral opposition to repressive governments, by seeking to address current crises of morality, poverty and conflict.[49] Jenkins explains this by arguing that the social and political world experienced by many African Christians is much like the world depicted in the Bible. He argues that Africans identify with the suffering of those who Jesus came to liberate, and are hence inspired to work for liberation themselves. Miller and Yamamori's global study of what they term 'progressive Pentecostalism' reveals similar trends of activism on behalf of the poor in various parts of the world.[50] Note, however, that while Miller and Yamamori do not claim that all expressions of Pentecostalism are 'progressive', their study does confirm trends and changes identified by Ranger and Jenkins.

Gifford – who wrote an afterword to Ranger's edited volume – remains sceptical about the role of charismatic Christianity in relation to democratization in Africa. He questions the spread and significance of the examples of socio-political engagement upon which Ranger and his contributors focus. For Gifford, the most significant scriptural paradigms in Africa remain the 'faith gospel' (or prosperity gospel) and 'demonic possession'. He contends that the 'demonic possession' paradigm undermines human agency by ascribing power to demons, 'divert[ing] attention from a more obviously political level of analysis'.[51] Gifford argues that as long as African Christians interpret the bible in such ways, then their Christianity will not help them to overcome repressive governments, poverty, or achieve a democratic political culture.

Progressive charismatic Christianity: Mount Pleasant Community Church

Mukonyora's recent research on 'salt of the earth' evangelicals in Zimbabwe, who could be considered part of Miller and Yamamori's progressive strand, indicates that this strand is more likely than others to promote democracy.[52] She claims that 'salt of the earth' evangelicals 'seek to function as ... "school(s) of democracy" in the sense that they emphasize Christian ideals of love, peace, and harmony and seek to oppose political injustice'.[53] This study engages with an example of the progressive variety in Zimbabwe, the Mount Pleasant Community Church.

I chose Mount Pleasant Community Church (MPCC) as a case study for the following reasons. First, I wanted to demonstrate how one small group of people from the wider yet often-overlooked progressive charismatic perspective try to deal with Zimbabwe's political and economic crises. Secondly, few recent studies focus on *congregations* in Zimbabwe. Most of the current information coming out of Zimbabwe focuses on prominent clerics or Christian organizations, such as the former Catholic Archbishop of Bulawayo Pius Ncube, Christian Alliance, the Evangelical Fellowship of Zimbabwe, or the Catholic Commission on Justice and Peace.[54]

MPCC is physically located in a relatively wealthy suburb near the University of Zimbabwe in Harare. People who attend the church are mainly well educated, young (under 35 years of age), and middle class. These factors make MPCC unusual in the Zimbabwean context.[55]

The most significant findings of the case study are related to a process of change within MPCC, which people call 'de-institutionalization'. The best way to understand de-institutionalization is to describe how it has occurred.[56]

De-institutionalization: changing structures, changing leadership

The term de-institutionalization refers to the way the MPCC congregation has sought to reduce or even eliminate structured events and activities. In interviews, people said they have done this because these events and activities were no longer helping them to develop their faith. Secondly, de-institutionalization refers to the fact that many congregation members now believe less than before in the authority of elders and other leaders. This is said to be an 'organic' process, occurring with the enthusiastic support of the elders, who were keen to stand down from their leadership roles, including fulltime paid employment by the congregation. The justification, the elders said, was that this was truer to the biblical model of leadership – the Apostle Paul, after all, was a tentmaker as well as a minister of the gospel. The elders – an Ndebele man and a white man – expressed these views to me in a joint interview in March 2007.

People dated the beginning of de-institutionalization to 2002, when people began to develop these ideas at once-per-week prayer meetings. By 2005, the prayer meetings were taking place five days a week. People said God spoke to them then, and God said that they were depending too much on the MPCC leaders and other structures to interpret the bible for them and to discern 'God's will' for their lives. People identified 'structures' as cell groups (that is, small bible study groups that meet during the week) and other organized activities such as men's breakfasts and women's fellowship meetings. Consequently, the cell groups were replaced by smaller 'discipleship groups'. Discipleship groups consisted of people from the congregation who met on a regular basis to pray, study the bible, and share a meal. These groups were intended to promote deeper spiritual growth, more meaningful relationships with others, and dependence upon God in the sense that people would no longer require elders or leaders to interpret the scriptures or 'God's will' for them. They were however discontinued in 2006, from which time regular participants in the prayer meetings encouraged others to attend prayer meetings and to meet informally in homes. The elders said they supported these developments at worship services. In my interviews, people at MPCC said some of the results of the changes outlined above were that they no longer expected the elders or other leaders in the congregation to 'spoon feed' them with interpretations of scripture or to discern 'God's will' for them.

Despite the process of de-institutionalization, elders and some lay leaders still prepared sermons for Sunday morning worship services. This was reported to me in interviews with elders and lay leaders, and I observed that such people would bring prepared sermon notes to services. But the participation of congregants in the services increased from 2002. By 2007, at least the first hour of a Sunday service was devoted to spontaneous prayer, worship and testimonies. Sometimes a congregant shared a spontaneous sermon, and the prepared sermon was never delivered. Elders said that this way of worshiping re-enforced the biblical idea of the 'priesthood of all believers', removing authority from the elders and placing it in *all* the people, where it rightfully belonged.[57]

This is unlike the authoritarian structure of congregational life that Maxwell documents in his study of the Pentecostal Zimbabwe Assemblies of God Africa (ZAOGA) denomination.[58] Rather, de-institutionalization at MPCC has produced a congregation in which many people felt empowered to think for themselves and contribute to decision-making within the congregation. All 18 people I interviewed said that they were now thinking and doing more for themselves. Others in the congregation also mentioned this in casual conversations.[59] This is notable, as many African cultures have been regarded as hierarchical or even dictatorial, presenting a view that elites often wield unchallenged power.[60] The voluntary laying down of power by the people in positions of authority in MPCC (even though this is on a small scale) provides an alternative to that generalization. On the other hand, some people at MPCC were concerned about the potential for leaders to 'abdicate' their roles and to allow the congregation to become too inward-looking, neglecting service to the poor when times got tough. They also worried that a congregation with so few 'structures' could be easily shaken by personality clashes and internal power struggles.[61]

De-institutionalization in the MPCC at the congregational level produced what I regard as an example of participatory democracy. Many members of the congregation rejected authoritarian leadership in favour of a form of equality whereby church members were encouraged to participate in all aspects of congregational life. This process is similar to that observed by Freston, and some of the scholars in Ranger's volume, who see churches in Africa as empowering people as they learn skills that can be transferred to participating in democratic politics.[62] Regarding the concerns of this article, we can note that the spiritual capital generated at MPCC produces a worldview which was participatory, anti-authoritarian and relationship-centred; it also dovetails well more generally with democratic principles in a wider political sense. The following sections explore how such a worldview developed at the micro-level through the articulation of empowering religious ideas, which were then nurtured and developed through networks of relationships.

Ideas and the development of spiritual capital

Research on 'new social movements' has emphasized the importance of ideas for encouraging political change. For example, members of such movements may develop ideas to justify the actions they take to try to bring about social and political change.[63] Similarly, people at MPCC developed ideas to justify the removing of structured activities and the redefinition of leadership that defines the de-institutionalization process. Many members of the church attach great importance to what is *said* during worship services and prayer meetings, interpreting these words as the prompting of the Holy Spirit or God's direct revelation. Through analysis of my interviews, field notes, and consultation with the elders, I identify four major discursive themes: (1) Relationships (with God and with others), (2) Acknowledging difficulties/injustices and yet persevering, (3) Waiting, and (4) Action through service. A detailed analysis of the content of these discursive themes is beyond the scope of this paper, although I have begun this elsewhere.[64]

These discourses are linked together, logically building upon each other and ultimately justifying *action* to serve the poor and in some cases to critique the government. The emphasis on action is crucial in a Zimbabwean context where charismatic Christians have either been accused of pietist withdrawal from society and politics or a passive adherence to the prosperity gospel.[65] The relationships between the discourses can be explained as follows. Discourses about relationships explain how trusting relationships are built. Trusting relationships allow people to freely and openly acknowledge the difficulties and injustices in their lives and in the wider society. This is not something that can be taken for granted in Zimbabwe, where it can be dangerous to criticize the government or even to imply that government policies are unjust. Then, once people start to talk about injustices, they move to speaking about patiently waiting for God's deliverance, and/or taking God-inspired action through service.

The way discourses build upon each other can be illustrated in the conduct of a prayer meeting in February 2007, where a handful of people gathered. The meeting started with a man called Simeon[66] reading Colossians 3:15/16:

> Let the peace of Christ rule in your hearts, since as members of one body you were called to peace. And be thankful. Let the word of Christ dwell in you richly as you teach and admonish one another with all wisdom, and as you sing psalms, hymns and spiritual songs with gratitude in your hearts to God.

This particular passage of scripture emphasizes the importance of *relationships* between individuals and God (let Christ rule in your hearts) and among individuals (teach and admonish one another).

Simeon's contribution was followed by a period of silence, during which time Ben entered the meeting. After silence for several minutes, he said that he was reading Psalm 33 during the day and found it encouraging. Ben read it, emphasizing the verses from 12 onwards:

> Blessed is the nation whose God is the Lord, the people he chose for his inheritance. From heaven the Lord looks down and sees all mankind; from his dwelling-place he watches all who live on earth ... no king is saved by the size of his army; no warrior escapes by his great strength. ...

This scripture emphasizes the idea that God is just, and even those rulers who abuse their power (no warrior escapes by his great strength) will one day face his judgment.

Then a man called Jabulani read I John 3:18: 'Dear children, let us not love with words or tongue but with actions and in truth.' He quoted from the book of James, where it talks about showing faith by your works. He said that love in action is difficult to implement when you think about the acts that the early church considered normal, such as, selling what they had and having all material goods in common. He posed the question to everyone: What do we do? Do we press on with this vision God has given? Or do we wait and then God has to bring it before us again? His implication was that people should be *acting* now on their faith.

Simeon then referred back to what Ben had said, noting that it was amazing that God meets our individual needs and helps us to meet others' needs. He said that the way others get to experience God is through the deeds that we do. He then read Psalm 96, emphasizing verses 10–13:

> Say among the nations, the Lord reigns. The world is firmly established, it cannot be moved; he will judge the peoples with equity. Let the heavens rejoice, let the earth be glad; let the sea resound, and all that is in it; let the fields be jubilant, and everything in

them. Then all the trees of the forest will sing for joy; they will sing before the Lord for he comes, he comes to judge the earth. He will judge the world in righteousness and the peoples in his truth.

Again, this scripture emphasizes God's just judgment. That, linked with prior points made about the need to put their faith in *action*, provides an example of how people utilized the bible to interpret their present situations and to justify doing something to change those situations for the better.

Later in the meeting, after prayers about meeting individual needs, such as, providing food for relatives and paying school fees, Ben quoted Romans 5:5 and said that we live in a poverty-stricken nation, where there is a 'terrible situation'. He thanked God for the groceries that people from MPCC purchased the day before for orphans and child-headed homes. He said that although none of them made a lot of money, they should not make excuses about being unable to help. His comment reflected a trend where people from the middle classes, like those at MPCC, had seen a dip in the real value of their salaries, due to inflation. Even some medical doctors in the congregation had set up small businesses on the side to try and make ends meet. He then quoted Psalm 33 again, saying the Lord 'loves righteousness and justice' and that he had promised to bring it about on earth. Ben then said that some of the economic policies in the country just were not fair. He mentioned the dual government and black market monetary exchange rates. He prayed that God would encourage people like the nineteenth century anti-slavery campaigner, William Wilberforce, that is, politicians who would do what was good and just and right for the benefit of the whole nation. This was an explicit critique of the government, articulated during a typical meeting. It was significant in that it highlighted injustice, locating its root in the dysfunctional *politics* of the country. It should be noted, however, that I never heard anyone at MPCC advocate direct action against the government. Rather, when they advocated action, they talked primarily about *service* to the poor and needy – those whose lives had become so difficult in large part due to unjust government policies.

In sum, we have explored examples of religious discourses that encouraged and justified action to serve the poor and, implicitly, to reform political leadership – issues crucial for democratization outcomes in Zimbabwe. There were, however, limits both to these discourses and how MPCC members understood them. For example, some MPCC people criticized what they saw as their congregation's unwillingness to speak out explicitly against the government, as organizations such as the Christian Alliance have done.[67] They believed this limited their congregation's potential to contribute to achieving justice in their country. I also asked some people if they thought that what their congregation was saying and doing was 'political', and they said 'no'. Perhaps surprisingly, MPCC members did not appear to make conscious links between what was happening in their congregation and wider social and political processes. While as a social scientist I may identify a worldview within MPCC that seems conducive to producing democratic citizens, many MPCC members saw themselves as doing God's work, meeting immediate needs and making the world around them just a little more bearable for others. Even so, people at the grassroots, including MPCC members are de facto creating democratic spaces, whereby they can develop their own ideas about their religion and the kind of society they want to live in. The ability to do this is itself essential to democratization. Now we turn to ways in which such ideas are spread within Zimbabwe.

Networks and the development of spiritual capital in Zimbabwe: impact on democratization

MPCC's emphasis on relationships ensures that most congregants have rich networks of relationships both within and without the congregation. This does not mean that people in other congregations or organizations do not participate in such networks. But everyone I talked with at MPCC said that de-institutionalization prompted them to cultivate their personal networks. This resulted in an increased level of social activism by people in the congregation. MPCC congregants also told me that those who already worked or volunteered for non-governmental organizations (NGOs) felt their work was better appreciated.[68] There were also new congregational initiatives to provide for orphans and widows in Harare's high-density suburbs, and in poor, rural areas, several hours' drive from the capital. MPCC includes a number of medical doctors among its members, so such activities also included medical missions whereby poor people received free health care. MPCC also has several sister congregations throughout Zimbabwe, associated with the United Kingdom-based New Frontiers Network of charismatic churches. MPCC publicizes the activities of these congregations and the Zimbabwe-based ministries of New Frontiers, including a widespread eco-farming project called 'Farming God's Way', based at another congregation in Harare. Several people I spoke with at MPCC had collaborated with or worked for the Farming God's Way initiative. Activities such as the medical missions and farming initiative drew on the particular strengths of people at MPCC and directly addressed the adverse effects of the economic and political crises by providing health care and a source of food.

The cultivation of such networks is crucial to democratization. Many MPCC members subsequently felt empowered to begin new initiatives to address the pressing social and economic needs brought on by the political crisis. They at least implicitly recognized that the state had failed to deliver on its developmental agenda and that as a result citizens would need to step in to undertake such activities to the extent they were able. The wider point is that democratization is not possible unless people believe that their actions to address social and political problems can make a tangible difference, even if it is small and incremental. Further, many people I spoke with in MPCC emphasized that their activism was not simply a form of philanthropic aid, rather it was aimed to help poor people take greater and better care of themselves. Thus, MPCC visits orphans, widows and the rural poor, suggesting practical tips on job training and farming. The spread of these skills is also important to democratization, as democratic politics is very difficult or impossible until or unless people's most basic economic and health needs are met.[69] In other words, assistance poor people receive from MPCC may help enable them to move beyond a concern with basic survival to a greater concern for political changes, including a demand for democracy. Finally, MPCC's participatory, anti-authoritarian and relationship-centred worldview might spread beyond the congregation by way of these networks. It is however beyond the scope of this article to examine if or to what extent the religiously-based discourses articulated at MPCC are present in other congregations and organizations in the country, including the issues of networks generally and whether people recognize that such ideas in particular stem from the MPCC. Further research focusing on how ideas and skills are transmitted through networks such as these is needed for a fuller understanding of the links between spiritual capital and how religious networks might facilitate democratization in Zimbabwe.

Conclusions: spiritual capital at the macro-level and the potential for democratization?

There is a great deal of confusion in the literature about spiritual capital and its relationship to democratization. Accordingly, part of the work of this article has been to develop a clearer conception of spiritual capital. This included both its micro-level aspects (including the religious ideas and networks of individuals) and its macro-level aspects (how religious ideas and practices might have a wider impact on culture, society and politics). The concept also is useful as an analytic framework for mapping diverse religious worldviews. But questions remain about the extent that spiritual capital can have an impact at the macro-level. Following Weber and Wuthnow, the next logical step is attempting to identify if or to what extent such religious worldviews pass into wider public consciousness.[70]

This article has identified a religious worldview at MPCC that is relationship-centred, participatory and anti-authoritarian. It has obvious resonances with a political worldview that might inform a desire for democratization and consequently if it were to spread more widely in Zimbabwe, it could potentially encourage a wider democratization process. As discussed, this can potentially happen as the relevant ideas and practices are transmitted by religious networks in the country. MPCC has well-established networks of relationships with other congregations and organizations within charismatic Christianity within Zimbabwe. But it is not clear that MPCC has developed strong networks with the mainline churches or with charismatic churches outside of the New Frontiers network, which could mean that other Christians may never learn about its ideas or practices.

In their work on contemporary Zimbabwean civil society, Raftopoulos and Alexander claim that church-based organizations and congregations are amongst the most active and prominent in the country. At the same time, they acknowledge that little is known about the extent that such organizations are able to spread their ideas and effective practices.[71] As a case study, my research at MPCC is similarly limited. This points to the necessity of a more ambitious research agenda, building on this first step to identify varieties of spiritual capital conducive to democratization. The next step is to evaluate if or how such varieties of spiritual capital are being spread, asking if they are reaching critical tipping points in which their ideas and practices could lead to widespread democratic changes.

This could in turn aid in our understanding of how Christian churches and organizations can contribute to a wider democratization process in Zimbabwe. It is clear that such churches enjoy high levels of citizen trust, thus carrying a moral authority that the government and some other civil society groups lack.[72] Indeed, ZANU-PF has recognized that some of the churches represent a challenge to its authority, as well as an alternative power base. For example, the BBC reported that many Zimbabweans believe that ZANU-PF was behind the 2007 sex scandal involving the government's most prominent critic, Archbishop Pius Ncube.[73] Certainly, compromising images of Ncube were prominent in *state-run* newspapers and television.[74] Ncube resigned his position as archbishop and has not been as prominent a public figure as he was before the scandal broke.[75] It seems ZANU-PF feels compelled to silence church-based critics who ground their discourses in biblical ideals of justice for the poor, and critiques of unjust leadership. Further, ZANU-PF has orchestrated its own campaigns of religiously-based rhetoric in an attempt to legitimate its positions, for example to justify farm seizures.[76] The fact that ZANU-PF appears to take religion so seriously indicates that in the Zimbabwean public sphere, religious discourses matter.

Whether these discourses and the actions that flow from them can contribute to wider progress of democratization in Zimbabwe remains to be seen. Research by the Institute for a Democratic Alternative in South Africa (IDASA) in 2008 indicated that of all civil society groups in Zimbabwe, the churches have been the most consistent in placing healing and reconciliation on the public agenda.[77] 'The Zimbabwe We Want,' a discussion document prepared for civil society organizations and government officials by the Zimbabwe Catholic Bishops Conference, the Evangelical Fellowship of Zimbabwe, and the Zimbabwe Council of Churches, identified important political issues to be addressed, including reconciliation of opposing groups.[78] It cannot be demonstrated definitively, but it may be the case that the churches' public discourses on reconciliation helped create a climate in which the new power-sharing government included a ministerial post for Healing, Reconciliation and Integration. Like the rebuilding of the economy, the rebuilding of trusting social relationships through a society-wide reconciliation process is an important precursor to democratization.

Finally, the MDC's Prime Minister, Morgan Tsvangirai, has indicated that he wishes to promote free expression and lift restrictions on the press.[79] But even as Tsvangirai toured Western nations in June 2009, wooing donors and seeking diplomatic respectability, Amnesty International warned that civil rights activists were still being arrested and that citizens still lived in fear.[80] It may be the case that with the advent of the power-sharing government, Christian churches, organizations and other civil society groups would become bolder in advocating and working for social and political change. But there are still many obstacles to overcome before democratization can be realized in Zimbabwe.

Acknowledgements

This research was funded in part by the Association for the Sociology of Religion's Fichter Grant and the Trinity College Dublin new lecturer's start-up fund. I am grateful to all at MPCC who so generously participated in the research. I wish to thank Karin Alexander, Jeff Haynes, Isobel Mukonyora, Terence Ranger, Jim Wellman and participants at the Luce Symposia for Religion and Human Security (Seattle, 2008 and 2009) for their insights as I developed this case study. Therese Cullen provided proofreading assistance and helpful comments.

Notes

1. Salih, 'African Liberation Movement Governments and Democracy'; Haynes, 'Religion and Democratization in Africa'; Merkel, 'Embedded and Defective Democracies'.
2. Salih, 'African Liberation Movement Governments and Democracy', 675–676; Merkel, 'Embedded and Defective Democracies'; Dahl, *Polyarchy: Participation and Opposition*.
3. Koelble and Lipuma, 'Democratizing Democracy'.
4. Ibid., 3.
5. Bratton, Chikwana and Sithole, 'Propaganda and Public Opinion in Zimbabwe'.
6. Moore, 'A Reply to the Power of Propaganda: Public Opinion in Zimbabwe 2004'.
7. Bhebe and Ranger, *The Historical Dimensions of Democracy and Human Rights in Zimbabwe*; Hill, *What Happens after Mugabe?*; Holland, *Dinner with Mugabe*.
8. Hill, *The Battle for Zimbabwe: The Final Countdown*.
9. Eppel, 'Gukurahundi: The Need for Truth and Reparation'; Reeler, 'Sticks and Stones, Skeletons and Ghosts'.
10. Raftopoulos, 'Unreconciled Differences: The Limits of Reconciliation Politics in Zimbabwe', xi–xii.
11. Between 1980 and 1997 '3.6 million hectares was transferred from large-scale white farmers to 71,000 black small-farmer households'. Sachikonye, 'Land Reform and Farm Workers', 69. The UK government supported this programme with £44 million. It claims that by 1996 £3 million of this funding had not been spent. It subsequently withdrew its financial support for land reform, claiming, 'we would support a land reform programme that was transparent, that was carried out within the rule of law, within a well-managed economic framework and was pro-poor. Those are the principles that the Zimbabwe government committed themselves to in 1998 but have not adhered to in practice'. FCO, 'UK Policy on Zimbabwe'.
12. FCO, 'UK Policy on Zimbabwe.'
13. Bond and Manyanya, *Zimbabwe's Plunge: Exhausted Nationalism, Neoliberalism and the Search for Social Justice*, 45.
14. Holland, *Dinner with Mugabe*, 138–9; Feltoe, 'The Onslaught against Democracy and Rule of Law in Zimbabwe in 2000', 197.
15. Hammar, Raftopoulos and Jensen, *Zimbabwe's Unfinished Business*; Raftopoulos, 'Current Politics in Zimbabwe: Confronting the Crisis'; Sachikonye, 'The Promised Land'.
16. Masunungure, 'Travails of Opposition Politics in Zimbabwe since Independence', 175–90.

17. Ranger, 'Historiography, Patriotic History and the History of the Nation: the Struggle over the Past in Zimbabwe'.
18. BBC News Online, 'Zimbabwe PM Jeered by UK Exiles'; BBC News Online, 'UK Announces £5 million Aid for Zimbabwe'; *Mail & Guardian*, 'Zim Government Making Progress, says Tsvangirai'.
19. BBC News Online, 'Rights in Zimbabwe "precarious"'.
20. Inglehart and Welzel, *Modernization, Cultural Change, and Democracy*, 287
21. BBC News Online, 'Zimbabwe Inflation Reaches 2,200 per cent'.
22. BBC News Online, 'Zimbabwe Abandons its Currency'.
23. Raftopoulos and Alexander, *Reflections on Democratic Politics in Zimbabwe*.
24. Ibid., 38.
25. Koelble and Lipuma, 'Democratizing Democracy', 22.
26. Ibid.
27. US Department of State, 'International Religious Freedom Report'.
28. Dube, *A Socio-Political Agenda for the Twenty-First Century Zimbabwean Church*, 8.
29. Putnam, 'Bowling Alone: America's Declining Social Capital'; Putnam, *Bowling Alone: The Collapse and Revival of American Community*. See also Coleman, 'Social Capital in the Creation of Human Capital'.
30. Norris and Inglehart, *Sacred and Secular: Religion and Politics Worldwide*, 192.
31. Iannaccone, 'Religious Practice: A Human Capital Approach'; Stark and Finke, *Acts of Faith: Explaining the Human Side of Religion*; Berger and Hefner, 'Spiritual Capital in Comparative Perspective; Malloch, 'Social, Human and Spiritual Capital in Economic Development'; Woodberry, 'Researching Spiritual Capital: Promises and Pitfalls'; Unruh and Sider, *Saving Souls, Serving Society: Understanding the Faith Factor in Church-based Social Ministry*; Haynes, *Religion and Development: Conflict or Cooperation?*
32. Carkoglu, 'Social vs. Spiritual Capital in Explaining Philanthropic Giving in a Muslim Setting: The Case of Turkey', 113.
33. Iannaccone, 'Religious Practice'; Iannaccone, 'The Consequences of Religious Market Structures: Adam Smith and the Economics of Religion'.
34. Stark and Finke, *Acts of Faith*.
35. Berger and Hefner, 'Spiritual Capital in Comparative Perspective'.
36. Haynes, *Religion and Development: Conflict or Cooperation?*, 109; see also Berger, *Pyramids of Sacrifice*.
37. Weber, *The Protestant Ethic and the Spirit of Capitalism*.
38. Ranger, *Evangelical Christianity and Democracy in Africa*; Haynes, 'Religion and Democratization in Africa'; Gifford, *African Christianity: Its Public Role*; Gifford, *The Christian Churches and the Democratisation of Africa*.
39. Haynes, 'Religion and Democratization in Africa', 87.
40. Ranger, *Evangelical Christianity and Democracy in Africa*.
41. There is considerable debate about how to define 'charismatic' Christianity and related traditions such as evangelicalism and Pentecostalism. Recent work by Ranger (2008), Jenkins (2006), and Freston (2001) point out the historical developmental links between these expressions of Christianity, and consider them part of a broader movement (see Gifford 2003, 2004 for an alternative perspective). I take that broad view, conceiving evangelical, Pentecostal, and charismatic Christianity as sharing core characteristics, as outlined in the main text of this article. In this article, I use the term 'charismatic' broadly to include these three expressions of Christianity, while acknowledging that there are significant differences between them. Throughout the text when I am discussing other authors' work, I use the term that they use in their own writing (i.e. Ranger and Mukonyora on evangelicalism or Miller and Yamamori on Pentecostalism).

42. Freston, chapters on 'Kenya', 'South Africa', and 'Zimbabwe' in *Evangelicals and Politics in Asia, Africa and Latin America*; see also Balcomb, 'From Apartheid to the New Dispensation: Evangelicals and the Democratization of South Africa'.
43. Haynes, 'Religion and Democratization in Africa'.
44. Ranger, *Evangelical Christianity and Democracy in Africa*, 17.
45. Ibid., 15.
46. See Freston, *Evangelicals and Politics in Asia, Africa and Latin America*.
47. Maxwell, 'Catch the Cockerel Before Dawn'; Maxwell, 'The Durawall of Faith'; Martin, *Tongues of Fire: The Explosion of Pentecostalism in Latin America*; Martin, *Pentecostalism: The World their Parish*; van Dijk, 'Pentecostalism and the Politics of Prophetic Power'.
48. Freston, *Evangelicals and Politics in Asia, Africa and Latin America*.
49. Ranger, *Evangelical Christianity and Democracy in Africa*, 23–8.
50. Miller and Yamamori, *Global Pentecostalism*.
51. Gifford, 'The Bible as a Political Document in Africa', 22; see also Gifford, *Ghana's New Christianity*.
52. Mukonyora, 'Foundations for Democracy in Zimbabwean Evangelical Christianity'.
53. Ibid., 136.
54. Raftopolous and Alexander, *Reflections on Democratic Politics in Zimbabwe*, 36–8; Mukonyora, 'Foundations for Democracy in Zimbabwean Evangelical Christianity'.
55. About 100–150 people regularly attend the main Sunday morning worship service. Its cultural or ethnic composition is about 80–85% Shona, 10–15% white, and 5% Ndebele, other Africans, Europeans, and others. The high percentage of Shona is due to the fact that the dominant ethnic group in Harare is Shona. Whites make up less than 1% of Zimbabwe's population, so they are 'over-represented' in the church. My research took place between February and April 2007. My methods were ethnographic, including participant observation at worship services and prayer meetings, as well as informal conversations and semi-structured interviews. I wanted to discover what people thought was important about their congregation and their hopes and concerns for Zimbabwe. I conducted 18 in-depth interviews. Participants in the interviews included seven Shona, seven white Zimbabweans, two Ndebele, one white European and one from another African nation. There were an equal number of females and males. Whites were over-represented in my interviews because there were more whites in the over-40 age group. Most people who had been attending the congregation for more than a few years were white, and in order to get an accurate picture about the early days of the congregation I needed to speak with them. MPCC began as a nearly all white congregation in 1997, so their perspectives were especially important for explaining how it became multicultural. The congregation met six days a week for either prayer or worship, and people interacted informally outside of church meetings on a daily basis. This meant that I also interacted with people from MPCC nearly every day.
56. Ganiel, 'Beyond Pietism and Prosperity'; Ganiel, 'Ethnoreligious Change in Northern Ireland and Zimbabwe'; Ganiel, 'Religion and Human Security in Zimbabwe'.
57. Interview with elders, March 8, 2007.
58. Maxwell, *African Gifts of the Spirit*.
59. All 18 interviews were conducted in Harare in February and March 2007. The identity of interviewees is confidential.
60. Davidson, *Black Man's Burden: Africa and the Curse of the Nation-State*; Moyo, *Dead Aid: Why Aid is Not Working and How there is Another Way for Africa*.
61. Two interviews with different congregants, March 5, 2007; interview with congregant, March 21, 2007.
62. Freston, *Evangelicals and Politics in Asia, Africa and Latin America*; Ranger, *Evangelical Christianity and Democracy in Africa*.

63. Touraine, *The Voice and the Eye: An Analysis of Social Movements*; Eyerman and Jamison, *Social Movements*; McAdam, McCarthy and Zald, *Comparative Perspectives on Social Movements*; see also Ganiel, 'Religion and Transformation in South Africa?'
64. Ganiel, 'Beyond Pietism and Prosperity'; Ganiel, 'Ethnoreligious Change in Northern Ireland and Zimbabwe'; Ganiel, 'Religion and Human Security in Zimbabwe'.
65. Gifford, 'The Bible as a Political Document in Africa'; Gifford, *Ghana's New Christianity*; Freston, *Evangelicals and Politics in Asia, Africa and Latin America*.
66. Names have been changed for the sake of confidentiality.
67. For examples, visit the website of the Christian Alliance, http://www.christianalliancezimbabwe.org/index.htm. This includes a News Room section with press releases, some of which directly criticize the government. Christian Alliance members also have been on the receiving end of violence by government forces, as occurred at a prayer meeting in Harare on March 10, 2007, when I was in the country conducting my fieldwork.
68. People at MPCC worked in a range of secular, religious, international and local NGOs. Given that the work of some NGOs has been hampered by the Zimbabwean government, I do not name the specific organizations here in order to protect the confidentiality of the organizations and the people working in them.
69. Moyo, *Dead Aid*, 42; see also Norris and Inglehart, *Sacred and Secular: Religion and Politics Worldwide*.
70. Weber, *The Protestant Ethic*; Wuthnow, 'How Religious Groups Promote Forgiving'.
71. Raftopoulos and Alexander, *Reflections on Democratic Politics in Zimbabwe*.
72. Dube, *A Socio-Political Agenda*; Raftopoulos and Alexander, *Reflections on Democratic Politics in Zimbabwe*.
73. BBC News Online, 'Zimbabwe's Dirty Tricks Brigade'.
74. BBC News Online, 'Zimbabwe Bishop "Victim of State"'.
75. BBC News Online, 'Mugabe Critic Quits as Archbishop'.
76. Chitando, 'In the Beginning was the Land: The Appropriation of Religious Themes in Political Discourses in Zimbabwe'.
77. IDASA, 'Southern African Regional Assessment Mission Zimbabwe'.
78. Zimbabwe Catholic Bishops Conference, the Evangelical Fellowship of Zimbabwe, and the Zimbabwe Council of Churches, 'The Zimbabwe We Want.'
79. BBC News Online, 'UK Announces £5 m Aid for Zimbabwe'.
80. BBC News Online, 'Viewpoint: Tsvangirai's Ambiguous Trip'.

Notes on contributor

Gladys Ganiel lectures in conflict resolution and reconciliation studies at the Belfast campus of the Irish School of Ecumenics, Trinity College Dublin. Her research interests include Pentecostal/charismatic Christianity, evangelicalism, religion and politics in Southern Africa, and the Northern Ireland conflict. She is the author of *Evangelicalism and Conflict in Northern Ireland* (Palgrave 2008) and numerous articles about religion and politics in Northern Ireland, South Africa and Zimbabwe.

Bibliography

Balcomb, Anthony. 'From Apartheid to the New Dispensation: Evangelicals and the Democratization of South Africa'. In *Evangelical Christianity and Democracy in Africa*, ed. Terence Ranger. Oxford: Oxford University Press, 2008.

BBC News Online. 'Viewpoint: Tsvangirai's Ambiguous Trip', June 24, 2009. http://news.bbc.co.uk/1/hi/world/africa/8112533.stm (accessed June 24, 2009).
BBC News Online. 'UK Announces £5 m Aid for Zimbabwe', June 22, 2009. http://news.bbc.co.uk/1/hi/world/africa/8112339.stm (accessed June 23, 2009).
BBC News Online. 'Zimbabwe PM Jeered by UK Exiles', June 20, 2009. http://news.bbc.co.uk/1/hi/world/africa/8110939.stm (accessed June 23, 2009).
BBC News Online. 'Rights in Zimbabwe Precarious', June 18, 2009. http://news.bbc.co.uk/1/hi/world/africa/8106735.stm (accessed June 23, 2009).
BBC News Online. 'Zimbabwe Abandons its Currency', January 29, 2009. http://news.bbc.co.uk/1/hi/world/africa/7859033.stm (accessed June 23, 2009).
BBC News Online. 'Zimbabwe Bishop "Victim of State"', September 23, 2007. http://news.bbc.co.uk/1/hi/world/africa/7009006.stm (accessed June 24, 2009).
BBC News Online. 'Zimbabwe's Dirty Tricks Brigade', September 13, 2007. http://news.bbc.co.uk/1/hi/world/africa/6991681.stm (accessed June 24, 2009).
BBC News Online. 'Mugabe Critic Quits as Archbishop', September 11, 2007. http://news.bbc.co.uk/1/hi/world/africa/6989101.stm (accessed June 24, 2009).
BBC News Online. 'Zimbabwe Inflation Reaches 2,200 per cent', April 26, 2007. http://news.bbc.co.uk/1/hi/business/6597993.stm (accessed June 23, 2009).
Berger, Peter. *Pyramids of Sacrifice: Political Ethics and Social Change*. New York: Basic Books, 1975.
Berger, Peter and Robert Hefner. 'Spiritual Capital in Comparative Perspective'. 2003. http://www.spiritualcapitalresearchprogram.com/pdf/Berger.pdf (accessed October 22, 2008).
Bhebe, Ngwabi, and Terence Ranger, eds. *The Historical Dimensions of Democracy and Human Rights in Zimbabwe*. Harare: University of Zimbabwe Publications, 2001.
Bond, Patrick, and Masimba Manyanya. *Zimbabwe's Plunge: Exhausted Nationalism, Neoliberalism and the Search for Social Justice*. London: Merlin Press, 2002.
Bratton, Michael, Annie Chikwana and Tulani Sithole. 'Propaganda and Public Opinion in Zimbabwe'. *Journal of Contemporary African Studies* 23, no. 1 (2005): 77–108.
Carkoglu, Ali. 'Social vs. Spiritual Capital in Explaining Philanthropic Giving in a Muslim Setting: The Case of Turkey'. In *Religion and the Individual: Belief, Practice, Identity*, ed. Abbey Day. Aldershot: Ashgate Publishing Ltd. 2008.
Chitando, Ezra. 'In the Beginning was the Land: The Appropriation of Religious Themes in Political Discourses in Zimbabwe'. *Africa* 75, no. 2 (2005): 220–39.
Coleman, James. 'Social Capital in the Creation of Human Capital'. *American Journal of Sociology* 94 (1998): 95–120.
Dahl, Robert A. *Polyarchy: Participation and Opposition*. New Haven, CT: Yale University Press, 1971.
Davidson, Basil. *Black Man's Burden: Africa and the Curse of the Nation-State*. London: James Currey, 1992.
Dube, Jimmy G. *A Socio-Political Agenda for the Twenty-First Century Zimbabwean Church: Empowering the Excluded*. Lewiston, NY: Edwin Mellen Press, 2006.
Eppel. 'Gukurahundi: The Need for Truth and Reparation'. In *Zimbabwe: Injustice and Political Reconciliation*, eds. Brian Raftopoulos and Tyrone Savage, 43–62. Cape Town: Institute for Justice and Reconciliation, 2004.
Eyerman, Ron, and Andrew Jamison. *Social Movements: A Cognitive Approach*. Cambridge: Polity Press, 1991.
FCO. 'UK Policy on Zimbabwe'. http://ukinsouthafrica.fco.gov.uk/en/working-with-south-africa/uk-policy-zimbabwe/ (accessed June 23, 2009).
Feltoe, Geoffrey. 'The Onslaught against Democracy and the Rule of Law in Zimbabwe in 2000'. In *Zimbabwe: The Past is the Future*, ed. David Harold-Barry, 193–223. Harare: Weaver Press, 2004.

Freston, Paul. *Evangelicals and Politics in Asia, Africa and Latin America*. Cambridge: Cambridge University Press, 2001.
Ganiel, Gladys. 'Religion and Transformation in South Africa? Institutional and Discursive Change in a Charismatic Congregation'. *Transformation: Critical Perspectives on Southern Africa* 63 (2007): 1–22.
Ganiel, Gladys. 'Ethnoreligious Change in Northern Ireland and Zimbabwe: A Comparative Study of Religious Havens'. *Ethnopolitics,* (2009, forthcoming).
Ganiel, Gladys. 'Religion and Human Security in Zimbabwe'. This paper was presented at the Luce Symposium on Religion and Human Security, Seattle: University of Washington, May 8–9, 2008 and May 7–8, 2009.
Ganiel, Gladys. 'Beyond Pietism and Prosperity: Religious Resources for Reconstruction and Reconciliation in Zimbabwe'. In African Peace and Conflict Network working paper, 2008. http://www.africaworkinggroup.org/files/Ganiel.pdf (accessed January 22, 2009).
Gifford, Paul, ed. *The Christian Churches and the Democratisation of Africa*. Leiden: E.J. Brill, 1995.
Gifford, Paul. *African Christianity: Its Public Role*. London: Hurst & Company, 1998.
Gifford, Paul. 'The Bible as a Political Document in Africa'. In *Scriptural Politics: The Bible and the Koran as Political Models in the Middle East and Africa*, ed. Niels. Kastfelt. London: Hurst & Company, 2003.
Gifford, Paul. *Ghana's New Christianity: Pentecostalism in a Globalising African Economy*. London: Hurst & Company, 2004.
Hammar, Amanda, Brian Raftopoulos, and Stig Jensen, eds. *Zimbabwe's Unfinished Business: Rethinking Land, State and Nation in the Context of Crisis*. Harare: Weaver Press, 2003.
Haynes, Jeffrey. 'Religion and Democratization in Africa'. *Democratization* 11, no. 4 (2004): 66–89.
Haynes, Jeffrey. *Religion and Development: Conflict or Cooperation?* Basingstoke: Palgrave, 2007.
Hill, Geoff. *The Battle for Zimbabwe: The Final Countdown*. Cape Town: Zebra Press, 2003.
Hill, Geoff. *What Happens After Mugabe? Can Zimbabwe Rise from the Ashes?* Cape Town: Zebra Press, 2005.
Holland, Heidi. *Dinner with Mugabe*. Johannesburg: Penguin Books, 2008.
Iannaccone, Laurence R. 'Religious Practice: A Human Capital Approach'. *Journal for the Scientific Study of Religion* 29 (1990): 297–314.
Iannaccone, Laurence R. 'The Consequences of Religious Market Structures: Adam Smith and the Economics of Religion'. *Rationality and Society* (1991): 156–77.
IDASA. 'Southern African Regional Assessment Mission Zimbabwe'. 2008.
Inglehart, Ronald and Christian Welzel. *Modernization, Cultural Change, and Democracy: The Human Development Sequence*. Cambridge: Cambridge University Press, 2005.
Jenkins, Philip. *The New Faces of Christianity: Believing the Bible in the Global South*. New York: Oxford University Press, 2006.
Koelble, Thomas A., and Edward Lipuma. 'Democratizing Democracy: A Postcolonial Critique of Convential Approaches to the Measurement of Democracy'. *Democratization* 15, no. 1 (2008): 1–28.
Mail & Guardian. 'Zim Government Making Progress, Says Tsvangirai', June 22, 2009. http://www.mg.co.za/article/2009-06-22-tsvangirai-zim-govt-making-progress (accessed June 23, 2009).
Malloch, Theodore Roosevelt. 'Social, Human and Spiritual Capital in Economic Development'. 2003. http://www.spiritualcapitalresearchprogram.com/pdf/malloch.pdf, (accessed October 22, 2008).

Martin, David. *Tongues of Fire: The Explosion of Pentecostalism in Latin America*. Oxford: Blackwell, 1980.
Martin, David. *Pentecostalism: The World their Parish*. Oxford: Blackwell, 2002.
Masunungure, Eldr. 'Travails of Opposition Politics in Zimbabwe Since Independence'. In *Zimbabwe: The Past is the Future*, ed. Eldr Masunungure, 147–92. Harare: Weaver Press, 2004.
Maxwell, David. 'Catch the Cockerel Before Dawn: Pentecostalism and Politics in Post-colonial Zimbabwe'. *Africa: Journal of the International African Institute* 70, no. 2 (2000): 249–77.
Maxwell, David. 'The Durawall of Faith: Pentecostal Spirituality in Neo-Liberal Zimbabwe'. *Journal of Religion in Africa* 35, no. 1 (2005): 4–32.
Maxwell, David. *African Gifts of the Spirit: Pentecostalism and the Rise of a Zimbabwean Transnational Religious Movement*. Oxford University Press: James Currey, 2007.
McAdam, Doug, John McCarthy and Mayer Zald. *Comparative Perspectives on Social Movements: Political Opportunities, Mobilizing Structures, and Cultural Framings*. Cambridge: Cambridge University Press, 1996.
Merkel, Wolfgang. 'Embedded and Defective Democracies'. *Democratization* 11, no. 5 (2004): 33–58.
Miller, David and Tetsunao Yamamori. *Global Pentecostalism: The New Face of Christian Social Engagement*. Berkeley: University of California Press, 2007.
Moore, David. 'A Reply to "The Power of Propaganda: Public Opinion in Zimbabwe 2004"'. *Journal of Contemporary African Studies* 23, no. 1 (2005): 109–19.
Moyo, Dambisa. *Dead Aid: Why Aid is Not Working and How There is Another Way for Africa*. London: Allen Lane, 2009.
Mukonyora, Isabel. 'Foundations for Democracy in Zimbabwean Evangelical Christianity'. In *Evangelical Christianity and Democracy in Africa*, ed. Terence Ranger. Oxford: Oxford University Press, 2008.
Norris, Pippa and Ronald Inglehart. *Sacred and Secular: Religion and Politics Worldwide*. Cambridge: Cambridge University Press, 2004.
Putnam, Robert. 'Bowling Alone: America's Declining Social Capital'. *Journal of Democracy* 6 (1995): 65–78.
Putnam, Robert. *Bowling Alone: The Collapse and Revival of American Community*. New York: Simon and Schuster, 2000.
Raftopoulos, Brian. 'Current Politics in Zimbabwe: Confronting the Crisis'. In *Zimbabwe: The Past is the Future*, ed. David Harold-Barry, 1–18. Harare: Weaver Press, 2004.
Raftopoulos, Brian. 'Unreconciled Differences: The Limits of Reconciliation Politics in Zimbabwe'. In *Zimbabwe: Injustice and Political Reconciliation*, eds. Brian Raftopoulos and Tyrone Savage, xi–xii. Cape Town: Institute for Justice and Reconciliation, 2004.
Raftopoulos, Brian and Karin Alexander. *Reflections on Democratic Politics in Zimbabwe*. Cape Town: Institute for Justice and Reconciliation, 2006.
Ranger, Terence O, ed. *Evangelical Christianity and Democracy in Africa*. Oxford: Oxford University Press, 2008.
Ranger, Terence O. 'Historiography, Patriotic History and the History of the Nation: the Struggle Over the Past in Zimbabwe'. 2003. http://cas1.elis.rug.ac.be/avrug/pdf06/ranger.pdf (accessed April 3, 2009).
Reeler, A.P. 'Sticks and Stones, Skeletons and Ghosts'. In *Zimbabwe: The Past is the Future*, ed. David Harold-Barry, 225–38. Harare: Weaver Press, 2004.
Sachikonye, Lloyd. 'Land Reform and Farm Workers'. In *Zimbabwe: The Past is the Future*, ed. David Harold-Barry, 69–76. Harare: Weaver Press, 2004.
Sachikonye, Lloyd. 'The Promised Land: From Expropriation to Reconciliation and Jambanja'. In *Zimbabwe: Injustice and Political Reconciliation*, eds. Brian

Raftopoulos and Tyrone Savage, 1–18. Cape Town: Institute for Justice and Reconciliation, 2004.
Salih, M.A. Mohamed. 'African Liberation Movement Governments and Democracy'. *Democratization* 14, no. 4 (2007): 669–85.
Smidt, Corwin, ed. *Religion as Social Capital*. Waco, TX: Baylor University Press, 2003.
'The Zimbabwe We Want: Towards a National Vision for Zimbabwe'. Discussion document of the Zimbabwe Catholic Bishops Conference, the Evangelical Fellowship of Zimbabwe, and the Zimbabwe Council of Churches, 2006. http://www.africamission-mafr.org/zimbabwe.doc (accessed June 24, 2009).
Touraine, Alain. *The Voice and the Eye: An Analysis of Social Movements*. Cambridge: Cambridge University Press, 1978.
Unruh, Heidi Rolland, and Ronald J. Sider. *Saving Souls, Serving Society: Understanding the Faith Factor in Church-Based Social Ministry*. Oxford: Oxford University Press, 2005.
US Department of State. 'International Religious Freedom Report', 2007. http://www.state.gov/g/drl/rls/irf/2007/ (accessed January 28, 2008).
van Dijk, Rijk. 'Pentecostalism and the Politics of Prophetic Power: Religious Modernity in Ghana'. In *Scriptural Politics: The Bible and the Koran as Political Models in the Middle East and Africa*, ed. Niels Kastfelt. London: Hurst & Company, 2003.
Weber, Max. *The Protestant Ethic and the Spirit of Capitalism*. London: Routledge, 2001.
Woodberry, Robert D. 'Researching Spiritual Capital: Promises and Pitfalls', 2003. http://www.spiritualcapitalresearchprogram.com/pdf/woodberry.pdf (accessed October 22, 2008).
Wuthnow, Robert. 'How Religious Groups Promote Forgiving: A National Study'. *Journal for the Scientific Study of Religion* 39, no. 2 (2000): 125–39.

Islam and democratization in Turkey: secularism and trust in a divided society

Ioannis N. Grigoriadis

Bilkent University, Ankara, Turkey

The history of Turkish modernization has been inextricably linked with the question of secularism. From the advent of the Turkish Republic in 1923, Islam was held responsible for the underdevelopment and eventual demise of the Ottoman Empire. Based on the laïcité of the Second French Republic, the secularization programme of modern Turkey's founder, Kemal Atatürk, entailed the full subjugation of Islam to the State, its eradication from the public sphere and its limitation into a very narrowly defined private sphere.

The transition of Turkey to multiparty politics in 1946 was linked with a rising role of Islam in the public sphere. Islam became a crucial element in the political vocabulary of peripheral political forces which challenged the supremacy of the secularist, Kemalist bureaucratic elite. While a number of military coups aimed – among other things – to control religion, Turkish political Islam showed remarkable resilience and adaptability.

Most recently, the transformation of the Justice and Development Party (*Adalet ve Kalkınma* Partisi – AKP) into the strongest proponent of Turkey's European Union (EU) integration brought Turkey closer than ever to EU membership, challenged the monopoly which the Kemalist elite enjoyed as the representative of Western political values and suggested a novel liberal version of secularism. Yet Turkey has been embroiled since 2007 in successive political crises which had secularism as their focal point. This article argues that the transformation of Turkish political Islam has produced an alternative, liberal version of secularism; yet, it has not resolved deep social divisions. Building a liberal consensus between religious conservatives and secularists is imperative for the resolution of deep social divisions in Turkey. The European Union as a guarantor and initiator of reform could play a major role in building trust between the secularist and the religious conservative segments of society.

In December 2007, Fazıl Say, a famous young Turkish pianist who after a shining international career decided to move back to Turkey in 2002 was interviewed by a German newspaper, *Süddeutsche Zeitung*. His remarks caused a controversy, as Say, speaking on behalf of the country's secularist elite touched upon a very sensitive issue: secularism in Turkey. The young artist said that he considered emigrating from Turkey due to the rise of Islamism in the country. In his own words:

> Our dreams are somewhat dead in Turkey. All ministers' wives wear headscarf. I want to move somewhere else ... I am waiting for the dialogue of the counter part for six years. There are some things that annoy me ... Turkey's music lover characteristic is being destroyed.[1]

Say's remarks caused a media sensation in Turkey. One of the most charismatic young Turkish artists, already acclaimed in Europe, who had returned to the country in 2004, at the peak of optimism about the country's European Union (EU) membership, was announcing his intention to emigrate for political reasons. His statement prompted various reactions from the ranks of the government party, the AKP. Prime Minister Recep Tayyip Erdoğan commented that 'the artists of this country do not abandon it'. Minister of Culture Ertuğrul Günay responded that 'His concerns are not founded. I do not understand his concerns about the future of Turkey, either.'[2] However, the bitterest reaction came from the Vice President of the AKP, Dengir Mir Mehmet Fırat, who said: 'Mr. Say is free to do so [emigrate]. I respect that and do not feel much sadness.'[3] One of the most interesting responses came from another renowned Turkish artist. Fashion designer Cemil İpekçi commented on Say's statement in an interview to the liberal Islamist newspaper *Zaman* as follows:

> I know Fazıl Say; he is a very nice person. But what does this 'those' mean? Those he calls 'those' get 70 percent of the vote. How does he make this division? These are the white Turks, 40,000 people to whom my family also belongs, who think that Turkey consists of Nişantaşı.[4] They do not see a Turkey of 65 million people, because these are the last outcries of a specific minority and dinosaurs.[5]

Say's reaction was however characteristic of a wider trend in Turkish society. The issue of secularism became increasingly pronounced in 2007, as the political dominance of the post-Islamist AKP raised concerns among Turkey's secularist elite regarding the future trajectory of the country. The year 2008 was marked by a closure case against the AKP filed by the country's chief prosecutor Abdurrahman Yalçınkaya. In the case it was claimed that the party had become a 'centre of anti-secular activities' threatening the republican nature of the Turkish state. While the court decision accepted the argument of the prosecutor, it fell short of closing the party.[6]

In fact, secularism has been a key political theme since the early twentieth century. The demise of the Ottoman Empire and the rise of republican Turkey were linked with a radical shift from pan-Islamism towards secularization.

Based on the secularism of the Second French Republic, the secularization programme of Kemal Atatürk entailed the full subjugation of Islam to the state, its eradication from the public sphere and its limitation into a very narrowly defined private space. This came under challenge with the rise of political Islam and an Islamist elite which challenged the supremacy of senior Kemalist figures, won political power by democratic means and suggested an alternative version of secularism, which did not oppose a public role for religion.

The summer 2007 presidential crisis[7] was illustrative of the relevance of this conflict to contemporary political developments. This article aims to explore the question of secularism in Turkey in light of recent developments in Turkish politics and society. It attempts to define the term 'secularism' and questions the consensus view that Turkey is indeed a secular state. It also explores different conceptualizations of secularism which lie at the heart of the contemporary debate in Turkey and are linked to a significant degree to the impact of globalization on Turkish society. It then examines the transformation of Turkish political Islam, its limits and evaluates the new version of secularism which the incumbent AKP government advocates. Amidst rising social tension, mutual distrust has aggravated relations between secularists and conservatives, as both sides have become caught in a vicious circle of claim and counter-claim regarding their motivations and goals. This article argues that an external actor with bearing on both factions such as the EU may indeed be instrumental in alleviating mutual distrust and helping build toleration for different lifestyles in Turkey.

Is Turkey a secular state?

Republican Turkey is often described as the 'only Muslim secular state', a 'model for the Islamic world'. Nonetheless, a closer examination of the term 'secular' reveals that this description is inaccurate.[8] The meaning of the term 'secular', colloquially understood as 'non-religious', is not limited to the separation of religious and political realms in Turkey. Instead, it involves a neutral stance toward different religious beliefs, as well as the phenomenon of religion in general. A genuinely secular state has no preferential links with any religion and neither promotes, nor obstructs religious belief among its citizens. The republican Turkish state fulfils neither of these conditions. Opposition to any religious form of expression within a – widely defined – public sphere shows the traditionally hostile approach of the Turkish state toward religion. For example, the ban on Islamic religious orders (*tarikat*) and religious attire, the headscarf issue and the eradication of religion from the public sphere are all indicative of a state which has long taken aggressive measures to put religious institutions under its firm control and promote a 'religion-free', 'rational' society. Religion was expected to fade away as a result of the consequential 'enlightenment' and 'modernization' of Turkish society and the associated upward economic and social mobility of its citizens.[9] As a result, the term 'assertive secularism' – rather than 'secularism' per se – more accurately describes state–religion relations in republican Turkey.[10] Nevertheless, the assertively secular character of the Turkish state has often been compromised as a result of political expediency. This compromise was not in the direction of original secularism, but rather toward championing a certain form of state religion.

Secular–ideological opposition to religion did not mean lack of state interest in the instrumental use of religion for political purposes. Sunni Islam, as a cementing factor of Turkish national identity and a counterweight to the perceived divisive influence of ethnic minority nationalism and leftist ideas, has been skilfully used since the founding years of the Republic; this also contradicted with the principle of secularism.[11] While Islam was purged from the public sphere in the early republican period, the state kept a firm control over it by banning the *tarikat*s and establishing the Directorate of Religious Affairs (*Diyanet İşleri Başkanlığı* – DİB).[12] Active intervention and control was viewed as the only means to secure the containment of the perceived threat from political Islam to the state's secular ideals and goals. This policy shift became institutionalized with the official championing by the 1980–1983 military regime of what was known as the 'Turkish-Islamic Synthesis' (*Türk-İslam Sentezi*), the introduction of mandatory religious primary education and clauses in the 1982 Constitution which strengthened the power of Sunni Islam.[13] The pro-Sunni bias evident in the policies of the Directorate of Religious Affairs, the mandatory instruction of Sunni Islam in state schools and the state-funded construction of mosques throughout the country – even in Alevi[14] villages – comprised clear manifestations of a pervasive bias in favour of Sunni Islam.[15] Especially when it came to the Alevi question, the assertively secular Turkish state suddenly became a Sunni one.[16]

This mixed legacy of animosity toward religion, state control and bias in favour of Sunni Islam forms the framework of state–society relations in republican Turkey. Turkey could, therefore, be characterized as a *sui generis* assertively secular state, in which long-term antireligious policies are matched by short-term instrumental use of Sunni Islam.[17] This situation created a serious obstacle in the process of Turkey's democratization, facilitated the politicization of Islam, and created an environment conducive to political conflict.[18]

The transformation of Turkish political Islam

The 'soft' coup of 28 February 1997 and the subsequent fall of the coalition government led by the Islamist Necmettin Erbakan crucially affected the course of political Islam in Turkey. At the domestic level, it became clear that any ideas about regime change and the introduction of the Islamic law were utterly unrealistic. This was due not only to the reaffirmation of the guardian role of the military in Turkish politics, but also to the lack of appeal of any Islamization programme to the vast majority of the people.[19] If a party with an Islamist political character could ever manage to claim a leading role in Turkish politics, this could only happen through its transformation into a conservative centre-right party with Islamic leanings.[20]

At the European level, the 2001 decision of the European Court of Human Rights (ECHR) to uphold the decision of the Turkish Constitutional Court on the closure of the Islam-leaning Welfare Party (*Refah Partisi* – RP) was a milestone event. On the one hand, Erbakan's decision to appeal to the ECHR against the closure of the RP undermined his rhetoric against European institutions and civilization. The establishment of an Islamic 'just order' in Turkey, which had been the perennial quest of the National View (*Milli Görüş*) movement,[21] implied the moral supremacy of the Islamic civilization over the European.[22] By appealing to the European Convention of Human Rights (ECHR), Erbakan tacitly acknowledged that 'Christian Europe' was an alternative and acceptable source of justice. The relativization of the concept of Islamic justice by the very person who had fought throughout his life for its establishment in Turkey undermined any belief in the superiority of Islamic civilization and showed that the Islamist political project in Turkey had reached its limits. The court ruled that, by closing the RP, the Turkish court did not violate Article 11 of the ECHR. The court held in July 2001 that

> the sanctions imposed on the applicants could reasonably be considered to meet a pressing social need for the protection of democratic society, since, on the pretext of giving a different meaning to the principle of secularism, the leaders of the Refah Partisi had declared their intention to establish a plurality of legal systems based on differences in religious belief, to institute Islamic law (the *Sharia*), a system of law that was in marked contrast to the values embodied in the Convention. They had also left in doubt their position regarding recourse to force in order to come to power and, more particularly, to retain power.[23]

This decision, which was made by the Third Section of the ECHR, was firmly upheld by the ECHR Grand Chamber in February 2003.[24] The ECHR decision demonstrated that Islamic extremism could not be protected by European liberal democratic institutions. Support of European political institutions for Turkish political parties under state persecution was not unconditional. Turkish political parties had to subscribe to European political values to be then able to claim European support. Like terrorism, Islamic fundamentalism or even traditional political Islam could not expect support from European courts.[25] The threat which 'Islamic fundamentalism' constituted for democratic principles and human rights was not underestimated, and the misuse of democratic institutions for undemocratic objectives could not be endorsed by European institutions

In the aftermath of the RP closure, ideological debate within the Virtue Party (*Fazilet Partisi* – FP), the party which succeeded RP as the representative of Turkish political Islam, showed a radical ongoing transformation. Many of its members attempted to break the vicious circle of state suppression by advocating a radical transformation of Islamist ideology. The establishment of an Islamic republic would no more be the ultimate aim. Allegiance to the secular principles of Western European democracy was instead adopted, and an amalgamation of Islamic values with Western political liberalism was attempted.[26] The quest for Islamic religious freedoms was now framed in the language of political liberalism and multiculturalism. Crucial for the rehabilitation of the hitherto Western image of 'corruption' was the experience of immigration to Western Europe for millions of Turkish citizens, who realized that they could more freely practice Islam in 'Christian' Germany than in 'Muslim' Turkey. The German legal order lacked the restrictions in the manifestation of Islamic religious belief in the public sphere, which hampered Islamic religious freedom in Turkey.[27]

This ideological trend within the Islamist intelligentsia obtained a political vehicle with the formation of the Justice and Development Party (*Adalet ve Kalkınma Partisi* – AKP) in the aftermath of the closure of the FP in 2001. The AKP leadership took pains to dissociate the new party from its Islamist past, and advertised itself as a moderate conservative party,[28] loyal to secularism.[29] The new ideology of the party was an amalgam of conservatism, liberalism, Islamic values and rightist political ideas. The term 'Islamist' was rejected as a description of the ideological identity of the party; the term 'conservative democratic' (*muhafazakâr demokrat*) was preferred.[30] The AKP was the first party from the Islamic political tradition to address the grievances of Turkey's pious Muslim population not in terms of Islamic justice or 'just order' (*âdil düzen*), but on the basis of a liberal and human rights agenda. The assertively secular character of the Turkish state was criticized, not from an Islamist but from a liberal perspective. Contested issues of major symbolic importance, like the headscarf and religious education, were now discussed as evidence of Turkey's democratic deficit. The liberal shift of the AKP was confirmed when – contrary to the tradition of the National View parties – it ardently supported Turkey's bid for EU membership.

The November 2002 elections became the big test case for the AKP political experiment: With 34.43% of the vote and 365 parliamentary seats the AKP formed a single-party government, while the traditionalist Islamic Felicity Party (*Saadet Partisi* – SP) gained only 2.49% and no seats. The AKP had succeeded in winning power, dominating the political agenda and ideology of Turkish political Islam and opening it to the influence of Western political ideas. The emphasis on Islamic morality as an antidote to chronic political corruption remained,[31] but the political priorities of the new government were different. After taking over power, the AKP and its leader Recep Tayyip Erdoğan vowed to pursue the reform steps necessary for Turkey to qualify for the start of EU accession negotiations. The prospect of EU membership provided a vision, which the majority of Turkish society shared.[32] The AKP leadership realized that the European Union could be of critical help in its effort to gain political legitimacy[33] and promote the sensitive, religion-related aspects of its political agenda. By becoming an ardent supporter and promoter of Turkey's EU membership, the AKP leadership challenged the monopoly of Kemalist elites in their advocacy of Westernization and EU membership. Raising the level of human rights protection in Turkey to the European standards fell within the scope of fulfilling the Copenhagen Criteria for the start of EU accession negotiations, and created the conditions for their successful completion. The reform of Turkey's human rights legislation would necessarily mean a redefinition of the public and private spheres in Turkish society. Many activities which would – until the reform – fall within the scope of the public realm, would now be transferred to the private realm and thus enjoy full protection under the new human rights legislation.[34] The prospect of EU membership and the EU monitoring of Turkish politics also provided a secure environment against any intervention by military and bureaucratic elites. This enabled the AKP government to implement its reformist political programme, which confirmed the transformation of the AKP from an Islamist to a conservative democratic party,[35] increasingly similar to the equivalent religious value-based Christian Democratic parties of Western Europe.

A new version of secularism in the making?

While Europe affirmed its opposition to Islamic fundamentalism by refusing to provide protection to the RP and Turkish political Islam was transformed, the question of how to protect freedom of religion against state practices remained open. Turkish political Islam traditionally viewed the secularist character of the Turkish state as a dire consequence of the Kemalist Westernization project. Europe was the historic cradle of assertive secularism and as such responsible for the antireligious character of the Turkish Republic. Nonetheless, with the rise of the AKP, Islamist intellectuals and politicians, alternative Western systems of regulating state–religion relations were explored. The fact that the AKP abandoned the Islamic state project for the sake of Western liberal democratic principles did not mean that it lost its sensitivity on issues of religious freedom; its argument, however, was now based upon political liberalism.[36] The establishment of a pluralist public sphere in Turkey was now suggested as the solution for the problems related to the public visibility of Islamic identity in Turkey.[37] This could be the starting point for the reform of Turkish secularism. This was inspired by French *laïcité* of the Second French Republic, the most antireligious system in the Western world and hardly compatible with the principles of Western European liberal democracy. It was, therefore, possible to argue for a reform of Turkish assertive secularism not on the basis of restoring Islamic law, but rather of introducing liberal principles.[38] This reform would aim at substituting a truly secular, religion-blind policy for the antireligious character of state policies as well as the bias in favour of Sunni Islam. This model of 'passive secularism' would be distanced from the French model of *laïcité* and could be more closely related to the United Kingdom or German models of secularism and Western European liberal standards.[39] It would protect state and religion from mutual interventions and protect Turkish democracy without obstructing the free religious expression of the majority of the Turkish people. In a treatise, which appeared on the official AKP website and could thus be considered to reflect the party's official views, Akdoğan, a scholar affiliated with the AKP, argued:

> The AKP understands 'secularism'[40] as an institutional stance and method, which ensures that the state remains neutral and keeps an equal distance from all religions and ideas; differences of religion and/or different confessions and ideologies can

be professed in social peace without them turning into conflict. The party thinks that, for secularism to work as an adjudicating institution (*hakem muessesi*) of the fundamental rights and freedoms under constitutional protection, it needs to be supported by democracy and operate in a conciliatory environment.[41]

Thus, the AKP accepted secularism as 'an indispensable condition of democracy and the guarantee of the freedom of religion and conscience',[42] while simultaneously linking it with democracy and human rights. This position attempted to reconcile the legacy of illiberal Turkish assertive secularism with respect for democratic principles and fundamental freedoms. Secularism should not mean the absence of religion from the public sphere, or the state control of religious institutions. The version of passive secularism that the AKP advocated did not eliminate religion from the public sphere, but required the state to adopt a neutral stance on religious issues and respect the freedoms of religion and conscience of its citizens.[43] The re-emergence of religion in the public sphere should not, therefore, be seen as a reassertion of militant political Islam, but as maturation in the process of democratization and transition from assertive to passive secularism. The introduction of such a secular system would mean the simultaneous abolition of Kemalist assertive secularism and Islamism in favour of a liberal democratic solution.[44] This became clear in the AKP political programme in 2004, where secularism was defined as an 'orienting principle for the state, but not for the individual', 'a means to freedom and social harmony' and 'a guarantee of freedom of conscience'.[45]

The appeal of this redefinition of secularism was not restricted to the leading circles of the AKP. Prominent Islamist intellectuals, who had once supported the establishment of an Islamic state in Turkey, became proponents of Turkey's European vocation.[46] The European Union was no more the arch enemy, but a *de facto* ally in their struggle against the Kemalist secularism and its iron fist, the military. The reform of assertive secularism could be achieved through Turkey's democratization, which only the process of Turkey's EU accession could guarantee. While democracy and human rights had been despised as prime examples of Western concepts, which had adulterated sound Islamic political thought, they now occupied the centre of Islamist political discourse,[47] offering a solution for the problem of secularism. The adoption of these principles of modernity resulted in a paradoxical situation whereby former Islamist intellectuals were defending human rights and democracy, pointing to the shortcomings of the Kemalist modernization project, which, despite professing modernity, had failed to deliver its proclaimed biggest blessings.[48]

The headscarf issue

The same liberal discourse was recently applied in a novel approach to the headscarf issue, one of the symbols of the secularist controversy in republican Turkey (also see Barras' article in this special issue). The ban on females' headscarf use in state institutions was one of the clearest manifestations of the assertively secular character of republican Turkey. The rise of an Islamic 'counter-elite' in the 1980s had resulted in the extreme politicization of the headscarf issue as the members of the new elite felt able to challenge the hegemony of the established secular elite. While retaining its original religious and traditional meaning, wearing the headscarf also achieved an explicitly political symbolic value. It became a political statement of a new rising and ambitious elite. Nonetheless, the argument in favour of females' headscarf use was still based on an Islamist discourse. The headscarf was understood as an indispensable element of female Islamic morality, and Islamic law failed to recognize the distinction between the public and the private sphere. The assertively secular principle of keeping religion outside the public sphere could not tolerate the most public manifestation of resistance to assertive secularism. The purge of the public sphere culminated in the aftermath of the 'soft' coup of 28 February 1997. The response to this campaign by the short-lived FP and, most importantly, the AKP, markedly differed in its content. Under the AKP, reference was made to the idea of 'universal human rights' embodied in international human rights conventions, and Islamic law was no more seen as the sole manifestation of justice. The right to education, the principle of non-discrimination, the freedom of religion as protected by the ECHR and other international human rights treaties were quoted in defence of the right of women to wear the headscarf. Even the solution suggested for the problem, based on a 'social consensus',[49] was borrowed from Western liberal thought.[50]

This shift in the AKP discourse was not well received by everyone. Many secularists saw the headscarf question as a litmus test for the commitment of the AKP to republican ideals. Another segment of the republican elites persistently doubted the motives of the AKP government, accusing it of having a secret agenda for the Islamization of Turkish state and society.[51] They argued that the AKP leadership could not have jettisoned its Islamist worldview within a few years. It was argued that it had actually been engaged in dissimulation (*takiyye*) by hiding its true intentions to establish an Islamic state, until the time was ripe.[52] Although such arguments were rather exaggerated, they were sometimes supported by clumsy attempts by the AKP to appease the Islamist part of its electoral base.[53]

The rise of the AKP to power in November 2002 did not signal a break with past state policies on the headscarf issue. Despite the explicit expectations of its electoral base, the AKP government normally abstained from openly raising the headscarf issue, in an effort to avoid polarizing the political scene and antagonizing the military and bureaucratic elites. Instead it opted to wait for the imminent decision of the ECHR on the issue, which was hoped to relieve the government of the political cost of reforming the headscarf legislation. The decision of the ECHR, however, in the case of *Leyla Şahin vs. Turkey* did not help these plans. As Barras shows in her contribution to this special issue, the court ruled that there was no violation of Article 9 (freedom of thought, conscience and religion) of the ECHR when the applicant was denied access to university examination and enrolment, because she wore a headscarf.[54] Although the ECHR decision did not help resolve the headscarf issue in Turkey, it had no profound impact on the liberal basis of the AKP public discourse.[55] However, it may have been one of the reasons for weakening its zeal to pursue EU-driven reform, which suffered a severe deceleration after 2004.

The symbolic significance of the headscarf issue was confirmed once again, when it became the focus of the confrontation between the AKP government and the bureaucracy in 2007. The constitutional amendment annulled by the Constitutional Court was meant to resolve a problem which has grown far beyond its original dimensions and has underlined the inability of Turkey's society to reach a liberal consensus to accommodate its diversity.

The Directorate of Religious Affairs

The AKP showed less determination in applying the same liberal discourse in the case of the Directorate of Religious Affairs (*Diyanet İşleri Başkanlığı* – DİB). The exponential growth of the activity of the Directorate since the 1980s has been one of the clearest indicators of the Islamist social and political resurgence. Its budget in 2007 was 38% bigger than the budget of the Ministry of Interior, 2.3 times that of the Ministry of Foreign Affairs and twice that of the Ministry of Culture.[56] Its personnel grew from 25,236 in 1970 to over 74,114 in 2004, while the number of mosques nearly doubled, from 42,744 in 1971 to 76,445 in 2004.[57] The expanding activity of the Directorate undermined the secular character of the Turkish state, given that it exclusively promoted Sunni Islam. Alevi associations and other religious minority representatives have repeatedly addressed their grievances about the Sunni bias of the Directorate and the absence of any funding programmes for Alevi religious houses of worship (*cemevi*). The reform of the Directorate was suggested by human rights organizations as a necessary step for the establishment of genuine secularism. Two possible solutions were suggested. The state should either cede control of the Directorate to the religious communities themselves, or maintain control of the Directorate, but guarantee the proportional representation of all religious groups in it, as well as their proportionate access to the Directory budgetary funds.[58] The prospect of Turkey's EU membership brought the Directorate to public attention, as EU Commission reports noted its unequal treatment of religious groups.[59] During the ensuing discussions on necessary reform steps, some human rights organizations suggested the transformation of the Directorate into an autonomous state authority, following the example of the Higher Education Council (*Yüksek Öğretim Kurulu* – YÖK). Other experts suggested the abolition of the Directorate and the takeover of its activities by the religious communities. Securing equal access of non-Sunni Muslims to the Directorate and its services was also underlined.[60] While the implementation of these proposals could contribute to the elimination of the Sunni bias of the Directorate, the AKP government did not display the same energy that it had shown in advocating the free profession of the Islamic faith in public space. Occasional statements by AKP officials – including Prime Minister Erdoğan himself – on Alevi grievances regarding the Directorate did not convey the expected level of sensitivity and loyalty to liberal principles when it came to recognizing Alevis as a separate religious group and not just as a branch of Sunni Islam.[61] It seems that the Sunni background of the AKP leadership has obstructed a liberal approach to the Directorate question, casting doubt about the depth of its liberal convictions.[62] Nonetheless, the existence of a persistent debate on how to bring the Directorate's role and functions in line with liberal and secular ideas does provide evidence that, although the AKP has failed in this case to play the role of a reform catalyst, the introduction of a new secularism has become a key issue in the country's political agenda.[63]

Secularism as the focal point of a major political crisis

2007 was a tumultuous year in Turkish politics. Both presidential and parliamentary elections took place in the summer of that year in a very tense political atmosphere in which secularism was the key political issue. A crisis erupted on 24 April 2007, when Prime Minister Erdoğan announced his decision to support the candidacy of Foreign Minister Abdullah Gül for the office of the Republic's President. Secularist media and civil society objected to the candidacy on the grounds that it prepared the abolition of secularism and the very principles of the Republic. The fact that Gül's wife Hayrünissa wore a headscarf and statements Gül had allegedly made in the 1990s as a member of the Islamist Welfare Party (*Refah Partisi*-RP) sufficed to declare his candidacy a threat for the Republic.

Civil society associations were soon also involved. On 14 April 2007, secularist associations organized a demonstration in Ankara to declare their determination to defend secularism and the spirit of the Republic. The demonstration, symbolically organized in front of *Anıtkabir*, Atatürk's mausoleum, gathered big crowds and was followed by similar demonstrations in Istanbul on 28 April 2007, and Izmir and other smaller cities on 14 May 2007. Large turnouts manifested the divide within Turkish society. The millions of Turkish citizens who demonstrated in Ankara, Istanbul, Izmir and other cities in defence of the secular values of the Republic represented the middle-class elites of the country who felt threatened by the meteoric rise of the AKP, the further reinforcement of the party-affiliated conservative elite and its prospective control of both highest state offices. Despite repeated statements by the AKP about its commitment to the secular principles of the Republic and its comprehensive reform programme, they insisted that the government party was performing *takiyye* – and that there was a hidden agenda to Islamize the country. The unease of a large part of Turkey's middle class about the rise of the AKP was matched with severe bureaucratic and military reaction.

The political turmoil took the dimensions of a constitutional crisis when the military and civil bureaucracy took a clear position against the government. On 27 May 2007, the General Staff issued a statement which appeared on its website. In an intervention for which the neologism 'e-coup' was coined, the military listed a number of incidents which adopted the claims that a rising Islamist activity comprised a serious threat for the Turkish Republic and warned that the Turkish military would not remain indifferent to such a development.

> During the last days, the problem which emerged in the Presidential election process has been focused on the debate of secularism. The Turkish Armed Forces follow this with concern. One should not forget that the Turkish Armed Forces are a party in these discussions and a definitive defender of secularism. The Turkish Armed Forces are definitively against the discussions and unfounded allegations made and, if necessary, will expose their stance and behaviour in an open and clear way ... The Turkish Armed Forces maintain their unshakeable decisiveness regarding the flawless implementation of their law-given duties to protect these features and maintains a firm belief in the binding character of this decisiveness.[64]

This direct political intervention of the military caused a major political crisis in a country with a long record of military coups. What made the situation worse was that the major opposition party, the secularist Republican People's Party (*Cumhuriyet Halk Partisi* – CHP) did not object to the military intervention into politics and its threats against the government but, on the contrary, seemed to endorse them. The situation was further aggravated on 1 May 2007. On that day, the Constitutional Court delivered a controversial opinion on the question of a quorum in the presidential elections, following an appeal by the CHP. The decision upheld the CHP's claim and made the election of an AKP-supported presidential candidate by the parliament impossible. While the legal basis of the decision was at best unsound, at the political level, this decision showed that the judiciary had in effect sided with the military in its opposition to the government party. The court decision stalled the presidential election process and led Prime Minister Erdoğan to call for early elections on 22 July 2007, as well as a constitutional referendum to establish the popular election of the president.

A tense election campaign came to an end with a triumphant victory for the incumbent AKP. With 46.7% of the vote, the government party scored a victory whose magnitude had been difficult to predict. Despite being in power for almost five years, the AKP increased its electoral appeal by more than 12% compared to the 2002 elections. This was the strongest proof that the party enjoyed the broad support of the public in its confrontation with the military and bureaucratic elites. By its vote, the Turkish people condemned the bureaucratic interventions and infringement of democratic practices. In fact, the sharp rise of the AKP's electoral strength could only be explained in terms of result of the political crisis. The polarizing effect of the military encroachment made many Turkish democratic citizens vote for the AKP, not because they approved of their political programme, but simply in order to protest against the military involvement.

Yet, more turmoil was to follow when the AKP government allied with the opposition Nationalist Action Party (*Milliyetçi Hareket Partisi* – MHP) to pass a constitutional amendment whose aim was to allow the use of the headscarf in university campuses. The CHP appealed against the amendment which was passed with a large majority in the Constitutional Court. The decision of the

Constitutional Court to annul the amendment appeared to set an alarming precedent, reinforcing claims by intellectuals about the rise of a 'juristocracy', a regime where the sovereignty does not belong to the people or the parliament but to the judiciary. Meanwhile, in March 2008, the Chief Prosecutor Abdurrahman Yalçınkaya filed a closure case against the AKP accusing it of having become a 'centre of anti-secular activity'.[65] The court's decision in July 2008 adopted the argument of the prosecutor but fell short of closing the government party. Instead, it set its future political initiatives on secularism under judicial scrutiny.[66]

Secularism and the fear of Turkey's Islamization

The backdrop to the political crisis was an increasing apprehension in Turkey's secular class about an encroaching Islamization threat. Justified or not, this fear did have a significant impact on the attitudes of a sizeable part of the Turkish people. The electoral victory of the AKP in the 2002 elections marked a milestone in the rise of a new Islamist 'counter-elite'. A new generation of well-educated, Western-oriented, religious and conservative professionals, who first appeared in the 1980s, was taking control of the country's government for the first time. During AKP rule, they further strengthened their position within the state administration, despite the opposition of the Republic's secularist President Ahmet Necdet Sezer and the opposition of the country's military and state bureaucracy. The election of Abdullah Gül to the President's office meant the takeover by the AKP of the last secularist bastion in executive power. For the first time since the 1950s, peripheral social forces which were hitherto marginalized in republican Turkish politics would assume control of the state.[67] This upset the secularist elites who had seen their political and social influence waning alarmingly in recent years. Their major participation in the 'republic's demonstrations', a series of secularist, anti-AKP demonstrations organized throughout Turkey in spring 2007, manifested their unease at the new constellation of powers in the Turkish political system. It also underlined their fear about the sustainability of a secular way of living in an AKP-dominated Turkey. Despite being a numerical minority in Turkish society, they enjoyed a disproportionate influence upon Turkish politics. However, as a consequence of Turkey's democratization, their position became untenable. As Turkey was transforming into a democratic society, political power gradually shifted from the secularist elite to the conservative social majority, which was very successfully represented by the AKP. Fazıl Say's reaction, underlined at the beginning of this study, also mirrored the inability of many Turkish secularists to adapt to this new environment. Cemil İpekçi's response pointed directly to that.

Confusion about the ongoing Islamization of Turkish society did not leave academia unscathed. Conflicting information and opinion polls allowed academics to defend antithetical positions on the issue of the Islamization of Turkish society. Two major surveys published in late 2007 announced conflicting results on the headscarf issue, which had the effect of increasing still further public attention.

The first survey argued that despite what many secularist Turks thought, the number of covered women as a percentage of the whole population had fallen.[68] It was only their rising public visibility and the fact that they were freer now to commute and participate in public life that jointly created the impression that the use of the headscarf was increasing in Turkey.[69] However, according to the second survey, there was a slight rise in the number of covered women as a percentage of the whole population. More significant though was the sharp rise of the percentage of women wearing the politically significant *türban*[70] among the covered women.[71] Fears about Turkey apparently impending Islamization were often linked to the transformation of the Turkish political Islam. Many secularists argued that Turkey was distancing itself from Europe and increasingly resembling Malaysia as an economically globalized but socially Islamic society.[72] In addition, many scholars pointed to the lack of a liberal consensus in Turkey as the root of more general social mistrust and conflict. In what Şerif Mardin called the 'neighbourhood's pressure' (*mahalle baskısı*),[73] Turkey's rising peripheral, conservative social class was attempting to impose its communitarian social values upon the secularist segment of the society. However, the core element of this stance, i.e. lack of respect for individual autonomy, did not pertain only to conservatives; it pervaded the whole of Turkish society. Thus the resolution of Turkey's deep social division on the issue of secularism remains inextricably linked with the rise of a liberal consensus which would allow the coexistence of different lifestyles. To this end, Turkey's EU membership could be of critical significance in terms of anchoring reform already made and triggering further liberalization.

Conclusion

Secularism has remained a focal point of Turkish politics throughout the history of republican Turkey. While Islamist political parties used to challenge secularism on Sharia-based arguments, the transformation of political Islam allowed for a liberal critique of Turkish secularism. The AKP advocated a version of secularism which would not ostracize manifestations of religious belief from the public sphere. Nonetheless, secularism remained a deeply divisive issue and led to consecutive political crises. Following his controversial election, President Abdullah Gül tried to convince everyone of the AKP government's commitment to the secular principles of the Republic. In his inauguration speech, he once more dismissed claims about the existence of a hidden Islamist agenda and added:

> The Turkish Republic is a democratic, secular, social state, governed by the rule of law. These features established through the non-amendable stipulations of our constitution are a whole and each of them is undoubtedly a fundamental value of our Republic. I will always be determined and resolved to advocate, without discrimination, each of these principles and to further strengthen them at every opportunity. Secularism, one of our foundational principles is a rule of social peace, as well as a model which allows for different ways of life within democracy, a system based on law and freedoms.[74]

Many expected that both President Gül and Prime Minister Erdoğan would give clear political signals of their intentions to respect religious freedom and advocate a tolerant version of secularism. Yet the country again became embroiled in a bitter confrontation between the AKP government and the secularist establishment. The closure case against the AKP in March 2008 on the grounds of being a 'focal point of anti-secular activity' brought secularism once again to the main stage of Turkish politics. The judicial process highlighted deep social divisions within Turkey, as well as the urgency of a liberal reconfiguration of the country's political system. While the AKP was spared closure, the July 2008 decision confirmed the allegations of the Chief Prosecutor about its 'anti-secular activities'. It is plausible to argue that a redefinition of state–religion relations in Turkey, so that Muslims, non-Muslims, atheists and agnostics enjoy equal respect for their beliefs is a necessary condition of the AKP-advocated liberal version of secularism. The implementation of such a reform could prove the sincerity of AKP commitments and reduce social cleavages, sharply manifested since April 2007. What is clearly missing, however, is a high level of mutual trust between Turkey's conservatives and secularists. In a country where a liberal culture of mutual toleration and respect for individual autonomy is not fully-fledged and social trust is a scarce resource, an external actor such as the European Union seems to be the actor best suited to act as arbiter and facilitate trust-building. The reinvigoration of Turkey's European integration process could perhaps provide the best framework for the development of mutual respect for different lifestyles within a tolerant society.

Notes

1. Hermann, 'Der Paukenschlag Des Pianisten'.
2. Günay's statement was of special importance, as he was himself one of the centre-left secularist politicians who decided to join the ranks of the AKP on the eve of the July 2007 elections.
3. Mağden, *Fazıl Say haksız mı?*
4. Nişantaşı is one of the most affluent, secularist boroughs of Istanbul.
5. Balta, 'Fazıl Say, Türkiye'yi Nişantaşı'ndan Ibaret Zannediyor'.
6. Ankara Bürosu, *Türkiye 'Oh' dedi*.
7. The prospect of the election of Abdullah Gül to the presidency of the country met with the fierce opposition of the secularist elite, because Gül's wife wears a headscarf. The publication of a military statement on the issue led to early elections in July 2007, which were won by the AKP by a wide margin.
8. Fuller, 'Turkey's Strategic Model: Myths and Realities', 52.
9. Gülalp, 'Whatever Happened to Secularization? The Multiple Islams in Turkey', 389–90.
10. On this, see Kuru, *Reinterpretation of Secularism in Turkey: The Case of the Justice and Development Party*.
11. This paradox was already observed in 1954 by Ali Fuat Başgil. See Başgil, *Din ve Laiklik*, 220, cited in Çakır and Bozan, *Sivil, Şeffaf ve Demokratik Bir Diyanet İşleri Başkanlığı Mümkün Mü?*, 107.
12. Kara, 'Diyanet İşleri Başkanlığı', 180–3.
13. This instrumental use of Islam, however, met with the opposition of Islamists. See Yılmaz, 'Darbeler ve İslâmcılık', 637–9.

14. Alevis are a syncretistic, heterodox Islamic group whose faith combines elements of Shiite Islam, Christianity, Shamanism and other Anatolian cultural heritage.
15. Göle, 'Secularism and Islamism in Turkey: The Making of Elites and Counter-Elites', 48–9.
16. Mahçupyan, 'Aleviler, Azınlık, Diyanet'.
17. Grigoriadis, *Trials of Europeanization: Turkish Political Culture and the European Union*, 105–7.
18. Toprak, 'Türkiye'de Laiklik, Siyasal İslam ve Demokrasi', 289.
19. Çarkoğlu and Toprak, *Türkiye'de din, toplum ve siyaset*, 17.
20. Grigoriadis, 'AKP and the Paradox of Islamic Europhilia', 66.
21. The National View (*Milli Görüş*) movement was founded by Necmettin Erbakan in the late 1960s and became the focal point for the rise of Turkish political Islam.
22. Erbakan frequently juxtaposed European power (*kuvvet*) against Islamic justice (*hak*).
23. European Court of Human Rights (ECHR), *Registrar's Press Release: Judgment in the Case of Refah Partisi (Welfare Party), Erbakan, Kazan and Tekdal vs. Turkey*. The full text of the decision is available at European Court of Human Rights, Refah Partisi [Welfare Party] and Others vs. Turkey (No. 41340/98, No. 41342/98 and No. 41334/98): Third Section, 2001, http://cmiskp.echr.coe.int/tkp197/view.asp?action=html&documentID=697494&portal=hbkm&source=externalbydocnumber&table=F69A27FD8FB86142BFO1C1166DEA398649.
24. European Court of Human Rights (ECHR), *Refah Partisi [Welfare Party] and Others vs. Turkey*.
25. Grigoriadis, 'AKP and the Paradox of Islamic Europhilia', 68.
26. For parallel developments in the field of *tarikat*s and the Fethullah Gülen movement, see Yavuz, 'Towards an Islamic Liberalism? The Nurcu Movement and Fethullah Gülen', 600–5.
27. Fokas, 'The Islamist Movement and Turkey–EU Relations', 154–5.
28. Jenkins, 'Muslim Democrats in Turkey?', 53–5.
29. Çağaptay, 'The November 2002 Elections and Turkey's New Political Era', 44.
30. Yılmaz, 'İslâmcılık, AKP, Siyaset', 613–17; and Akdoğan, 'Adalet ve Kalkınma Partisi', 625–31. Dağı suggested the term 'post-Islamist' to explain the transformation of the AKP ideology. See Dağı, 'Rethinking Human Rights, Democracy, and the West: Post-Islamist Intellectuals in Turkey'.
31. Heper and Toktaş, 'Islam, Modernity, and Democracy in Contemporary Turkey: The Case of Recep Tayyip Erdoğan', 173.
32. This was manifested in numerous opinion polls throughout the 2000s. Although public support for Turkey's EU membership fell significantly after 2005, it has not waned out.
33. Dağı, 'Transformation of Islamic Political Identity in Turkey: Rethinking the West and Westernization', 31.
34. Grigoriadis, 'AKP and the Paradox of Islamic Europhilia', 67.
35. On the conservative nature of the AKP, see Aktay, *İslâmcılıktaki Muhafazakârlık Bakiye*, 348–50.
36. Dağı, 'Transformation of Islamic Political Identity in Turkey: Rethinking the West and Westernization'.
37. Cizre and Çınar, 'Turkey 2002: Kemalism, Islamism, and Politics in the Light of the February 28 Process', 327.
38. Grigoriadis, 'The First "Muslim Democratic" Party? – The AKP and the Reform of Political Islam in Turkey', 26–7.
39. See Kuru, *Reinterpretation of Secularism in Turkey: The Case of the Justice and Development Party*.
40. Assertive secularism is here used as a synonym of secularism.

41. Akdoğan, *AK Parti ve Muhafazakâr Demokrasi*, 6.
42. İnsel, 'The AKP and Normalizing Democracy in Turkey', 304.
43. See Alpay, 'AB, Türkiye ve İslam'.
44. On this, see Kuru, *Reinterpretation of Secularism in Turkey: The Case of the Justice and Development Party*.
45. Heper and Toktaş, 'Islam, Modernity, and Democracy in Contemporary Turkey: The Case of Recep Tayyip Erdoğan', 176.
46. Ali Bulaç is a primary example of this shift. His argument on the 'three generations of Islamist politics' is illuminating. See Bulaç, 'İslâm'ın Üç Siyaset Tarzı Veya İslâmcıların Üç Nesli', 48–50. See also Dağı, 'Rethinking Human Rights, Democracy, and the West: Post-Islamist Intellectuals in Turkey', 143–9.
47. Some authors even came to the point of discovering human rights courts during the Islamic 'Era of Felicity'. See Şahin, 'İslam'da İnsan Hakları Mahkemesinden Bir Örnek!'.
48. Dağı, 'Rethinking Human Rights, Democracy, and the West: Post-Islamist Intellectuals in Turkey', 141.
49. Bulaç, 'CHP, Anadolu Solu ve Başörtüsü'.
50. Dağı, 'Rethinking Human Rights, Democracy, and the West: Post-Islamist Intellectuals in Turkey', 142.
51. Coşar and Özman, 'Centre-Right Politics in Turkey after the November 2002 Election: Neo-Liberalism with a Muslim Face', 66.
52. Heper and Toktaş, 'Islam, Modernity, and Democracy in Contemporary Turkey: The Case of Recep Tayyip Erdoğan', 160; and Belge, 'Takiye Tartışması'.
53. The short-lived proposal to penalize adultery during the reform of the Turkish Penal Code in August 2004 is a prime example.
54. See European Court of Human Rights (ECHR), *Leyla Şahin vs. Turkey*, 26. This decision came under heavy attack by European human rights organizations, which diagnosed a dangerous illiberal shift in the ruling of the court, following the emergence of a headscarf question in EU member states like France.
55. Many pious Turks thought that the ECHR was applying double standards against Islam. In any case the decision only ruled that headscarf restrictions in higher education did not violate the freedom of religion according to the ECHR. It neither justified nor posed any obstacles to the lifting of the restrictions themselves. See Akyol, 'Anayasa, Laiklik, Siyaset'.
56. Ankara Bürosu, *Diyanet bütçesi 37 kurumu solladı*.
57. See Çakır and Bozan, *Sivil, Şeffaf ve Demokratik Bir Diyanet İşleri Başkanlığı Mümkün mü?*, 73–4. Nonetheless, the rise in the number of mosques should not only be attributed to increasing religiosity, but also to rising welfare.
58. Kara, 'Diyanet İşleri Başkanlığı', 194–6.
59. Commission of the European Communities, *2004 Regular Report on Turkey's Progress towards Accession*, 44–5.
60. Çakır and Bozan, *Sivil, Şeffaf ve Demokratik Bir Diyanet İşleri Başkanlığı Mümkün Mü?*, 110–17.
61. Age-old Sunni prejudices of Alevi Islam survived in the AKP. A statement of Prime Minister Recep Tayyip Erdoğan spoke volumes about the level of intolerance on the Alevi issue among Sunni Muslims. When asked during a television interview on his opinion on the Alevi question he replied that Alevism is not a religion and added: 'If Alevism means to love Ali and follow his path, I am also Alevi. I am one of those who struggle to live like Ali. I am more Alevi than them.' See Soykan, 'Alevi Tepkisi Artıyor'. See also Erdem, 'Cemevi Sosyal Tesismiş'.
62. Grigoriadis, 'EU-Beitrittsprozeß Und Säkularismus in Der Türkei', 29.
63. Çakır and Bozan, *Sivil, Şeffaf ve Demokratik Bir Diyanet İşleri Başkanlığı Mümkün Mü?*, 336–9.

64. Genelkurmay Başkanlığı, *Basın Açıklaması (Ba-08/07)* [Press Statement].
65. Ankara Bürosu, *Yargıtay Başsavcısı AKP'nin kapatılmasını istedi*.
66. Tahincioğlu, *AKP'ye 'ciddi ihtar'*.
67. On centre-periphery relations in republican Turkey, see the classical Mardin, 'Center-Periphery Relations: A Key to Turkish Politics?'.
68. Çarkoğlu and Toprak, *Religion, Society and Politics in a Changing Turkey*, 62–9.
69. Istanbul Bürosu, 'Örtülü Kadın Azaldı Malezya Olmuyoruz!' ['Headscarved Women Decreased, we do not become Malaysia!'].
70. Women who wore the *türban* and not a simple headscarf expressed their dissidence against the secularist politics of republican Turkey.
71. Erdem, 'Gündelik Yaşamda Din, Laiklik ve Türban 1: Türbanın Hızlı Yükselişi'.
72. On this, see Mert, *Türkiye ve Malezya*.
73. Çakır, *Şerif Mardin: Mahalle Baskısı-Ne demek istedim*.
74. Ankara Bürosu, '11. Cumhurbaşkanı Abdullah Gül'ün TBMM Genel Kurulu'ndaki Konuşmasının Tam Metni: Özgürlük ve Laiklik Vurgusu' ['Full Text of the Speech of the 11th President of the Republic Abdullah Gul at the Turkish Grand National Assembly: Emphasis on Freedom and Secularism'].

Note on contributor

Dr Ioannis N. Grigoriadis is Assistant Professor at the Department of Political Science, Bilkent University. He completed his undergraduate studies at the University of Athens, where he studied Law. In 2002 he obtained a Master of International Affairs (MIA) and a Certificate of Middle Eastern Studies from the School of International & Public Affairs (SIPA), Columbia University. In 2005, he earned a PhD in Politics at the School of Oriental and African Studies (SOAS), University of London. He has taught at Turkish universities (Sabanci University, Isik University) for three years. Between 2007 and 2009 he was Lecturer at the Department of Turkish and Modern Asian Studies, University of Athens. His research interests include European, Middle Eastern and energy politics, nationalism and democratization.

Bibliography

Akdoğan, Yalçın. 'Adalet ve Kalkınma Partisi'. In *İslamcılık*, ed. Yasin Aktay, *Modern Türkiye'de Siyasi Düşünce*, 620–31. İstanbul: İletişim, 2004.
Akdoğan, Yalçın. *AK Parti ve Muhafazakâr Demokrasi* [*AK Party and Conservative Democracy*]. Ankara: AK Parti Yayınları, 2004.
Aktay, Yasin. 'İslâmcılıktaki Muhafazakârlık Bakiye'. In *Muhafazakârlık*, ed. Ahmet Çiğdem, *Modern Türkiye'de Siyasi Düşünce*. İstanbul: İletişim, 2003.
Akyol, Taha. 'Anayasa, Laiklik, Siyaset' ['Constitution, Secularism, Politics']. *Milliyet*, April 27, 2007.
Alpay, Şahin. 'AB, Türkiye ve İslam' ['EU, Turkey and Islam']. *Zaman*, October 9, 2004.
Balta, İbrahim. 'Fazıl Say, Türkiye'yi Nişantaşı'ndan Ibaret Zannediyor' [Fazil Say thinks that Turkey consists of Nisantasi]. *Zaman*, December 16, 2007.
Başgil, Ali Fuat. *Din ve Laiklik* [*Religion and Secularism*], İkinci Baskı. ed. İstanbul: Kubbealtı Neşriyat, 2003.
Belge, Murat. 'Takiye Tartışması' ['The Debate about Dissimulation']. *Radikal*, November 8, 2002.
Bulaç, Ali. 'CHP, Anadolu Solu ve Başörtüsü' ['CHP, the Anatolian Left and the Headscarfs']. *Zaman*, July 3, 2002.

Bulaç, Ali. 'İslâm'ın Üç Siyaset Tarzı Veya İslâmcıların Üç Nesli' ['Three Political Ways of Islam or Three Generations of Islamists']. In *İslamcılık*, ed. Yasin Aktay. *Modern Türkiye'de Siyasi Düşünce*. İstanbul: İletişim, 2004.
Bürosu, Ankara. '11. Cumhurbaşkanı Abdullah Gül'ün TBMM Genel Kurulu'ndaki Konuşmasının Tam Metni: Özgürlük ve Laiklik Vurgusu'. *Radikal*, August 29, 2007.
Bürosu, Ankara. 'Diyanet Bütçesi 37 Kurumu Sollad?' ['The Directorate of Religious Affairs outmarched 37 Institutions']. *Hürriyet*, October 24, 2006.
Bürosu, Ankara. 'Türkiye "Oh" Dedi' ['Turkey says "Oh"']. *Radikal*, July 31, 2008.
Çağaptay, Soner. 'The November 2002 Elections and Turkey's New Political Era'. *Middle East Review of International Affairs (MERIA)* 6, no. 4 (2002): 42–8.
Çakır, Rusen. 'Şerif Mardin: Mahalle Baskısı-Ne Demek Istedim'. NTVMSNBC, May 28, 2008.
Çakır, Ruşen, and İrfan Bozan. *Sivil, Şeffaf ve Demokratik Bir Diyanet İşleri Başkanlığı Mümkün Mü? [Is a Civil, Transparent and Democratic Directorate of Religious Affairs Possible?]* İstanbul: TESEV Yayınları, 2005.
Çarkoğlu, Ali, and Binnaz Toprak. *Değişen Türkiye'de Din, Toplum ve Siyaset*. İstanbul: TESEV, 2006.
Çarkoğlu, Ali, and Binnaz Toprak. *Religion, Society and Politics in a Changing Turkey*. Istanbul: TESEV, 2007.
Cizre, Ümit, and Menderes Çınar. 'Turkey 2002: Kemalism, Islamism, and Politics in the Light of the February 28 Process'. *South Atlantic Quarterly* 102, no. 2/3 (2003): 309–32.
Commission of the European Communities. *2004 Regular Report on Turkey's Progress Towards Accession* [SEC(2004) 1201]. Brussels: European Union, 2004.
Coşar, Simten, and Aylın Özman. 'Centre-Right Politics in Turkey after the November 2002 Election: Neo-Liberalism with a Muslim Face'. *Contemporary Politics* 10, no. 1 (2004): 57–74.
Dağı, İhsan D. 'Rethinking Human Rights, Democracy, and the West: Post-Islamist Intellectuals in Turkey'. *Critique: Critical Middle Eastern Studies* 13, no. 2 (2004): 135–51.
Dağı, İhsan D. 'Transformation of Islamic Political Identity in Turkey: Rethinking the West and Westernization'. *Turkish Studies* 6, no. 1 (2005): 21–37.
Erdem, Tarhan. 'Gündelik Yaşamda Din, Laiklik ve Türban 1: Türbanın Hızlı Yükselişi'. *Milliyet*, December 3, 2007.
Erdem, Zihni. 'Cemevi Sosyal Tesismiş' ['Cemevis were Social Premises']. *Radikal*, May 1, 2005.
European Court of Human Rights (ECHR). 'Leyla Şahin vs. Turkey'. Strasbourg: Fourth Section, 2004.
European Court of Human Rights (ECHR). 'Refah Partisi [Welfare Party] and Others vs. Turkey'. Third Section, 2001.
European Court of Human Rights (ECHR). 'Refah Partisi [Welfare Party] and Others vs. Turkey'. Grand Chamber, 2003.
European Court of Human Rights (ECHR). 'Registrar's Press Release: Judgment in the Case of Refah Partisi (Welfare Party), Erbakan, Kazan and Tekdal vs. Turkey'. Strasbourg, 2001.
Fokas, Effie. 'The Islamist Movement and Turkey–EU Relations'. In *Turkey and European Integration: Accession Prospects and Issues*, ed. Mehmet Uğur and Nergis Canefe. London & New York: Routledge, 2004.
Fuller, Graham E. 'Turkey's Strategic Model: Myths and Realities'. *Washington Quarterly* 27, no. 3 (2004): 51–64.
Genelkurmay, Başkanlığı. 'Basın Açıklaması (Ba-08/07)'. Ankara: Genelkurmay Başkanlığı, 2007.

Göle, Nilüfer. 'Secularism and Islamism in Turkey: The Making of Elites and Counter-Elites'. *Middle East Journal* 51, no. 1 (1997): 46–58.
Grigoriadis, Ioannis N. 'AKP and the Paradox of Islamic Europhilia'. *Turkish Policy Quarterly* 3, no. 1 (2004): 65–70.
Grigoriadis, Ioannis N. 'EU-Beitrittsprozeß und Säkularismus in der Türkei' [Turkey's EU Accession Process and the Question of Secularism]. *Südosteuropa Mitteilungen* 47, no. 2 (2007): 20–31.
Grigoriadis, Ioannis N. 'The First "Muslim Democratic" Party? – The AKP and the Reform of Political Islam in Turkey'. In *Moderate Islamists as Reform Actors: Conditions and Programmatic Change*, ed. Muriel Asseburg. Berlin: Stiftung Wissenschaft und Politik, 2007.
Grigoriadis, Ioannis N. *Trials of Europeanization: Turkish Political Culture and the European Union*. New York, NY: Palgrave Macmillan, 2008.
Gülalp, Haldun. 'Whatever Happened to Secularization? The Multiple Islams in Turkey'. *South Atlantic Quarterly* 102, no. 2/3 (2003): 381–95.
Heper, Metin, and Toktaş Şule. 'Islam, Modernity, and Democracy in Contemporary Turkey: The Case of Recep Tayyip Erdoğan'. *Muslim World* 93, no. 2 (2003): 157–85.
Hermann, Rainer. 'Der Paukenschlag Des Pianisten' ['The Drumbeat of the Pianist']. *Frankfurter Allgemeine Zeitung*, December 18, 2007.
İnsel, Ahmet. 'The AKP and Normalizing Democracy in Turkey'. *South Atlantic Quarterly* 102, no. 2/3 (2003): 293–308.
Istanbul, Bürosu. 'Örtülü Kadın Azaldı Malezya Olmuyoruz!' *Radikal*, September 28, 2007.
Jenkins, Gareth. 'Muslim Democrats in Turkey?' *Survival* 45, no. 1 (2003): 45–66.
Kara, İsmail. 'Diyanet İşleri Başkanlığı' ['Directorate of Religious Affairs']. In *İslamcılık*, ed. Yasin Aktay, *Modern Türkiye'de Siyasi Düşünce*. İstanbul: İletişim, 2004.
Kuru, Ahmet T. 'Reinterpretation of Secularism in Turkey: The Case of the Justice and Development Party'. In *Transformation of Turkish Politics*, ed. M. Hakan Yavuz. Salt Lake City: University of Utah Press, 2006.
Mağden, Perihan. Fazıl Say Haksız mı? ['Is Fazil Say Wrong?'] *Radikal*, December 16, 2007.
Mahçupyan, Etyen. 'Aleviler, Azınlık, Diyanet' ['Alevis, Minority, Directorate of Religious Affairs']. *Zaman*, November 1, 2004.
Mardin, Şerif. 'Center-Periphery Relations: A Key to Turkish Politics?'. *Daedalus* 102, no. 1 (1973): 169–90.
Mert, Nuray. 'Türkiye ve Malezya'. *Radikal*, October 2, 2007.
Şahin, Ahmet. 'İslam'da İnsan Hakları Mahkemesinden Bir Örnek!' *Zaman*, December 14, 2004.
Soykan, Timur. 'Alevi Tepkisi Artıyor'. *Radikal*, October 9, 2004.
Tahincioğlu, Gökçer. 'AKP' ye "Ciddi Ihtar"' ['Serious Warning to the AKP']. *Milliyet*, July 31, 2008.
Toprak, Binnaz. 'Türkiye'de Laiklik, Siyasal İslam ve Demokrasi' ['Secularism, Political Islam and Democracy in Turkey']. *Uluslararası Atatürk ve Çağdaş Toplum Sempozyumu*, ed. *Demokrasi ve Gençlik Vakfı*. İstanbul: İş Bankası Kültür Yayınları, 2002.
Yavuz, M. Hakan. 'Towards an Islamic Liberalism? The Nurcu Movement and Fethullah Gülen'. *Middle East Journal* 53, no. 4 (1999): 584–605.
Yılmaz, Murat. 'Darbeler ve İslâmcılık' ['Coups and Islam']. In *İslamcılık*, ed. Yasin Aktay, *Modern Türkiye'de Siyasi Düşünce*. İstanbul: İletişim, 2004.
Yılmaz, Nuh. 'İslâmcılık, AKP, Siyaset'. In *İslamcılık*, ed. Yasin Aktay, *Modern Türkiye'de Siyasi Düşünce*. İstanbul: İletişim, 2004.

The Fethullah Gülen movement and politics in Turkey: a chance for democratization or a Trojan horse?

İştar B. Gözaydın

Department of Humanities and Social Sciences, Istanbul Technical University, Maslak, Istanbul, Turkey

Since 1923 the official ideology of republican Turkey has been strictly secular. However religious networking has always been a very important component of the socio-structural system in the country. Over time, the republican regime sought to stifle development of such networking, while at the same time also promoting changes in this regard. For 50 years – between 1930 and 1980 – Islamic networks in Turkey developed market relations that promoted strategies to improve the economic position of their members. In this context, several 'new' religious groups emerged, including the Fethullah Gülen movement. This article is concerned with the democratic involvement of the Fethullah Gülen movement in recent democratization in Turkey.

This article is concerned with the Fethullah Gülen movement and its relationship to democratization in Turkey. The article seeks to advance three arguments:

Firstly, the post-Ottoman, republican decision-making elite in Turkey introduced laicist[1] policies and legislation in order not only to change the superstructure of the country towards a Western model but also to 'modernize' Turkish society more generally. For them, traditional beliefs threatened the seemingly ambitious project of modernity. Consequently, the Republic of Turkey's founding elite implemented policies to remove religion from the public realm and reduce it to a matter of faith and practice of the individual. As a result, the principle of religious freedom amounted only to a protection of 'individualized religion'. Paradoxically, many of the strongest supporters of laicism actually consider themselves religious, and would be offended to be perceived as agnostics or atheists.

Secondly, such policies found widespread acceptance in society. Nevertheless, many Turks preferred to remain faithful to their traditional beliefs. Over time, especially during the last decades, political Islam, a modern ideology with roots in the nineteenth century, has become more visible in the political arena in Turkey. The result is that over the last 80 years, that is, since the demise of the Ottoman Empire and the introduction of the post-Ottoman republican regime after World War I, divisions between the two worldviews deepened in Turkey. It is important to understand that this was not a religious 'revival'[2] as many scholars in the field claim. This is because, while a political allegiance to 'religion' has always been a part of the Turkish social body,[3] it has noticeably grown in the last few decades, paralleling a wider – some say, worldwide resurgence – of religion. In Turkey, it became especially visible from the 1990s, spearheaded by a new emerging Islamic bourgeoisie. In addition, it seems clear that Turkey's domestic policies in the 1980s, a time of civil conflict and economic liberalization, encouraged social conservatism and the rise of political Islam.

Finally, Fethullah Gülen, the spiritual leader of a large community of religious activists, is a prominent religious figure who is currently living in self-imposed exile in the United States. Since the 1980s, his movement has grown to comprise several million followers and sympathizers, including important business groups and politicians in Turkey. His movement is known as the Gülen movement. Its ostensible aims and ideals are comparable to the Roman Catholic Jesuits: both give major emphasis to secular education, which in the case of Gülen amounts to hundreds of institutions all over the world. In addition, the 'movement'[4] also works to advance transnational interfaith dialogue.

A brief account of state, society and religion in republican Turkey

After the foundation of the Turkish Republic in 1923, the state elite tried to secure the system they were structuring through a series of laicist legal regulations. Laicist reforms abolished the caliphate, that is, the erstwhile religious leadership, established a state monopoly over education, disestablished the institution of the *ulema* (doctors of Islamic law), rejected Islamic law and adopted a modified version of the Swiss Civil Code, Latinized the alphabet, and, in 1928, struck out the sentence in the Constitution of 1924 which stated that the Turks were necessarily Muslims.[5]

The republican leader, Mustafa Kemal Atatürk, sought to remove religion from the public and social realm, 'to confine it to the conscience of people', and make it a set of beliefs that would not go beyond their personal lives. Thus his aim was to reduce religion to a matter of individual faith and prayer. Henceforward, the principle of freedom of religion and conscience was to protect only *individualized* religion and prayers. Religion was to stay a personal issue and only to necessitate state intervention if it concerned and objectified the social order.[6] The 'Turkish Republic' was designed to be a strictly temporal state. Mustafa Kemal stated this clearly: 'We get our inspirations not from the heavens or invisible things but directly from life.'[7] The state's purpose in this period was to secularize not only the state and the 'political' realm, but also society and the 'social' environment.

It is plausible to argue that this is the biggest single difference between Republican and Ottoman modernizations in Turkey.

Those referred to as 'Kemalist nationalists' preferred what may seem a risky path, although it was actually not so: they declared that all ties with the Islamist and the Ottoman past were now cut off. Instead, they wanted to connect to what they regarded as a utopian, 'universal civilization', epitomized at the time by the modern nation-states of Western Europe.[8] However, while the Kemalists denied Islam as a civilization project, they continued to imagine the Turkish nation as Muslim.[9] As a result, two 'very different conceptions of life'[10] existed side-by-side in Turkey: the secular and the religious.

> Those in the secularist camp are troubled by the 'fact' that a significant part of the population in Turkey does not think the way they do, and are not convinced by the assurances of those in the Islamist camp that if the latter capture power they will respect the secularists' life styles. Consequently, the secularists are hostile to virtually anything that smacks of Islam. In turn, those in the Islamist camp have lost all hope that the secularists will eventually accept them into their fold, and, as a result, have adopted an equally uncompromising attitude.[11]

A new middle class became visible from the 1980s,[12] which, while accepting the ethical standards and cultural values of the traditional order, also adopted the 'rational' business rules and the profit motive of the capitalist market system.[13] As the late Ernest Gellner put it: 'Of the Western monotheisms, Islam is the most Protestant. That is Islam ... has certain appropriate 'Protestant' features: rule orientation, strict Unitarianism, a kind of completeness, the stress on the doctrine, and the finality of doctrine.'[14] Now, if this is a correct sketch of Islam, and if the Weberian thesis is correct, then the new Turkish Islamic middle and upper middle classes are very good examples of a capitalist spirit in Turkey, both as believers and entrepreneurs. Although coming not exactly from the same spiritual/philosophical sources, many of the cadres of the ruling AKP (Adalet ve Kalkınma Partisi/Justice and Development Party),[15] as well as many followers of Fethullah Gülen, would fall into this category.[16] This 'Islamic bourgeoisie' evolved from two sources: (1) the state's neo-liberal economic policies that created conducive economic conditions, and (2) developing transnational financial networks, consequential to deregulation and the opening of the Turkish economy to external networks. Most Islamic entrepreneurs are first generation college graduates, children of an Anatolian-based petty bourgeoisie who benefited from Turgut Özal's[17] neo-liberal economic policies in the 1980s and early 1990s. These policies had the effect of increasing such people's social mobility, allowing them to establish their own medium-sized and small-sized firms.[18] When the Özal government privatized the economy, education, and telecommunication networks, well-organized Muslim groups were empowered to carve new economic and social spaces for themselves.

In February 1997, the mayor of Sincan, a town on the outskirts of Ankara, organized 'Jerusalem Day', to call for the liberation of that city from Israeli control. The mayor was from the 'pro-Islamic' Welfare Party,[19] a partner of the then extant coalition government. The Iranian ambassador was invited and, making anti-secular statements, he called for the establishment of Islamic law in Turkey, while the crowd demonstrated in support of Hamas and Hizbullah, two Islamist groups waging armed struggle against Israel.[20] Laicist forces in Turkey were infuriated and appalled by the rally so close to the capital, and the generals of the Turkish Joined Forces responded by sending tanks through Sincan as a warning. The mayor was arrested, the Iranian ambassador declared *persona non grata*, and an investigation launched against the Welfare Party. Ahmad notes that by this act, 'The Welfare Party had provided the generals with a pretext to curb the Islamic movement and they did so, with what is described as a soft or "post-modern" coup', known as 'the February 28th regime'.[21]

28 February was the date of a National Security Council meeting where the Chief of the General Staff and the commanders of the different forces demanded the implementation of the 18 measures designed to check the growth of 'religious fundamentalism'.[22] On 18 June 1997, faced with pressure from the military and the high judicial institutions, Prime Minister Erbakan (Welfare Party) presented his resignation to President Demirel. As a result, a new government was established, led by Mesut Yılmaz, the leader of the centre right/liberal Motherland Party. Despite this, the army remained very active politically.

In subsequent general elections, held on 3 November 2002, the Justice and Development Party (AKP) got 34% of the vote and won nearly two-thirds of the seats in the parliament. AKP, born partly out of the pro-Islamist Fazilet Partisi (Virtue Party) persistently rejects the nomenclature, 'Islamist'. Instead, it defines itself as a conservative democratic party, and emphasizes not only the democratic character of its party organization and spirit of teamwork but also the importance of consensus-seeking in politics.[23] Five years later, in June 2007, the AKP recorded another resounding victory in general elections, increasing its share of the popular vote to over 46%. However in the local elections in 2009 the Party got 'only' 38.8% of the votes, a significant decline compared to 2007. The period of the rise of the AKP to power in Turkey was also the time of growing significance for the Gülen movement.

Fethullah Gülen and the 'Gülen Movement'[24]

> Gülen is the product of the Struggle against Communism Foundations of the 1960s. Look ... The inner state sees everything acceptable as long as they are under their control. If something goes beyond its control that immediately becomes a threatening element. Gülen has a claim as 'educating a golden generation'. This is Turco–Islamic elitism. Just as the Jesuit priests had ... 'We will educate a golden generation in the schools. Later we will dominate the world with these elites, we will govern it'. That is his idea.
>
> Ahmet İnsel interviewed by Neşe Düzel, 'Fethullahçıları Derin Devlet Yarattı (*Fethullahists* were created by the inner state)', *Taraf* daily, January 14, 2008, 11.

General elections took place in 1995 in Turkey. The increasing popularity of the pro-Islam Refah Partisi seemed to offer the threat of 'religious fundamentalism' to laicist circles. Gülen emerged then as a counter-effect to the apparent rise in religious fundamentalism. He presented a non-political profile although also managing to give the firm impression that the political Islam of the Welfare Party was henceforward to face strong opposition from a milder, 'apolitical' version of Islam from within the Turkish Islamic community.[25]

The organisation's founder, Fethullah Gülen (b.1941),[26] seems to have preferred not to be particularly visible to larger audiences than his own circles until 1995 when he started giving interviews to almost all of the major daily newspapers and television channels in Turkey.[27] The Fethullah Gülen movement is represented in Turkey and abroad through many organizations and publications. In Turkey the movement controls the daily *Zaman* newspaper and the *STV (Samanyolu)* television network.

Numerous conferences, meetings, symposiums have been organized by Gülen groups cooperating with prestigious academic institutions. For example, recent events have included: 'The Muslim World in Transition: Contributions of the Gülen Movement', which was held on 25–27 October 2007 at the House of Lords in London organized by the School of Oriental and African Studies, the London School of Economics and the Leeds Metropolitan University.[28] There was also a symposium entitled 'Islam in Turkey Today' hosted by Columbia University in New York on 2–3 November 2007.[29] This was followed shortly after by the 'International Conference on Peaceful Coexistence: Fethullah Gülen's Initiatives for Peace in the Contemporary World', held on 22–23 November 2007 at Erasmus University Rotterdam, the Netherlands.[30] Finally, there was 'Practitioners, Faith Based Organizations and Global Development Work', a conference organized as part of a joint Berkley Center for Religion, Peace and World Affairs and Luce Foundation project on religion and international relations on 17 December 2007 at Georgetown University's Doha Campus.[31]

Despite his adhesion to a 'moderate' Islam, Gülen became one of the targets of the '28 February regime', and as a result removed himself to the United States where he has lived since 1999, claiming that he is in the USA to receive medical treatment.

Gülen was born in a village in Erzurum province, well known as the home of a very conservative and highly nationalistic population. He left primary school education in 1949, and commenced a religious one. In 1959 he was appointed by the official Presidency of Religious Affairs to be an associate imam (that is, the man who leads prayers in a mosque) in Edirne, a north-western province of Turkey, near to the border with Greece. In 1966 he was appointed as a preacher in Izmir, Turkey's third largest city, located in the Aegean Region. After a military 'intervention' on 12 March 1970, he was arrested and released seven months later. In 1975 he initiated summer camps called '*nur kampları*'(the light camps) for low-income families' teenage children of the Aegean region. At the same time, he continued to work for the Presidency of Religious Affairs until September 1980, resigning his post in 1981. From 1979 he wrote articles for the periodical *Sızıntı* (rivulet) and others, under the pseudonym Abdülfettah Şahin. Following his motto that 'founding a school is better than a mosque', his followers started to establish schools and dormitories in Holland in the late 1980s and in Germany from 1994. During that year, Gülen founded the Journalists and Writers' Foundation (*Gazeteciler ve Yazarlar Vakfı*), and began to become better known.

Gülen was strongly influenced by Bediüzzaman Said Nursi (1877/1878?–1960, the 'Nonpareil of Our Times'),[32] and still shows him a great deal of respect. Bediüzzaman was an Islamic thinker from Turkey of Kurdish origin and the author of the *Risale-i Nur* (*The Epistle/Treatises of Light*), a near-6,000 page commentary on the Koran.[33] Gülen's teachings draw on the heterodox traditions of the Turkish Sufi tradition and refer heavily to the ideas of the medieval mystic poet Mevlana Celalledin-I Rumi (founder of the order of 'whirling dervishes'). The Gülen belief system emphasizes the Turkish traditions of Islamic practice over orthodox Sunni doctrines. In addition, the Gülen movement also has a nationalist focus, in that it envisages an Islamic world shaped by an 'enlightened' Turkish culture rather than a 'reactionary' Arab one.[34]

Following Nursi's teaching, the Gülen movement[35] has avoided political issues, including the relationship between religion and secularism.[36] On the other hand, in the late 1990s, Turkey's Journalists and Writers' Foundation together with the Gülen movement began to organize the Abant Workshops with the aim of seeking to ameliorate socio-political polarization and to search for a new social consensus in Turkey. The annual workshops involve around 50 Turkish intellectuals from different ideological backgrounds.[37] The first workshop in 1998 was devoted to Islam and Secularism. Its press declaration emphasized that God's anthological sovereignty is compatible with the political sovereignty of the people.[38] The second workshop also examined the relationships among state, society and religion.[39]

Fethullah Gülen specifically stresses the compatibility of Islamic ideas and practices with the market economy, and his followers control a complex web of businesses and significant broadcast and print media in Turkey and in Central Asia.[40] The movement is very well financed by its sympathizers and it uses these funds to disseminate its literature and establish many hundreds of colleges and universities not only in Turkey but also in Central Asia, Russia, the Balkans, Africa, and, more recently, Latin America and Nepal. Regarding the movement's business interests, many commentators suspect strong lines of patronage between the present AKP government and the Gülen movement. Under the current AKP administration, a number of business groups owned by avowed members of the movement have grown rapidly with the help of state contracts and concessions.[41] The 'Business Life Solidarity Association' (abbreviated to ISHAD in Turkish) is another key organization for fostering the movement's business ties – particularly in countries other than Turkey.[42] ISHAD members are reputed to provide the main sources of funding for the movement.[43]

Many Turkish commentators (and some members of the Turkish judiciary) appear to suspect the movement of sinister intentions, particularly towards the secular establishment in Turkey and the Turkic republics. However, there are no grounds to suspect ties to radical Islamist or terrorist groups and even Fethullah Gülen's most outspoken opponents have not suggested any such ties. The Gülen group presents itself as a civil society movement and not as an evangelical or political force. Naturally, much of Turkey's laic establishment is deeply suspicious of the group's intentions. The fiercely secularist State Security Court prosecutor Nur Mete Yüksel indicted Fethullah Gülen in 2000 for activities against secularism and for seeking to establish a theocratic state. The indictment alleged that: 'The Fethullah Gülen group has been assessed as the strongest and most influential reactionary formation of this country with their:

- Efforts to appear as modest Islam thanks to their ostensibly accepting democratic methods,
- Using as a device for their aims the schools they have set up at home and abroad with the approval of a sizable part of the people,
- Claim to spiritual leadership, not only in Turkey, but also in the world,
- Exploitation of the established government system through their acceptance by political parties and some state cadres,
- Financial power, whose source is unknown and which keeps active their religious and political structure.'[44]

The trial (in absentia) of Fethullah Gülen in May 2006 concluded with his acquittal on all charges noted in the bullet points above, with the help of changes made in related laws by the current AKP government. However, the judgement was appealed against, and it was not until June 2008 that the acquittal was finally made official.

The movement's educational activities

'portar parte del peso delle schuole'[45]

Neglect of the intellect ... would result in a community of poor, docile mystics. Negligence of the heart or spirit, on the other hand, would result in crude rationalism devoid of any spiritual dimension. ... It is only when the intellect, spirit and body are harmonized, and man is motivated toward activity in the illuminated way of the Divine message, that he can become a complete being and attain true humanity.[46]

Fethullah Gülen has always focused his attentions on education.[47] He started to put his thoughts into practice in the 1970s, when he established his own community (*cemaat*), delivering public lectures to thousands of listeners, which were recorded and sold throughout the country. From this time, Gülen began to attract people who supported his ideas with money and volunteers. Specific community houses, so called 'houses of light' (modified Nurcu-*dershanes*),[48] were established utilizing private flats or houses. In the Nurcu-*dershanes*, Islamic education was and is taught on the basis of both Nursi's writings and Gülen's teaching, making use of the latter's tapes. These units make up Gülen's own *cemaat*, the nucleus of his educational network, which is however much larger than the *cemaat* itself.[49]

He also expressed his thoughts on the issue in his writings.

> Science also can be described as comprehending what things and events tell us, what the Divine laws reveal to us, and striving to understand the Creator's purpose. Created to rule creation, we need to observe and read, to discern and learn about our surroundings so that we can find the best way to exert our influence and control. When we reach this level, by the decree of the Exalted Creator, everything will submit to us and we will submit to God. ... There is no reason to fear science.[50]

Gülen, seizing both national and global opportunities, advanced his goal of training a new elite that he named the 'golden generation' armed with both modern sciences[51] and Islamic ethics. It seems that he now moved beyond leading a purely religious movement to one which had both social and educational connotations, while presenting himself as a 'modern' educator and social innovator.[52] This educational mobilization, in turn, has shaped the worldview and practices of the Gülen movement. Those trained in the summer camps he had initiated in the 1970s became the teachers of the new generation of teachers, ones who carried the ethical message of Islam all over the world. It may be argued that the movement was first transformed by its educational practices while it was seeking to transform the society.[53] 'Serving humanity by means of education' seemed to become Gülen's motto to initiate educational institutions of all levels all around the world:

> First of all, education is a humane service, for we were sent here to learn and be perfected through education. ... I encouraged people to serve the country in particular, and humanity in general, by means of education. I called them to help the state educate and raise people by opening schools. Ignorance is defeated through education, poverty through work and the possession of capital, and internal schism and separatism through unity, dialogue, and tolerance. However, as every problem in human life ultimately depends on human beings themselves, education is the most effective vehicle regardless of whether we have a paralyzed social and political system or one operating with a clockwork precision. ... Schools have been opened in places ranging from Azerbaijan to the Philippines and from St. Petersburg (the capital of Czarist Russia) and Moscow (the capital of communist Russia, and with the help and reference of our Jewish fellow citizen and prominent businessman Üzeyir Garih[54]) to Yakutsky. These schools have been opened in almost all countries, except for those, like Iran, that don't give their permission.[55]

Several journalists and academicians have been invited to visit these institutions. It is reported that the Gülen schools pay special attention to their curriculum in terms of 'sensitivities' of the country where they are located:

> The Central Asian schools are not run by a central financial institution. Entrepreneurs came from various Turkish cities and opened schools in different cities. The teachers, whose teaching is top quality, graduated from the best universities in Turkey. ... None of these schools give religious education. Religion is taught, but none of the

teachers have been educated in theology. With their well-equipped labs and curriculum, the schools follow the pattern of the Turkish Anadolu high schools. Girls do not cover their heads. The purpose is not to introduce religion as a set of norms, but to bring up students according to universal moral standards.[56]

This observation indicates that Fethullah Gülen has been able to undertake an educational programme designed not to upset secular sensibilities, at least not immediately and not in its public forms. As Vicini notes, 'Adherents are not required to bring any outward sign that marks their Islamic inclination. In places linked to movement's activities – from schools to dormitories, to administrative centres of foundations – no sign of Muslim faith is present. Rather, there we can find – at least in Turkey – Atatürk busts and Turkish flags. From this point of view Gülen has given to Islam a public form that is suitable for secular rules of appearance.'[57]

Fethullah Gülen also appears to have much interest in social sciences education, in addition to natural sciences and technology:

When Turkey was knocked out by its adversaries technologically, it was decided to turn all superior minds in this direction so that they would study physics and chemistry and transfer high technology to Turkey as soon as possible. But it seems that some who gave priority to the social sciences also will be among those who will manage the future. ... Raising a leader is tied, in part, to respect for free thought. A seed has the strength to sprout in the soil's bosom and grow. If the air is beneficial to growth and if it reaches water, the sapling will grow taller. People are like that. There shouldn't be any pressure. People should be able to express themselves. People, even geniuses, are not directed to their essential capabilities. This system must change. Students should choose what they want to study. Both high school and the university need this flexibility. An untalented, incapable team is controlling this nation's destiny.[58]

The Gülen movement's educational mission is at its core and in its praxis, remarkably similar to the centuries-old Jesuit educational tradition.[59] Ignatius of Loyola, initiator of the Society of Jesus or so-called *Jesuits*, a Christian religious order of the Roman Catholic Church, sent his companions as missionaries around Europe to create schools, colleges, and seminaries in the 1550s.[60] The Jesuits were founded at the threshold of the counter-reformation, a movement whose purpose was to reform the Catholic Church from within and to counter the Protestant Reformers, whose teachings were spreading throughout Catholic Europe. Gülen's initiation appears to be with a similar sentiment, as a reaction to republican Turkey's official ideological approach to Islam. By the time of Ignatius' death in 1556, the Jesuits were already operating a network of 74 colleges on three continents. Some of these institutions were local, but some others like *Collegio Germanico* were admitting students from various countries of Europe, including Poland, England and Scotland, and even two from Turkey by 1565.[61] A precursor to liberal education, the Jesuit plan of studies incorporated the Classical teachings of Renaissance humanism into the Scholastic structure of Catholic thought.

Finally, the Gülen school curriculum reflects a similar approach of combining modern sciences with Islamic ethics. Since the 1990s, the Gülen movement has presented its educational mission as a cure for identity conflicts, a bridge between local and global groups, and a basis for interfaith dialogue.

The movement's interfaith dialogues

> Applaud the good for their goodness; appreciate those who have believing hearts; be kind to the believers. Approach unbelievers so gently that their envy and hatred would melt away. Like a Messiah, revive people with your heart.[62]

> ...Interfaith dialogue is a must today, and the first step in establishing it is forgetting the past, ignoring polemical arguments, and giving precedence to common points, which far outnumber polemical ones[63]

Angelo Giuseppe Roncalli (25 November 1881–3 June 1963), was made *Vicaire Apostholique* (Apostolic Delegate) to Turkey and Greece from 1935 to 1945. He became known as Blessed John XXIII following his beatification, and was elected as the 261st Pope of the Roman Catholic Church and sovereign of Vatican City on 28 October 1958.[64] Pope John XXIII instituted the Second Ecumenical Council of the Vatican (often referred to as Vatican II), the 21st Ecumenical Council of the Church. Vatican II commenced in 1962 under the auspices of Pope John XXIII and ended in 1965 under the direction of Pope Paul VI, following the former's death. It is likely that Pope John XXIII's familiarity with other faiths and cultural traditions was consequential in the Council's initiation of various interfaith relations including those with non-Christian religions. The Declaration on the Relation of the Church to Non-Christian Religions (*Nostra Aetate*) was enacted as a by-product of Vatican II. It urged Catholics to enter, with prudence and charity, into discussion and collaboration with members of other religions. (See Troy's contribution in this special issue for further discussion of this issue.)[65]

Starting in the early 1990s, Gülen was the first spiritual leader in Turkey to express his views on the necessity of interfaith dialogues:

> The goal of dialogue among world religions is not simply to destroy scientific materialism and the destructive materialistic worldview; rather, the very nature of religion demands this dialogue. Judaism, Christianity, and Islam, and even Hinduism and other world religions accept the same source for themselves, and, including Buddhism, pursue the same goal. As a Muslim, I accept all Prophets and Books sent to different peoples throughout history, and regard belief in them as an essential principle of being Muslim. A Muslim is a true follower of Abraham, Moses, David, Jesus, and all other Prophets. Not believing in one Prophet or Book means that one is not a Muslim. Thus we acknowledge the oneness and basic unity of religion, which is a symphony of God's blessings and mercy, and the universality of belief in religion. So, religion is a system of belief embracing all races and all beliefs, a road bringing everyone together in brotherhood. ... Regardless of how their adherents implement their faith in their daily lives, such generally accepted values as love, respect, tolerance, forgiveness, mercy, human rights, peace, brotherhood, and freedom exalted

by religion. Most of them are accorded the highest precedence in the messages brought by Moses, Jesus, and Muhammad, as well as in the messages of Buddha and even Zarathustra, Lao-Tzu, Conficius, and the Hindu prophets ....

There are many common points for dialogue among devout Muslims, Christians, and Jews. ... there are just as many theoretical or creedal reasons for Muslims and Jews drawing closer to one another as there are for Jews and Christians coming together. Furthermore, practically and historically, the Muslim world has a good record of dealing with the Jews: There has been almost no discrimination, and no Holocaust, denial of basic human rights, or genocide. On the contrary, Jews always have been welcomed in times of trouble, as when the Ottoman State embraced them after their expulsion from Andalusia.[66]

Well before the significant increase in dialogue activities in the post-9/11 world, Gülen had established the Journalists and Writers Foundation in 1994. It appears that from this time he was intent on promoting dialogue and tolerance among all strata of the society in Turkey and elsewhere. In the context of the Intercultural Dialogue Platform, Gülen has held talks with many religious leaders and institutions, such as Pope John Paul II (1998), Greek Eucumenical Patriarch Bartholomeos (1996),[67] Sepharadic Chief Rabbi of Israel Eliyahu Bakshi Doron (1999), as well as a number of Turkish religious leaders.

The Foundation also functions as a think tank on related issues. The movement tries to bring together scholars and intellectuals regardless of their ethnic, ideological, religious and cultural backgrounds (an initiative known as 'The Abant Platform'). This platform is the first of its kind in Turkey, an environment where intellectuals could agree to disagree on sensitive issues such as laicism, secularism, peaceful co-existence, 'faith and reason' relations, and the status of one of Turkey's minority religious groups, the Alevis.

Gülen's dialogue and peaceful coexistence discourse was also replicated in institutions abroad, like the Dialogue Society established in 1999 in London and the Rumi Forum established in 2000 in Washington DC. There are now hundreds of dialogue associations and charities all over the world founded by the movement's Muslim and non-Muslim volunteers said to be motivated by Gülen's teachings. Through these charities, these volunteers initiate and engage in interfaith and intercultural dialog with people of different faiths, backgrounds, and cultures.

As a result of these activities, Gülen and his associates were strongly criticized by two groups: hardline secularists and some Islamists. The two differed in the ways and reasons for which they criticized Gülen. Hardline secularists rebuked him based on the contention that in order to get into contact with other faiths' representatives, some sort of an authorization is required. Since Gülen was not appointed by the state, he had no right to speak to someone like Pope John Paul II on his own behalf.[68] Radical Islamists' reaction to Gülen's visit were slightly different. They considered Gülen's initatives as a humiliation. A Muslim should not go and visit a non-Muslim. They also believed that for such a prominent Muslim religious leader to visit other religious leaders would cause some Muslims to convert.[69]

In Gülen's opinion, interfaith dialogues have five main reasons: saving modern humans from materialism; all religions have the same sources and natures; the Koran's call to interfaith dialogue; religious tolerance as a purpose of human life; and love as the essence of being requests tolerance. He repeatedly rejects fundamentalist, violent, and exclusivist interpretations of religion.[70] Instead, Gülen emphasizes the importance of pragmatist reasoning to serve what he sees as the common goal of all religions: to fight materialism and to revive the existence of God in people's lives. In other words, he appears to be seriously concerned not only with religion per se, but also with the question of how to to improve the religious life of contemporary humans so as to increase both tolerance and interfaith dialogues. He prefers as a method of dialogue to forget the divisive arguments of the past and to concentrate on common points that religions share.[71]

In the context of 'dialogue', it is interesting to observe Gülen's construction of 'otherness'. Kösebalaban analyses Gülen's conception of foreign policy through the application of a constructivist theoretical framework.[72] Kösebalaban distinguishes three perceptions of the 'other' defined by varying degrees of separation that shape Gülen's national security identity: (1) a strong degree of common identification with the Turkic world, (2) a lack of common identification with the West but a desire to integrate with Western institutions, (3) a strong lack of common identification with Iran. These conceptions may be useful in interpreting Gülen's expressions like the following:

> To devotees, the value of their ideals transcends that of the earthly ones to such an extent that it is almost impossible to divert them from what they seek – God's gratuitous consent – and lead them to any other ideal. In fact, stripped entirely of finite and transient things, devotees undergo such a transformation in their hearts to turn to God that they are changed because they recognize no goal other than their ideal. Since they devote themselves completely to making people love God and to being loved by God, dedicating their lives to enlightening others, and, once again, because they have managed to orient their goal in this unified direction, which in a sense contributes to the value of this ideal, they avoid divisive and antagonist thoughts, such as 'they' and 'we', 'others' and 'ours'.[73]

Concluding remarks

We have seen that the Gülen movement is a faith-based network with organizational structures and a focus of discourse that has developed as a consequence both of Turkey's unique political history and global events since the end of the Cold War in the early 1990s. During this time, Fethullah Gülen has managed to lead his followers into the modern world while retaining their religious framework. Their education initiatives concerning all around the world, as well as inter-faith dialogue activities, seem to emanate from a desire to be involved in agenda setting at both Turkish and global levels. Despite most members having a specific national background in Turkey, the movement appears to be a religious actor which wants to be both assertive in making its points while also showing willingness to listen to other points of view. Fostering the movement's global business ties among members that are reputed to provide the main sources of funding for the movement seems to be an objective inextricable from the aim to be an actor in global politics. Although already there is quite an impressive amount of literature on the Gülen movement[74] very few critical ones exist, and almost no serious work has been done yet on issues like the role of his followers in Central Asia, or the impacts of the graduates of the educational institutions all over the globe, founded by members of the community.

In sum, in order to understand the nature of the movement, it is necessary to refer to Fethullah Gülen's thinking.[75] For Gülen, Kemalist Turkey's 'top-down' imposition of a dogmatic secularism has distanced swathes of Turkish society from the governing elite. Gülen prefers to draw inspiration from the Ottoman model of state–society relationships. Although the empire's rulers were guided by their faith, the Ottoman system of governance was not theocratic. Public laws were formulated on the basis of the state's needs rather than in accordance with Islamic law (Shari'a). For Gülen, the state has a functionally secular responsibility to provide internal and external security and stability for its citizens. Gülen is not in favour of the political implementation of Shari'a, though the freedom to express one's faith should be respected. Gülen believes that there is no necessary contradiction between Islam and modernity. Indeed, Turkish Islam's more adaptable and less doctrinal Sufi traditions have enabled Turkey, with its democratization, free market economy, and secular political system, to incorporate aspects of modernity barely found elsewhere in the Muslim world. A key to his thinking is that Islam should positively embrace science, reason, democratization, and tolerance. It may be said that Gülen's support of democracy back in the 1990s was instrumental in facilitating in Turkey many practising Muslims' internalization of democracy.[76]

In this context, Park notes the following:

> [T]he more one perceives the movement as a more-or-less hierarchical, disciplined, and 'conspiratorial' organization that seeks to penetrate and undermine the Turkish state and society from within, the more one is inclined to adopt an essentially political interpretation of the movement's activities. This is precisely the model of the Gülen movement that many in Turkey's elite hold, and fear. On the other hand, although the movement's lack of transparency and the weakness of its internal democracy and capacity for self-criticism are unsettling, this does not necessarily render it an extremist phenomenon. Neither Gülen nor the movement that takes his name is overtly politicized, and in the absence of hard evidence to the contrary, the movement will seem benign to many – unless of course one is ideologically opposed to challenges to Turkey's existing order, as many in Turkey are, or inherently uneasy about any faith-inspired movement.[77]

Finally, this article has sought to underline that Turkish democracy is at a stage where it is necessary for consistent checks and balance to be in place covering all interested parties along the political spectrum. This is particularly the case if we understand democracy in terms of the rule of law. The latter should be created by the will of majority in a democratically elected legislature, involving popular participation, competition, consent, and sufficient protection of both individual and minority rights then it is not legitimate to try to exclude any movement from the political realm. This is the case as long as the above mentioned constituents of a democratic regime are consistently respected and honoured by all, government and governed alike.

Acknowledgements

I want to express my gratitude to the Birkbeck Institute for the Humanities, University of London, for the fellowship that allowed me to carry out my work in London in spring 2009. I would also like to thank Dr Özcan Keleş for his valuable comments on an earlier version of this article.

Notes

1. I use the term laicists to mean those who prefer the state's control of religion as opposed to secularism which implies the separation of state and religion. As Rex Ahdar and Ian Leigh point out, 'The longstanding French policy of *laicité* exemplifies ... desire to restrict, if not eliminate, clerical and religious influence, over the state. ... The modern Islamic society of Turkey is similarly an example of a state founded on strongly secular principles where restrictions on individual religious liberty have been introduced to prevent pressure being exerted by the predominant religious group' (Ahdar and Leigh, *Religious Freedom in the Liberal State*, 73). For a comprehensive argumentation on the terms laic and secular, and their derivatives, see Davison, 'Turkey, a "Secular" State? The Challenge of Description'. I totally agree with Davison in his arguments, thus I prefer to use the term 'laicist' for republican state practice in Turkey. Furthermore, laiklik (laicité) is the concept that is preferred by the Republican decision-making elite of Turkey in both legislation and other legal regulations.
2. For such usage see, Esposito, *Islamic Revivalism*; Davison, *Secularism Revivalism in Turkey*; Howe, *Turkey Today: A Nation Divided over Islam's Revival*, 7, 8, 15, 305; Kramer, *A Changing Turkey: The Challenge to Europe and the United States*, 55–84; Karpat, *The Politicization of Islam*, 527; Nachmani, *Turkey: Facing a New Millennium*, 90; Vertigans, *Islamic Roots and Resurgence in Turkey*. I assert that 'revival' may only be used for the revitalizations of the religious orders (see Mardin, *Religion and Social Change in Modern Turkey*, 149) in the nineteenth century, part of the emergence of political Islam – which in fact is a modern ideology (see Türköne, *Siyasi İdeoloji Olarak İslamcılığın Doğuşu*).
3. For a very illuminating work on reconstitution of the *process* that led to the emergence of the current party of government, the Justice and Development Party (AKP), see Mardin, 'Turkish Islamic Exceptionalism Yesterday and Today'.
4. Followers of Gülen have been reluctant to use the term 'movement'. Several other terms have been suggested, including, 'community' (*cemaat*) and network. Hakan Yavuz justifies his use of the term, movement, as follows. I agree with this usage: 'I use the term *movement*, because a movement has a collective goal that it intends to achieve through a collective engagement. In order to achieve it, you need networks. The Gülen movement consists of a number of networks, organized horizontally. In this loose network system, the traditional values and idioms of the community play an important role. ... As a movement, it incorporates the network and community, or communal ethos. I would consider it as a movement based on the re-imagining

of Islam and consisting of loose networks under the guidance and leadership of Fetullah Gülen.... These networks are not necessarily organized in hierarchical terms. But we see three circles. The first is the core circle around Gülen. The second circle consists of those who give their time and labour in order to achieve the collective goals of the movement. The third circle consists of those who are sympathizers: sometimes they support the movement by writing an article in the media, or they give money, or they support the movement in other ways .... So you have a number of circles, but each circle includes a number of networks. When we examine these networks, there is a sense of solidarity and of the Islamic ethos of brotherhood. This is the glue that joins these networks together' (Mayer, 'The Gülen Movement').

5. Zürcher, *Turkey: A Modern History*, 194.
6. Actually this was a political/legal enforcement of the 'secularization thesis' (see Casanova, *Public Religions in the Modern World*, 17–39), and 'privatization of religion' (see Luckmann, *The Invisible Religion*) by adopting the right to individual belief, 'a product of the only legitimate space (that was) allowed to Christianity by post-Enlightenment society' (Asad, *Genealogies of Religion*, 45).
7. Atatürk, *Söylev ve Demeçler*, 389.
8. Gülalp, *Kimlikler Siyaseti: Türkiye'de İslamın Temelleri*, 35.
9. Turkey is often defined as a predominantly Muslim country; Islamists especially delight in repeating at every opportunity that 99% of Turkish people are Muslim. But this is mostly a definition given to them by the secular state. Unless declared otherwise, every child born in Turkey is registered as Muslim and this is clearly indicated in every person's government-issued identity card. ... '"Muslim" is evidently a social identity conferred upon the Turkish people by the "secular" state' (Gülalp, 'Whatever Happened to Secularization?', 394; also see Meeker, *A Nation of Empire*, 51–4).
10. Howe, *Turkey Today: A Nation Divided over Islam's Revival*, 243.
11. Heper, 'Review of "Turkey Today: A Nation Divided over Islam's Revival"', 150.
12. For overviews of the 'new middle class', see İnsel, 'The AKP and Normalizing Democracy in Turkey', 297; Raudvere, 'Where Does Globalization Take Place?', 168, n. 2.
13. Kemal Karpat makes a very similar statement for the last decades of Ottoman times (Karpat, *The Politicization of Islam*, 21).
14. Gellner, 'The Turkish Option in Contemporary Perspective', 234.
15. For the religious lineage that takes us to Turkey's current prime minister, Recep Tayip Erdoğan, see Mardin, 'Turkish Islamic Exceptionalism Yesterday and Today', 15–18.
16. See, Selçuk Uygur, '"Islamic Puritanism" as a Source of Economic Development: Contributions of the Gülen Movement', a paper presented at the 'Muslim World in Transition: Contributions of the Gülen Movement', conference that was held on October 25–27, 2007, at the House of Lords in London organized by SOAS, the London School of Economics and the Leeds Metropolitan University, online at http://en.fgulen.com/content/view/2453/53/
17. Turgut Özal (1927–1993), a Turkish political leader, prime minister and the eighth president of Turkey. As prime minister and later president, he transformed the economy of Turkey by paving the way for the privatization of many state sectors.
18. Yavuz, 'The Role of the New Bourgeoisie in the Transformation of the Turkish Islamic Movement', 5.
19. A series of pro-Islamic parties have been represented over time in parliament with almost the same group of founders since the 1970s: National Order Party (Milli Nizam Partisi), founded on 26 January 1970 – banned on 20 May 1971; National Salvation Party (Milli Selâmet Partisi), founded on 11 October 1972 – closed on 12 September 1980; Welfare Party (Refah Partisi), founded 1983 – banned on 22 February 1998; Virtue Party (Fazilet Partisi), founded 1998 – banned on 22 June 2001; Felicity Party (Saadet Partisi), founded on 20 July 2001.

Religion and Democratizations 189

20. In addition to having an Islamist movement to be represented in parliament, Turkey also has a number of active small and medium-sized radical Islamist groups. For a recent report published in September 2007 by the Washington Institute for Near East Policy on the 'reemergence of Hizbullah in Turkey' see Çakır, 'The Reemergence of Hizbullah in Turkey'.
21. According to Turkish National Security Council decision no. 406, the Erbakan government was instructed to implement 18 directives initiated by 'the principle of laicité [that] should be strictly enforced and laws should be modified for that purpose, if necessary'. For these directives see Yavuz and Esposito, *Turkish Islam and the Secular State*, 275–6.
22. Ibid.
23. In an article Erdoğan is quoted as saying 'Let me be quite open and clear in stating a fact – we don't find it appropriate to mix religion and politics . . . . We are not Muslim democrats, we are conservative democrats. Some in the west portray us as (Muslim democrats) but our notion of conservative democracy is to attach ourselves to the customs and the traditions and the values of our society, which is based on the family. This is a democratic issue, not a religious one (Boland, 'Eastern Premise').
24. Gülen himself rejects the name 'Gülen Movement in both his writings and interviews, as well as the tag 'Fethullahists'. Recently he was said to have requested academics not to use such terms, but instead to use 'movement of ones united for high humanitarian values' (Yüksek, *insani değerler etrafında birleşmiş insanların hareketi*) (samanyoluhaber.com – 10 January 2008).
25. For a very insightful analysis of the 'movement', see Laçiner, 'Seçkinci bir geleneğin temsilcisi olarak Fethullah Hoca Cemaati'.
26. Some sources report his birth date as 10 November 1938. Nurettin Veren, an ex-follower who later became a fierce opponent, claims that this is Gülen's symbolic invention to indicate his role as a saviour of Islam by dating his birth to the very day Mustafa Kemal Atatürk died. See, Veren, *Kuşatma: ABD'nin Truva Atı Fethullah Gülen Hareketi*, 9.
27. 23–28 January 1995: Ertuğrul Özkök-Hürriyet; 30 January 1995: Nuriye Akman-Sabah; 3 July 1995: Ateş Hattı/Reha Muhtar-TRT 1; 6 July 1995: InterStar TV: news; 13–23 August 1995: Eyüp Can: Zaman; 20 August 1995: Oral Çalışlar-Cumhuriyet.
28. See http://www.gulenconference.org.uk/
29. See http://www.islaminturkeytoday.org/
30. See http://www.gulenconference.nl/
31. See http://berkleycenter.georgetown.edu/42589.html
32. Şerif Mardin, a very prominent sociologist that has been working on religion, state and society in Turkey since the 1970s, is the author of a milestone book on Bediüzzaman Said Nursi published in 1989. Recently many books and other academic works have appeared in English. See, Abu-Rabi, *Islam at the Crossroads*; Vahide, *Islam in Modern Turkey* (actually she is also the author of a previous book on Bediüzzaman of 1992 under the name Mary Weld, *Bediuzzaman Said Nursi*); Markham and Özdemir, *Globalization, Ethics and Islam*. Also for a detailed biography of Bediüzzaman Said Nursi in English, see http://www.ayetulkubra.com/rnkdiller/eng/english_hayat.htm
33. For *Risale-i Nur* collection in English see http://www.risale-i-nur.org/
34. For the Gülen movement's contributions to Turkey's potential leadership of the 'Turkic world', see Yılmaz, '*Ijdihad* and *Tajdid* by Conduct'.
35. For overviews of the significance of the movement, see Yavuz, 'Towards an Islamic Liberalism?', and Aras, 'Turkish Islam's Moderate Face'.
36. Kuru, 'Reinterpretation of Secularism in Turkey', 141.

37. For an argument on Gülen's efforts to reveal a dynamic interpretation of Islam that is compatible with and at the same time critical of modernity and Muslim tradition, rather than creating an eclectic or hybrid synthesis of modernity and Islam, see Kuru, 'Fethullah Gülen's Search for a Middle Way Between Modernity and Muslim Tradition'.
38. For the texts of the first four *Abant Declarations* see Yavuz and Esposito, *Turkish Islam and the Secular State*, 251–6. Also see, http://en.fgulen.com/content/category/148/265/18/
39. See *İslam ve Laiklik* (Islam and Laicité) (1998) Gazeteciler ve Yazarlar Vakfı, Istanbul; *Din, Devlet, Toplum* (Religion, State and Society) (2000) Gazeteciler ve Yazarlar Vakfi, Istanbul.
40. Eickelman, 'Islam and Ethical Pluralism', 123–7.
41. Hendrick, 'Transnational Religious Nationalism', 16.
42. See, http://www.ishad.org.tr/ishad_english.asp
43. The projects sponsored by the Gülen-inspired movement are numerous, international and costly in terms of human and financial capital. Critics of the movement often question the financing of these initiatives – with some convinced of collusion with Middle Eastern governments, others (within Turkey) suspicious that Western governments are financially backing the projects. For a response to such questions, see Helen Rose Ebaugh and Dogan Koc, 'Funding Gülen-Inspired Good Works: Demonstrating and Generating Commitment to the Movement', a paper presented at the 'Muslim World in Transition: Contributions of the Gülen Movement', conference that was held on October 25–27, 2007, at the House of Lords in London organized by SOAS, the London School of Economics and the Leeds Metropolitan University, online at http://en.fgulen.com/content/view/2519/53/
44. The author has a copy of the indictment dated 22 August 2000, entitled: 'Republic of Turkey, ANKARA, State Security Court, Prosecutor's Office'. No other bibliographical details are available.
45. 'Every Jesuit must bear his part of the burden of the schools.' *Monumenta paedagogica Societatis Jesu* (1965–1986/2nd edn) v.3, Monumenta Historica Societatis Iesu, Rome, 305–06.
46. Gülen, *Prophet Muhammad: Aspects of his Life*, 105–06.
47. 'The main duty and purpose of human life is to seek understanding. The effort of doing so, known as education, is a perfecting process though which we earn, in the spiritual, intellectual, and physical dimensions of their beings, the rank appointed for us as the perfect pattern of creation. . . . Education is different from teaching. Most people can teach, but only a very few can educate. Communities composed of individuals devoid of a sublime ideal, good manners, and human values are like rude individuals who have no loyalty in friendship or consistency in enmity.' ('Education from Cradle to Grave' from a summary of his series of articles published in monthly *Sızıntı*, No: 26–41, March 1981–June 1982). See, http://en.fgulen.com/content/view/777/16/
48. The *dershane* is a venue for social and cultural activities and interaction.
49. Agai, *Zwischen Diskurs und Netzwerk*, 136–53; Yavuz and Esposito, *Turkish Islam and the Secular State*, 32.
50. Gülen, *Criteria or Lights of the Way*, 59–61.
51. 'Science also can be described as comprehending what things and events tell us, what the Divine laws reveal to us, and striving to understand the Creator's purpose. Created to rule creation, we need to observe and read, to discern and learn about our surroundings so that we can find the best way to exert our influence and control. When we reach this level, by the decree of the Exalted Creator, everything will submit to us and we will submit to God. . . . There is no reason to fear science. The danger does not lie with science and the founding of the new world it will usher in, but rather with

ignorance and irresponsible scientists and others who exploit it for their own selfish interest. ... Although science might be a deadly weapon in the hands of an irresponsible minority, we should not hesitate to adopt both it and its products and then use them to establish a civilization in which we can secure our happiness in this world and the next. It is pointless to curse machines and factories, because machines will continue to run and factories to operate. Science and its products will begin to benefit us only when people of truth and belief begin to direct our affairs.' (Gülen, 'İlim ve Tekniğe Küskünlük').

52. Agai, 'The Gülen Movement's Islamic Ethic of Education'.
53. For an informative work and critical analysis of the Gülen community that focuses on educational institutions in Central Asia, see Balcı 2005.
54. For Üzeyir Garih's comments about these schools, 'As far as I saw, these schools are giving secular education. I visited many of them to see whether they are Muslim missionary institutions established on Islamic standards and pursuing an Islamic unity. I saw that they are not. Students are raised very well.' see, *Hürriyet* daily, April 11, 1996.
55. 'Educational Services Spreading Throughout the World', see http://en.fgulen.com/content/view/778/16/[0]
56. Ali Bayramoğlu, *Yeni Yüzyıl* daily, October 31, 1996.
57. Vicini, 'Gülen and Sources in Islam for Interfaith Dialogue'.
58. Sevindi, *Fethullah Gülen ile Global Hoşgörü ve New York Sohbeti*, 118.
59. For differences between the two communities see Michael David Graskemper, 'A Bridge to Inter-religious Cooperation: The Gülen–Jesuit Educational Nexus', a paper presented at the 'Muslim World in Transition: Contributions of the Gülen Movement', conference that was held on October 25–27, 2007, at the House of Lords in London organized by SOAS, the London School of Economics and the Leeds Metropolitan University, online at http://en.fgulen.com/content/view/2511/53/
60. Höpfl, *Jesuit Political Thought: The Society of Jesus and the State*, 426.
61. O'Malley, *The First Jesuits*, 235.
62. Fethullah Gülen, quoted in Ünal and Williams, *Advocate of Dialogue*, 23.
63. Ibid., 244–5.
64. In 2000 Roncalli's name was given to the street where the Vatican Embassy is located in Istanbul; thus the name of the street was changed from *Ölçek Sokak* to *Roncalli Sokağı*.
65. Troy, '"Catholic Waves" of Democratization? Roman Catholicism and Its Potential for Democratization'.
66. 'Fethullah Gülen's Speeches and Interviews on Interfaith Dialogue' see, http://en.fgulen.com/content/view/1334/11/. Note however that Turkey's Presidency of Religious Affairs has also made 'dialogue' a part of its agenda from 1998. However recently it has become a concept that has been expressed more and more by the authorities: 'I believe that one of the most effective steps to solve such problems is to establish ways for strong dialogue among religions as well as cultures. Such a dialogue will not only help to wipe out the prejudices of the followers of different faiths, but also contribute to solve the above-mentioned problems. I believe that lack of sincere dialogue causes the discourse of the clash of civilizations to gain ground.' ('Peace and Tolerance', a speech made by Ali Bardakoğlu, the President of Religious Affairs in the Conference on Peace and Tolerance II, co-sponsored by Appeal of Conscience Foundation and Greek Orthodox Patriarchate in Istanbul, November 7–9, 2005).
67. For 'Repercussions from Gulen–Bartholomeos Meeting' see, http://en.fgulen.com/content/category/148/252/11/
68. See Necip Hablemitoglu, *Yeni Hayat* (*New Life*), Issue 52.
69. See, Mehmet Sevket Eygi, 'Papalikla Gizli Anlasma' [Secret agreement with Papacy], *Milli Gazete* (*National Gazette*), May 26, 2000.

70. See, Y. Alp Aslandogan and Bekir Cınar, 'A Sunni Muslim Scholar's Humanitarian and Religious Rejection of Violence Against Civilians', a paper presented at the 'Muslim World in Transition: Contributions of the Gülen Movement', conference that was held on October 25–27, 2007, at the House of Lords in London organized by SOAS, the London School of Economics and the Leeds Metropolitan University, online at http://en.fgulen.com/content/view/2463/53/.
71. An interesting comparison would be with Benedict Anderson that asserts the necessity for amnesia to become a nation in *Imagined Communities*. For an opposing view, see Pim Valkenberg, 'Fethullah Gülen's Contribution to Muslim–Christian Dialogue in the Context of Abrahamic Cooperation', a paper presented at the 'Muslim World in Transition: Contributions of the Gülen Movement', conference that was held on October 25–27, 2007, at the House of Lords in London organized by SOAS, the London School of Economics and the Leeds Metropolitan University, online at http://en.fgulen.com/content/view/2138/31/.
72. Kösebalaban, 'The Making of Enemy and Friend', 172–3.
73. Gülen, *Kırık Testi*, 100.
74. A substantial amount of these works appear to be, to say the least, 'extremely flattering' like comparisons of Fethullah Gülen with most prominent names of intellectual history as Confucius, Plato, Kant, Mill, and Sartre (see, Caroll, *A Dialogue of Civilizations*). Other works, however, especially many written by Turks, highlight a conspiracy theory between the movement and hardline Islamists in Turkey. In addition, there are other, more objective works. See, for example, Balcı, *Orta Asya'da Islam Misyonerleri: Fethullah Gülen Okulları*; Hendrick, 'Transnational Religious Nationalism' (the author of this unpublished paper is about to complete a PhD dissertation on Gülen networking); Koyuncu-Lorasdağı, 'Globalization, Modernization, and Democratization in Turkey'; Özyürek, 'Feeling Tells Beter than Language'; Park, 'The Fethullah Gülen Movement'; Toprak et al., *Türkiye'de Farklı Olmak: Din Ve Muhafazakarlık Ekseninde Ötekileştirilenler*, 144–70; Turam, *Between Islam and the State*; White, *Islamist Mobilization in Turkey*, 111–13, 207, 278; Yavuz and Esposito, *Turkish Islam and the Secular State*.
75. Articles, speeches, interviews, etc. by Fethullah Gülen can be found at the movement's website at http://www.fgulen.org.
76. In an interview undertaken by the present writer with one of the followers of the movement on March 20, 2009, I was told that, 'I think it is important to recall and consider Gülen's views on democracy, state and politics in context. One of Gülen's early public speeches on democracy was at the launch of the Journalists and Writers Foundation in 1994. There he said that there can be no return from democracy; that while not perfect it is the best form of governance and that we should strive to perfect it further. From a personal point of view, I remember this statement having an effect on me as a teenager wondering whether I could internalise this value and whether doing so would run contrary to my faith. Many practising Muslims had similar dilemmas – including perhaps our current prime minister. It is no exaggeration to say that at the very least a significant proportion of the conservative practising Muslims of Turkey were extremely ambivalent about internalising democracy. They were happy to utilise it, but couldn't bring themselves to sincerely accepting it as a viable (and religiously permissible) form of governance. The stumbling block was their understanding of faith, religion and society. They were taught that accepting democracy will lead to disbelief; at the most it must be exploited to be subverted, but that's it. It was at this juncture that Gülen came out strongly supporting democracy. He didn't just argue that Islam "permist" democracy but has increasingly argued that it in fact necessitates "democratic engagement" which is important for me. You might be interested in watching his most recent video clip on this released just this week. His support of

democracy back in the 1990s was instrumental in facilitating the practising Muslim mass' internalisation of democracy.' (Interview with Özcan Keleş of the The Dialogue Society at the society's headquarters in London)
77. Park, 'The Fethullah Gülen Movement'.

Note on contributor

İştar Gözaydın is Professor of Law and Politics in the Department of Humanities and Social Sciences at Istanbul Technical University, Turkey. She is also the head of the Department of Politics Studies affiliated with the Department of Humanities and Social Sciences at Istanbul Technical University. She has studied at New York University School of Law and Georgetown University International Law Institute, and holds an LLD degree from Istanbul University. Since 1995 Professor Gözaydın has produced and presented a radio programme on Acik Radyo [Open Radio] in Istanbul.

Bibliography

Abu-Rabi, Ibrahim M. *Islam at the Crossroads: On the Life and Thought of Bediuzzaman Said Nursi*. Albany, NY: State University of New York Press, 2003.
Agai, Bekim. 'The Gülen Movement's Islamic Ethic of Education'. In *The Emergence of a New Turkey: Democracy and the AK Party*, ed. M. Hakan Yavuz. Salt Lake City: The University of Utah Press, 2003.
Agai, Bekim. *Zwischen Diskurs und Netzwerk – Das Bildungsnetzwerk um Fethullah Gülen (geb. 1938). Die flexible Umsetzung modernen islamischen Gedankenguts*. Hamburg: EB-Verlag, 2004.
Ahdar, Rex, and Ian Leigh. *Religious Freedom in the Liberal State*. Oxford and New York: Oxford University Press, 2005.
Aras, Bülent. 'Turkish Islam's Moderate Face'. *Middle East Quarterly* 5, no. 3 (1998): 23–9.
Asad, Talal. *Genealogies of Religion: Discipline and Reasons of Power in Christianity and Islam*. Baltimore, MD and London: The John Hopkins University Press, 1993.
Atatürk, Mustafa Kemal. *Söylev ve Demeçler* [Speeches and statements]. In *The Grand National Assembly and Republican People's Party General Meetings: 1919–1938*, v. 1. Istanbul, 1945.
Balcı, Bayram. *Orta Asya'da Islam Misyonerleri: Fethullah Gülen Okulları* [Muslim missionaries in Central Asia: the schools of Fethullah Gülen]. Istanbul: İletişim, 2005.
Caroll, B. Jill. *A Dialogue of Civilizations: Gülen's Islamic Ideals and Humanistic Discourse*. NJ: The Light, Inc. & the Gülen Institute, 2007.
Boland, Vincent. 'Eastern Premise'. *Financial Times*, December 3, 2004.
Çakır, Ruşen. 'The Reemergence of Hizbullah in Turkey'. *Policy Focus no. 74*. Washington, DC: The Washington Institute for Near East Policy, 2007.
Casanova, José. *Public Religions in the Modern World*. Chicago and London: The University of Chicago Press, 1994.
Davison, Andrew. *Secularism Revivalism in Turkey*. New Haven, CT and London: Yale University Press, 1998.
Davison, Andrew. 'Turkey, a "Secular" State? The Challenge of Description'. *South Atlantic Quarterly* 102, nos. 2/3 (2003): 333–50.
Eickelman, Dale F. 'Islam and Ethical Pluralism'. In *Islamic Political Ethics: Civil Society, Pluralism and Conflict*, ed. Sohail H. Hashmi, 116–34. Princeton, NJ and London: Princeton University Press, 2002.
Esposito, John L. *Islamic Revivalism*. Occasional Paper no.3. Washington, DC: American Institute for Islamic Affairs: The Muslim World Today, 1985.

Gellner, Ernest. 'The Turkish Option in Contemporary Perspective'. In *Rethinking Modernity and National Identity in Turkey*, ed. Sibel Bozdoğan and Reşat Kasaba, 233–44. Seattle, WA and London: University of Washington Press, 1997.

Gülalp, Haldun. *Kimlikler Siyaseti: Türkiye'de İslamın Temelleri* [*Identity Politics: Roots of Islam in Turkey*]. Istanbul: Metis, 2003.

Gülalp, Haldun. 'Whatever Happened to Secularization? The Multiple Islams of Turkey'. *South Atlantic Quarterly* 102, nos. 2/3 (2003): 381–95.

Gülen, Fethullah. 'İlim ve Tekniğe Küskünlük' ['Regretting Science and Technology']. *Sızıntı* 2, no. 19 (August 1980).

Gülen, Fethullah. *Criteria or Lights of the Way*, vol. 2, 12th edn. Izmir: Fountain Publications, 1998.

Gülen, Fethullah. *Prophet Muhammad: Aspects of his Life*, translated by Ali Ünal. Fairfax, VI: The Fountain, 2000.

Gülen, Fethullah. *Kırık Testi* [*Broken Jug*]. Istanbul: Gazeteciler ve Yazarlar Vakfı, 2004.

Hendrick, Joshua D. 'Transnational Religious Nationalism: Globalization, Muslim Networks, & The Turkish Movement of M. Fethullah Gülen'. *yayınlanmamış bildiri*: A Different Approach to Debates on Political Islam – Micro-Level Studies International Conference, Ben Gurion University of the Negev, Israel, Haziran 2–4, 2008.

Heper, Metin. 'Review of "Turkey Today: A Nation Divided over Islam's Revival"'. *The Middle East Journal* 55, no. 1 (2001): 150–1.

Höpfl, Harro. *Jesuit Political Thought: The Society of Jesus and the State, c.1540–1630*. Cambridge, MA and London: Cambridge University Press, 2004.

Howe, Marvine. *Turkey Today: A Nation Divided over Islam's Revival*. Colorado and Oxford: Westview Press, 2000.

İnsel, Ahmet. 'The AKP and Normalizing Democracy in Turkey'. *South Atlantic Quarterly* 102, nos. 2/3 (2003): 293–308.

Karpat, Kemal H. *The Politicization of Islam: Reconstructing Identity, Faith, and Community in the late Ottoman State*. Oxford and New York: Oxford University Press, 2001.

Kösebalaban, Hasan. 'The Making of Enemy and Friend: Fethullah Gülen's National Security Identity'. In *Turkish Islam and the Secular State: The Gülen Movement*, ed. M. Hakan Yavuz and John L. Esposito. New York: Syracuse University Press, 2003.

Koyuncu Lorasdağı, Berrin. 'Globalization, Modernization, and Democratization in Turkey: The Fethullah Gülen Movement'. In *Remaking Turkey: Globalization, Alternative Modernities, and Democracy*, ed. E. Fuat Keyman, 153–77. Lanham, MD: Lexington Books, 2007.

Kramer, Heinz. *A Changing Turkey: The Challenge to Europe and the United States*. Washington, DC: Brookings Institution Press, 2000.

Kuru, Ahmet T. 'Fethullah Gülen's Search for a Middle Way Between Modernity and Muslim Tradition'. In *Turkish Islam and the Secular State: The Gülen Movement*, ed. M. Hakan Yavuz and John L. Esposito. New York: Syracuse University Press, 2003.

Kuru, Ahmet T. 'Reinterpretation of Secularism in Turkey'. In *The Emergence of a New Turkey: Democracy and the AK Party*, ed. M. Haka Yavuz. Salt Lake City: The University of Utah Press, 2006.

Laçiner, Ömer. 'Seçkinci bir geleneğin temsilcisi olarak Fethullah Hoca Cemaati' ['Fethullah Hodja Community as a Representative of an Elitist Tradition']. *Birikim* 77 (September 1995): 3–10.

Luckmann, Thomas. *The Invisible Religion*. New York: Macmillan, 1967.

Mardin, Şerif. *Religion and Social Change in Modern Turkey: The Case of Bediüzzaman Said Nursi*. Albany, NY: State University of New York Press, 1989.

Mardin, Şerif. 'Turkish Islamic Exceptionalism Yesterday and Today: Continuity, Rupture and Reconstruction in Operational Codes'. In *Religion and Politics in Turkey*, ed. Ali Çarkoğlu and Barry Rubin, 3–23. London and New York: Routledge, 2006.
Markham, Ian, and Ibrahim Ozdemir. *Globalization, Ethics and Islam: The Case of Bediuzzaman Said Nursi*. London: Ashgate Publishing, 2005.
Mayer, Jean-François. 'The Gülen Movement: A Modern Expression of Turkish Islam – Interview with Hakan Yavuz (July 21, 2004)'. *Religioscope*, 2004. http://religion.info/English/interviews/article_74.shtml.
Meeker, Michael M. *A Nation of Empire: The Ottoman Legacy of Turkish Modernity*. Berkeley: University of California Press, 2002.
Nachmani, Amikam. *Turkey: Facing a New Millennium*. Manchester and New York: Manchester University Press, 2003.
O'Malley, John W. *The First Jesuits*. Cambridge, MA and London: Harvard University Press, 1993.
Özyürek, Esra G. 'Feeling Tells Better than Language: Emotional Expression and Gender Hierarchy in the Sermons of Fethullah Gülen Hocaefendi'. *New Perspectives on Turkey* 16 (Spring 1997) 41–51.
Park, Bill. 'The Fethullah Gulen Movement'. *MERIA Journal* 12, no. 4 (2008).
Raudvere, Catharina. (2004). 'Where Does Globalization Take Place? Opportunities and Limitations for Female Activists in Turkish Islamist Non-Governmental Organization'. In *Globalization and the Muslim World: Culture, Religion, and Modernity*, ed. Birgit Schaebler and Leif Stenberg, 166–87. New York: Syracuse University Press, 2004.
Sevindi, Nevval. *Fethullah Gülen ile Global Hoşgörü ve New York Sohbeti* [*Global tolerance and New York chat with Fethullah Gülen*], 4th edn. Istanbul: Timaş, 2002.
Toprak, Binnaz, İrfan Bozan, Tan Morgül and Nedim Şener. *Türkiye'de Farklı Olmak: Din Ve Muhafazakarlık Ekseninde Ötekileştirilenler* [*To be Different in Turkey: Otherisation in Terms of Religion and Conservatism*]. İstanbul: Boğaziçi Üniversitesi Yayınları, 2008.
Troy, Jodok Troy. '"Catholic Waves" of Democratization? Roman Catholicism and Its Potential for Democratization'. *Democratization* 16, no. 6 (2009): 1093–114.
Turam, Berna. *Between Islam and the State: The Politics of Engagement*. Stanford, CA: Stanford University Press, 2007.
Türköne, Mümtazer. *Siyasi İdeoloji Olarak İslamcılığın Doğuşu* [*Emergence of Islamism as a Political Ideology*]. Istanbul: İletişim, 1991.
Ünal, Ali, and Alphonse Williams. *Advocate of Dialogue*. Fairfax, VI: The Fountain, 2000.
Vahide, Şükran. *Islam in Modern Turkey: An Intellectual Biography of Bediüzzaman Said Nursi*. Albany, NY: State University of New York Press, 2005.
Veren, Nerettin. *Kuşatma: ABD'nin Truva Atı Fethullah Gülen Hareketi* [*Siege: Fethullah Gülen movement as a Trojan horse for the US*]. Istanbul: Siyah Beyaz, 2007.
Vertigans, Stephen. *Islamic Roots and Resurgence in Turkey: Understanding and Explaining the Muslim Resurgence*. Westport, CT and London: Praeger, 2003.
Vicini, Fabio. 'Gülen and Sources in Islam for Interfaith Dialogue' 2007. http://en.fgulen.com/content/view/2473/53/.
Weld, Mary. *Bediuzzaman Said Nursi*, 2nd edn. Istanbul: Sözler Publications, 1992.
White, Jenny B. *Islamist Mobilization in Turkey: A Study in Vernacular Politics*. Seattle, WA and London: University of Washington Press, 2002.
Yavuz, M. Hakan. 'Towards an Islamic Liberalism? The Nurcu Movement and Fettullah Gülen'. *Middle East Journal* 53, no. 4 (1999): 584–605.
Yavuz, M. Hakan, and John L. Esposito. *Turkish Islam and the Secular State: The Gülen Movement*. New York: Syracuse University Press, 2003.

Yavuz, M. Hakan. (2006) 'The Role of the New Bourgeoisie in the Transformation of the Turkish Islamic Movement'. In *The Emergence of a New Turkey: Democracy and the AK Party*, ed. M. Hakan Yavuz, 136–59. Salt Lake City: The University of Utah Press, 2006.

Yılmaz, İhsan. '*Ijdihad* and *Tajdid* by Conduct'. In *Turkish Islam and the Secular State: The Gülen Movement*. New York: Syracuse University Press, 2003.

Zürcher, Erik J. *Turkey: A Modern History*. London, New York and Istanbul: I.B. Tauris & Co Ltd, 1993.

A rights-based discourse to contest the boundaries of state secularism? The case of the headscarf bans in France and Turkey

Amélie Barras

Department of Government, London School of Economics, London, UK

For the last two decades the human rights discourse has been increasingly used across the world – one could argue that there has even been a globalization of human rights. This discourse has also been intrinsically linked to positivism, enlightenment and secularism. It is with this in mind that this article looks at how religious Muslim individuals and groups in France and Turkey have been appropriating the human rights discourse and its national, regional and international legal channels to challenge state secular policies and redefine the relationship between religion and the state. By looking into two specific case studies – the work of the Collective Against Islamophobia in France (CCIF) and the *Merve Kavakci case v. Turkey* presented at the Strasbourg European Court of Human Rights (ECHR) – I investigate if groups and individuals have found through the use of this 'authorized narrative' a space where they can propose a new plural ethos that can better co-exist with their piety. This is a space where they can offer a more plural and de-centralized vision of secularism. To complement this analysis, I also highlight some of the possible paradoxes found within the human rights discourse – paradoxes that might enlighten us on the challenges of using such a discourse, particularly to ask for the right to display publicly one's religion. In other words, I attempt to shed some light on whether the use of a rights-based discourse by religious rights groups and individuals can help resolve democratically disputes between the religious and the secular – encouraging perhaps the democratization of secularism in specific contexts.

In 2004, France passed a law banning all 'conspicuously' worn religious symbols from public schools. What caught my attention at that time was that students in headscarves who protested against this law were using slogans that stressed the incompatibility of those laws with their human rights: 'Right to School, Right to Knowledge'.[1] In the same vein, I discovered that the rights based discourse was also used by religious groups and individuals to challenge strict secular policies in Turkey, and this led to the creation of broader coalitions with secular human rights groups. I found this to be quite an interesting phenomenon, particularly because Muslim individuals and groups, in both countries, had until the late 1980s, been using a religious discourse to frame their claims. It seemed, therefore, that they were now re-appropriating a discourse considered by many as secular to try to protect their rights.[2] Thus, the separation between secularism and Islam, stressed by many in the literature seemed, at least in this case, to be suddenly quite blurred. From that starting point, I felt compelled to analyse thoroughly how groups were using this discourse in response to states' strict secular laws, and to what extent it offered them a space where secularism and piety could co-exist. This would be a space where perhaps they could pluralize their state's vision of secularism. Most of the works on French *laïcité* and Turkish *laiklik* (terms are discussed below) adopt a state-centred approach, where there is an attempt to understand why and how states have been favouring a vision of secularism that limits the visibility of religious symbols in the public sphere.[3] In the first part of this article I will look at state secularism in both France and Turkey. In the second section I supplement this with a 'bottom-up' approach, analysing some of the means of contestations responding to this specific interpretation of secularism, and their possible limits. My overall aim is to investigate and understand how religious Muslims affected by this interpretation, in both countries, have sought to cope with it and have found 'acceptable' ways to question it.

A brief overview of the similarities between secularism in France and in Turkey

Secularization is a global hegemonic phenomenon that has taken various forms in different societies. In the first part of this article, I am specifically interested in state secularism – that is, a political and legal scheme implemented by states in relation to their societies, as part of their policy to manage and control religion. Indeed, it is important here to underline that although secularization seems to have touched in one way or another every corner of the world, the way it has been received and implemented, as a state policy, has been much influenced by specific historical and political experiences of countries. As a matter of fact, in France and in Turkey *laïcité* and *laiklik* (a derivative of *laïcité*) are respectively used to refer to secularism.[4] Yet, it is relevant to stress that some scholars are wary of translating these terms into 'secularism', as their meanings remain very context specific.[5]

Laïcité in France

The term *laïcité* appeared quite recently in the French language. As it has never been defined clearly, it has become a term, like 'democracy', that does not have an agreed definition, and thus can be invested with different meanings. Yet, while its 'signified' is open for contestation, its 'signifier' nevertheless remains, in my view, extremely powerful in the French context.

The *Conseil d'Etat* (the highest judicial entity in France) sees the law of 1905 (where the term *laïcité* does not appear) as central in defining and providing a legal framework to the term.[6] This law, often referred to as the law of separation, regulates the status of religions in France by preventing the state from subsidizing or extending special recognition to any religion. For the *Conseil d'Etat*, *laïcité* also implies the neutrality of the state with regards to religion, which should not favour or discriminate against any type of religion. The practicalities of this neutrality have unfolded throughout the jurisprudence of the last decades, where it is stipulated that state representatives (i.e. providers of public services) are required to be neutral, and therefore not represent publicly any religions (for instance, they are not allowed to wear visible religious symbols, or engage in proselytizing activities).[7] Yet, until 2004, this same jurisprudence also clearly underscored a key point: this neutrality requirement should not affect users of public services, and therefore should not, in principle, be applied to students in schools.[8] This is quite important as it means that the *Conseil d'Etat*, from the late 1980s to 2004, did not see a direct incompatibility between students wearing the headscarf and the principle of *laïcité*. This point was clearly underlined in its November 1989 *Opinion* after the first significant case of students wearing the headscarf in school erupted:[9]

> The wearing by **students of signs through which they intend to express their religious belonging to a religion is not per-se incompatible with the principle of laïcité** if it constitutes an exercise of freedom of expression and a manifestation of belief.[10]

In its *Opinion*, the *Conseil d'Etat* made a difference between students wearing religious signs, which were not seen in themselves to be incompatible with *laïcité*, and the actions that could result from the wearing of such signs – including, proselytizing, breaching of the assiduity principle (e.g., missing classes for religious reasons) and requests that would endanger students' safety (e.g., wearing the headscarf during sports or chemistry classes) – which, were described as disturbing the public order, and therefore undermining *laïcité*. This *Opinion* led to a case by case jurisprudence, where every situation had to be analysed individually in its context.[11]

However, this interpretation of *laïcité* has been the source of many contestations. Indeed, different French governments (variously dominated by the left and the right) tried to end this case by case jurisprudence through the release of several ministerial circulars,[12] giving guidelines to school administrators to ban all religious symbols from public schools. Although these ministerial circulars did not have the legal binding power of the *Conseil d'Etat*'s case law, they represented a vision of *laïcité* where religious symbols became in themselves incompatible with *laïcité*. This movement reached its highpoint with the passing of the 2004 law preventing 'conspicuously' worn religious symbols in primary and secondary schools.[13] The public debates leading to this law gave a good sense of the interpretation of *laïcité*, which unfolded at that time. Indeed, the *Commission Stasi* (a body put in place, in 2003, by the former French President, Jacques Chirac, which recommended passing this law), and the government that endorsed the law (as well as several civil society groups and intellectuals) seemed to have invested *laïcité* with being a common good – similar to a public morality – superior to religion, and being responsible for preserving the public sphere from the divisive nature of the religious.[14] President Chirac expressed this idea in his speech of 17 December 2003 and noted that *laïcité* is:

> The privileged place for meetings and exchanges, where **everyone can come together** bringing the best to the national community. **It is the neutrality of this public space that enables different religions to harmoniously co-exist.**[15]

In other words, preserving neutrality can justify prohibiting any signs perceived as disrupting this 'coming together' of citizens. The public sphere thus becomes a space where ethnic, religious and other characteristics are erased (everyone, is therefore 'equal'). As Bowen notes, this notion of a protected public sphere goes much further than the law of 1905 and the jurisprudence of the *Conseil d'Etat* that only requires, as I have shown, that the state and its agents be neutral, an issue that does not extend to students and ordinary citizens.[16] Bowen and Göle highlight a key concern in this regard: the aim of forbidding religious symbols in the public sphere is defined by how one defines what is the public sphere. That is, should the state forbid the wearing of headscarves only in schools, or does this also extend to other public spaces such as hospitals, city halls, parliaments, and perhaps even the street?[17]

What is equally interesting in this definition of *laïcité* and its practical implementation, particularly with the law of 2004, is how the state has denied agency to students who wear headscarves.[18] This has the result of not treating them as fully fledged free-thinking citizens, but rather objectifying them into victims that have to be saved from religious values imposed by their faith. For Göle this behaviour is a way of avoiding to address a rather disturbing modern reality, in which individuals are at the same time subject of their own actions, and yet also publicly expressing their bond to a belief other than in the nation-state.[19]

Laiklik in Turkey

The Republic of Turkey was established as a secular state by Mustapha Kemal (Atatürk) in 1923. This attachment to secularism is reiterated in Article 2 of Turkey's current constitution:

> The Republic of Turkey is a democratic, secular (laik) and social State based on the rule of law, respectful of human rights in a spirit of social peace, national solidarity and justice, adhering to the nationalism of Atatürk and resting on the fundamental principles set out in the Preamble.[20]

The creation of this new secular Republic came with several key symbolic reforms to separate the public and religious sphere. Among them it is worth citing the abolition of the Caliphate (in 1923), the retraction of the provision in the Constitution declaring Islam the state religion, the closing of religious courts, the abolition of the *Sharia* (Islamic law), the introduction of a new civil code based on the Swiss one, and the banning of traditional headgear for men, the fez, in 1925.[21] To McGoldrick these reforms were: 'inspired by the evolution of the nature of society in the nineteenth century and sought first and foremost to create a religion free zone in which all citizens were guaranteed equality without distinction on the grounds of religion or denomination'.[22]

It is worth noting that the main difference between French *laïcité* and Turkish *laiklik* is that the idea of separation between state and religion underpinning the French 1905 law is not present in Turkey.[23] Indeed, in Turkey the state has openly and publicly controlled Islam through its State Directorate of Religious Affairs ('*Diyanet*') under the supervision of the Prime Minister. The *Diyanet* is responsible for nominating religious officials, including Imams and muezzins, as well as controlling Islamic religious education and training. As Gökariksel and Mitchell explain, this control aims to promote a state republican Islam.[24]

However, despite this difference, *laiklik*, like French *laïcité*, has never been clearly defined and has therefore been at the source of many divisive debates. The idea of creating a public sphere free of religious symbols seems to have also been of prime importance for secular elites in Turkey. This has been particularly so since the mid-1980s, where one notices a growth of a new Islamic economic, cultural and political elite.[25] Indeed, it is in the 1980s and even more importantly after the 1997 soft coup, when the Islamic party in power was forced to step down and secular military elites purged Islam from the public sphere, that the state started to actively implement a headscarf ban in schools, universities and state buildings.[26] The first set of regulations on dress was issued in July 1981 and prohibited both students and teachers from wearing the headscarf in educational institutions. A circular issued by the Higher-Education Authority, followed in December 1982, banning the headscarf in all lecture halls. McGoldrick underlines that although these guidelines were contested, the Constitutional Court in its 7 March 1989 judgement confirmed that this ban was necessary to preserve secularism and democracy:

> The Constitutional Court observed that freedom of religion, conscience and worship, which could not be equated with a right to wear any particular religious attire, guaranteed first and foremost the liberty to decide whether or not to follow a religion. It explained that, once outside the private sphere of individual conscience, freedom to manifest's one's religion could be restricted on public-order grounds to defend the principle of secularism.[27]

This background can help us trace similarities between the French and Turkish cases. Indeed, it seems that in both cases the headscarf is perceived as particularly disturbing because it violates the state idea of a confined religion (more specifically of a confined Islam). Religion is understood as a threat to both Republican secular French and Turkish identities that should supersede all other affiliations in the public realm. It introduces the idea that citizens can have more than one identity in the public sphere. This brings us to the idea that secularism symbolizes here: not only the neutrality of the state (and its employees), but also the neutrality of the public sphere and of its subjects. In both countries, extending the boundaries of this neutrality has taken great importance over the last decades, and bans on the headscarf can be read as a symbol *par excellence* of this effort. Gökariksel and Mitchell offer an interesting analysis of this phenomenon. For them, the state has been using secularism as 'a technology of governance' to create a modern universal 'unattached and unbiased liberal subject' justifying their attempt to 'discipline' and control in the public sphere the body of Muslim women marked by non-neutral particularities.[28]

In sum, secularism seems to have become in both countries an inevitable hegemonic signifier. I would argue that it is specifically the rather contested nature of the term that has allowed groups and individuals to find space to question or reshape its meaning. The two case studies below are illustrative of this phenomenon. Indeed, they provide an analysis of how Muslims groups and individuals have been using a rights-based discourse to challenge the boundaries of state secularism both in Turkey and France, and to propose a definition of secularism that seems to be more compatible with their religious ethos.

Contesting the boundaries of state secularism

> Le Fort calls human rights the **'generative principle of democracy'** for, it is through the promotion of an 'awareness of rights' – the dissemination of democratic discourse to new areas of the social, the radicalisation of the concept of human rights, and the institutionalisation of democratic principles – **that disempowered political subjects can win their struggles for recognition**.[29]

The rights-based discourse can be quite powerful particularly because, as Wilson precisely puts it, law is a form of violence that constitutes authority.[30] Consequently, using and appropriating rights-based discourses can enable individuals to gain authority – becoming therefore active subjects in a particular situation. Moreover, as I will demonstrate through my Turkish case study, the fact that human rights are considered by many to be a product of the enlightenment and the secular era, and that there is an international framework protecting them, allows domestic groups not only to seek legitimacy for their claims at the international level but also to network with transnational actors.[31] This international dimension is particularly noteworthy, as it implies that the struggle to define or redefine secularism is not solely located at the level of the nation state, but extends well beyond it.

The case study of the Collective against Islamophobia in France (CCIF)

The CCIF was established in 2003 in response to increasing acts of 'Islamophobia' in France. It is an association made up of 20–30 volunteers/activists and one permanent lawyer. Although the organization does not consider itself to be a Muslim organization, most of its members are second or third generation French

Muslims.[32] The CCIF is of particular interest, in my view, because it could be considered to be the first litigating group on issues related to religious freedom and the public presence of Islam in France. Prior to its creation, Muslim associations were engaged in political lobbying, but no group was specialized in legal work.[33]

The CCIF activities are threefold. They have first created an '*Observatoire de l'Islamophobie*' (observatory of Islamophobic acts) responsible for making a list of 'Islamophobic' written and oral statements and acts occurring in France,[34] and publicizing them in an annual report. They have also set up a legal clinic made up of lawyers providing support to victims of 'Islamophobia'. The aim is to help them contact legal authorities and when necessary provide legal support for cases. Finally, they regularly conduct sensitization activities with citizens, civil society organizations, and politicians.

Pre-occupations with the 2004 law

The members of CCIF were quite preoccupied by the 2004 law on 'conspicuously' worn religious symbols, as they perceived it as going against the spirit of *laïcité* laid out by the *Conseil d'Etat*, which guaranteed the neutrality of the state, freedom and equality of religion and a respect for plurality. They expressed two central concerns with the law.[35] First, this law had extended the principle of neutrality to users of public services (i.e. school children) a provision that was not outlined in the law of 1905 or in the *Opinion* of the *Conseil d'Etat*, and this, in their view, was setting a dangerous precedent for extending this rule to other users. Secondly, the law went against the principle of state neutrality that underpins their definition and legal understanding of *laïcité*, where the state started to judge which religious expressions in themselves were compatible with *laïcité* and which were not in the public sphere regardless of whether the believer's actions had been disturbing public order.[36] This was something that, until 2004, the *Conseil d'Etat* jurisprudence had explicitly avoided doing.

Extension of the 2004 law to other public spaces

> Contrary to the idea conveyed, laïcité's purpose is not to exclude religion and its practice from the public sphere. **On the contrary, laïcité guarantees the neutrality of the State, right to religious freedom (even if this does not please rigid secularists), and the respect for pluralism**. Indeed, there is no religious freedom without total neutrality from the State and its representatives guaranteeing the equality of treatment of users ... **This is why the demands linked to neutrality of public agents in the exercise of their function are not applicable to the situation of users. It is true that this is not the case anymore for schools (legal exception based on the March 15th 2004 law), yet this remains the case in hospitals and in all administrations**.[37]

Interestingly, since 2004, CCIF's members' work has been driven by their first concern with the law. Indeed, they have recorded many cases related to the extension of the ban of the headscarf by public institutions beyond primary and secondary school students. Since this extension of the law has no legal basis they have been using a rights-based argument focusing on the *Conseil d'Etat*'s jurisprudence to demonstrate what they see as this illegality.[38] They have been providing legal support to a variety of different cases. One of their major cases, for instance, won in front of the High Authority Fighting against Discrimination and for Equality (HALDE) in May 2007. It related to mothers who wanted to volunteer as chaperones during their children's school outings, but who were not allowed to do so, because they were wearing a headscarf.[39] The main argument of the CCIF was that schools had no legal grounds to prohibit the participation of those women, as they were not state employees or students (for whom legal restrictions on wearing the headscarf exist). What is noteworthy here is that the CCIF read this prohibition as a direct violation of the principle of *laïcité*, which, in their view, legally protects the right to religious freedom, not solely in the private sphere, but more importantly in the public sphere. It has also defended other cases, where women were not allowed to enter city halls because they were wearing a headscarf (e.g., to participate in a naturalization ceremony or be wedding witnesses), or were prohibited from following university classes, evening classes, passing driving exams, participating in internship programmes, voting during regional elections (2005), and so on.

A reading of the CCIF press releases and reports shows that it opposes the 'objectivity' of national and international law, including human rights treaties signed by France (such as the International Covenant on Civil and Political Rights or the European Convention of Human Rights,), to the arbitrary behaviour of public institutions. The organization seems to underline a dislocation in French society, where public institutions with responsibility to protect the basic tenets of the Republic (Equality, Liberty and Justice) are instead becoming a field of discrimination. One can conclude that these activists have invested themselves with the civic responsibility of scrutinizing the unfair implementation of republican *laïcité*, and in so doing ensuring that a 'true' *laïcité* prevails: 'Each time the CCIF is seized, it proceeds to a recall of the law',[40] 'This decision constitutes a victory of the law against arbitrariness'.[41]

Guardian of a pre-2004 jurisprudence

It is interesting to note that since the passing of the 2004 law in France, one can notice a shift in the jurisprudence of the *Conseil d'Etat*, which has been promoting a vision of secularism closer to the spirit of the 2004 law.[42] In other words, agreeing that a religious sign in itself, worn in school, can be a threat to *laïcité* – embracing, most likely, a political attempt to fix the meaning of *laïcité* at least on school grounds. This trend might also be expanding to other cases, for instance, the *Conseil d'Etat* ruled in 2008 on a case where it confirmed a decision to refuse French nationality to the wife of a French citizen because of her 'radical' practice of religion.[43] One of the reasons that led to this judgment was based on the fact that the woman was wearing a niqab, i.e., a veil that covered all her face except for her eyes. This did not allow her, in the eyes of the judges, to integrate into French society.[44] The CCIF released a press statement on the issue strongly criticizing the *Conseil d'Etat* for its decision. The CCIF considered that the *Conseil d'Etat* was not equipped to judge on the 'radicalism' of a religious practice, and that this decision would simply reinforce discrimination against Muslims:

> With this decision the Conseil d'Etat is creating a dangerous precedent with regard **to the fundamental right to the freedom to express one's religion**. Indeed, the drifts noted by the CCIF in the administration against women and men of Muslim faith aiming at limiting the right to express one's faith, will from now on, be more numerous, and their perpetrators, reinforced by this decision, will give themselves the arbitrary permission to judge on the opportunity to give a right or not to a citizen of Muslim faith ... **The CCIF was promoting in front of international instances the lucidity with which French justice was dealing with questions of Islam and its followers within society. Justice seemed to be one of the last barriers against heinous aggressions and discriminatory practices** ... The law and justice need to take the upper hand over the arbitrary and blinded hate....[45]

One could ask therefore whether the CCIF, along with other Muslim religious activists in France, were not turning into the guardians of a *laïcité 'ante'* 2004 promoted by the *Conseil d'Etat*. A *laïcité* that, in their view, followed the legal canvas put in place by the 1905 law, and preserved the neutrality of the state that restrained itself from interfering or judging the religious *per se* – in other words, allowing for the public co-existence of believers and non-believers.[46]

The 'paradoxes' of rights – can the rights-based discourse really succeed in achieving greater religious freedom?

As I argued above, the use of a rights-based discourse – and specifically of a human rights discourse – can be a very powerful tool because it situates itself within the accepted discursive field resonating with the values of a secular society. Yet, certain paradoxes come out of this usage. Wendy Brown, borrowing the expression of Gayatri Spivak, argues that rights are 'that which we cannot not want'[47] since they succeed in attenuating or redressing particular violations, and, yet, they still often fail to challenge the causes leading to those violations. This, I would argue, could enlighten us regarding some of the limits on using a rights-based discourse to ask for greater religious freedom in France and, in addition, to help reshape state secularism. Indeed, as I have shown in the case study above, a legal argument led activists to focus on specific individual violations. This may result in redressing certain trends, but not necessarily in addressing the reasons behind why they happen first in schools, and increasingly in other public spaces across France, and are supported by a majority of policy makers and a wide range of citizens. One might even argue that locating and focusing the problem within individual cases may depoliticize the debate around *laïcité*, avoiding therefore issue of addressing difficult political questions – which might, go beyond issues of religious freedom – linked to a certain exclusive conception of French citizenship, and collective life. Furthermore, following Brown and Vakulenko, one could also wonder if this over-legalization of religious concerns does not lead to a greater regulation of the religious, therefore limiting religious freedom.[48] Indeed, legal authorities are asked to decide which behaviour and dress are considered to be religious and which of those are acceptable in the public sphere. This implies increased public scrutiny of the believer's body and his/her reasons for wearing certain types of clothing. For instance, inquiries are conducted not only by legal agents but also by public administrators and citizens on whether one is considered to be a 'user' or a 'provider' of public services, whether one's choice to wear a bandana, a hat or other types of headgear in school is motivated by fashion or for religious reasons, whether one is wearing a religious sign out of 'free' choice, whether a public space is considered to be 'too' public for allowing particular religious symbols, whether certain attires are considered to be to be 'too' religiously 'radical' to be worn in certain public spaces, and so on. Ironically, this scrutiny seems to participate to the defining of who is an 'acceptable' modern religious subject and who is not in the Republic. In other words, rights are quite ambivalent here since they appear, as Brown rightly argues, to be politically 'essential' but at the same time rather politically 'regressive'.[49]

Using transnational human rights mechanisms: Merve Kavakci v. Turkey

The Merve Kavakci case illustrates quite well, in my view, another facet of using a human rights discourse in relation to religious issues in a democracy. Indeed, it can be a way to access transnational human rights mechanisms to question the limits of state secular policies. These mechanisms have been used increasingly in Turkey over the last decade.[50]

It is important to remember that unlike France, where religious rights groups and activists were able, at least until 2004, to use national courts to seek redress,[51] in Turkey, complaints linked to religious freedom, and in particular related to the wearing of the headscarf in the public sphere, have rarely been won in national courts. This is so because the jurisprudence of high courts and of the Constitutional Court in Turkey has promoted a republican vision of secularism, aiming to regulate and limit the visibility of religion in the public sphere.[52] In my view, this perhaps best explains the importance of resorting to international human rights mechanisms to find spaces to voice complaints. This use of human rights appears representative of a wider discursive shift in Turkey, where religious actors who were resorting, in the 1980s, to a religious idiom to present their religious claims, have increasingly been using a human rights language considered by many to be more inclusive and to resonate beyond religious circles.[53] Moreover, one also needs to understand that this increased use of international human rights platforms is linked to a rather new socio-economic reality marked by a growing, relatively well-educated Muslim bourgeoisie in Turkey, which has the financial means to engage in such transnational activities.

The case

The Merve Kavakci case is particularly interesting in three respects. First, it is a case that was won in April 2007 against Turkey at the European Court of Human Rights (ECHR).[54] Although the court did not base its ruling on Article 9 of the European Convention on Human Rights (article protecting freedom of thought, conscience and religion), it still marked a precedent in the ruling of the court, and received quite extensive media coverage. The case is also noteworthy because, in parallel to being presented at the ECHR, Merve Kavakci worked with international secular groups and presented her case in different international forums. Finally, we can again note, through the use of a rights-based discourse that there seemed to be an attempt to renegotiate the boundaries of state secularism, and to propose a model more compatible with individual religious piety.

Merve Kavakci was the first woman elected in Turkey running for an Islamist party, known as the Virtue Party, and choosing to wear a headscarf. In 1999, after her election, Kavakci walked into parliament to take her oath wearing her headscarf. Although the dress code regulation in parliament did not mention a ban on the wearing of religious signs, the mainstream, i.e., non-religious, parties saw this move as an offensive challenge against the secular roots of Turkey. As a result, Kavakci was forced out of parliament without taking her oath, and saw her Turkish citizenship revoked.[55] She, and two of her former colleagues, were banned from politics for five years, followed by the closure of the Virtue Party by the Constitutional Court.[56] Kavakci used her right to go to the European Court of Human Rights: 'To find worldly justice.'[57] On 5 April 2007, the court ruled that Turkey was in violation of Article 3, Protocol 1 of the European Convention on Human Rights, which mandates that states 'ensure the free expression of the opinion of the people in the choice of the legislature'.

It is important to underline that, although the court ruled in favour of Kavakci, its judgement remained somewhat ambivalent. Indeed, as in previous judgements, the court was keen to be seen to uphold the 'secular' character of Turkey. Accordingly, in this judgement the court first underlined that the measures taken by Turkey, in the Kavakci case, were appropriate in the context of state attempts to preserve public order:

> The court noted that the temporary restrictions imposed on the applicants' political rights had been intended to preserve the secular nature of the Turkish political system. Given the importance of that principle for democracy in Turkey, **it considered that the measure had pursued legitimate aims, namely the prevention of disorder and protection of the rights and freedoms of others.**[58]

Having stipulated this, the judgement then specified that the sanctions given were still considered to be disproportionate:

> **the sanctions imposed on the applicants were serious and could not be regarded as proportionate to the legitimate aims pursued.** The Court therefore concluded that there had been a violation of Article 3 of Protocol No.1.[59]

International forums – finding a space to voice concerns?

Despite the reservations of the ECHR, one should note that bringing a case to the court offers quite a valuable platform for networking and engaging in lobbying activities. Such activities can end up not being limited to regional human rights instances, but can extend, for example, to the United Nations and other international forums and to collaboration with a variety of international non-governmental organizations.

The Merve Kavakci case is representative of this process. Indeed, Kavakci received the support of the International Parliamentary Union (IPU) based in Geneva, which adopted a resolution at its 171st annual session affirming the illegality of the Turkish Constitutional Court decision on her case: 'The IPU fears ... that Ms. Kavakci was not only arbitrarily prevented from assuming here mandate and duties as an elected representative of the Turkish people, but may also have been deprived of her membership without any valid legal basis, and according to a procedure not provided for under Turkish law',[60] and which testified, as a third party, in her favour at the ECHR.

In the same vein, she was also helped by the Becket Fund for Religious Liberty, a United States-based foundation providing international legal aid to individuals who feel that their religious freedom has been breached.[61] The Fund provided legal advice for her case at the ECHR, as well as a space for her to testify in front of the former United Nations Commission for Human Rights (known, today, as the Human Rights Council), where she stressed, among other things, that women should have the right to choose to be religious, and to express it.[62]

In sum, the creation of transnational networks seem to be of significant importance, as it puts issues of religious freedom on the international agenda, and offers a space to propose an alternative vision of secularism more compatible with some individuals' religious piety.[63] I would argue that in this case the support and the influence of several United States non-governmental organizations including, Human Rights Watch or the Becket Fund are particularly noteworthy. Indeed, these groups not only supported some individuals affected by the headscarf ban, helping to reinforce the legitimacy of their claims, but they also publicly positioned themselves in favour of a different interpretation of secularism, compared to the Turkish state. In fact, in a personal interview with the author, Merve Kavakci stressed that Turkish *laiklik* ought not to be confused with American secularism, as in the Turkish case the state exercises a total monopoly over religion, and so there is therefore no true separation between religion and the state.[64] Indeed, she underlined that there are many types of secularisms and that the concept does not necessarily imply a respect for human rights.[65] She suggested that Turkey should embrace a model closer to the American one, where the state poses neither as a religious nor a non-religious entity, and where the individual right to freedom of religion is protected. Similar to the French case, it is interesting here to underscore how the human rights discourse is used to promote a type of secularism where the state restrains itself from controlling the religious subject. The slight difference is that, in the Turkish case, we seem not to be faced with actors who defend a type of *laïcité 'ante'* – a *laïcité* symbolized by the pre-2004 *Conseil d'Etat*'s jurisprudence – but rather, that are trying to re-invent a new type of *laiklik* compatible with their religious piety.

Limits of using Article 9 at the ECHR

It is useful to come back to the actual *Kavakci v. Turkey* judgement, as I think it can enlighten us on some of the limits of using the ECHR to ask for greater religious freedom. It is important to note that Kavakci considered that there had also been a violation of Article 9 of the ECHR.[66] Indeed, for her, both her citizenship and political mandate were taken away because she expressed her religious convictions by wearing her headscarf in parliament. She underlined that there was no legal basis for doing so, as the internal dress code for MPs did not preclude the right to wear the headscarf.[67] However, the court did not examine separately this violation, and only looked at the violation of Article 3, Protocol 1.

This, in my view, is particularly noteworthy, and reflects an attempt by the court not to interfere in Turkey's secular politics. It is significant here to mention the *Leyla Sahin v. Turkey* case for which the Grand Chamber of the ECHR gave a judgement in November 2005. Leyla Sahin was a medical student in Turkey who was not allowed to continue studying in Turkish university because she was wearing a headscarf. She also decided to seize the ECHR court claiming that there was a violation of Article 9 of the Convention. The court, in this case, ruled in favour of Turkey, as it found that the restrictions were justified in light of Article 9 (2) which stipulates that freedom to express one's religion can be restricted if those limitations are 'prescribed by the law and are necessary in a democratic society in the interests of public safety, for the protection of public order, health and morals, or for the protection of the rights and freedoms of others'. Moreover, to justify the validity of those limitations the court strongly stressed the 'special' political and social context of Turkey where 'the majority of the population, while professing a strong attachment to the rights of women and a secular way of life, adhered to the Islamic faith'.[68] Therefore, the ECHR in its judgement left a wide margin for the state's actions in Turkey by endorsing its view that the headscarf could be perceived, in this particular context, as a threat to both secularism and democracy.

This trend to give a wide margin of interpretation and 'delegating the final authority concerning the legalization of religious symbols' to the state, seems to have been a way for the court to avoid tackling these difficult questions directly at the supranational level.[69] Therefore, one could wonder, particularly in view of the nature of Article 9 (2) that leaves an important leeway for national opinion, if resorting to this article to resolve concerns related to religious freedom and secularism is fruitful, or if on the contrary it does not confirm the validity of national case law and might reinforce polarization in society.[70] Indeed, as Gökariksel and Mitchell argue, the *Sahin* decision was used by fervent secularists in Turkey as a quasi-universal truth stressing that it was 'legally binding and final'.[71] Opposite to this, Muslim democrats and Islamists became very disillusioned with the court, as this ruling symbolized for them the: 'failure of European liberalism and democracy' and was considered to be 'an additional evidence of European bias against Muslim'.[72]

Building on the above comments, one could argue that in the Merve Kavakci case, the possibility of litigating on Article 3, Protocol 1, might have given the opportunity to the court to avoid pronouncing on Article 9. It is important in my view to briefly consider one of the reasons that might explain why there seems to be considerable tension around this article, and more specifically around the right to express one's religion publicly. Wendy Brown highlights that one of the key notions present in a rights-based language is the idea of sovereignty of the individual[73] – in other words his or her autonomy. This implies that rights give the individual the possibility to 'choose' his or her own life. In the case of the right to religious freedom, this would signify that people should be allowed to make 'free' autonomous choices concerning their religious belief, and how they wish to express it. I agree with Lewis and Vakulenko that this notion of autonomous 'free' choice that underpins the right to religious freedom may be problematic on two levels when it comes to asking for the right to wear the headscarf.[74] First of all, as Vakulenko underlines, although women and girls are requested in their discourse to demonstrate that they are wearing the headscarf out of 'free' choice (i.e. that it has not been imposed on them) for it to be considered a human right, the fact that this practice is often perceived as irrational or anti-egalitarian, makes their 'free' choice questionable.[75] Hence, suspicion surrounds whether this choice is really a 'free' choice and not an imposed one. The second level that might shed light on our first argument is linked to the fact that the notion of 'free' choice might not necessarily be fully compatible with the choice of following one's religious duty.[76] Indeed, as Lewis stresses:

> As far as the believer herself is concerned, it may be more appropriate to say not that she chooses her faith but **that her faith, or God, chooses her**. So it becomes not a question of exercising individual rational decision-making power between a plurality of competing paths but rather a matter of eternal, absolute, divinely ordained duty.[77]

Therefore, some believers might be asking for the 'sovereign' right to choose to obey God, and express this duty publicly.[78] It would be worth asking ourselves if this idea of religious piety can co-exist with the modern liberal understanding of 'autonomous/sovereign' individuals that seems to underpin many decisions of the jurisprudence and discourses on 'universal' human rights. Moreover, it may be the case that this tension between duty and 'free' choice, present in the right to religious freedom, explains, in part, the weak jurisprudence of the ECHR on this right, and why, ironically, issues related to religious freedom might be easier to litigate by using other rights than the right to religious freedom.[79] In my view, these tensions are clearly representative of the paradox of 'universal' human rights which 'are sooner or later entangled in their contextual particularism and are incapable of fulfilling their universal function'.[80] Indeed, many human rights are considered to be 'universal' norms deriving their authority 'not from heaven but from earth'.[81] It is perhaps by reference to this particular 'secular' vision of rights that one can shed light on some of the difficulties of reconciling it with claims based on the right to express one's allegiance to God publicly.[82]

Concluding thoughts

The rights-based discourse is an interesting means of contesting nationally and internationally the boundaries of state secularism both in France and in Turkey. It is a powerful and most importantly 'legitimate' discourse as it is considered by many to be modern, a product of the enlightenment and of the secular rational state. In France, as I have underlined, the use of this discourse and legal procedures at the national level seems to have, at least until 2004, been quite successful to address individual complaints. On the other hand, the Turkish Constitutional Court has proposed a rather less liberal interpretation of *laiklik*, which explains the importance given to seeking justice beyond the national state. In my view, using the human rights discourse to access regional and international forums is particularly noteworthy, as it does not only offer a platform for possible redress, but more importantly creates an interesting space to voice concerns around restrictions put on the right to religious freedom by states' secular policies. It is also relevant to underline that in both cases the contestation does not happen at the level of the signifier (i.e. secularism) but rather at the level of the signified (i.e. its definition). Indeed, secularism *per se* does not seem to be the object of contestation, rather the rights-based discourse is used here to attempt to 'adjust' the boundaries of secularism for it to be more compatible with expression of individual public piety.

However, the question of the success of this rights-based discourse still remains open. Indeed, as I have briefly touched upon in this article, although human rights seem to give a certain political agency to the religious subject, it also links to the greater regulation and control of the religious – not quite squaring with claims for greater religious freedom. Moreover, a greater consideration of the right to religious freedom – and more particularly the right to public piety – seems to highlight a paradox, where a 'universal' discourse carries 'particular' visions of the world. Indeed, tensions surrounding this right might be explained in part because piety is difficult to grasp with a liberal frame of reference that centres on a specific idea of autonomy and sovereignty of the individual. Yet, by seriously addressing this tension, we may be pushed to realize that other paradigms, not just those dominated by a certain understanding of 'free' choice and individual autonomy, exist and are worthwhile exploring.[83]

Building on this, it might be meaningful for interested scholars not solely to focus on a state-centric approach to secularism, but also to complement it with a study of the different ways secularism can be understood, lived and practised. In so doing, one might find that some interpretations of the term allow for the peaceful co-existence of different *'ethical-imaginaries'*[84] – interpretations that might be more compatible with a plural democracy. However, I wonder if we are yet ready for such a co-existence that would most likely imply questioning the supreme authority of our liberal values, or rather our understanding of some of those values.

Acknowledgments

Field research for this paper was made possible through a doctoral grant from the Canadian Social Research Council and a grant from the University of London Central Research Fund. I am very grateful for the insightful comments I received from panellists and participants at the 9th Mediterranean Research Meeting (Florence, Italy, March 2008), ISA annual meeting (New York, USA, February, 2009), Religion and Democratization Conference (London, UK, April 2009) and University of Geneva Political Science's lunch seminar (Geneva, Switzerland, May 2009), where earlier versions of this article were presented. Finally, I am indebted to my PhD thesis supervisor, Dr John Chalcraft, for the many discussions we had on several of the ideas developed in this article, and to Professor Jeffrey Haynes for taking the time to provide thoughtful comments and feedback on drafts of this article. I bear, of course, responsibility for any shortcomings.

Notes

1. 17 January 2004, protests in Paris. Author's translation.
2. By secular discourse, I am referring to non-religious discourses. For a general discussion of why some scholars argue that human rights are 'secular' please see: Evans, 'Religion, Law and Human Rights: Locating the Debate', and Asad, 'What Do Human Rights Do? An Anthropological Inquiry'.
3. For instance, see: Bowen, *Why the French Don't Like Headscarves*; Gunn, 'Religious Freedom and Laïcité'; Scott, *Politics of the Veil*; Gökariksel and Mitchell, 'Veiling, Secularism, and the Neoliberal Subject'; McGoldrick, *Human Rights and Religion*; Salton, 'Veiled Threats?'.
4. It is important to note that both countries have been marked by a tradition of laicism conveying the idea that the state controls, limits, restricts and in some instances even pushes religion from the public sphere. For more information on this see, Ahdar and Leigh, *Religious Freedom in the Liberal State*. In addition, Hurd (*Politics of Secularism in International Relations*) provides an insightful analysis of this tradition, as well describing how it differentiates itself from Judeo-Christian secularism.
5. Bowen (*Why the French Don't Like Headscarves*) and Troper ('French Secularism, or Laïcité') explain how secularism only reflects partially the meaning of *laïcité*. Davison ('Turkey a "Secular" State?') offers a similar argument for the Turkish term *laiklik*.
6. The 9 December 1905 law is known as the law putting an end to the conflict between the state and religious orders that had been dividing France, and implementing a new legal regime regulating relations between the state and religions. Without referring explicitly to *laïcité*, it is understood by the Conseil d'Etat (*Rapport Public 2004*, 258) as defining its two main principles: freedom of conscience and the principal of separation. Indeed through its Article I, the law affirms freedom of conscience, and by correlation of religion: '*The Republic ensures freedom of conscience. It guarantees the free exercise of cults under the restrictions announced thereafter in the interest of public order*' (author's translation). Article II of the law recognizes the principle of separation between church and state, which stipulates: '*The Republic does not recognize, gives salaries or subventions to any cult. Consequently, starting from the 1st of*

January following the promulgation of this law, spending related to the exercise of cults will be suppressed from state's, departments', and communes' budgets' (author's translation) – through the latter Article the 1905 law ended the regime of recognized religion in France. For more information as well as a full reading of the law please see Conseil d'Etat, *Rapport Public 2004*, 258–60 and 405–15. One should note that the term *laïcité* is not mentioned in this law, and only appears for the first time in the French Constitution of 1946, and then later in the Constitution of 1958 – yet nowhere in those texts is *laïcité* defined.

7. Conseil d'Etat, *Rapport Public 2004*, 337. This is, also, well explained in the *Kherouaa Affair* (1992) and the *Avis Marteaux* (2002) of the *Conseil d'Etat*.
8. The year 2004 marked the passing of the law prohibiting conspicuously worn religious symbols in schools. From then the jurisprudence of the *Conseil d'Etat* followed the spirit of this law.
9. *Opinions* (also known as *Avis*) by the *Conseil d'Etat* are recommendations to the government on specific issues. Although they are not legally binding, they are generally followed by the government. This particular *Opinion* was released after the first important headscarf affair erupted in 1989, known as the *Creil Affair*. It is important to note that there was, in the late 1980s, an increase in the number of girls wearing the headscarf in schools in France. Different reasons are given for this from identity politics to changes in immigration policies. For more information, see for example, Cesari, *Etre Musulmans en France*; Kepel, *Banlieues de l'islam*; Ternisien, *France des Mosquées*; Gaspard and Khosrokhavar, *Foulard et République*; Laurence and Vaisse, *Integrating Islam*.
10. Conseil d'Etat, *Avis no. 346.893*, November 27, 1989. Author's translation, emphasis added.
11. McGoldrick notes (*Human Rights and Religion*, 70), that out of 49 expulsions' cases considered from 1989 to 2003 by the *Conseil d'Etat*, 41 were reversed – a trend which emphasizes the quite liberal interpretation by the *Conseil d'Etat* of *laïcité*.
12. A ministerial circular in France is issued by a member of the executive and its role is to guide the administration in their day to day duties – examples of those regarding the headscarf are the *Jospin Circulaire* (1989) and the *Bayrou Circulaire* (1994).
13. Although this law refers to all 'conspicuously' worn religious symbols, a majority of commentators point out that it specifically targeted the wearing of headscarves in schools. In fact, it has been referred to as: *'la loi sur le foulard'* (the law on the headscarf). In this vein, it is also interesting to note that the members of the *Commission Stasi's* acknowledged in their report that the public debates around passing a law were centred exclusively on the wearing of the headscarf by young girl (Stasi, *Rapport de la Commission*, 57).
14. To better understand the above, it is useful to note, as Bowen (*Why the French Don't Like Headscarves*, 13–20) reminds us, the importance that France gives to the state. In France, many believe that individuals acquire freedom through the state and not freedom from the state. This explains why there might not necessarily be a contradiction between promoting *laïcité* and regulating the visibility of religion. Indeed, if one considers that *laïcité* is invested with the power to preserve and foster the common good, this mission may require that freedom of religion, in some cases, be restrained to the private sphere or one's conscience – even if this does not necessarily square with the widespread idea that *laïcité* implies the strict separation of religion and the state.
15. Chirac, 'Discours prononcé pas Monsieur Jacques Chirac'. Author's translation, emphasis added.
16. Bowen, *Why the French Don't Like Headscarves*, 29.
17. Bowen, *Why the French Don't Like Headscarves*; Göle, 'Laïcité républicaine et l'Islam public'.

18. It is interesting to note that the *Commission Stasi*, in charge of deciding if a law should be implemented, interviewed only one French woman wearing the headscarf. For more information see, Bouzar, *Intégrisme, Islam et Nous*, 94.
19. Göle, 'Laïcité républicaine et l'Islam public'.
20. Turkish Constitution, 1982, Article 2.
21. For further information on the secular reforms in Turkey as well as on the religious dress regulations, please see, Berkes, *Development of Secularism in Turkey*; McGoldrick, *Human Rights and Religion*, 133; Davison, 'Turkey a "Secular" State?'.
22. McGoldrick, *Human Rights and Religion*, 133.
23. This difference between France and Turkey, in my view, might need to be nuanced. Indeed, one could wonder – especially after the passing of the 2004 law – if in spite of the fact that the idea of separation is present in a certain legal understanding of *laïcité*, whether some interpretations of the term might not also be attempting to control the type of religious expressions allowed in the Republic. For discussions going in this direction please see, Mahmood, 'Secularism, Hermeutics, and Empire'; Bowen, 'View from France'; Göle, 'Laïcité républicaine et Islam public'.
24. Gökariksel and Mitchell, 'Veiling, Secularism and the Neoliberal Subject', 149. It is interesting to note that, through this control, the state is privileging a particular understanding of Sunni Islam – an understanding used to define the boundaries of Turkish citizenship.
25. In 1980 the Turkish state introduced 'The Turkish Islamic Synthesis', where greater religious liberalism was permitted. This neo-liberal climate allowed Islamic politics, economy and culture to develop. However, Mitchell and Gökariksel ('Veiling, Secularism, and the Neoliberal Subject', 149) explain, that this opening remained heavily controlled by the state.
26. In 1997 the military demanded that the Welfare Party ruling the country at the time in coalition with the centre-right True Faith Party restore secularism. Concretely, they demanded the restriction of Imam Hatip schools (religious schools), an increase in mandatory secular education from five to eight years and greater control of religious orders. The party came to a stalemate, as it was too divided on those issues, and resigned. This 'soft' coup was backed up by the Constitutional Court, which later expelled the Party's leader from parliament, banned him from political participation for five years and seized all the party's assets (Esposito, 'Introduction: Islam and Secularism', 6).
27. McGoldrick, *Human Rights and Religion*, 135.
28. Gökariksel and Mitchell, 'Veiling, Secularism and Islamist Politics', 147.
29. Smith, *Laclau and Mouffe*, 8, emphasis added.
30. Wilson, 'Human Rights, Culture and Context', 18.
31. A parallel can be traced here with Soysal's *Limits of Citizenship* argument who considers that the concept of national citizenship needs to be revisited. Indeed in her view, international human rights have rendered membership multiple, where identity unfolds not only at the national, but also at the regional and global level. In our case, I would argue that secularism cannot be solely analysed at the national level anymore, but one needs also to understand how the secular settlement is being renegotiated at the international level in particular through the use of human rights. Yet, this international networking does not mean that national models of religious governance are necessarily undermined. Indeed, as I will show, in the last part of my Turkish case analysis, in some instances international judgements can reinforce national authority.
32. Lila Charef, lawyer for CCIF and Samy Debah member of CCIF, Paris, France, in discussion with the author, 13 November 2007, Paris, France.

33. The CCIF could be compared, on a much smaller scale, to conservative Christian public litigation firms in the US defending the presence of religion in the public sphere. For more information on those firms see: Hacker, *Culture of Conservative Christian Litigation* and Brown, *Trumping Religion*.
34. One should note that this is quite a novelty in France, as the use of the term 'Islamophobia' created many controversies, especially among secular human rights organizations that seem to have particular difficulties to address issues related to religious discriminations. Despite this fact, it is noteworthy that over the last couple of years many of those same organizations have started an internal reflection on the issue, and some have even adopted it in their programme of work (e.g. *Mouvement Pour l'Amitié des Peuples et Contre le Racisme* (MRAP)). For a scholarly discussion on the term 'Islamophobia', as well as more broadly on this phenomenon in France please see: Geisser, *Nouvelle Islamophobie*.
35. CCIF, *Bilan de la loi du 15 mars*.
36. Building on this, it is interesting to note that President Chirac in his December 2003 speech preceding the passing of the law mentioned that discrete religious signs, such as small crosses, stars of David, or hands' of Fatima were still allowed in schools. One could wonder here, to what extent the state is deciding what is religiously allowed and what is not – giving, even, a religious dimension to signs that might traditionally not have one. For a full reading see, President Chirac, 'Discours relatif au respect du principe de *laïcité*.
37. CCIF, *Bilan de la loi du 15 mars*. Author's translation, emphasis added.
38. For an example of this please see CCIF, 'Fiche Pratique 3: Les Signes Religieux et l'Enseignement Supérieur'.
39. CCIF, 'Communiqué concernant les mamans voiles exclues'.
40. CCIF, 'Discrimination à l'égard des mères des élèves'. Author's translation.
41. CCIF, 'Montreuil- L'arrêté du maire'. Author's translation.
42. The *Conseil d'Etat*'s case *Union Francaise pour la Cohésion Nationale v. Ministère de l'Education Nationale* (October 2004) contesting the validity of the Circular Fillon (a circular giving instructions on how to implement the 2004 law), and the case *Mlle X* (October 2004), regarding a student expelled from school because she was wearing a bandana, are illustrative of this.
43. Conseil d'Etat, *Mme M*.
44. It is important to note that it is the first time that such a judgment was given in France. Indeed, as Le Bars ('Une marocaine en burqa') underlines, French citizenship had until then been refused to people who had spoken publicly in favour of a 'radical' vision of Islam, but not because someone was considered to practice 'radically' a religion.
45. CCIF, 'Conseil d'Etat une décision dangereuse'. Author's translation, emphasis added.
46. In sum, the 1905 law and the jurisprudence of the *Conseil d'Etat* have been used here as political resources to underline the inconsistencies in the implementation of *laïcité*, and to justify claims for the restoration of a 'true' *laïcité*.
47. Brown, 'Suffering Rights as Paradoxes', 230.
48. Ibid., 235; and Vakulenko, 'Islamic Dress in Human Rights Jurisprudence', 8.
49. Brown, 'Suffering Rights as Paradoxes', 239.
50. Merve Kavakci brought her case at the ECHR (*Affaire Kavakci c. Turquie*), but this is not the only transnational human rights mechanism used. Religious rights activists in Turkey have also, for instance, been using United Nations mechanisms, such as submitting shadow reports on the headscarf issue to the CEDAW (Convention on the Elimination of All Forms of Discrimination against Women) committee (2005 and 2010), and actively lobbying with members of this committee.

51. The situation seems to have been changing after the passing of the 2004 law on religious symbols. Indeed, because redress cannot be sought nationally regarding cases of school exclusions, grievances have been sent to UN Special Rapporteurs (e.g. *UN Special Rapporteurs on Freedom of Religion and Beliefs*), to UN Human Rights Committees, and to the ECHR.
52. McGoldrick, *Human Rights and Religion*, 135–7, provides interesting information on judgements of the Constitutional Court regarding secularism and religious freedom.
53. This is illustrated by, for instance, Turkish faith-based NGOs (e.g. *Mazlumder*, *AKDER*, Capital Women Platform, etc.) that have been since the mid-1990s increasingly framing their concerns with a human rights language – a language which has enabled them to collaborate with international NGOs and actors to ask for greater religious freedom in Turkey. For further information on this discursive shift see: Dagi, 'Rethinking Human Rights' and 'Turkey's AKP in Power'; Yavuz, *Islamic Political Identity in Turkey*.
54. Although there are still few cases underlining the limits of Turkish secular system that have been brought at the ECHR these are important because they represent the first pieces of jurisprudence at the EU level touching specifically on questions related to secularism and the wearing of religious symbols in the public sphere. Among interesting cases filed on the issue we can note the case of *Karaduman v. Turkey* (1993) and ECHR, *Sahin v. Turkey* (2005).
55. The official reason given for revoking her citizenship was that Merve Kavakci had acquired US citizenship prior to her election without obtaining formal permission from the Turkish authorities. Yet, it is relevant to highlight that authorities have generally never been strict about citizens informing them when they acquire double nationality (Cemrek, 'How Could the Rights to Education and Representation Challenge National Security?', 57).
56. The Virtue Party was banned in 2001 by the Constitutional Court, which accused the party of anti-secular activities, including advocating for the choice to wear the headscarf in state universities and in public places.
57. Merve Kavakci in discussion with the author, 11 September 2007, Washington, DC, USA. It is relevant to note that two other colleagues of Ms Kavakci, Mr Silay and Ms Ilicak, also brought their cases to the ECHR and won. However, Ms Kavakci was the only one wearing the headscarf, and who alleged that there had been, also, a violation of Article 9 of the Convention (freedom of thought, conscience and religion) and Article 14 (prohibition of discrimination).
58. ECHR, *Kavakci v. Turkey, Silay v. Turkey and Ilicak v. Turkey*, emphasis added.
59. Ibid, emphasis added.
60. International Parliamentary Union, 'Resolution Adopted Unanimously by the IPU Council'.
61. For more information see, Becket Fund for Religious Liberty, http://www.becketfund.org/.
62. Kavakci, 'Statement at the UN Commission for Human Rights'.
63. It is relevant to note, here, that several activists, members of religious rights' NGOs (e.g. *AKDER*, Capital Women Platform and *Mazlumder*), whom I interviewed in Turkey in 2008, stressed the crucial importance of this international networking whether it be at the EU level, or more broadly at the UN or with INGOs, to counteract the influence of 'kemalist' networks – which did not advocate for greater religious freedom in Turkey (in particular with regards to the wearing of religious symbols in the public sphere), nor underline the limits of Turkish secularism.
64. Merve Kavakci in discussion with the author, 11 September 2007, Washington, DC, USA.

65. Merve Kavakci makes a similar point in her testimony in front of the UN Commission for Human Rights (Kavakci, 'Statement at the UN Commission for Human Rights').
66. Article 9 protects the freedom of thought, conscience and religion. For a full reading of Article 9 see the European Convention on Human Rights (ECHR): http://www.hri.org/docs/ECHR50.html.
67. *Kavakci c. Turquie.*
68. *Sahin v. Turkey.*
69. Vakulenko, 'Islamic Dress in Human Rights Jurisprudence', 4. This trend, to rely on local jurisprudence when dealing with questions related to the public expression of religion, does not seem to be limited to Turkey. Indeed, two judgements released in December 2008 on the wearing of the headscarf in French public schools – *Kervanci v. France* and *Dogru v. France* – confirmed the importance given to local contexts in judgements related to the notion of secularism.
70. Vakulenko, 'Islamic Dress in Human Rights Jurisprudence', 4, and Lewis, 'What Not to Wear', offer an enlightening discussion of the limits of Article 9, and more generally human rights to resolve questions related to religious dress in the public sphere.
71. Gökariksel and Mitchell, 'Veiling, Secularism and the Neoliberal Subject', 158.
72. Ibid.
73. Brown, 'Suffering Rights as Paradoxes', 239.
74. Vakulenko, 'Islamic Dress in Human Rights Jurisprudence' and Lewis, 'What Not to Wear'.
75. Vakulenko, 'Islamic Dress in Human Rights Jurisprudence', 4.
76. It is worth highlighting that there are many theological debates related to whether the headscarf is or is not a religious requirement. Asking this type of question in our case does not really help us, as many individuals are convinced that it is their religious duty to do so, and are demanding for the right to live according to what they think is dutiful.
77. Lewis, 'What Not to Wear', 6, emphasis added.
78. Indeed several religious women members of Turkish religious rights-based organizations, who advocated against the headscarf ban in Turkey and whom I interviewed in 2008, argued that they were wearing the headscarf because of piety, and related notions such as duty, virtue or the marking of ethical boundaries. The headscarf was often described as embodying one's relationship with God, and one's daily efforts to be morally closer to him. Saba Mahmood, *Politics of Piety*, exposes similar findings in her research on piety and the Mosque movement in Egypt.
79. It is interesting to note that religious rights groups in Turkey (e.g. *Mazlumder*, *AKDER*, Capital Women Platform, *Ozgurder*) are increasingly framing their grievances against headscarf bans as violations of the rights to education, to labour, to freedom of expression, or to gender equality, and less as a religious freedom issue.
80. Laclau, in Torfing, *New Theories of Discourse*, 181.
81. Asad, 'What Do Human Rights Do?', 22.
82. Many religious rights activists, whom I interviewed in Turkey in 2008, explained that they made a difference between the legal framework protecting human rights, a product of secular nation-states, and the origins of human rights. Indeed, for them, human rights were inclusive and universal precisely because they were 'God-given' rights – given to every human being at birth. This vision of the origins of rights can again make us wonder about the different 'particular' understandings of rights located within the notion of 'universal'.
83. Mahmood, 'Secularism, Hermeutics and Empire', offers an insightful discussion on the limits of liberal understanding of autonomy and free choice to fully grasp religiousness.
84. Mahmood, *Politics of Piety*, Epilogue; 'Secularism, Hermeutics, and Empire', 343.

Notes on contributor

Amélie Barras is currently finishing her PhD thesis at the London School of Economics in the Department of Government. She specializes in comparative politics, with a focus on secularism, Islam and human rights.

Bibliography

Ahdar, Rex, and Ian Leigh. *Religious Freedom in the Liberal State*. Oxford: Oxford University Press, 2005.
Asad, Talal. 'What Do Human Rights Do? An Anthropological Inquiry'. *Theory & Event* 4, no. 4 (2000).
Becket Fund for Religious Liberty. 'ECHR: Turkey at Fault for Expelling Merve Kavacki from Parliament for Wearing Muslim Headscarf'. Press release, April 11, 2007. http://www.becketfund.org/index.php/Article/657.html (accessed October 1, 2009).
Berkes, Niyazi. *The Development of Secularism in Turkey*. Montreal: McGill University Press, 1964.
Bouzar, Dounia. *L'Intégrisme, L'Islam et Nous* [*Fundamentalism, Islam and Us*]. Paris: Plon, 2007.
Bowen, John. *Why the French Don't Like Headscarves, Islam, the State and Public Space*. Princeton, NJ: Princeton University Press, 2007.
Bowen, John. 'A View from France on the Internal Complexity of National Models'. *Journal of Ethnic and Migration Studies* 33, no. 6 (2007): 1003–16.
Brown, Wendy. 'Suffering Rights as Paradoxes'. *Constellations* 7, no. 2 (2000): 230–41.
Brown, Steven. *Trumping Religion: The New Christian Right, The Free Speech Clause, And The Courts*. Tucaloosa and London: University of Alabama Press, 2002.
CCIF. *Le Bilan de la Loi du 15 Mars 2004 et de ses effets pervers* [*Assessment of 15 March 2004 Law and its Perverse Effects*]. 2005. http://www.islamophobie.net (accessed October 1, 2009).
CCIF. 'Montreuil – L'arrêté du maire Montreuil a été annulé' ['Montreuil – The Montreuil Mayor's Decisions has been Annulled'], Press release, October 22, 2005. http://www.islamophobie.net (accessed October 1, 2009).
CCIF. 'Discrimination à l'égard des mères des élèves – les dégâts de la loi du 15 mars 2004' ['Discrimination against Mothers wearing the Headscarf – The Damages of 15 March 2004'], Press release, December 8, 2005. http://www.islamophobie.net (accessed October 1, 2009).
CCIF. 'Communiqué concernant les mamans voilées exclues des activités scolaires' ['Press Release concerning Mothers wearing the Headscarf Excluded from Partaking in School Activities'], Press release, June 13, 2007. http://www.islamophobie.net (accessed October 1, 2009).
CCIF. 'Conseil d'Etat une décision dangereuse' ['A Dangerous Decision of the Conseil d'Etat'], Press release, July 13, 2008. http://www.saphirnews.com/CCIF-Conseil-d-Etat-une-decision-dangereuse_a9310.html (accessed October 1, 2009).
CCIF. 'Fiche Pratique 3: Les Signes Religieux et l'Enseignement Supérieur' ['Legal Note 3: Religious Symbols and Higher Educotion'], legal note, 2004. http://www.islamophobie.net (accessed October 1, 2009).
Cemrek, Murat. 'How Could the Rights to Education and Representation Challenge National Security? The Headscarf Conflict in Turkey Revisited'. *Human Security Perspectives* 1, no. 2 (2004): 52–8.
Cesari, Jocelyne. *Etre Musulmans en France: Associations, Militants et Mosquées* [*To be Muslims in France: Associations, Militants and Mosques*]. Paris: Edition Khartala, 1994.

Chirac, Jacques. 'Discours prononcé par Monsieur Jacques Chirac, Président de la République relatif au respect du principe de la laïcité dans la République' ['Speech pronounced by Mr Jacques Chirac, President of the Republic related to the Respect of Laïcité in the Republic'], Palais de l'Elysée, Paris, France December 17, 2003. http://www.elysee.fr/elysee/interventions/discours_et_declarations/2003/ decembre/discours_prononcepar_m_jacques_chirac_president_de_la_republique_ relatif_au_respect_du_principe_de_laicite_dans_la_republique-palais_de_l_elysee.2829. html (accessed October 1, 2009).
Conseil d'Etat. *Rapport Public 2004: Jurisprudence et avis de 2003, Un siècle de laïcité* [*Public Report 2004: Case Law and Opinions of 2003, a Century of Laïcité*]. Paris: La Documentation Française, 2004.
Conseil d'Etat. 'Port de signe d'appartenance à une communauté religieuse' ['Wearing of Signs Indicating a Belonging to a Religious Community'], Avis no. 346.893, November 27, 1989.
Conseil d'Etat. 'M. Kherouraa et autres' ['M. Kherouraa and Others'], Judgement, November 2, 1992.
Conseil d'Etat. 'Mlle Marteaux', Avis no.217017, May 3, 2002.
Conseil d'Etat. 'Union Francaise pour la Cohésion Nationale v. Ministère de l'Education Nationale' ['French Union for National Cohesion v. Ministry of National Education'], Judgement (req.no.269077), October 8, 2004.
Conseil d'Etat. 'Mlle X', Judgement (req.no.272926), October 8, 2004.
Conseil d'Etat. 'Mme M', Judgement (req. no. 286798). May 26, 2008.
Dagi, Ihsan. 'Rethinking Human Rights, Democracy and the West: Post-Islamist Intellectuals in Turkey'. *Critique: Critical Middle Eastern Studies* 13, no. 2 (2004): 135–51.
Dagi, Ihsan. 'Turkey's AKP in Power'. *Journal of Democracy* 19, no. 3 (2008): 26–30.
Davison, Andrew. 'Turkey a "Secular" State? The Challenge of Description'. *The South Atlantic Quarterly* 102, no. 2/3 (2003): 334–50.
ECHR. *Merve Kavakci c. Turquie*, Application no. 71907/01, April 5, 2007.
ECHR. *Leyla Sahin v. Turkey*, Application no. 44774/98, November 10, 2005.
ECHR. *Dogru v. France*, Application no. 27058/05, December 4, 2008.
ECHR. *Kervanci c. France*, Application no. 31645/04, December 4, 2008.
ECHR Registrar. *Kavakci v. Turkey, Silay v. Turkey and Ilicak v. Turkey*, Press release, April 5, 2007.
Esposito, John. 'Introduction: Islam and Secularism in the Twenty-First Century'. In *Islam and Secularism in the Middle East*, ed. Azzam Tamimi and John Esposito. London: C. Hurst & Co, 2000.
European Commission. *Karaduman v. Turkey*, Application no. 16278/90, May 3, 1993.
Evans, Malcolm. 'Religion, Law and Human Rights: Locating the Debate'. In *Law and Religion in Contemporary Society: Communities, Individualism and the State*, ed. Peter Edge and Graham Harvey. Burlington: Ashgate Publishing, 2000.
Gaspard, Françoise, and Farhad Khosrokhavar. *Le Foulard et la République* [*The Headscarf and the Republic*]. Paris: Découverte, 1995.
Geisser, Vincent. *La nouvelle islamophobie* [*The New Islamophobia*]. Paris: Editions la Découverte, 2003.
Göle, Nilufer. 'La Laïcité républicaine et l'Islam Public ['Republican Laïcité and Public Islam']. Revue Pouvoirs, September 2005'.
Gökariksel, Banu and Katharyne Mitchell. 'Veiling, Secularism, and the Neoliberal Subject: National Narratives and Supranational Desires in Turkey and France'. *Global Networks* 5, no. 2 (2005): 147–65.
Gunn, Jeremy. 'Religious Freedom and Laïcité: A Comparison of the United States and France'. *Birgham Young University Law Review* no. 2 (2004): 420–502.

Hacker, Hans. *The Culture of Conservative Christian Litigation*. Lanham: Rowan & Littlefield Publishers, Inc, 2005.
Hurd, Elizabeth. *The Politics of Secularism in International Relations*. Princeton, NJ: Princeton University Press, 2008.
International Parliamentary Union. 'Turkey: Case No TK/66 – Merve Safa Kavakci, Resolution Adopted Unanimously by the IPU Council at its 171 session', Resolution, Geneva, Switzerland, September 27, 2002. http://www.ipu.org/hr-e/171/Tk66.htm (accessed October 1, 2009).
Kavakci, Merve. 'Statement at the UN Commission for Human Rights', UN Commission for Human Rights, Geneva, Switzerland, March 23, 2005. http://www.becketfund.org/index.php/Article/373.html (accessed October 1, 2009).
Kepel, Gilles. *Les banlieues de l'Islam* [*The Suburbs of Islam*]. Paris: Le Seuil, 1987.
Laurence, Jonathan, and Justin Vaisse. *Integrating Islam: Political and Religious Challenges in Contemporary France*. Washington, DC: Brookings Institution Press, 2006.
Le Bars, Stéphanie. 'Une Marocaine en burqa se voit refuser la nationalité française' ['French Nationality is Refused to a Moroccan Woman wearing the Burqa']. *Le Monde*, July 11, 2008'.
Lewis, Tom. 'What Not to Wear: Religious Rights, the European Court, and the Margin of Appreciation'. *International and Comparative Law Quarterly* 56 (2007): 395–8.
Mahmood, Saba. *Politics of Piety: The Islamic Revival and the Feminist Subject*. Princeton, NJ: Princeton University Press, 2005.
Mahmood, Saba. 'Secularism, Hermeutics, and Empire: The Politics of Islamic Reformation'. *Public Culture* 18, no. 2 (2006): 323–47.
McGoldrick, Dominic. *Human Rights and Religion: The Islamic Headscarf Debate in Europe*. Oxford: Hart Publishing, 2006.
Salton, Herman. 'Veiled Threats? Islam, Headscarves and Religious Freedom in America and France'. PhD diss. University of Auckland, 2007.
Scott, Joan. *The Politics of the Veil*. Princeton, NJ: Princeton University Press, 2007.
Smith, Anne-Marie. *Laclau and Mouffe, The Radical Democratic Imaginary*. London: Routledge, 1998.
Soysal, Yasemin. *Limits of Citizenship: Migrants and Post-national Membership in Europe*. Chicago, IL: The University of Chicago Press, 1994.
Stasi, Bernard. *Rapport de la Commission de Réflexion sur l'Application du Principe de Laïcité dans la République Remis au Président de la République le 11 Décembre 2003* [*Report of the Commission on the Application of the Principle of Laïcité in the Republic given to the President of the Republic on 11 December 2003*]. Paris: Documentation Française, 2004.
Ternisien, Xavier. *La France des Mosquées* [*The Mosques of France*]. Paris: Editions Albin Michel, 2002.
Torfing, Jacob. *New Theories of Discourse: Laclau, Mouffe, and Zizek*. Oxford: Blackwell, 1998.
Troper, Michel. 'French Secularism, or Laïcité'. *Cardozo Law Review* 21 (2000): 1267–84.
Vakulenko, Anastasia. 'Islamic Dress in Human Rights Jurisprudence: A Critique of Current Trends'. *Human Rights Law Review* (2007): 1–14.
Wilson, Richard. 'Human Rights, Culture and Context: An Introduction'. *Human Rights, Culture and Context: An Anthropological Perspectives*. London: Pluto Press, 1997.
Yavuz, Hakan. *Islamic Political Identity in Turkey*. New York: Oxford University Press, 2003.

The problematic nature of religious autonomy to minorities in democracies – the case of India's Muslims

Ayelet Harel-Shalev

Ben-Gurion University of the Negev, Israel

This article focuses on the ambivalent effect of religious autonomy in India and the outcome for democracy in the country. The Indian constitution guarantees autonomy to its religious minorities, and promises the minorities the freedom independently to manage their religious affairs in addition to a proportional share of the budget. At the same time, the constitution emphasizes the aspiration to legislate 'uniform personal laws' for all the citizens of India in accordance with the principles of secularism, equality and with India's self-definition as a civic nation. This recommendation has however remained a 'dead letter' until today. In this domain, the state has constituted a civic law for Hindus, which adjusts Hinduism to democratic principles. In this sense, the state has nationalized Hinduism, and the government has assumed authority and reformed Hindu civic and marriage laws. However, although they have tried, the state's legal and political institutions have not interfered thus far with Muslim marriage and religious laws. Muslims are committed to the Sharia while Hindus must obey the state's civic laws. By avoiding enforcement of affirmative action for Muslims in the spheres of political representation or public employment, while simultaneously prohibiting Hindus' group rights, and providing religious autonomy to the Muslim minority, the Constitution, which stresses so-called secularism as well as minority protection, intensifies the conflict between these two governance principles. The conclusion is that this situation not only leads to ideological conflicts and resource competition but also, overall, threatens the stability of India's democracy.

Introduction

The leading classical model of the state in the West is a democratic nation state. This model corresponds to the idea of liberal democracy, as the Westminster model suggests.[1] Nonetheless, many conflicts between indigenous communities, and modern 'identity politics' disputes, spring from a 'hole' in the political theory underlying modern liberal democracy.[2] This 'hole' is related to the degree of 'group rights'[3] that liberal societies allow groups compared to individuals.

In theory, liberal democracy is indifferent to distinctions among citizens. The liberal tradition has conceived of citizenship as a universalizing and homogenizing concept where all citizens are supposed to be treated as equals.[4] Accordingly, it has declared that the modern nation state is 'the citizen's state' – and therefore, labelled it 'a civic nation state'. Yet, many researchers doubt the suitability of the liberal democracy model to deeply divided societies in general[5] and to post-colonial societies in particular.[6] One of the reasons for this uncertainty is that deeply divided societies, which comprise several indigenous communities, are often 'dragged' into inevitable conflicts which raise the question: Who owns the state? Or, more precisely, which ethno-national community has hegemony over the homeland? Moreover, many deeply divided states offer different group rights[7] and create a 'differentiated citizenship', rather than a universalistic one.[8] Since citizenship in deeply divided societies usually does not fit the ideal-type of universalistic citizenship – as the liberal tradition suggests – we need to deconstruct the citizenship discourse in these states in order to analyse the status of the relevant minority groups. It is also important to examine what it means in terms of laws, court rulings, and public policy.[9]

Deeply divided India is considered in the academic literature on democracy to be a deviant case.[10] There are many social divisions in India, including ethnic, linguistic, regional, caste-based, and religious. Nevertheless, despite the intense challenges, the democratic ethos in India has remained a major part of India's political system and self-identity. Moreover, most of the country's conflicts remain mainly at the local level and do not spread to the entire sub-continent, except one: the Hindu Muslim divide.[11] The conflict between Hindus and Muslims in India is a major schism that threatens the survival of the Indian democracy.

Independent India was established over 60 years ago in the midst of a violent partition process and severe competition between Hindus and Muslims. Still, the Indian state grants equal civic rights to all citizens, regardless of religion or ethnic origin. India is not defined in its official documents as 'a Hindu state', but instead as a secular democracy that is formally neutral in terms of the different homeland communities, both majority and minorities. As such, India corresponds well to the ideal type of 'liberal democracy', and therefore, it has established constitutional civil rights and universal citizenship in line with its self-definition as a secular state, that is, a civic nation state.[12]

As a formally liberal democracy, India's founding fathers chose not to establish a democratic regime based on power sharing, with respect to the Hindu–Muslim divide. Quite the opposite: India's constitution is based, to a large extent, on the majoritarian Westminster model.[13] The dominant Hindu leaders of colonial India rejected the demand of Muslim leaders to establish a cooperative Hindu–Muslim government; thus they actually pushed the Muslims to aspire to establish a separate state of their own: Pakistan.[14]

In practice, Indian governance often rests on majoritarianism as one of its governing principles, frequently showing preference to the Hindu community and displaying attitudes opposing equality and universal citizenship. During an early meeting of its Constituent Assembly, the transnational status of the Urdu language, which is identified with Muslims, was cancelled, and Hindi was retained as the Indian official transnational language.[15] Affirmative action is extended to members of lower caste Hindus, but Muslims, as a separate, weak and underrepresented community, are ineligible for its benefits.[16] Every current call for affirmative action for the whole Muslim community has been perceived as a demand for further partition of India.[17] Moreover, the political powers in India have suppressed secessionist demands in Punjab, Assam, and Kashmir with an iron fist, yet been relatively lenient with the Hindu Right, which wishes to reform India to become 'a Hindu and democratic state', and this caused the Right's ideology both to expand and to radicalize.[18]

We must not forget, however, that along with entitling all its citizens to equal civic rights, India recognizes minority groups' rights and autonomy. The autonomy of religious minorities is recognized within the spheres of education and religion, resulting in the award of rights that have occasionally conflicted with the state's liberal laws. Surprisingly, minorities enjoy more group rights than does the Hindu majority. The Constituent Assembly formulated the constitution with the expectation that the majority would forego these rights for the sake of Indian unity; Hindus are, consequently, not entitled to manage autonomously their education system or even their holy places, the state does that for them.

Religious autonomy in India

Analysing India's religious sphere is a complex undertaking. This article examines this issue comprehensively. The Indian constitution guarantees autonomy to its religious minorities, and it promises minorities the freedom independently to manage their religious affairs, as well as a proportional share of the state's budget in religious affairs. At the same time we can trace, through the aspirations of the founding fathers, the wish for a civil, religious unification for the sake of equality and secularity. For example, in the country's early days, the Indian Constituent Assembly recommended the legislation of 'uniform personal laws' for all the citizens of India in accordance with the principles of secularism and with its self-definition as a civic nation. This recommendation later became Article 44 of the Indian constitution: 'Uniform Civil Code for Citizens: The state shall endeavour to secure for citizens a uniform civil code throughout the territory of India'. This article remains undone until today.

Apart from Article 44, the Indian Constitution contains no direct reference to the personal laws maintained by India's various religious communities. However, Article 372 states that, although existing laws will remain in force, they will be subject to the stipulations of other Constitution articles until Parliament revises those original laws.[19] The Indian Constitution therefore guarantees many rights – such as civil rights and the right to equality – that often clash with the personal laws upheld by the separate religious communities. Nonetheless, Article 13 states that the laws passed prior to independence in 1947 would be valid as long as they did not conflict with the Fundamental Rights granted by the Constitution.[20] In cases of conflict, the previous laws would be treated as void. With the Constitution superseding all other laws, conflicts between personal laws and the principles guiding the Constitution – especially in the area of human rights – represented serious constitutional and judicial predicaments for the government. During the Indian democracy's infancy, India's Supreme Court ruled that the distinctive personal laws were to be upheld until otherwise determined.[21] For several decades, this decision provided the escape hatch required by the judicial system and other government agencies to avoid intervention in religious affairs.[22]

Hindu Personal Law was nevertheless revised by the parliament during the 1950s to adapt it to the conditions of democratic society. Traditional Hinduism is extremely rigid with respect to all matters of social hierarchy and the caste system; therefore, its principles frequently contradict the Constitution's liberal values. Despite this inherent collision, the independent country's first prime minister, Jawaharlal Nehru, and his colleagues succeeded in introducing some revisions that revised the law so that it might fit the modern climate.[23] The Hindu Code Act of 1954–1956 was, in effect, applicable to all Hindus belonging to all the castes and living throughout the country.[24] During the same period, the Untouchability (Offences) Act, 1955 was passed; this law made it illegal to discriminate against the Untouchables (*Dalits* or, the *Fifth Varna*) in any way, shape, or form.[25] The new 'Hindu civic code' further prohibits discriminations regarding who may enter the temples; it prohibits the 'sati' custom; it prohibits polygamy and other traditional, non-democratic customs. In this sense, the state has nationalized Hinduism, and the government assumed authority and reformed Hindu civic and marriage laws.

Each revision was accompanied by a chorus of objections voiced by orthodox Hindus, who perceived these laws as gross state interventions into the community's religious affairs.[26] The new laws cancelled almost every reference to castes; they also gave women many rights, including divorce. The government was resolute in its attempt to implement its revisions to the Hindu Personal Law at the same time that it refused to submit to the pressures imposed by numerous Hindu organizations.[27] Hindu resistance to government policy in this area was tireless because, among other things, the Muslims refused to revise their own Personal Law in any way. Official activity in the area of Hindu Personal Law was consequently perceived by Hindu nationalists as anti-Hindu.

Legislation of the Hindu Civil Code Act made Parliament directly responsible for Hindu personal law in the family and social life spheres; the objections of the Hindu religious elite were disregarded.[28] From this position of power, the government took upon itself to revise Hindu law as it saw fit.[29] Inconsistencies were not, however, avoided. Although they tried, the state's legal and political institutions have not interfered thus far with Muslim marriage and religious laws.

This created an incomparable situation, where Muslims in India are entitled to polygamy, while Hindus are prohibited from marrying more than one wife, due to the civic law. The Muslim women pay the price.[30] Liberal Hindus and Muslims alike complained that this state of affairs contradicted the Constitution's Article 15, which stipulates that discrimination – of any group – on the basis of religion was inherently unconstitutional.

Following submission of a petition requesting nullification of a prior regional court ruling convicting several Hindus of polygamy, the issue was brought before the High Court in the State of Bombay in 1952.[31] The court supported the heavy penalties inflicted on the polygamists while arguing that such penalties were necessary to make the law effective, a position rationalized by the fact that the purported discrimination was not committed on the basis of religion.[32] The court also ruled that the state was authorized to introduce gradual reforms into the various personal laws, and that it was perfectly legitimate to begin such reforms with the Hindu religion.[33] By means of this announcement, considered to be in harmony with the respective legislation, the court hoped to encourage state adoption of the Uniform Civil Code. These arrangements eventually became an inseparable part of India's fragile system for distributing minority rights.

There were a few exceptions, nonetheless. Galanter and Krishnan[34] identify two cases where court intervention in Muslim Personal Law did not arouse a public storm.[35] The Supreme Court ruled in these cases that according to India's criminal law, women were eligible to receive alimony beyond the three-month post-divorce period (the *idatt*) set by the Muslim Sharia. Muslims expressed no public objections to the rulings because, Galanter and Krishnan claim, the presiding judge, Krishna Iyer, did not hand down a universal judgment abrogating the Sharia; he limited his decisions to the specific women demanding additional compensation.

A subsequent case, known as the Shah Bano case, set a controversial precedent in 1985 – it was the first time that the courts openly contravened Muslim personal law by ruling as unjust the alimony due divorced women according to the Sharia.[36] Crucially, the court also declared that Indian civil law was legally superior to the Sharia. The case involved a woman, Shah Bano, who had petitioned the court to force her husband to pay her alimony after he divorced her following 46 years of marriage. Her petition was based on Article 125 of India's Federal Criminal Code (CrPC), which states that a husband is to pay his former spouse a standard payment every month. In her plea, Shah Bano claimed that her former husband did not provide her with sufficient means to maintain herself. In his defence, her husband argued that the Sharia required him to transfer only a designated amount (known as the *mahr*) during the three-month duration of the *idatt*. Hence, he was not required to provide his ex-wife with additional support.

The High Court in MP ruled that in addition to the *mahr* paid during the *idatt*, the husband was to pay his ex-wife monthly alimony as dictated by the CrPC. The husband then appealed to India's Supreme Court, which sustained the 23 April 1985 decision handed down by the High Court in MP. As part of its decision, India's Supreme Court declared that secular law was superior to religious law;

hence, the husband was to abide by the CrPC. The verdict opens with the following sentence: '[T]his appeal does not involve any constitutional importance.' Arguably, the judges were convinced that this decision, like those in the other two cases cited, touched on the mere conventional attributes of the law; however, it is much more likely that they were well aware of its highly charged potential impact and wanted to minimize public outrage.

The Shah Bano case also gave the courts an opportunity to state their positions regarding India's progress toward a universal and uniform personal law. And so, India's Supreme Court declared that previous court reluctance to intervene in Muslim personal law was misguided:[37] The Supreme Court thus ruled that in the name of 'justice', Indian state law was superior to Muslim personal law in this case but refrained from basing its decision on the argument that Muslim personal law interfered with the exercise of fundamental rights. Had the courts made use of this argument, Muslim personal law could have been nullified according to Article 13 of the Constitution. Instead, the court's refusal to invalidate Muslim personal law effectively waived the opportunity for the parliament to reform the law. At the time, according to Dhavan and Nariman,[38] the court was apparently insufficiently reformist to attempt such a move.

Nevertheless, conservative Muslim figures and organizations were infuriated by the decision; it argued that the ruling represented a red flag before Islam in general and India's Muslims in particular. Tahir Mahmood,[39] a Muslim jurist and public figure, argued that the court was ignorant and uninformed about Islam, which is why it had handed down such a flawed decision. Mahmood likewise held that the Constitution invoked the formulation of a *uniform* personal law but not one law held *in common*, which implied that the minority communities were to approach this goal independently of any state dictates.[40] An extensive protest campaign, organized by the *All India Personal Law Board*, was subsequently waged with the participation of the Muslim press, religious institutions and mosques, and local communities. Its platform stated that the Shah Bano decision represented a death knell to Islamic identity in India.[41] Other organizations, like the *Muslim Majlis–e-Mushawarat*, led by Syed Shahabuddin, announced that should the decision not be reversed, Muslims would treat the Indian Republic Day as 'a black day'.[42] Importantly – although their voices were lost in all the noise – more moderate, liberal Muslims, in addition to numerous academics, concurred with the Supreme Court decision.[43]

The issues raised in the Shah Bano decision were of singular importance both to Indian women generally and to Muslim women in particular.[44] But conservative Muslim interests were able to transform the ruling in the case into a threat to Muslim identity and self-respect within the confines of India.[45] There were two conflicting themes: the principle of civic equality and democratization versus Muslim values and minority's autonomy. Although the court's intent was protection of Muslim women's individual civil rights, ironically many Muslims perceived the Shah Bano decision as an attack on Muslim personal law and the Muslim community.

Rajiv Gandhi, India's Prime Minister during this controversy in 1985–1986, initially supported the court but later reversed his position in response to pressure from Muslim members of his party (Congress). Consequential demonstrations and riots held by Muslims throughout India also played their part. To quell the unrest, Prime Minister Rajiv Gandhi assigned Ziaur Rahman Ansari, a Muslim cabinet member, to the task of investigating the issue. Doing so provided him with the support needed to formulate a legislative proposal declaring Sharia superiority to civil law in matters of divorce and personal law. Parliamentary debates on the subject were lengthy, with many objecting to the proposal on the grounds of its un-democratic and anti-constitutional character. Liberal Muslims also strongly opposed the proposal. Arif Mohammed Kahn, a Muslim, resigned from the cabinet in response to the proposal's 'inhumane' and 'anti-Islamic' elements.[46] Despite the strong bipartisan antagonism, the proposal was passed and signed into law on 5 May 1986.[47] The new law (Muslim Women's Protection of Rights in Divorce Bill, 1986) effectively turned back the clock by transforming Muslim women into second class citizens. It prevented them from exercising their rights according to article 125 of the federal CrPC and shifted responsibility for a divorced woman's support to her family rather than her ex-husband. Sharia decrees regarding the *mahr* remained intact.

The parliament's response, observed in the new law that overturned the Shah Bano verdict, succinctly captured government policy toward Muslim personal law and Muslim orthodoxy; it also reflected the poor quality of state efforts to implement a Uniform Civil Code (UCC).[48] India's democratic, secular republicanism had floundered with the government's choice not to intervene in the practice of Muslim personal law. By doing so, it also accepted the orthodox segments of the Muslim community as its sole representatives. Professor Zoya Hasan, a distinguished Muslim political scientist, claims that the proposal overturning the court ruling was defective and a perversion of the basic principle of equality.[49] Muslims, especially Muslim women, were again placed beyond the reach of justice and equality.

The ironically entitled 'Muslim Women's Protection of Rights in Divorce Bill' was passed after a campaign headed by the slogan 'What Muslims want'. It reflects the Hindu public's attitude of 'them [the Muslims] and their laws' as opposed to 'we and our customs'.[50] Moderate and liberal Muslims, who had maintained that the Shah Bano decision was not at all detrimental to Islam, were not included in the debate,[51] and neither were Muslim women. It was Orthodox Muslim forces who made the call.[52] Former Supreme Court Justice Iyer wrote a public letter addressed to Rajiv Gandhi stating that the new law was unjust and unconstitutional.[53] Nonetheless, several moderate politicians backed Rajiv Gandhi because the amendment appeared to promote community autonomy in the face of excessive parliamentary power.[54]

Liberal political scientists, including Baxi and Hasan, argued that parliament was not authorized to act contrary to the Constitution, to differentiate between Muslim women and the rest of the population, or to undermine their civil rights.

By passing legislation that circumvented the Supreme Court, parliament had violated several of the Constitution's articles.[55] Several petitions were subsequently filed, such as in the *Maharshi Avadhesh case*, which called for nullification of the 'Supreme Court circumvention law' due to its incongruity with the Constitution.[56] The Supreme Court dismissed the petitions and ruled that it had stated its position in the Shah Bano case and was unwilling to comment further given that the matter was before the legislature.[57]

Much later, in 1995, another Supreme Court decision deviated from its previous non-intervention policy. In the case of Sarla Mudgal,[58] the president of Kalyani, a social action organization, petitioned the Supreme Court in the name of a group of Muslim and Hindu women who were victims of a gap in personal law legislation. India's Supreme Court decided that this case was appropriate for reviewing its position on the existing distinctive personal laws. By doing so it stressed that Hindu personal law had voluntarily introduced liberalizing and democratizing reforms and revisions over the years, since the 1950s, whereas Muslim personal law had persistently refrained from doing so. Similarly, the judges argued that a Uniform Civil Code would hasten national integration and prove that the minorities were prepared to renounce the two nation theory. Within their verdict, they note that numerous Muslim states, such as Syria, had revised their personal laws but that only a minority of India's Muslims was unwilling to do the same:[59]

> In the Indian republic, there was to be only one nation – the Indian nation – and no community could claim to remain a separate entity on the basis of religion .... The desirability of a uniform code can hardly be doubted. But it can concretize only when the social climate is properly built up by society's elites, statesmen amongst leaders who instead of gaining personal mileage rise above and awaken the masses to accept the change.
> ...We, therefore, request the Government of India, through the Prime Minister of the country, to take a fresh look at Article 44 of the Constitution of India and endeavour to secure for the citizens a Uniform Civil Code throughout the territory of India .... We further direct the Government of India through the Secretary, Ministry of Law and Justice to file an affidavit of a responsible officer in this Court ... indicating therein the steps taken and efforts made, by the Government of India, towards securing a 'Uniform Civil Code' for the citizens of India ....[60]

In a still later case, in 1997, a petition presented by the Ahmedabad Women's Action Group[61] gave the Supreme Court an opportunity to revert to its former policy of non-intervention. The petition referred to two issues: the first, a petition to nullify a '*triple talaq*' allowing Muslim males to validate a divorce simply by declaring aloud, three times, 'you are divorced'; the second issue expressed the group's uncertainty about the constitutionality of the 'Supreme Court circumvention law' regarding divorce among Muslim women.[62] In a lengthy opinion, the Supreme Court reiterated its previous position and added that although it is necessary to prevent discrimination and to promote efforts to enact a Uniform Civil Code, the issue had been referred to the legislature. The court was therefore uninterested in creating a situation of 'dual proceedings'.

The court likewise submitted that progress be made in implementing Article 44 with respect to the formulation of a Uniform Civil Code, although it relegated its own proposal to the rather low level of 'a recommendation to Parliament'. Numerous Hindu organizations and Muslim women's groups supported the court's recommendation, but orthodox Muslims were still unprepared to do so.[63] On 23 June 2002, the All India Muslim Personal Law Board announced at a meeting in Hyderabad that Muslims were to continue to carry out their religious charges according to the Koran and the Sharia. Their audience was encouraged not to fear the Hindu 'terrorists' and 'fascists' who were attempting to interfere with their practice of Islam.[64]

By analysing the policy sphere of Muslim religious autonomy in India, we can note a major contradiction between the proclaimed aspirations of a democratic state and its stance towards one of its non-ruling minorities. In short, the multicultural Indian state did not succeed in awarding all its diverse communities the same level of civic and democratic rights.

To intervene or not to intervene? A theoretical perspective

The fact that the Indian government changed the Hindu personal law, and did not change the Muslim personal law, had various consequences. Political theorists disagree about the appropriate policy in such matters.[65] From a communitarian perspective, there is a need for religious self-rule and the state's understanding of both communities' special needs and unique self-identity. Communitarians, such as Amitai Etzioni, Charles Taylor, or Philip Selznick, consider both non-liberal and liberal communities as constitutive collectives in democratic legal cultures because communities are central to the formation of human identity and prime agents for the fulfillment of human needs and interests.[66] Therefore, communities should be protected, and communities should protect the identity practices that the state attempts to marginalize or even eliminate.[67]

On the other hand, legal pluralists, such as Robert Cover, who are, to a large extent, suspicious of state-made law, justify its intervention in communal matters, *if* the communal order generates instances of discrimination between minority members.[68] Whereas individuals often enjoy some level of personal autonomy and protection in most communities, liberal theoreticians, as Chandran Kukathas, argue that it is appropriate for the state to compel members of some communities to relinquish their collective identities and adjust themselves to identities, even if alien to their tradition, since they assume that liberal values and civic rights are sufficient in order to protect all citizens.[69]

Noting this theoretical controversy, it would appear that nationalization of Hindu personal law indicates that the state essentially views Hindus as 'the state' and minorities as foreign elements. By avoiding enforcement of affirmative action for Muslims in the spheres of political representation or public employment, while simultaneously prohibiting Hindus' group rights, the Constitution, which stresses so-called secularism as well as minority protection, actually intensifies the conflict between these two governance principles while also bringing about ideological conflicts and resource competition, and, as a result, it is possible to argue that it threatens the stability of India's democracy.[70]

The question of whether the world's religious systems, including Hinduism and Islam, are compatible with democracy is discussed in length in the academic literature.[71] This research acknowledges the problematic nature of combining religion and state, and does not assume that one religion or another is incompatible with democracy. Furthermore, Smith notes that Pakistan, a Muslim state, reformed its Muslim personal law, introducing changes, including: making the taking of a second wife conditional on the consent of the first wife, and raising the minimum age of marriage from 14 to 16 years.[72] He concludes that India's Muslims have retained a static, stringent, and outdated personal law that undermines the principles of equality and human rights, unlike other religious communities that were apparently more successful in taking meaningful steps toward a Uniform Civic Code.[73] In sum, many conservative Muslim figures and organizations in India view state non-intervention into Muslim personal law as a cornerstone of secular democracy. Hence, this segment of the orthodox Muslim community views itself as the highest authority with respect to any conflict with the government over Muslim personal law.[74]

Religious autonomy to the Muslim minority in India – a political analysis

We have seen that the Uniform Civic Code is a highly charged and complex subject; it may be one of the main causes of conflict in India's political arena, perhaps threatening the stability of the country's democracy. Certainly, some Muslims have met the aspirations motivating the Uniform Civic Code with hatred and suspicion.[75] India's liberal Constitution, therefore, may appear irrelevant in the context of the Muslim personal law. Furthermore, despite declarations, India's governments have been reluctant to exercise their power and have therefore allowed conservative Muslims to enjoy considerable autonomy in this particular area.

The political elite, like the government, perceives orthodox Islam as the hegemonic authority over all decisions pertaining to the Muslim community. The government's preference for non-intervention in religious affairs has been sustained over the years even though inter-communal peace was bought, to some degree, with the denial of human rights and increased stratification, contrary to the spirit of the Indian Constitution. The government has used non-intervention to try to increase stability, maintain public order and reduce minority-government tensions. As mentioned above, the courts have also avoided conflict with those responsible for minority religious affairs, despite the judicial system's liberal interpretations of the Constitution.[76]

Initially formulated during the early days of independence, an informal status quo has apparently been achieved. This amounts to a formal declaration from the state to endeavour to secure a uniform civil code for all its citizens, yet simultaneously the government and other state institutions refrain from practically intervening in Muslim minority internal affairs, even if by doing so the state undermines the value of equality before the law, guaranteed to all India's citizens by the Indian constitution. The cases presented above, of Muslim reaction to state initiatives of change to Muslim personal law, lends support to the proposition that in India any government-initiated attempt to change the status quo in the area of personal law – as opposed to efforts that originate from within the Muslim community itself – incites conflict so bitter that it might threaten the integrity of Indian democracy.

Nevertheless, religious autonomy to the Muslim minority is a double-edged sword. On the one hand it can contribute to collective memory, culture, and identity of the minority. On the other, it may reduce the Muslim minority's participation in Hindu dominated society and politics, and present it as a fundamentalist and less modern community compared to other societal groups.[77]

India is defined as a secular state that does not wish to see the regular interaction of religion and politics in the political realm. Although it was established by its founding fathers as 'a neutral state', generally termed as 'a state of its citizens'; a major part of the dominant Hindu community in India, especially since Jawaharlal Nehru's death, considers itself as the legitimate 'owner' of the state, or the 'core nation'.[78] Such perceptions suggest a special, less good, status for India's non-assimilated minorities, notably the large Muslim minority (13.4% of the population of more than 1.03 billion people) that is often perceived by various state agencies as a potential fifth column, 'potential Pakistani agents', or simply as 'foreigners'.[79]

Syed Shahabuddin, a leading Muslim intellectual, told this writer: 'I feel that being a Muslim in India is like wearing a yellow star in Europe during World War II'. While it may be that this comparison is exaggerated, provocative, and inappropriate, it is impossible to deny his feelings. Shahabuddin explained that discrimination is not performed systematically, as that is forbidden by law. But, in spite of the prohibition on filling in one's religion in official forms, Muslims can be identified by their family names. According to Shahabuddin, a Muslim feels like a less equal citizen in every field of life in India.[80]

As mentioned above, the Muslim community is under-represented in both the political realm and public employment. The state does not apparently choose to change this state of affairs by effective means of affirmative action. In addition, there is state neglect of the Muslim language, Urdu. Moreover, despite the numerous rights to which the Muslim minority is entitled, there is a serious gap between the levels of personal security afforded the Hindu majority in comparison with that provided to minorities, including Muslims. Sadly, inter-communal violence between Hindus and Muslims is all too frequent. India has witnessed frequent, almost yearly communal disturbances, which became more common after Nehru's death in 1964.[81] Overall, since India's independence, more than 12,000 citizens have been killed in communal violence (not including partition in 1947 between India and Pakistan, which cost the lives of half a million). Most of the victims over the years were Muslims.

In this context, we can note a harsh reality, whereby the Muslim minority in India is often anxious about its life and property while the government and its various arms cannot or do not want to protect it.[82] Chandhoke observes that when the history of communal riots and the active participation of the agencies of the state in these riots are addressed, then it becomes evident that the state has not only failed in its agenda of protecting the minorities, but can even be accused of practising discrimination against minority communities, including Muslims.[83] In brief, the various government authorities in India do not do enough to protect the Muslim minority community at the most crucial level: the right to live. It is precisely in the 'secular' Indian democracy, that the lives of the Muslim minority are not valued enough and they do not get appropriate protection.[84] There is a very large difference between the formal definition of the state and actual daily life in India's secular democracy.

Citizenship defined by civic and universalistic, rather than ethnic or religious criteria which would guarantee a principle of inclusion in India's democracy, has been eroded by majoritarian notions of the nation-state.[85] In the view of the current writer, this process is not surprising. In India, the vast pluralism, the trauma of the subcontinent partition, and the constant tension regarding Pakistan has led to four fundamental characteristics of the Indian state: (1) the principle of maintaining territorial unity and thus intolerance for any separatist or secessionist movements; (2) the principle of protecting democracy and a declared commitment of tolerance toward minorities; (3) the principle that the Muslim minority should be entitled to collective rights in the fields of education and religion but that no affirmative action should be put into place in either the public or the private spheres; and (4) the principle that India will not give up (informal) Hindu hegemony of the country.

While these principles are complex and sometimes contradictory, they do help us outline the policies of India's government and its institutions. Hinduism, multilingualism, Muslim demand for widespread autonomy, and secularism as the formal ideology of the state have been hallmarks of the Indian state since its independence. The central contradiction in India is its definition as a secular state, a principle it often fails to uphold. Rather, it frequently acts according to Hindu values and emphasizes Hindu dominance. This fact is evident even in Supreme Court verdicts which typically rule in favour of the minority in India. The court claims time and again, that Hinduism is a tolerant faith, which enables other religions to reside in India. 'It is that tolerance that has enabled Islam, Christianity, Zoroastrianism, Judaism, Buddhism, Jainism and Sikhism to find shelter and support upon this land.'[86] Intentionally or not, this repeated claim implies who is the natural resident in India and who is the 'guest'.

The Muslims in India are entitled to formally equal citizenship, due to the state's claimed secularism and liberal system of laws. In addition, the Indian constitution grants many collective rights. But if the viewpoint shifts from the legal status to the socio-political status, from the level of rights to the level of actualization of those rights, a different picture is revealed: After peeling, metaphorically, the formal layers of the onion of citizenship and deconstructing the citizenship discourses in various levels, it seems clear that Muslims are often excluded from India's mainstream. The meaning of the word 'Us' in the Indian context is in many cases – the Hindu people.[87] Apparently, inclusive formal citizenship does not guarantee equal citizenship for the minority in deeply divided societies.

Conclusion

This article has presented an overview of a very complicated political game of 'give and take' that is taking place in the large and intriguing Indian democracy. Particularly in the spheres of language and minority representation, spheres in which group rights are most needed, the state does not tolerate compromises. It is precisely the religious autonomy sphere that the state is willing to compromise 'for the sake of Indian unity'. The price for this decision is a low status for Muslim women in particular and an offence to the equality principle in general. The article has illustrated how the political establishment in India grants India's Muslims collective rights in this sphere, not because such a decision is constitutionally right but rather in order to maintain inter-communal stability.[88] Intentionally or unintentionally, however, the government policy in this matter supports the formation of negative stereotypes about the minority community, whom many Hindu perceive as backward, fundamentalist, and conservative.

Moreover, by choosing this policy, the state unintentionally encourages the Hindu Right. Paradoxically, it seems that minimal intervention in religious autonomy, such as setting the minimum age for marriage, and prohibiting polygamy, is a cost that the Muslim minority in India should pay, in order to enhance their status in society, and to align according to democratic norms – especially the equality principle. Other Muslim societies and Muslim minorities in the world, as well, were willing to set limited changes to the Muslim personal law.[89]

India, which is defined as a secular democracy, and grants its minority citizens numerous rights, and even has their symbols on national emblems, has nevertheless shifted over the last few decades toward a framework of ethnic democracy,[90] adopting national-Hindu elements for the definition of the collective social good. In fact, many Hindus believe that, whether the recognition of Hindu dominance is constitutional or not, Hindus should benefit from political and cultural dominance concerning shaping the nation's future.[91] India, a proclaimed secular democracy, does not always act according to its self-definition. At the same time, the state does not intervene in Muslim personal law. This policy has ambivalent consequences. Based on research findings, this article has sought to show that giving full religious autonomy to the Muslim minority might not be the best way to practise democratic norms in India, as well as to protect the minority in its multifaceted multicultural society.

Acknowledgments

The author thanks the editor of this special issue, Jeff Haynes, for his constructive comments. In addition, the author would like to mention several institutions and organizations that have generously assisted and funded the research at different stages, for which she is profoundly grateful – The Faculty of Social Science and the Department of Political Science, Tel-Aviv University; The David Horowitz Research Institute on Society and Economy, Tel-Aviv University; Israel Foundations Trustees; The Gilo Center for Citizenship, Democracy and Civic Education, The Hebrew University of Jerusalem; The Kreitman Foundation, Ben-Gurion University of the Negev, Israel.

Notes

1. For a concise presentation of ideal-types of democracies, see Smooha, 'Types of Democracy'.
2. Fukuyama, 'Identity, Immigration and Democracy', 6.
3. Collective or group rights are rights that are granted to certain citizens because they belong to a certain cultural group; rights which stem from the group differentiation. For more details about granting collective rights to minorities, see: Jamal, 'Collective Rights to Indigenous Minorities'; Saban, 'A Lone (Bi-Lingual) Cry in the Dark?'.
4. Barber, *Strong Democracy*; Turner and Hamilton, *Citizenship: Critical Concepts*.
5. Brubaker, 'National Minorities'.
6. Wimmer, 'Who Owns the State?'.
7. Jamal, 'Collective Rights to Indigenous Minorities'.
8. The liberal idea of citizenship – 'the universal citizenship' – tends to separate citizens from non-citizens; and to entitle an equal status to all citizens of the state. Differentiated citizenship is a concept that attempts to empower legal cultures that perceive groups as a way to incorporate individuals into a liberal political culture. To read more about 'differentiated citizenship', see Kymlicka, *Multicultural Citizenship*, 51–2, 95–6; Kook, 'Towards a Rehabilitation of Nation Building'. To read about the distinction between the terms 'universal citizenship' and 'differentiated citizenship', see Jamal, 'Beyond Ethnic Democracy'.
9. Shafir and Peled, *Being Israeli*.
10. Mcmillan, 'Deviant Democratization in India'.
11. Varshney, 'India Defies the Odds'.
12. Citizenship laws in India demand that the state regard each citizen as an individual and not as a member of any religious congregation. That is to say, Indian citizenship is universal. The Indian government does not limit the granting of citizenship according to criteria of ethnicity, religion, race, culture, or language.
13. Mcmillan, 'Deviant Democratization in India', 743.
14. It should be mentioned that there were other reasons for the partition, such as British influence, internal Muslim power conflicts, etc. To read more see: Hasan, *Legacy of a Divided Nation*; Weiner, *The Indian Paradox*; Bose and Jalal, *Nationalism, Democracy and Development*, Chapter 16.
15. In the original plan, Hindustani (an oral tongue that combines Hindi and Urdu and is written in two different scripts: the Devanagari and the Arabic-Persian) was designated as the national language. Following the partition's confirmation in 1947, many Hindus felt the need to 'take revenge on Urdu'. As one expression of this sentiment, members of the Constituent Assembly proposed deleting Urdu from the draft constitution. Accordingly, the following proposal was raised on 15 July 1947, one month before independence: 'That in clause 21, the words "or in Hindustani" should be deleted ... for the words "Hindustani (Hindi or Urdu)", the word "Hindi" would be substituted' (Constituent Assembly, Orders of the Day, 18). Muslims in the Assembly vigorously opposed this action (*Constituent Assembly Debates* (CAD) IX 34, 1339–458). The majority of delegates, however, voted in favour of legislation approving Hindi written in the Devanagari script as the sole official

language of the union (CAD; IX 34, 1486–91; Schedule 343 (1)). For a review on the status of English as an 'associate official language' in India, see Harel-Shalev, *The Status of Minority Languages*, 25–7.
16. For a detailed description of the representation of Muslims in India, and reading on the Muslim partial eligibility to reservations, see The Sachar Report, 189–214.
17. Bhargava, 'On the Persistent Political Under-Representation of Muslims in India'.
18. Basu, 'The Transformation of Hindu Nationalism?', 397.
19. The Constitution of India, article 372.
20. The Constitution of India, article 13.
21. *State of Bombay v. Narasu Appa*. 1952 AIR Bombay, 85 and other cases, decided by India's Supreme Court. For further details see: Mahmood, *Personal Laws in Crisis*, 14–5.
22. For more details, read Hasan, 'Communalism, State Policy and Question of Women's rights'.
23. Ibid, 6. Nehru attempted to introduce changes as early as 1951; however, because the political constellation was inappropriate at the time, his preliminary attempts failed.
24. Galanter, *Law and Society in Modern India*, 156. The collection of laws regulating Hindu personal affairs legislated during 1954–1956, under the inclusive title 'the Hindu Code Act'. It includes the Hindu Marriage Act, 1955; the Hindu Succession Act, 1956; the Hindu Minority and Guardianship Act, 1956 and the Hindu Adoptions and Maintenance Act, 1956.
25. 'Untouchability' refers to a social practice in Hinduism of excluding a specific minority group by regarding them as 'ritually polluted' and segregating them from the mainstream. The *untouchables* (known also as *Harijans* or *Dalits*) are treated as individuals who represent the lowest status in society, even below the Hindu caste system. To read more about this custom, see Galanter, *Law and Society in Modern India*; Weiner, 'Minority Identities'.
26. To learn more about the political struggles re the Hindu civic law, read Newbigin, 'The Codification of Personal Law and Secular Citizenship'.
27. On the fierce Hindu resistance to revision of the Personal Law see Smith, *India as a Secular State*, 277–91.
28. Galanter, 'The Displacement of Traditional Law in Modern India', 252.
29. Jacobsohn, *The Wheel of Law*, 33–4.
30. To read more about the particularly low status of women with respect to marriage and divorce, see Hasan, 'Communalism, State Policy and Question of Women's rights'.
31. *State of Bombay v. Narasu Appa*. 1952 AIR Bombay, 84. Hereinafter Narasu Appa.
32. In a later case, the Supreme Court of UP ruled that polygamy is not 'a required practice' of Hinduism. Therefore, state law was not in question and polygamy was definitely prohibited. For details see: *Ram Prasad v. State of UP*, AIR 1957, Allahabad, 411.
33. Narasu Appa case, 87.
34. Galanter and Krishnan, 'Personal Law and Human Rights', 113–14.
35. *Bai Tahira v. Ali Hussain Fisalli*, 1979 AIR 362; *Fazlunbi v. Kahder Vali*, 1980 AIR 1730.
36. *Shah Bano Begum v. Mohd. Ahmed Khan* 1985 AIR, 0945, SCR (3) 844. hereinafter Shah Bano case.
37. Ibid.
38. Dhavan and Nariman, 'The Supreme Court and Group Life', 274.
39. Mahmood, *Statute Law Relating to Muslims in India*.
40. Mahmood, *Personal Laws in Crisis*.
41. 'The Shah Bano Verdict', *The Statesman*, October 10, 1985.

42. This expression has also been attached to the government decision to allow Hindus to pray in the Ram temple/Babri Mosque in Ayodhya. See: Govt. of India, *The Ninth Annual Report of the Minority Commission*, 171; Rajgopal, *Communal Violence in India*, 54.
43. Zoya Hasan, interview with the author, Delhi, August 8, 2002; Khurshid, interview with the author, Delhi, September 3, 2002.
44. Menon, 'Women and Citizenship', 241–66.
45. Hasan, 'Communalism, State Policy and Question of Women's Rights'.
46. Lok-Sabha Debates (hereinafter LSD), May 5, 1986, 17(45), 451.
47. LSD, 1986, 17(45), 610–24.
48. The decision to propose the legislation also reflects state policy toward women in general and Muslim women in particular. This policy contradicted the platform published by Rajiv Gandhi and the Congress, in which he declared his intention to promote women's rights as partners in state development. *Election Manifesto*, Congress I, 1982, 1989.
49. Hasan, 'Religion and Politics in a Secular State', 283.
50. Ibid., 266.
51. Raghubir, 'Shah Bano Judgment and the Aftermath'.
52. Basu, 'Women and Religious Nationalism in India', 3–4; Hasan, 'Communalism, State Policy and Question of Women's Rights'.
53. Iyer, 'Muslim Women Bill Unjust'.
54. LSD, 1986, 317, 390.
55. Baxi, 'The Shah Bano Reversal', 89–94.
56. *Maharshi Avadhesh v. Union of India*, 1994 Supp 1 SCC 0713.
57. Following is a synopsis of the remarks made in the Maharshi Avadhesh case: 'This is a petition by a party in person under Article 32 of the Constitution. The prayers are twofold. The first prayer is to issue a writ of mandamus to the respondents to consider the question of enacting a common Civil Code for all citizens of India. The second prayer is declare Muslim Women (Protection of Rights on Divorce) Act, 1986 as void being arbitrary and discriminatory and in violation of Articles 14 and 15 of the Fundamental Rights and Articles 44, 38, 39 and 39-A of the Constitution of India. The third prayer is to direct the respondents not to enact Shariat Act in respect of those adversely affecting the dignity and rights of Muslim women and against their protection. These are all matters for the legislature. The Court cannot legislate in these matters. The writ petition is dismissed.'
58. *Sarla Mudgal, President, Kalyani and others v. Union of India and others*; AIR 1995 SC 1531. Among the petitioners, the Hindu Meena Mathur complained that her husband had converted to Islam and taken a Muslim woman as a second wife; as a result, she was now inadequately protected by the law because no personal law statute applied to women in her specific position. In this case, the constitutional issue was whether a person who had married according to Hindu civil code and had converted to Islam was eligible to marry another woman being that Hindus were forbidden to practice bigamy.
59. Ibid.
60. Ibid.
61. *Ahmedabad Women's Action Group v. The Union of India* (1997) 3 SCC 573.
62. Hasan, 'Minority Identity and its Discontents', 38.
63. The only item giving evidence of some progress in Muslim willingness to revise Muslim personal law is unilateral accelerated divorce, commonly practiced by Sunni Muslims. The Supreme Court in Allahabad ruled that the '*triple talaq*' was illegal and that only full divorce proceedings would be considered valid. India's Supreme Court confirmed this decision. 'Muslim Differs on Talaq Procedure',

The Statesman, New Delhi, April 19, 1994; 'Apex Court Review of Triple Talaq', *Hindustan Times*, New Delhi, July 11, 1994. The matter was again reviewed by the Supreme Court in 2001; see: *Daniel Latifi v. Union of India*, 2001 7 SCC 740. In the latter case, numerous Muslims exhorted Muslims to act as courageously as those Hindus who had fought *suttee* (a Hindu practice in which a widow is burned on the grave of her husband; it was declared illegal during the 1956 reform of Hindu personal law) and the discrimination perpetuated by the old Hindu personal law. They also encouraged reform of Muslim personal law, nullification of polygamy and ending 'cruel' divorces, which were anti-Islamic in spirit. Engineer, 'The Role of Muslim Intellectuals'. The High Court in Bombay also ruled the *triple talaq* to be illegal; see: 'Bombay HC: Triple *Talaq* Not Good Enough for Divorce', *The Times of India*, New Delhi, January 21, 2007.

64. Editorial. *Muslim India*, 236, August 2002, 376.
65. Rizzo, Abdel-Latif and Meyer, 'The Relationship between Gender Equality and Democracy', 1151; Evans and Need, 'Explaining Ethnic Polarization', 653; Levey, 'Equality, Autonomy, and Cultural Rights', 215–49.
66. Etzioni, *New Communitarian Thinking*; Selznick, *The Moral Commonwealth*; Taylor, *Sources of the Self*.
67. Barzilai, *Communities and Law*, 34.
68. Minow et al. *Narrative, Violence and the Law*, 13–49; 95–172; 203–38.
69. Kukathas, 'Are There Any Cultural Rights?'. To read more about the liberal school, see Barzilai, *Communities and Law*, 31–3, 303.
70. The current policy simultaneously causes a radicalization of the Hindu right wing; prohibits several civil rights from segments of society; and nonetheless dealing with minority's dissatisfaction from its status in the Indian society.
71. Stepan, 'Religion, Democracy and the Twin Toleration'.
72. Smith, *India as a Secular State*, 422.
73. Ibid., 123.
74. To read more about the judicial and political struggles regarding the Muslim personal law, see All India Muslim Personal Law Board website, at http://www.aimplboard.org (accessed June 10, 2009).
75. Vanaik, *The Furies of Indian Communalism*, 46.
76. Had the Indian Supreme Court used the plea of Muslim personal law hurting fundamental rights in its verdicts re the Muslim personal law, the Muslim personal law was nullified based on Article 13 of the constitution, but the court refrained from doing so.
77. Vanaik, *The Furies of Indian Communalism*, 46; Hasan, 'Religion and Politics in a Secular State'.
78. Brubaker, *Nationalism Reframed*; Pandey, 'Can A Muslim Be an Indian?'; Hasan, *Legacy of a Divided Nation*.
79. Hasan, *Legacy of a Divided Nation*; Shahabuddin, 'Communal Violence – A Challenge to Plurality', 104–17.
80. Shahabuddin, interview with the author, Delhi, September 4, 2002.
81. The incidents of communal violence were frequent, both under the rightist BJP leadership as well as under the Congress party-led coalitions. Violence takes place mainly in Urban India, in the northern and western states. For a detailed analysis of inter-communal riots in India, see Varshney, *Ethnic Conflict and Civic Life*; Brass, *The Production of Hindu–Muslim Violence*.
82. Baxi, 'Notes of Holocaustian Politics', 77.
83. Chandhoke, *Beyond Secularism*, 65.
84. Basu, 'When Local Riots are not Merely Local'; Aslam, 'State Communalism', 278, 280–1.

85. For a further discussion of the erosion of the universalistic citizenship discourse in India, see Hasan, 'Religion and Politics in a Secular State'.
86. *Dr M. Ismail Faruqui and others v. Union of India and others*, 1994, (6) SCC 360. Paragraph 159.
87. Varshney, *Ethnic Conflict and Civic Life*.
88. The reason a uniform matrimony law was not legislated in the early days of India is that India's founders did not want to cause too strong a jolt to the Muslim public, who felt persecuted and insecure in the years that succeeded the partition. During the first years of India's independence the Congress Party established precedent in acquiescing to demands from the religious sector so that even today it is hard to overturn that precedent and reform the Muslim matrimony law to enforce equality for India's Muslim women and the general population.
89. Even Islamic states like Syria and Pakistan initiated adjustments in the Muslim personal law. Another example could be found within the Muslim minority in Israel; since all citizens in Israel (Jews, Christians, and Muslims) are confined to minimum age of marriage civic law, and to prohibition of polygamy.
90. Ethnic democracy is characterized by four elements: 1. All citizens enjoy identical individual civil rights; 2. certain collective rights are granted to ethnic minorities; 3. One ethnic group, which constitutes the majority, legally governs the country and is regarded as if were an absolute majority; 4. The dominant group's ideological and practical commitment to the democratic idea. It is not a liberal democracy, but a flawed one. Smooha, Types of Democracy.
91. Varshney, *Ethnic Conflict and Civic Life*, 57.

Note on contributor

Ayelet Harel-Shalev is a Post-Doctoral Fellow in the Politics and Government Department, Ben-Gurion University. Her forthcoming book is titled *The Challenge of Sustaining Democracy in Deeply Divided Societies: Citizenship, Rights, and Ethnic Conflicts in India and Israel* (Rowman & Littlefield 2010). It is based partly on her PhD dissertation, which won the Israeli Political Science Association (ISPSA) prize for outstanding doctoral dissertation, 2006. She is specializing in comparative political studies; Indian politics and society; ethnic conflicts; and Israeli politics and society.

Bibliography

Ahmedabad Women's Action Group v. the Union of India, 1997 3 SCC 573.
'Apex Court Review of Triple Talaq'. *Hindustan Times*, New Delhi, July 11, 1994.
Aslam, Mohammad. 'State Communalism and the Reassertion of Muslim Identity'. In *The State, Political Processes and Identity*, ed. Z. Hasan, S.N. Jha, and R. Khan, 270–82. New-Delhi: Sage, 1989.
Bai Tahira v. Ali Hussain Fisalli, 1979, AIR 362.
Barber, Benjamin R. *Strong Democracy: Participatory Politics for a New Age*. Berkley: University of California Press, 1992.
Barzilai, Gad. *Communities and Law: Politics and Cultures of Legal Identities*. Ann Arbor: University of Michigan Press, 2003.
Basu, Amrita. 'Women and Religious Nationalism in India: An Introduction'. *Bulletin of Concerned Asian Scholars* 25, no. 4 (1993): 3–4.
Basu, Amrita. 'When Local Riots are not Merely Local'. In *State and Politics in India*, ed. Partha Chatterjee, 390–435. New Delhi: Oxford University Press, 1997.

Basu, Amrita. 'The Transformation of Hindu Nationalism?'. In *Transforming India: Social and Political Dynamics of Democracy*, ed. Francine R. Frankel, Zoya Hasan, Rajeev Bhagava, and Balveer Arora, 378–404. New Delhi: Oxford University Press, 2000.

Baxi, Upendra. 'The Shah Bano Reversal: Coup against the Constitution'. In *Inhuman Wrongs and Human Rights*, ed. Upendra Baxi, 89–94. New Delhi: Har-Anand Publication, 1994.

Baxi, Upendra. 'Notes of Holocaustian Politics'. *Seminar* 513 (May 2002): 77–83.

Bhargava, Rajeev. 'On the Persistent Political Under-Representation of Muslims in India'. Paper presented at the 'Multiculturalism and the Antidiscrimination Principle' conference, Ramat-Gan College of Law, December 10–12, 2005.

'Bombay HC: Triple *Talaq* Not Good Enough for Divorce'. *The Times of India*, New Delhi, January 21, 2007.

Bose, Sugata Ayesha Jalal, ed. *Nationalism, Democracy and Development: State and Politics in India*. New Delhi: Oxford University Press, 1999.

Brass, Paul. *The Production of Hindu-Muslim Violence in Contemporary India*. Seattle: University of Washington Press, 2005.

Brubaker, Rogers. 'National Minorities, Nationalizing State and External National Homelands in the New Europe'. *Daedalus* 124, no. 2 (1995): 107–32.

Brubaker, Rogers. *Nationalism Reframed: Nationhood and the National Question in the New-Europe*. Cambridge: Cambridge University Press, 1996.

Chandhoke, Neera. *Beyond Secularism: The Rights of Religious Minorities*. New Delhi: Oxford University Press, 1999.

Congress I party. *Election Manifesto*, 1982, 1989.

Daniel Latifi v. Union of India, 2001 7 SCC 740.

Dhavan, Rajeev and Fali S. Nariman. 'The Supreme Court and Group Life'. In *Supreme But Not Infallible*, ed. B.N. Kirpal, A.H. Desai, G. Subramanium, R. Dhavan, R. Ramachandran, Chapter 14. New Delhi: Oxford University Press, 2000.

'Editorial'. *Muslim India* 236. August 2002, 376.

Engineer, Ashgar Ali. 'The Role of Muslim Intellectuals'. *The Hindu*, New Delhi, August 28, 1998.

Etzioni, Amitai. *New Communitarian Thinking: Persons, Virtues, Institutions, and Communities*. Charlottesville: University Press of Virginia, 1995.

Evans, Geoffrey, and Ariana Need. 'Explaining Ethnic Polarization over Attitudes Towards Minority Rights in Eastern Europe: A Multilevel Analysis'. *Social Science Research* 31, no. 4 (2002): 653–80.

Fazlunbi v. Kahder Vali, 1980, AIR 1730.

Fukuyama, Francis. 'Identity, Immigration and Democracy'. *Journal of Democracy* 17, no. 2 (2006): 5–20.

Galanter, Marc. 'The Displacement of Traditional Law in Modern India'. In *Law and Society in Modern India*, ed. Marc Galanter. New Delhi: Oxford University Press, 1989.

Galanter, Marc. *Law and Society in Modern India*. New Delhi: Oxford University Press, 1997.

Galanter, Marc, and Jayanath Krishnan. 'Personal Law and Human Rights in India and Israel'. *Israel Law Review* 34 (2000): 101–33.

Govt. of India. *The Ninth Annual Report of the Minority Commission*, for 4.1986-3.1987, Delhi, 1987.

Harel-Shalev, Ayelet. *The Status of Minority Languages in Deeply Divided Societies*. Tel-Aviv: Harold Hartog School of Government and Policy, TAU, 2005.

Hasan, Mushirul. 'Minority Identity and its Discontents: Ayodhya and its Aftermath'. *South Asia Bulletin* 14, no. 2 (1994): 38.

Hasan, Mushirul. *Legacy of a Divided Nation: India's Muslims since Independence*. New Delhi: Oxford University Press, 2001.

Hasan, Zoya. 'Communalism, State Policy and Question of Women's Rights in Contemporary India'. *Bulletin of Concerned Asian Scholars* 25, no. 4 (1993): 5–15.
Hasan, Zoya. 'Religion and Politics in a Secular State: Law, Community and Gender'. In *Politics and the State in India*, ed. Zoya Hasan, 269–89. New Delhi: Sage, 2000.
Hasan, Zoya. 'Interview with the author', Delhi, August 8, 2002.
Indian Parliament. Lok-Sabha Debates (hereinafter LSD)
Iyer, Krishna. 'Muslim Women Bill Unjust'. *Indian Express*, New Delhi, March 4, 1986.
Jacobsohn, Gary J. *The Wheel of Law*. Princeton, NJ: Princeton University Press, 2003.
Jamal, Amal. 'Beyond Ethnic Democracy: State Structure, Multicultural Conflict and Differentiated Citizenship in Israel'. *New Political Science* 24, no. 3 (2002): 411–31.
Jamal, Amal. 'Collective Rights to Indigenous Minorities – Theoretical and Normative Aspects'. In *The Status of the Arab Minority in the Jewish Nation State*, ed. Elie Rekhess and Sara Ozacky-Lazar, 27–44. Tel-Aviv: Dayan Center, TAU, 2005.
Khurshid, Salman. Interview with the author, Delhi, September 3, 2002.
Kook, Rebecca B. 'Towards a Rehabilitation of Nation Building and the Reconstruction of Nations'. In *Ethnic Challenges to the Modern Nation State*, ed. Shlomo Ben-Ami, Yoav Peled and Alberto Spektorowski, 42–64. Houndmills, Basingstoke: Macmillan, 2000.
Kukathas, Chandran. 'Are there any Cultural Rights?'. In *The Rights of Minority Cultures*, ed. Will Kymlicka, 228–55. Oxford: Oxford University Press, 1995.
Kymlicka, Will. *Multicultural Citizenship*. Oxford: Clarendon, 1995.
Levey, Geoffrey Brahm. 'Equality, Autonomy, and Cultural Rights'. *Political Theory* 25, no. 2 (1997): 215–49.
Maharshi Avadhesh v. Union of India, 1994, Supp 1 SCC 0713.
Mahmood, Tahir. *Personal Laws in Crisis*. Delhi: Metropolitan Book Co. 1986.
Mahmood, Tahir. *Statute Law Relating to Muslims in India—A Study in Constitutional and Islamic Perspective*. New Delhi: Institute of Objective Studies, 1995.
Mcmillan, Alistair. 'Deviant Democratization in India'. *Democratization* 15, no. 4 (2008): 733–49.
Menon, Nivedita. 'Women and Citizenship'. In *Wages of Freedom: Fifty Years of the Indian Nation-State*, ed. Partha Chatterjee, 241–66. New Delhi: Oxford University Press, 1998.
Minow, Martha, Michael Ryan, and Austin Sarat, eds. *Narrative, Violence and the Law: The Essays of Robert Cover*. Ann Arbor: University of Michigan Press, 1992.
'Muslim Differs on Talaq Procedure'. *The Statesman*, New Delhi, April 19, 1994.
Newbigin, Eleanor. 'The Codification of Personal Law and Secular Citizenship'. *Indian Economic & Social History Review* 46, no. 1 (2009): 83–104.
Pandey, Gyanendra. 'Can A Muslim Be an Indian?'. *Comparative Studies of Society and History* 41, no. 4 (1999): 608–29.
Raghubir, Malhotra. 'Shah Bano Judgment and the Aftermath'. *The Economic Times*, New Delhi, March 30, 1986.
Rajgopal, P.R. *Communal Violence in India*. New Delhi: Uppal Publishing House with Center for Policy Research, 1987.
Ram Prasad v. State of UP, AIR 1957, Allahabad, 411.
Rizzo, Helen, Abdel-Hamid Abdel-Latif, and Katherine Meyer. 'The Relationship between Gender Equality and Democracy: A Comparison of Arab versus Non-Arab Muslim Societies'. *Sociology: The Journal of the British Sociological Association* 41, no. 6 (2007): 1151–70.
Saban, Ilan. 'A Lone (Bi-Lingual) Cry in the Dark?, Following *Adalah et al. v. Tel-Aviv-Jaffa et al.* Case'. *Iyunei Mishpat* 27 (2003): 109–38.
Sachar, Rajinder Head. 'Social, Economic and Educational Status of the Muslim Community of India report'. New Delhi, 2006. Hereinafter The Sachar Report.

Sarla Mudgal, President, Kalyani and others v. Union of India and others, AIR 1995 SC 1531.
Selznick, Philip. *The Moral Commonwealth: Social Theory and the Promise of Community*. Berkeley: University of California Press, 1992.
Shafir, Gershon, and Yoav Peled. *Being Israeli – The Dynamics of Multiple Citizenship*. Cambridge: Cambridge University Press, 2002.
Shah Bano Begum v. Mohd. Ahmed Khan, AIR, 1985 SC 0945, SCR (3) 844. Hereinafter Shah Bano case.
Shahabuddin, Syed. 'Communal Violence – A Challenge to Plurality'. In *Communal Riots in Post Independence India* ed. Ashgar Ali Engineer. 2nd ed, 104–17. Hyderabad: Sangam Books, 1991.
Shahabuddin, Syed. Interview with the author, Delhi, September 4, 2002.
Smith, D. Eugene. *India as a Secular State*. Princeton: Princeton University Press, 1963.
Smooha, Sammy. 'Types of Democracy and Modes of Conflict Management in Ethnically Divided Societies'. *Nations and Nationalism* 8, no. 4 (2002): 423–31.
State of Bombay v. Narasu Appa (1952), AIR Bombay, 84. Hereinafter Narasu Appa.
Stepan, Alfred. 'Religion, Democracy and the Twin toleration'. *Journal of Democracy* 11, no. 4 (2000): 37–57.
Taylor, Charles. *Sources of the Self: The Making of Modern Identity*. Cambridge: Harvard University Press, 1989.
The Constitution of India, article 372, article 13.
'The Shah Bano Verdict'. *The Statesman*, October 10, 1985.
Turner, Bryan S. and Peter Hamilton. *Citizenship: Critical Concepts*. London: Routledge, 1994.
Vanaik, Achin. *The Furies of Indian Communalism*. London: Verso, 1997.
Varshney, Ashutosh. 'India Defies the Odds: Why Democracy Survives'. *Journal of Democracy* 9, no. 3 (1998): 36–50.
Varshney, Ashutosh. *Ethnic Conflict and Civic Life: Hindus and Muslims in India*. Ann-Harbor, MI: Yale University Press, 2002.
Weiner, Myron. *The Indian Paradox*. Newbury Park, CA: Sage, 1989.
Weiner, Myron. 'Minority Identities'. In *Politics in India*, ed. Sudipta Kaviraj, 241–53. New-Delhi: Oxford University Press, 1997.
Wimmer, Andreas. 'Who Owns the State? Understanding Ethnic Conflict in Post-Colonial Societies'. *Nations and Nationalism* 3, no. 4 (1997): 631–66.

Conclusion: religion, democratization and secularization

Jeffrey Haynes

London Metropolitan University, UK

The overarching theme of this special issue was the attempts by various religious actors – Christian, Muslim, and Jewish – to try to assert their values and pursue their goals in variable political circumstances. We saw that they sought to do this in contexts characterized not only by secularization and political changes, some of which emanate from within countries, but also as a result of external pressures, often a consequence of globalization.

The countries and regions upon which we focused in this special issue are not unique. In other words, a large number of countries around the world now feature increasingly vocal political contributions from various religious actors. Sometimes they have been ascendant and now they appear to be in decline. For example, in officially secular India, there have been numerous examples of militant Hinduism in recent years, including the emblematic storming and destruction of the Babri Masjid mosque by Hindu militants at Ayodhya in 1992. Nearly 20 years ago, this event was widely seen as instrumental in transforming the country's political landscape, to the extent that a Hindu nationalist political party, the Bharatiya Janata Party (BJP), grew in the 1990s to swift political prominence, briefly to appear dominant. From the mid-1990s, the BJP served in several coalition governments and until 2004 was the leading party in government. Elections in that year however confirmed the return to prominence of the secular Congress party, the 'natural' party of government for many years since India gained its independence in 1947.[1] In addition, in Israel Jewish religious parties regularly serve in government and do so in the current Netanyahu administration; the religious right has been a consistent political presence in the USA, with a significant voice at election times; the Muslim world is widely and often heavily influenced by political Islamism; and the Roman Catholic Church played a leading role in recent turns to democracy in, *inter alia*, Spain, Poland, and numerous Latin American and African countries. Overall, we have seen numerous examples of recent religious involvement in politics in various parts of the world, in both domestic and international contexts; in many cases, various religious actors collectively have major impacts upon both democratization and democracy.

In recent years, scholars have identified a range of religious actors with a variety of political goals. This special issue has examined political activities of selected religious actors in primarily Christian, Muslim and Jewish contexts, in Europe, the Middle East and Sub-Saharan Africa. The basic hypothesis of the contributors was that various religious actors – including Islamist groups and various Christian entities – have an impact – sometimes a considerable impact – upon issues of democratization, democracy, and secularization in these countries and regions.

Contributors worked from an understanding that, around the world in recent years, numerous religious actors of various kinds demonstrably do affect a range of political outcomes in various ways. However, despite this recognition, there is still a relative lack of clear understanding regarding what they *do*, of importance in enabling us to understand clearly *why*, *how* and *when* religious actors act politically. To conceptualize these issues we sought to answer a key question in the special issue: *Why, how and when do religious actors seek to influence political outcomes, in particular in relation to secularization and democratization in various countries and regions*? This question did not of course arise in a vacuum. It followed three decades of religion's 'reintroduction' into politics, following associated processes of deprivatization.

Religion and the 'return' to politics

The background is that prior to the eighteenth century and the subsequent formation and development of the modern (secular) international state system, religion was a key ideology that often stimulated political conflict between societal groups both within and between countries. Following the Peace of Westphalia in 1648 and subsequent development of centralized states first in Western Europe and then via European colonization to most of the rest of the world, the political importance of religion declined around the world, including as an organizing ideology both domestically and internationally.

In the early twenty-first century, however, there is clear resurgence of political involvement involving a range of religious entities. This has been especially noticeable in the post-cold war era (that is, since 1989) in all regions of the world, including among the so-called 'world religions' (Buddhism, Christianity, Confucianism, Hinduism, Islam and Judaism). Although what started this development is open to question, many scholars would agree on the importance of the Islamist Iranian revolution of 1978–1979 as a key event that definitively marked the 'reappearance' of political religion in global politics. This was such an epochal event because the government of putatively 'modern' and 'secular'

Iran decided to remove religion from the public realm in the interests of 'progress' and 'development', like Turkey decades before, and pursue a consciously Western-derived, secular development model.

But that was not all. Over the last three decades, scholars have sought to explain numerous examples of religious actors acting politically around the world, including in Europe, that most apparently secular of regions. While in Europe it was long believed that religion was increasingly marginal in terms of its public role, in recent years political controversies have raged over issues such as the wearing of headscarves in schools in France and elsewhere, as Barras explains in her article, and the mention of Christianity in the putative European Constitution. More generally, as the contributions in this special issue by Künkler and Leininger and Barras individually emphasize, religious issues are of growing importance in many European polities and in an overall European context. A recent book edited by Byrnes and Katzenstein[2] focuses on effects that the recent enlargement of the European Union (EU) – to include countries with different and stronger religious traditions, including, putatively, Turkey – may have on the EU as a whole, especially on its presumed homogeneity and assumed secular nature. When examined through the focal point of the region's main transnational religious communities – Catholicism, Protestantism, Orthodoxy and Islam – it is clear that various religious factors are not stepping stones but stumbling blocks towards Europe's further integration. This is because each of the religious traditions are putting forward concepts of European identity and European union that differ substantially from how the European integration process is generally understood by political leaders and scholars. Rapid secularization in Western Europe over the last few decades has not however substantially diminished the continuing unease with which many non-Muslim Europeans consider the presence of Islam and European Muslims in their midst, as Barras's article highlights. Exacerbated by 11 September 2001, the subsequent American and British involvement in Afghanistan and Iraq, the March 2004 Madrid bombs and those in London on 7 July 2005, societal unease has centred on several concerns. Both secular European elites and Europe's religious Muslim citizens have been concerned with the issue of how to assimilate and incorporate different cultural backgrounds into the societal and political fabric of their countries and by extension Europe overall. There is also however another factor: a fundamental division between the 'secular' – regarded by many Europeans as 'normal', 'progressive', and 'enlightened' – and the 'religious' – widely regarded as 'backward' and 'reactionary'.

Clearly, the issue of the role and position of Muslims in relation to issues of secularization and democracy is central to our understanding more generally of the nature of the relationship between religion and politics in Europe. However, among religious actors not only Muslims seek to pursue political and societal goals. Davie (2000) reminds us that it is not only Islam which falls into this context in Europe. She underlines that there is a particular emphasis in the region on (1) currents of religion outside the mainstream churches, (2) the significance of the religious factor more generally in European societies, and (3) how

Europe fits in overall parameters of faith around the world. Davie is particularly interested in what she calls 'European exceptionalism'. This is a reference to patterns of religion in Europe that are not prototypical of global religiosity, but peculiar to the European continent. It follows that the relatively low levels of religious activity in modern Europe are not simply the result of early modernization; they are part of what it means to be European and need to be understood in these terms. In a more recent book, Davie[3] examines Europe from the outside, asking what forms of religion are widespread in the modern world but do not occur in most parts of Europe. One important example she notes is Pentecostalism, a religious tradition close to the charismatic Christianity that Ganiel examines in Zimbabwe in her article in this special issue.

Ramadan argues that Islam can and should feel at home in Europe and elsewhere in the West.[4] He focuses on Islamic law (*Sharia*) and tradition in order to analyse whether Islam is in conflict with 'Western' ideals, including liberal democracy. According to Ramadan, there is no contradiction between them. He also identifies several key areas where Islam's universal principles can be 'engaged' in the West, including education, inter-religious dialogue, economic resistance and spirituality. As the number of Muslims living in the West grows, the question of what it means to be a Western Muslim becomes increasingly important to the futures of both Islam and the West. While the media are focused, some would say obsessed, on radical political Islam, Ramadan claims a 'silent revolution' is sweeping Islamic communities in the West, as Muslims actively seek ways to live in harmony with their faith within a Western context. 'Western' Muslims, both women and men – living, *inter alia*, in Denmark, France, Germany, the Netherlands, Spain, the United Kingdom and the United States – are now in many cases reshaping their religion into one that is faithful to the principles of Islam, albeit increasingly contoured by European and American cultures, and definitively rooted in Western societies. Roy also examines the issue of Muslims in the West.[5] He is interested in the prejudices and simplifications used in much popular culture and media in the West regarding Muslims. Like Ramadan, Roy explores how individual Muslims are reacting to (not necessarily against) globalization and westernization, informed by various political and social issues.

Religion, secularization and democratization

Captured both in the title of the special issue and in the contents of its two constitutive sections, our general concern was to examine what happens when religion interacts or overlaps with democratization in various countries and regions. We also had two specific concerns: first, how religion can challenge or support democratization attempts, and secondly, how this may come about in contexts of secularization. The first section of the special issue focused upon the issue of religious actors' involvement in democratization in specific countries and regions in Europe, Africa, the Middle East and Asia. The second section examined how religious actors attempt to act politically, including in relation to democratization, in circumstances characterized by secularization. Our examples here included: Turkey, France and India.

We saw that, despite globalization and the associated development of transnational communities and networks, neither transnational Islamic citizenship (the *umma*) nor regional citizenship (EU) nor any other forms of what might be called post-national citizenship have replaced *national* citizenship; nor is there any indication that such a development might occur in the near future. In other words, *individual* rights and *nation*-states are the typical fundaments of membership rules and citizenship in individual countries. In Safran's recent edited book,[6] contributors examine the political roles of religion in various countries and regions, focusing on Western and East-Central Europe, North America, the Middle East and South Asia. The conclusions were that many countries in these regions are comparable in three main ways: (1) they are committed to constitutional rule, (2) embrace a more or less secular culture, and (3) feature formal guarantees of freedom of religion. Yet in all the cases examined in the special issue, religion affects politics and political systems in some form of legal establishment, semi-legitimation, subvention, and/or selective institutional arrangements. In addition, its role is also reflected both societally and politically in other ways, including in relation to: cultural norms, electoral behaviour and public policies. The overall finding is that while relationships between religion and politics come in many varieties in different countries, all are faced with three major challenges: modernity, democracy and the increasingly multi-ethnic and multi-religious nature of many societies.

Troy's article in this special issue focuses upon the transnational role of the Roman Catholic Church in encouraging democratization. In relation to Poland, for example, a country where Catholics comprise 95% of the population, the main issue was the political role of the Catholic Church in relation to the post-World War II communist regime, underwritten by the Soviet Union until its dissolution in 1991. Poland is now beset by various 'moral conflicts', where secular and religious world views collide. What this leads to is that, despite continuing processes of individual detachment from traditional religion, both the secular state and 'non-religious' parts of society are obliged to accept the involvement of often resurgent religious communities in the public realm, involving in many cases a focus on often controversial issues of relevance to religion, covering local, national and sometimes international concerns, as troy explains. For example, under current conditions of swift and significant biotechnological developments and corresponding European efforts to harmonize policy regulations, national policies in all European countries are increasingly influenced by moral questions, as Barras' article underlines in relation both to France and Turkey. Note however this does not mean that religion necessarily gains the upper hand in such debates nor is able to achieve the results it would prefer.

While concerns about, for example, the legalization of genetic engineering or euthanasia pose ethical problems to all liberal democracies, the quest for a liberal abortion regime and an agreed legal status for homosexual partnerships are also particularly salient issues, especially in predominantly Catholic and Orthodox Christian societies, both in Europe and elsewhere. In predominantly Catholic Poland, as Troy notes, this was not the outcome that was necessarily expected following the decline of communist rule and subsequent democratization. Nevertheless, because the theme of societal values – especially those concerning family life and sexual ethics – are fundamental to the Catholic Church's teaching and societal position, it is hardly surprising that these concerns have become increasingly significant.

Out of the closet: the public and political role of religion

Casanova noted nearly 20 years ago, that 'religion continues to have and will likely continue to have a public dimension'.[7] All the contributions to this special issue abundantly support Casanova's perceptive observation, while taking the basic observation further, furnishing both nuance and detail. In relation to the Roman Catholic Church, for example, religious deprivatization in post-communism (Poland), post-Franco (Spain) or past-Marcos (the Philippines) influenced significantly how the Church saw its societal and religious position: resolutely to defend what it sees as its corporate interests, as well as those of its 'flock', in the public sphere. The recent era of democratic transition and in some cases eventual democratic consolidation also impacted upon wider relationships: between society, public religion and politics in the context of a 'moral conflict', an issue of key importance to the wider issues of both democratization and secularization in the society.

When we turned in the special issue away from Europe, we saw similar examples of involvement of religious entities in a range of political questions. For example, both Baumgart-Ochse and Jamal separately examined the issue of the relationship between politics and religion in contemporary Israel, in a context informed by concerns about morality in modern circumstances of, *inter alia*, globalization. They noted that, against the predictions of the secularization paradigm that forecasted the public demise of religion and consequent irrelevance for public life, religion actually has lost none of its social and political significance in Israel. Indeed, it consistently plays a central role in political and social life. Over the years, Casanova has described this sequence of events as a process of religious deprivatization which refuses secularization's imperative: to relegate religion to the margins of society and keep it there.[8] Instead, in Israel religion has developed over the last three or four decades as a political force to be reckoned with.

Israel is an archetypical example, which highlights a more general conclusion: around the world, religious movements of various kinds now regularly, often persistently, clash with secularizing trends to try to protect their preferred religiously-oriented way of life,[9] in what is sometimes referred to as a 'culture war'. In Israel, the notion of culture war refers to a tense social and political context, characterized by a growing schism between two poles – the 'religious' and the 'secular' – polarized by different values and moving towards what some see as an 'inevitable' clash over the precise boundaries of state and society. While dramatic events and statements at times give credence to the thesis, overall however the evidence of a culture war in Israel, waged both locally and globally, involving an advancing, confident secularism and an equally resilient, resurgent religion, is inconclusive. As a consequence, the issue becomes something different: not only how and in what contexts religion and secularism are advancing or withdrawing but also in what realms are these dynamics operating and how the issue affects conceptions of citizenship in Israeli. As a result, what we see is not a 'culture war' between two coherent groups of citizens with set agendas – but rather different struggles waged in different realms, involving different constituencies and with different levels of political intensity.

Comparing the case of Israel with other countries enables us to conclude that the former is a highly volatile example of a world trend of increasing but varied secular–religious clashes with, on the one hand, a territorial debate strongly informed by religious dogma and, on the other hand, a secularizing public sphere in the context of a societal religious resurgence. Two major developments underscore the concern of a culture war. The first is the overlap between religiosity/secularity and hawkish/dovish perceptions that turns the question of Israel's future borders into a religious debate. The second development is the erosion of status quo church–state arrangements, which once defined the role of religion in public life in Israel, from the regulation of marriage to the observation of the Sabbath as a day of rest.

Moving on from a focus on democratization, which occupied the first section of the special issue, the second key theme of the special issue is the relationship between secularization, democratization and democracy. Among other relationships, articles in the special issue focused on the often-noted social and political resurgence of Islam in the Muslim world; Turkey was the main case study in this regard, with separate articles from Grigoriadis, Gözaydın and Barras. Collectively, their findings underscore an often-repeated point: there is a widespread rise of political Islam or 'Islamism', which may incorporate local, national, regional and/or international networks. In addition, Gözaydın highlights a relatively little known, but important, phenomenon: connections between political Islam, so-called 'Islamic economics', and transnational Islamist business networks in Turkey. The relevant transnational networks are reflective of processes of globalization and its pervasive forces that foster extensive, sometimes unexpected, linkages involving various actors and spheres. Religion-based networks are no exceptions in this overarching trend.

This focus on Turkey includes a perusal of what is sometimes known as *homo-Islamicus*, with reference to 'Islamic economics', epitomizing what may be understood as an ideational legitimacy which fits in well philosophically with current, dominant discourses of neo-liberalism. Islamic finance institutions in Turkey facilitate the workings of Islamic economics. Turkey is a particularly interesting example as it is a country which is often to be 'looking West while moving East', a reference to the country's European aspirations albeit with roots in

Muslim culture. As both Grigoriadis and Gözaydın note, Islamic business in Turkey has strong linkages with the recent upsurge of political Islam, not least involving serving members of the current government, under the control of the AK Party (Justice and Development Party). Their concern was to understand the interaction of both transnational and national Islamic business networks; expansion of Islamic finance and ideational factors sometimes referred to as the so-called 'quiet Islamic Reformation' or 'Islamic Calvinism' which they claim is taking place in Turkey at the present time.

Overall, their contributions highlight that Islamic capital began to be an important factor in Turkey's economy from the 1980s, with connections to the recent unprecedented and emphatic rise of political Islam in the country. In short, we saw the development of intertwined processes: the rise of transnational Islamist networks of business which facilitated dispersion of new ideas; and connections between these networks and political Islam. We saw political outcomes linked to emergence, development and expansion of Islamic networks involving various economic actors.

The issue of secularization and its impact on social and political processes is also the concern of Harel-Shalev's case study on India. Her article highlights the ambivalent effect of religious autonomy in India and the outcome for both continued democratization and the status of democracy in the country. She explains that the Indian constitution guarantees autonomy to its religious minorities, and promises the minorities the freedom independently to manage their religious affairs in addition to a proportional share of the budget. At the same time, the constitution emphasizes the aspiration to legislate 'uniform personal laws' for all the citizens of India in accordance with the principles of secularism, equality and with India's self-definition as a civic nation. Nevertheless, as Harel-Shalev notes, this recommendation has remained just that: a proposal that has not been implemented. The state has constituted a civic law for Hindus, which links Hinduism to democratic principles. In this sense, the state has nationalized Hinduism, and the government has assumed authority and reformed Hindu civic and marriage laws. However, although they have tried, the state's legal and political institutions have not interfered thus far with Muslim marriage and religious laws. It is assumed that India's Muslims are committed to the *Sharia* – while Hindus must obey the state's civic laws. By avoiding enforcement of affirmative action for Muslims in the spheres of political representation or public employment, while simultaneously prohibiting Hindus' group rights, and providing religious autonomy to the Muslim minority, the Constitution, which stresses so-called secularism as well as minority protection, intensifies the conflict between these two governance principles. Harel-Shalev's conclusion is that this situation leads both to ideological conflicts and resource competition as well as posing a threat to the stability of India's democracy.

Jamal provides evidence for the highly controversial nature of the role of Islamist parties in the Middle East. In many cases, for example the Muslim Brotherhood in Egypt, Islamist movements have decided to take part in conventional politics; often, with considerable electoral success. Nevertheless, Jamal opines that such attempts to play the 'game' of political participation are typically treated with considerable suspicion by domestic governments, domestic political opponents and international actors, including the United States and the European Union. On the other hand, there is a quandary, especially for the external actors. It is this: not to recognize the political clout of Islamists in a political system seeking regeneration is to make democratization very difficult or impossible to achieve. Thus, some scholars and policy-makers see Islamism as a potential pro-democracy resource, while others see them as enemies of democracy and potentially authoritarian. Such polarizing attitudes are generally the product of an attempt to establish what can be considered the true nature of such movements, particularly with respect to their democratic credentials and commitment. Central to this question is the relationship between democracy and secularization: what should the relationship between them be? Jamal's case study of Egypt and Turkey provides no clear answer to this difficult question.

There is also an ambiguity in Ganiel's case study of Zimbabwe, and the social and political role of a specific charismatic church in that country. She notes that, not just in Zimbabwe but also in Africa more generally, charismatic Christianity has been caricatured as an inhibitor of democratization. Its adherents are said either to withdraw from the rough and tumble of politics ('pietism') or to preach a prosperity gospel that encourages believers to pour their resources into their churches in the hope that God will 'bless' them. Both courses of action are said to encourage such people to be politically quietist, with no interest in democratization or other forms of political activity. This is said to thwart democratization. This article utilizes an ethnographic case study of a 'progressive' charismatic congregation in Harare, Zimbabwe, in 2007, to provide evidence that 'pietism' and 'prosperity' are not the only options for charismatic Christianity. Drawing on the concept of 'spiritual capital,' it argues that some varieties of charismatic Christianity have the resources to contribute to democratization. For example, this congregation's self-styled 'de-institutionalization' process is opening up new avenues for people to learn democratic skills and develop a worldview that is relationship-centred, participatory, and anti-authoritarian. The article concludes that spiritual capital can be a useful tool for analysing the role of religions in democratizations. It notes, however, that analysts should take care to identify and understand what variety of spiritual capital is generated in particular situations, focusing on the worldviews it produces and the consequences of those worldviews for democratization.

Overall, the special issue shows clearly that the interaction of religion and politics in relation to both democratization and secularization is rich, multifaceted and complex. We saw that generally it is now common for religious political actors to be heavily involved in questions of secularization and democratization, albeit with variable outcomes. We also observed that religious actors of various kinds can also influence political outcomes in countries that are already democratic and secular, such as India and Israel.

Notes

1. At the time of writing (late 2009), the secular Congress Party is still the largest party in parliament, with 206 seats, following elections earlier in the year. The breakdown of seats in the 543-seat Lok Sabha was: Congress and allies: 262; BJP and allies: 157; and 'Others': 124 (http://www.indian-elections.com/).
2. Byrnes and Katzenstein, *Religion in an Expanding Europe.*
3. Davie, *Europe: The Exceptional Case.*
4. Ramadan, *Western Muslims and the Future of Islam.*
5. Roy, *Globalised Islam. The Search for a New Ummah.*
6. Safran, *The Secular and the Sacred: Nation, Religion and Politics.*
7. Casanova, *Public Religions in the Modern World*, 66.
8. Casanova, *ibid*, and 'Religion, Secular Identities and European Integration'.
9. Haynes, *The Politics of Religion.*

Bibliography

Byrnes, Timothy, and Peter Katzenstein, eds. *Religion in an Expanding Europe*. Cambridge: Cambridge University Press, 2006.

Casanova, José. *Public Religions in the Modern World*. Chicago: University of Chicago Press, 1994.

Casanova, José. 'Religion, Secular Identities and European Integration'. In *Religion in an Expanding Europe*, ed. Timothy Byrnes and Peter Katzenstein, 65–91. Cambridge: Cambridge University Press, 2006.

Davie, Grace. *Religions in Modern Europe: A Memory Mutates*. Oxford: Oxford University Press, 2000.

Davie, Grace. *Europe: The Exceptional Case. Parameters of Faith in the Modern World.* London: Darton, Longman and Todd, 2002.

Haynes, Jeffrey, ed. *The Politics of Religion*. London: Routledge, 2006.

Ramadan, Tariq. *Western Muslims and the Future of Islam*. Oxford and New York: Oxford University Press, 2003.

Roy, Olivier. *Globalised Islam. The Search for a New Ummah*. London: Hurst and Co. 2004.

Safran, William, ed. *The Secular and the Sacred: Nation, Religion and Politics.* London: Frank Cass, 2002.

INDEX

affirmative action 223, 229–30
Africa 58, 132–3, 136–8 see also Zimbabwe
Akdoğan, Yalçın 160–1
Alexander, Karin 134–5, 144
Aloni, Shulamit 87
Anderson, John 58, 79
Ansari, Ziaur Rahman 227
Arafat, Yasser 75, 88, 89–90, 92
Atatürk, Kemal 14, 109–10,156, 159, 161, 164, 175–6, 182, 186, 200
authoritarian regimes
  defining democratization 5–6
  Egypt, state-religion relations in 113–17, 123
  elections 6
  processes of democratization, case studies on 19, 20, 22, 25–30, 43
  Turkey, state-religion relations in 110
autonomy 19, 210–11, 223–33

Barak, Ehud 90–2
Barras, Amélie 162
Baxi, Upendra 227–8
Bayat, Asef 39
Beck, Ulrich 4
Ben Gurion, David 118
Berger, Peter 136
Bowen, John 200
Brattan, Michael 133
Brown, Nathan 114–15
Brown, Wendy 205, 206, 210
Butterfield, Herbert 66
Byrnes, Timothy 244

capitalism 55, 60

Carkoglu, Ali 136
Casanova, José 24, 55, 63, 110, 247
Catholic Church
  Africa 58
  'Catholic Wave' 12, 18, 53–66
  civil society 63, 65
  comparative justice 63–4
  democratization and democracy 54–62, 64–6, 242–3, 246
  'end of history' 54
  foreign policy 57, 63–6
  freedom of religion 56
  homogenized culture 73
  human rights 54, 57, 61
  identity 65
  international organizations, participation in 62
  Jesuits 182–3
  liberalization 54, 60, 65–6
  modernity, pluralism of 59
  moral appeal, loss of 3
  papal encyclicals, importance of 63, 64
  Poland 1, 4, 61, 62, 246–7
  political theology 57–8
  politics 57–66
  processes of democratization, case studies on 20, 23, 24, 31–5, 38–9, 41
  secularism 59–60, 61, 66
  separation between Church and state 54–5
  social justice 56–7, 61, 63–4, 66
  South America 58, 61–2
  state–church relationship 59–62
  status quo versus change 55–9
  subsidiarity 61

tradition and political outcomes
  60–3
transnational actor, as 62–3
transnational mobilization 9
twin toleration, secularism and
  59–60
United Nations 57
universalism 64
values 54, 66
Vatican II 54, 55–9, 61, 63
West Germany 23, 24, 31–2, 35,
  38–9, 41
Central and Eastern Europe 1, 2 see
  also individual countries
Chandhoke, Neera 232
charismatic Christianity 12–13,
  138-46, 245, 250
Chikwana, Annie 133
Chirac, Jacques 199–200
Christianity see also Catholic Church;
  Protestantism
  charismatic Christianity 12–13,
    138-46, 245, 250
  Coptic Christians 112–13, 116
  Egypt, state-religion relations in
    112–13, 116
  Orthodox churches 20, 23, 24–5,
    29–42
  other religions, compared with 2
  processes of democratization, case
    studies on 20, 23, 24–5, 29–42
  United States, religious right in
    1, 242
  Zimbabwe 135–46, 245, 250
citizenship 222–3, 232–3, 246
civil religion 8–9
civil society 3–4, 9–10, 34, 43, 63,
  65, 180
clash of civilizations 63
Cold War 54
colonialism 136–7
Communism 1, 61, 62, 246–7
communitarianism 229
comparative justice 63–4

consolidation of democracy 5–6, 12,
  20, 22, 24, 34–9
constitutions
  European Union 244
  Georgia 32
  India, Muslims in 223–5, 229–30,
    249
  Indonesia 32–3
  Mali 33–4, 37
  processes of democratization, case
    studies on 30–4, 43
  Ukraine 32
covenantalism 117, 123
Cover, Robert 229

Dahl, Robert A 133
Davie, Grace 244–5
de Juan, Alexander 80
de-democratization 12, 20, 22, 34–42,
  88–90
definition of democratization 5–6
definition religion 6–7
demonic possession 137–8
deprivatization 3–4, 247
Dhavan, Rajeev 226
Diamond, Jared 54
discrimination and equality 108–9,
  122, 223-33, 249
Don-Yehiya, Eliezer 117
Dowty, Alan 86
dress see headscarf bans

Eastern Europe 1, 2 see also
  individual countries
economics 176, 187–8, 248–9
education
  headscarf bans in Turkey 162–3
  India, Muslims in 223
  Israel 120
  Turkey 109–10, 157, 161, 175,
    178–9, 180–3
  Egypt, state-religion relations in
    122–4
  authoritarianism 113–17, 123

Coptic Christians 112–13, 116
deinstitutionalization of religion 123
elections 113–16, 250
freedom of religion and freedom from religion 113
grand Mufti 113
institutionalization of Islam 112–13, 115
Islamic movements 113–17, 249–50
liberalization 116–17
moderates 114–16
non-Muslims 112–13, 116
pluralism, rejection of 115
political elite 113–16, 124
political parties 113–17
radicalization 114–16
self-defence, participation in elections as 114–15
Shari'a law 112–13, 115
women 112, 116
Eisenstadt, Shmuel N 80
Elazar, Daniel 117, 123
elections
 authoritarianism 6
 Egypt, state-religion relations in 113–16, 120
 elites, control by 6
 Islamist movements 1
 Israel and Palestine 84–5, 86
 processes of democratization, case studies on 20
 Turkey 123, 159, 164–6, 177–8
 United States 1
 Zimbabwe 134
elites
 control 6
 defining democratization 6
 Egypt, state-religion relations in 113–16, 124
 headscarf bans in Turkey 162, 201
 Turkey 112, 123, 166, 174, 181, 186
'end of history' 54

Erbakan, Necmettin 157–8, 177
Erdoğan, Recep Tayyip 155, 159, 163–5, 168
establishmentarianism 10
Etzioni, Amitai 229
European Convention on Human Rights 15, 157–8, 162–3, 207–11
European exceptionalism 245
European Union 14, 111, 112, 155, 159–60, 163, 167–8, 244, 248–9
Evangelical Protestantism 59

family law 37, 119–20, 223–31, 233, 249
Fethullah Gülen movement 15, 174–87
Foucault, Michel 109
Fox, Jonathan 24
Fradkin, Hillel 115
France see headscarf bans in France
freedom from state control 19
Freedom House status 21, 113
freedom from religion 105–6, 113
freedom of religion
 Catholic Church 56
 Egypt, state-religion relations in 113
 headscarf bans 162, 203–11
 Israel, state-religion relations in 119–20
 processes of democratization, case studies on 30, 33, 34, 43
 state-religion relations 105–6, 112, 160, 168, 174
 Turkey, state-religion relations in 112, 160, 168, 174
Freston, Paul 137
Fukuyama, Francis 54
fundamentalists see radicalization or fundamentalism

Galanter, Marc 225
Gandhi, Rajiv 227
Gellner, Ernest 176
gender see women

Georgia 19, 23, 25–30, 32, 34, 36–42
Germany 19, 23–32, 35, 38–41, 44
Gifford, Paul 137–8
Gill, Anthony 58–9
globalization 156, 246–7
Gökariksel, Banu 201, 202, 209–10
Göle, Nilufer 110–11, 200
group and individual religiosity 7
Gül, Abdullah 164, 166, 167–8
Gülen movement 15, 174–87

Haklai, Oded 83
Hamzawi, Amr 114–15
Haqqani, Husain 115
hard-liners and soft-liners 6
Harvard Research Project on
  Religious and Social Affairs
  18–19, 30
Hasan, Zoya 227
Hasenclever, Andreas 80
Haynes, Jeffrey 58, 136–7
headscarf bans
  autonomy 210–11
  Collective against Islamophobia in
    France (CCIF) 202–6
  contesting the boundaries of
    secularism 202–6
  counter-elite in Turkey 162
  democracy 209
  education, access to 162–3
  elites 162, 201
  European Convention on Human
    Rights 15, 162–3, 207–11
  France 15, 197–206, 211–12, 244
  freedom of religion 203–6,
    208–11
  human rights 162, 197–8, 202,
    204–11
  international forums, use of 206–9
  Islamization 162, 166–7
  laicism 198–200, 203–6, 209, 211
  legal support 203–4
  liberalism 161–3
  manifestation of belief 199

neutrality 199–200, 202, 203, 205
  political parties 162–3, 165–6, 207
  political symbol, scarf as a 162
  public opinion 166–7
  public sphere 162, 200–4
  schools, students in 199–200,
    203–4
  secularization 156, 167, 197–8,
    200–2, 206–9, 211–12
  sensitization activities 203
  separation of religion and state
    11–12, 199, 200
  state institutions 161–2,
    165–6, 201
  state secularism 198–202,
    205–8, 211–12
  thought, conscience and religion,
    freedom of 162, 207, 209–11
  Turkey 15, 156, 161–7, 200–2,
    206–11
  United States 208
  universities 162–3, 165–6, 209–10
  West 162–3
Hefner, Robert 136
Heydemann, Steven 114
human rights
  Catholic Church 54, 57, 61
  headscarf bans 162, 197–8, 202,
    204–11
  India, Muslims in 223–4, 230
  Israel 77–8, 120, 122, 123
  Turkey, state-religion relations in
    157–8, 159–63
  Zimbabwe 134–5
Huntington, Samuel P 24, 40, 53,
  55–6, 60, 122
Hurd, Elizabeth Shakman 59

identity 65, 104, 109–12, 222, 229
importance, retention and increase of
  social 4
increase in religiosity and
  spirituality 3
India, Muslims in 16, 221–33

affirmative action 223, 229–30
autonomy 223–33
Bharatiya Janata Party (BJP) 1, 242
bias towards Hindus 223, 232
caste system 224
citizenship 222–3, 232–3
communitarianism 229
Constitution 223–5, 229–30, 249
Dalits or untouchables 224
democracy 221–2, 224, 227, 230, 233, 249
discrimination and equality 223–5, 227–9, 231–3, 249
education 223
human rights 223–4, 230
identity 222, 229
language 223, 231
liberal democracy 222
majoritarianism 222–3, 232
militancy 242
minority rights 16, 223–30, 233, 249
nationalism 1, 242
Pakistan 222, 230–2
partition 222–3
personal laws 223–31, 233, 249
polygamy 225–6, 230, 233
secessionism 223, 232–3
secularism 222–3, 227, 229–33, 249
Shari'a law 227, 249
social divisions 222
state religion relations 230–1
violence between communities 222, 231, 242
Westminster model of state 221–2
women 227–8, 233
Indonesia 19, 22–3, 25–41
influence of religious organizations, decline in 3
Inglehart, Ronald 134, 135–6
institutionalization
    deinstitutionalization 123, 138–40, 143
    Egypt, state-religion relations in 108, 112–13, 115, 122–3
    Israel, state-religion relations in 117–18, 121–4
    popular religion 106–8, 123
    processes of democratization, case studies on 23
    secularization 23–4
    state-religion relations 104–8, 110, 112, 122–4, 161
    'twin toleration' 59–60
    Turkey, state-religion relations in 109–10, 123, 161
    Zimbabwe 138–40, 143
Iranian Revolution 1979 2, 243–4
Islam see headscarf bans; India, Muslims in; Islamic movements; Muslims
Islamic movements
    Egypt, state-religion relations in 113–17, 124, 249–50
    elections 1
    headscarf bans in Turkey 162, 166–7
    mobilization 9
    moderates 124
    resurgence of religion 59
    state-religion relations 124
    Turkey 4, 110–12, 122, 124, 155–68, 176–8, 184, 248
Israel
    Arab citizens of Israel, status of 13–14, 84–5, 86, 89, 93, 118
    armed conflicts and use of force 76–80, 85, 88–92, 122
    colleges, establishment of religious 84
    communal politics, settler movement in 83–4
    conversion process 119–20
    covenantalism 117, 123
    culture war 117
    de-democratization 88–90
    deinstitutionalization of religion 123

democracy and democratization 13, 75–93, 104–5, 117–19, 121, 123–4
dietary laws 121
discrimination 120, 122
education 120
electoral system 84–5, 86
family law 119–20
freedom of religion 119–20
fundamentalists 1, 80–2, 88
Gush Emunim 82–3, 90
historical evolution of politicized religion 80–2
human rights 77–8, 120, 122, 123
Intifadas 76, 85, 88, 91–2
institutionalization of religion 108, 117–18, 121–4
institutionalization of religious jurisprudence 118, 124
integrationist political theology 82–4
Jewishness, meaning of 117–19, 123–4
liberal democracy 76–8, 87–9, 93
marriage and divorce 119–20, 122, 248
nationalism 78–9, 81, 86, 88–9, 91, 117
non-Jews, status of 118, 123
Oslo peace process 13, 75–6, 80–2, 85–93
Palestine 13, 75–6, 80–2, 85–93
Palestinian Authority 88, 90, 92–3
Palestine Liberation Organization 85–6
political parties 82–3, 87, 89, 91–2, 118–21, 124, 242
redemption, signs of 81
re-escalation 88–90
religious holidays 120–2, 248
religious Zionists 82, 88–93
secular Zionists 81–2
secularism 117, 119–20, 247–8
securitization by elites 80, 91–2
self-rule for Palestine 86, 88, 90, 92
settler movement 76, 80–4, 88–93, 122
state-religion divide 76, 85, 86–9, 93, 104–5, 108, 117–23
status quo document 118, 121
suicide bombings 88–90
theo-democracy 79
Turkey 165–7
ultra-orthodox establishment, hegemony of 119–20
United States 91–2
women 120, 122
Zionists 76, 80–3, 87–93, 118

Jenkins, Philip 137
Jesuits 182–3

Kadioglu, Ayse 111
Kahn, Arif Mohammed 227
Kant, Immanuel 77, 78, 90
Katzenstein, Peter 244
Kavakci, Merve 15, 207–9, 210
Keyman, Faut 109–10
Koelble, Thomas A 133, 135
Kook, Abraham Isaac HaCohen 81–2
Kook, Zvi Yehuda HaCohen 82
Korany, Bahgat 115
Kösebalaban, Hasan 185
Krishnan, Jayanath 225
Kukathas, Chandran 229

laicism
 definition 198–200
 France 160, 198–200, 203–6
 headscarf bans 198–200, 203–6, 209, 211
 state-religion relations 104
 Turkey 110, 123, 160, 174–5, 177–8, 180
language 223, 231
Levi, Gideon 121–2
Lewis, Tom 210
liberalization and liberalism

Catholic Church 54, 60, 65–6
defining democratization 5
Egypt, state-religion relations in 116–17
headscarf bans in Turkey 161–3
India 222
Israel and Palestine 76–8, 87–9, 93
Turkey, state-religion relations in 111–12, 158–60, 175
Lipuma, Edward 133, 135

Mady, Abdel-Fattah 84
Mahmood, Tahir 226
majoritarianism 222–3, 232
Mali 19, 23, 25–31, 33–41
manifestation of belief 159, 160, 199
Mann, Michael 79
Mansfield, ED 78, 80
Mardin, Şerif 150, 167
marriage and divorce
    India, Muslims in 223–31, 233, 249
    Israel, state-religion relations in 119–20, 122, 248
    polygamy 225–6, 230, 233
Maxwell, David 137, 139
McGoldrick, Dominic 201
McHenry Jr, Dean 84
Merkel, Wolfgang 132–3
minorities 16, 223–30, 233, 249
Mitchell, Katharyne 201, 202, 209–10
modernization and modernity 2–3, 59, 80, 109–11, 161, 174, 186
Mubarak, Hosni 116
Mugabe, Robert 133–4
Mukonyara, Isabel 138
multi–vocal religious traditions 2
Muslims see also headscarf bans; India, Muslims in; Islamic movements
    Egypt, state-religion relations in 104–5, 108, 112–17, 122–4, 249–50
    Iranian Revolution 1979 2, 243–4
    processes of democratization, case studies on 20, 23, 25–30, 32–41
    secularization 244–5
    Shari'a law 112–13, 115, 186, 230–1, 245
    social and political features of Muslim countries 1–2
    state-religion relations 11
    Sufism 179, 186
    Western Muslims 245
Mustafa, Hala 113

Nariman, Falis S 226
nationalism
    India 1, 242
    Israel 78–9, 81, 86, 88–9, 91, 117
    Turkey 176, 179
Ncube, Pius 138, 145
Nehru, Jawaharlal 224, 231
Netanyahu, Benjamin 89–90, 242
networks 143–4, 174, 176
neutrality 199–200, 202, 203, 205
Norris, Pippa 135
Norton, Augustus Richard 113
Nursi, Bediüzzaman Said 179, 180–1

organizational forms 23, 39–40
Orthodox churches 20, 23, 24–5, 29–42
Ottolenghi, Emanuele 118
Özal, Turgut 176

Pakistan 222, 230–2
Palestine see Israel and Palestine
Peace of Westphalia 243
Peres, Shimon 88
personal laws 223–31, 233, 249
Philpott, Daniel 56, 59, 79–80, 107–9
pluralism 59, 115
Poland 1, 4, 61, 62, 246–7
political parties
    Egypt, state-religion relations in 113–17

Index

headscarf bans in Turkey 162–3, 165–6, 207
Israel 82–3, 87, 89, 91–2, 118–21, 124, 242
Turkey 110–12, 124, 155–67, 176–80, 249
politics see also political parties
activism 2–4, 8
Catholic Church 4, 9, 57–66
civil society 9–10
defining democratization 5
democracy 105
deprivatization and political change 3–4
fundamentalists 79–80
group religiosity 7
headscarf bans in Turkey 162
Islamic movements 4, 9
mobilization 9
Muslims 4, 9, 157–60, 162, 175, 245, 248–9
Poland 4
political society 9
processes of democratization, case studies on 23, 37–43
representation 2–3
socio-political power 9
state-religion relations 105, 107
popular religion, institutionalization of 106–8 123
post-colonialism 137
power, exercise of 7
pressure groups, religious groups as 9
private, religion as
civil religion 8–9
deprivatization and political change 3
headscarf bans in Turkey 162, 200–2
modernization 2
reversal of privatization 12
state-religion relations 8, 109, 111, 156–7, 160, 174, 175

Turkey, state-religion relations in 109, 111, 156–7, 160, 174, 175
processes of democratization, case studies on role of religious actors in
authoritarian rule, erosion of 19, 20, 22, 25–30, 43
case selection and methodology 20–5
Catholicism 20, 23, 24, 31–5, 38–9, 41
Christian–Orthodox churches 20, 23, 24–5, 29–42
civil society 34, 43
consolidation of democracy 20, 22, 24, 34–9
constitutions 30–4, 43
constructive role 22, 25–39
de-democratization 20, 22, 34–42
democracy 30–4, 44
destructive role 22, 25–39
elections 20
factors conditioning the role of religious actors 39–42
family law 37
freedom from state control 19
freedom of religion 30, 33, 34, 43
gender 37
Georgia (1987–2007) 19, 23, 25–30, 32, 34, 36–42
Harvard Research Project on Religious and Social Affairs 18–19, 30
Indonesia (1991–2007) 19, 22, 23, 25–41
institutionalization 23
legal autonomy 19
legal position of religious actors 40–2
majority religion, special status of 41–2
Mali (1877–2007) 19, 23, 25–31, 33–41

Muslim countries 20, 23, 25–30, 32–41
obstructive role 22, 25–39
organizational form of religious actors 23, 39–40
politics 23, 37–43
Protestantism 19, 20, 23, 24, 31, 34–5, 38–9, 41
radical groups 43
religious actors, role of 12, 18–44
reorganization of religious sphere 34, 37
replacements, transplacements and transformations 24–5
secularism and secularization 22–5, 32–3
state-religion relations 22–5, 30, 32–3
transnational linkages 19
Ukraine (1987–2007) 19, 23, 24–41
West Germany (1945–1969)19, 23–32, 35, 38–41, 44
Protestantism
  capitalism 55, 60
  Evangelical Protestantism 59
  processes of democratization, case studies on 19–20, 23–4, 31, 34–5, 38–9, 41
  West Germany 23, 24, 35, 38–9, 41
public opinion 166–7
public sphere 4–5, 162, 200–4
Putnam, Robert 135

Rabin, Yitzhak 75, 86–9, 91–3
radicalization or fundamentalism
  Egypt, state-religion relations in 114–16
  Israel and Palestine 1, 80–2, 88
  processes of democratization, case studies on 12, 18–44
  Turkey 112, 158, 160, 177–80, 184
Raftopoulos, Brian 133–4, 144
Ramadan, Tariq 245
Ranger, Terence O 136–7

Rawls, John 60
resurgence of religion 59, 61, 175, 243–4, 248
Roman Catholics see Catholic Church
Roncalli, Angelo Giuseppe (Pope John XXIII) 183
Roy, Olivier 245
Russia 29, 40

Safran, William 246
Sahin, Leyla 162–3, 209–11
Salih, MA Mohamed 132–3
Sason, Talya 84
Say, Fazil 155, 166
secularization and secularism
  Catholic Church 59–60, 61, 66
  democratization 245–7
  deprivatization 247
  headscarf bans 156, 167, 197–202, 205–12
  India, Muslims in 22–3, 227, 229–33, 249
  institutional secularism 23–4
  Israel, state-religion relations in 117, 119–20, 247–8
  modernization 2
  pre-condition for democracy, as being 23–4
  pressure groups, religious groups as 9
  processes of democratization, case studies on 22–5
  separation of religion and state 24, 32–3
  state-religion relations 8–9
  Turkey 109–12, 155–68, 175–80, 182, 184, 186, 244
securitization of religious referent objects 80
Selznick, Philip 229
separation between religion and state 54–5, 109–10, 123, 156–7, 199, 200
Shahabuddin, Syed 226, 231

Shari'a law 112–13, 115, 186, 230–1, 245
Sharon, Ariel 92
Sithole, Tulani 133
Smith, D Eugene 230
Snyder, JL 78, 80
social construction of religious identity 104
social justice 56–7, 61, 63–4, 66
social movements 9–10, 140, 143–4, 181
Somer, Murat 112
South America, Catholic Church in 58, 61–2
spiritual capital 13, 135–8, 140–4
spirituality, increase in 3
state-religion relations 10–16
  British establishmentarianism 10
  Catholic Church 59–62
  civil religion arrangements 8–9
  comparative study 13–14, 103–24
  culture 11
  deinstitutionalization of religion 123
  democracy 104–24
  differentiations 107–9
  discrimination and intolerance 108–9
  dynamic, as being 105, 123–4
  Egypt 104–5, 108, 112–17, 122–4
  elections 113–16, 250
  elites 113–16, 124
  France, Islamic dress in 11–12
  freedom of religion and freedom from religion 105–6, 113
  India, Muslims in 230–1
  institutionalized religion 104–8, 123–4
  integration 104, 107, 123
  Islamic movements 113–17, 249–50
  Israel 76, 85–7, 89, 93, 104–5, 108, 117–24, 247–8
  laicism 104
  liberalization 116–17
  models 107–9
  Muslims 11
  pluralism 115
  political and religious authority, relationship between 107
  political parties 113–17
  politicization of religion 105
  popular religion, institutionalization of 106–8, 123
  pressure groups, religious groups as 9
  privatization 9, 12
  processes of democratization, case studies on 22–5, 30, 32–3
  radicalization 114–16
  secularism 8–9, 24, 32–3
  Shari'a law 112–13, 115
  Turkey 14–15, 104–5, 109–12, 122–4, 154–68
  'twin tolerations' 106–7, 124
  women 112, 116
Stepan, Alfred 59–60, 106–7
Sufism 179, 186

Taylor, Charles 209
terrorism 88–90, 244
Tocqueville, Alexis de 66
transitions to democracy 5–6, 12 see also processes of democratization, case studies on role of religious actors in
transnational linkages 19
Tsvangirai, Morgan 145–6
Turkey
  28 February regime 178
  Abant Platform 184
  Alevis 163–4, 184
  authoritarianism 110
  civil society group, as 180
  conferences, meetings and symposiums 178
  counter-elite 166
  cultural identity 110, 112
  democracy 111–12, 156, 158, 161, 166, 174, 186–7

denationalization 111–12
Directorate of Religious Affairs 109, 157, 163–4, 200
economics 176, 187–8, 248–9
education 157, 175, 178–9, 180–3
elections 123, 159, 164–6, 177–8
elites 112, 123, 166, 174, 181, 186
European Court of Human Rights 157–8, 162–3
European Union membership 14, 111, 112, 155, 159–60, 163, 167–8, 244, 248–9
Fethullah Gülen movement 15, 174–87
freedom of religion 112, 160, 168, 174
fundamentalists 158, 160, 177–8
funding 179
globalization 156
headscarf issue 156, 161–3, 164, 165–7
human rights 157–8, 159–63
identity 109–12
institutions and education, control of 109–10, 161
institutionalization of religion 112 123
integration 111
interfaith dialogues 183–5
Islamist movements 4, 110–12, 122, 124, 155–68, 176–8, 184, 248
Israel 176–7
Jesuits 182–3
Kurds 111
laicism 104, 110, 160, 174–5, 177–8, 180
liberalization 111–12, 158–60, 175
manifestation of belief 159, 160
media 178
middle class 110, 164, 175–6, 206
military 123, 157, 164–5, 177, 201
modernity 109–11, 161, 174, 186
nationalists 176, 179
networks 174, 176

'otherness' 185
Ottoman empire 14, 109, 154–6, 174–5, 186
political Islam 157–60, 162, 175, 248–9
political parties 110–12, 124, 155–67, 176–80, 249
presidential crisis 2007 14, 156, 165
private, religion as 109, 111, 156–7, 160, 174, 175
radical groups, ties to 112, 158, 160, 177–80, 184
religious orders, bans of 156–7
resurgence of religion 175
rule of law 186–7
secularism 109–12, 155–68, 175–80, 182, 184, 186, 244
separation of religion and state 109–10, 123, 156–7
Shari'a law 186
social movement, as 181
state–religion relations 14–15, 104–5, 154–68, 200
Sufism 179, 186
Sunni Islam, bias towards 157, 160, 163–4
think tank 184
Turkish-Islamic synthesis 157
United States, exile in the 175, 178
workshops 179
'twin toleration' 59–60, 106–7, 124

Ukraine 19, 23–41
United Kingdom, establishmentarianism in 10
United Nations (UN) 57
United States
  Christian Right 1, 242
  elections 1
  Gülen, Fethullah, exile of 175, 178
  headscarf bans in Turkey 208
  Israel and Palestine 91–2
  spiritual capital 135–6
universalism 64

Vakulenko, Anastasia 206, 210
values 12, 54, 66, 133
Vatican II 54, 55–9, 61, 63, 183
Vicini, Fabio 182
violence
  India, Muslims in 222, 232, 242
  Israel and Palestine 76–80, 75, 88–92, 122

Weber, Max 55, 60, 136, 144, 176
Weigel, George 61
Welzel, Christian 134
West Germany 19, 23–32, 35, 38–41, 44
Wilson, Richard 202
women
  Egypt, state-religion relations in 112, 116
  India, Muslims in 227–8, 233
  Israel, state-religion relations in 120, 122
  processes of democratization, case studies on 37
  Shari'a law 112
Wuthnow, Robert 144

Yamamori, Tetsumao 137
Yilmaz, Hakan 110–11
Yilmaz, Mesut 177

Zimbabwe 12–13, 132–46

agriculture 133–4
charismatic Christianity 12–13, 138–46, 245, 250
Christianity 135–46, 245, 250
de-institutionalization of churches 138–40, 143
democracy 133–4, 138, 140, 142–5, 250
elections 134
human rights 134–5
ideas and spiritual capital 140–3
land reform 133–4
macro-level, spiritual capital at 144–6
Mount Pleasant Community Church 138–46
Movement for Democratic Change (MDC) 134–5
networks 143–4
non-governmental organizations (NGOs), volunteering for 143
Operation Murumbatsvina 135
opposition groups 134–5
power-sharing 134, 145–6
reconciliation 133, 145
relationships 140–1, 143
social movements 140, 143–4
spiritual capital 13, 135–8, 140–4
ZANU-PF 133–4, 145
Zionists 76, 80–3, 87–93, 118

For Product Safety Concerns and Information please contact our EU
representative GPSR@taylorandfrancis.com
Taylor & Francis Verlag GmbH, Kaufingerstraße 24, 80331 München, Germany

www.ingramcontent.com/pod-product-compliance
Lightning Source LLC
Chambersburg PA
CBHW051631230426
43669CB00013B/2264